BEHIND THE THISTLE

BEHIND THE THISTLE

Playing Rugby for Scotland

DAVID BARNES

and

PETER BURNS

BIRLINN

First published in 2010 by
Birlinn Limited
West Newington House
10 Newington Road
Edinburgh
EH9 1QS

www.birlinn.co.uk

ISBN: 978 1 84158 653 3

British Library Cataloguing-in-Publication Data
A catalogue record for this book is available from the British Library.

Typeset by Iolaire Typesetting, Newtonmore
Printed and bound in Slovenia by arrangement with Associated Agencies, Oxford

CONTENTS

I am under no illusions as to how fortunate I have been to spend the last six years being paid to watch rugby matches and to speak to sporting legends. During that time I have been constantly impressed by the down to earth intelligence and humour of the international stars I have met – and I have often wondered how their achievements on the rugby field have coloured their lives.

This book is an attempt to get under the skin of these giants of the game so that we can understand what makes them tick and appreciate the individual qualities a character needs in order to successfully play rugby at the highest level.

Every Scottish rugby fan has wondered at some point what it would be like to join that exclusive club of Scotland internationalists. Alas only a very small proportion of us ever get to realise that dream while the rest can only stand on the sidelines and marvel. This book is a celebration of those who have pulled on the blue jersey, but also a tribute to the rest of us who live in the slipstream of our sporting heroes.

This book is also for Johanne Barnes, our children, Maisie and Robbie, and in memory of Russell Bruce and Frank Coutts, who both contributed to this book but passed away before its publication.

David Barnes, September 2010

I remember the first time my father took me to Murrayfield. It was 17 February, 1990 and I was eight years old. I can still vividly remember the scent of cigar and pipe smoke mixing with the sweet tang of alcohol on the breath of those sitting near us and the waxy smell of Barbour jackets in the air (we were sitting in the East Stand, after all). There was a great hubbub and energy in the ground as the stands and terraces filled before kick-off, and I can still remember my jolt of surprise when a train raced along the track behind the south terrace and sounded its horn in salute to the gathering throng. Minutes later cheers and applause broke out as a cockerel was released onto the pitch and was shooed away by the security marshals. The rousing melodies of the pipe band began to echo around the ground as the clock ticked closer to the hour-mark and then the teams emerged. We stood in respectful silence for La Marseillaise as ripples of French support sang their hearts out before the rest of the ground erupted into Flower of Scotland; it was a noise the like of which I had never heard before – a deafening cry to arms. And in those few minutes, from passing through the turnstiles to the moment the kick-off was struck, Murrayfield and that Scottish jersey had captured my heart forever.

This book is for every fan who, like me, has dreamed the dream of playing for Scotland, and for all those great and wonderful players who have had the honour of doing so. It is also for my father, who instilled his love of the game in me; for my mother, who has long endured my obsession with it; for my wife Annabelle, who lovingly puts up with me droning on endlessly about it; and for our daughter Isla, who will no doubt love something else entirely.

Peter Burns, September 2010

The authors would like to thank everyone who has given their time so generously to assist in the preparation of this book. Those whom we interviewed are too many to name individually but their thoughts are included in the pages which follow.

Thanks must also go to all at Birlinn, who have been incredibly enthusiastic about this project from the start and just as incredibly patient at the time it has taken to come together.

Watching Scotland play international rugby has been one of the greatest privileges of my life. Ever since that first occasion when I marched down Princes Street with my dad, my wee hand in his, on my way to Murrayfield for the first time, every occasion when Scotland has played has been special to me. It remains a huge disappointment to me that I never got the chance myself to pull on the famous jersey, listen to the last-minute team talk and run out to play the auld enemy at Murrayfield. I have spent my entire life wishing that I could somehow have played, even just once, for Scotland in a full international. It would have meant more to me than anything else I can think of in a sporting context. When I played in that final trial at our national ground, just entering the dressing room was a thrill in itself. I was awestruck.

Bill McLaren (1923-2010)
The Voice of Rugby

FOREWORD

I didn't know what rugby was until I was eleven. In Tarbolton, the little mining village in Ayrshire where I was born and raised, sport meant football, racing pigeons, whippets, pitch-and-toss and more football. I doubt if anyone in the place had any idea where Murrayfield was, let alone been there.

It was only when I made it into Ayr Academy that I was introduced to the sport which would play a defining role in the remainder of my life. I was hooked straightaway. I loved the physicality, the brutality and the camaraderie of it. Before long the game had become the be-all and end-all of my life, and like all rugby-mad youngsters the possibility of one day representing my country was a dream that I harboured quietly but determinedly.

I was fortunate enough to go on and realise that dream. The fact that I had to wait so long before winning my first cap against England in 1969 made the achievement all the more satisfying.

You never know how you are going to cope with becoming an international player until you have lived through it. I've seen people freeze up, I've seen others who couldn't stop talking as they tried to overcome their nerves, but for me the feeling was of complete exhilaration. I couldn't wait to get into the dressing room and get my hands on the blue jersey, and when we got in there I grabbed it off the peg and pulled it down over my shoulders as quickly as possible, just in case the selectors changed their minds. I was twenty-six years old and had waited a long time to get hold of that strip, and it would have taken a brave man to try and prise it away from me then.

Much of that day is a haze, but I remember sitting in the changing room at 2.50pm. Jim Telfer, the captain, was giving his pep talk, with a few special words of encouragement for myself and fellow debutant Billy Steele. *Open the doors*, I thought. *Let me get out there and at them.* I had waited all my life for that moment.

In many ways, rugby has changed beyond recognition from the game which I played. Money has been a major factor in this. Guys are now bigger, stronger and far better drilled. The need to provide entertainment means that the rules have been changed to suit the spectator rather than the player. But the fundamental character of the game is still the same. It is a game for tough but fair men, who revel in the conviviality of team sport rather than the more private glory which comes with success in individual pursuits.

In my role as president of the Scottish Rugby Union, I have been able to spend a lot of time in recent months meeting individuals and watching games at grassroots level, and I am in no doubt that the twelve year old boys I see now – running, passing, kicking and tackling, emulating their heroes in the dark blue of Scotland – are motivated by the same things as me and my pals were way back in the 1950s: the adrenalin rush of a ruthlessly physical contest, the deep sense of satisfaction which comes from knowing that you have gone toe-to-toe with a worthy adversary and not let your teammates down, and ultimately the burning ambition to one day be deemed good enough to represent your nation in a full-blooded international. Money might be a welcome bonus to today's young rugby players but I'm sure the sport itself is still the real draw.

This book is for everybody who has shared that dream of running out at Murrayfield in that dark blue jersey with the thistle on their left breast, the adrenalin pumping through their veins, a wall of sound in front of them, and a nation at their back.

Ian McLauchlan, September 2010

1

LIGHT FROM THE SHADOWS

M URRAYFIELD *Stadium, the fortress heart of Scottish rugby, sits sternly to the west of Edinburgh's city centre. From the heights of the West Stand, one can gaze out across the city to the Lions Haunch and the crags of Arthur's Seat, and to the glorious sight of Edinburgh Castle perched on its dark outcrop of volcanic rock, while to south the Pentland Hills rise high above the suburbs, hemming in the city limits before rolling away to the south.*

Murrayfield Stadium is a towering bastion of concrete and steel girders, one of the great arenas of the modern rugby world. It has had many faces since it first opened in 1925, but at its heart the field of battle has remained a constant.

When the land was purchased in the early 1920s, a stand was built on the west side of the pitch and three embankments were raised to the north, south and east to pen in this new theatre of dreams. It was finished just in time to host Scotland's final game in the 1925 Championship, where a last-gasp Herbert Waddell drop-goal overcame England to secure Scotland's first ever Grand Slam in front of a world record-breaking crowd of over 70,000 spectators.

But during the Second World War, the Five Nations Championship slipped into hibernation. The stadium was converted into a supply depot for the Royal Army Service Corps and, until 1944 when it was derequisitioned and the home tie in the annual Scotland versus England services international was played, the turnstiles lay still. During the war the armed services played these games over two legs, home and away, and before the return to Murrayfield in 1944, the first two home matches were played at Inverleith.

Although the toll was not as great as it was in the First War, Scotland lost a generation of players to the Second, with 15 capped internationalists alone killed in action. Returning on leave to life in a country ravaged by the horrors of war and reeling from its impact, Scotland's rugby players found solace in the game that they

---

Opposite: Scotland and England line up for the pre-match playing of God Save the King at Twickenham in 1947. *Press Association.*

held so dear. Pulling on the dark blue jersey, even if it wasn't in a full international, was still the greatest honour to be bestowed to a Scottish player – and one that many individuals would go to great extremes to realise.

When, at last, the war ended, international rugby returned with a series of Victory Internationals held in 1946 between the Home Nations and the touring New Zealand Army, before the Five Nations Championship was revived in 1947.

RUSSELL BRUCE (Glasgow Academicals and the Army)
8 Caps: 1947–49 (plus six Victory Internationals in 1946)

I played in several of the service internationals during the war, and when the war finished I captained the Rhine Army side until I was demobbed in February 1946. During that period, I also came home quite often to play for the British Army because they didn't have a stand-off in the country which suited them.

So I got a very nice trip home from France every couple of weeks in a first class sleeper, which was set aside for me with all my papers in it. The number of times Generals and Field Marshals came along and said, 'Who's this Major Bruce occupying a sleeper while I can't get one?'

An aerial view of Murrayfield during the Scotland–England Victory International match in 1946. *Press Association.*

But one time they changed the starting terminus from Genapp to somewhere else, which meant I went to the wrong place and missed the connection. I was stranded. Then my driver said, 'Why don't we just motor overnight to Calais?'

I said, 'What a wonderful idea – but I doubt we'll have enough petrol to get all the way there.'

'Don't worry,' he said. 'I know a depot where the Canadians have got petrol – we'll go and bribe a jerry can from them – that should see us to Calais.'

So we headed over to the depot and did a deal with these Canadian chaps and then headed off. We drove all through the night in this open-top jeep; it was quite an adventure and we really had to hare it along all these winding roads in the pitch dark, but it was worth it. It meant an awful lot to get back and play in those games.

But when we eventually got to Calais I was put under arrest because my papers explaining that I was on leave to go and play rugby in Bristol for the Army against the touring New Zealand Army had been on the train and I didn't have anything to prove that what I was telling them was true. Fortunately, they put me on the ferry and when I got to Dover they phoned up the Army Sport Control Board, and were told, 'Yes, we're expecting a Major CR Bruce – we thought he would be here last night.' So they finally released me and I was able to head off to join up with the rest of the team.

It was quite interesting because having spent a night in a jeep then the next night under arrest I was a bit of a write-off against the Kiwis – which was quite beneficial when they played Scotland later in the tour. Billy Munro, who was at inside centre, and I played particularly well in that game and we won 11-6. A few years later, when I played for the Barbarians alongside the New Zealand half-back Fred Allen, he told me that when they were discussing the Scotland team before the match they had written me off as a no-hoper because I had played so badly for the Army. We were the only team to beat the Kiwis on that tour, which was quite an achievement – especially when you consider that Scotland have never beaten New Zealand in all the years since then. That result really stands out and should be remembered more than it is, because it was a special victory and it was wonderful to be part of it.

The Kiwis were a great team – full of power and pace, and they were all monstrously big and fit, and because they were on a tour they were much better prepared than we were. But we really stuck in as a team and were cheered on wonderfully by the Murrayfield crowd; we wanted to enjoy ourselves whenever we played for Scotland, so we attacked whenever we could and at times *we* looked like the touring team because things just worked so well between the players.

We played against rugby league players in the army at that time because during the war the two codes joined forces and played under union rules. Things soon went back to normal, with the two codes once again separated, but

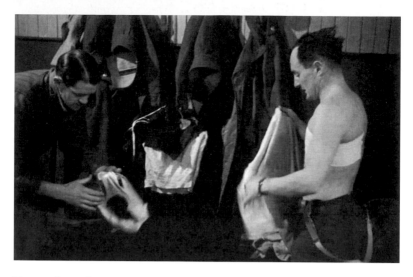

Players from the New Zealand Army rugby team in the changing room at Murrayfield, 1946. *Hulton Getty Archive*

when we played France for the first time after the war, on New Year's Day 1947, we found that their professionals were there playing as amateurs again. So we asked them why they had decided to come back to union, and they told us it was more lucrative.

It had been a different story in Scotland, where they remained very strict

The players in action during Scotland's momentous victory over the New Zealand Army. *Hulton Getty Archive*

about keeping union and league apart, despite what went on elsewhere during the war. In 1944 the Army Sport Control Board decided to organise a special game in Bradford for the amateurs versus the professionals, and I was lucky enough to be asked to play at fly-half for the amateurs, alongside the great Haydn Tanner of Wales. But I got a letter from Frank Moffat of the SRU telling me that if I played against the professionals I would never be considered for Scotland again.

FRANK COUTTS (Melrose and the Army)
3 Caps: 1947 (plus two Victory Internationals in 1946)

When I was first selected for Scotland, for our Victory International against Wales in March 1946, I was stationed in Denmark and I honestly think I would never have found out I had been picked were it not for a Corporal in Copenhagen who rang through and told me. He said he had taken the liberty of booking me a plane to Prestwick on the Thursday and that the fare was about £33 . . . it took me 18 months to get that refunded. I don't think the SRU were mean, they were just *canny*.

There was five men – Donnie Innes, Iain Henderson, Ralph Sampson, William Murdoch, William Young – who played for Scotland both before and after the war, and the famous story is that when they turned up to play for the first time since hostilities had ceased, they each found that there was no strip for them to put on, and Harry Simpson, the secretary, said, 'You got your jerseys before the war.'

When they first re-introduced the National Trial after the war we all turned up at Murrayfield and the great innovation was that we all had to have our height and weight measured. So I stepped up onto the weighing machine.

'Where's your penny, Mr Coutts?'

I had to pay a penny to be weighed. Harry Simpson certainly liked to keep a tight ship!

There was no office at Murrayfield, they worked out of a lawyers' office on Coates Crescent, and you'd sneak in on a Friday and say to the Secretary-Treasurer, 'Mr Simpson, sir, do you think I might have two tickets for my parents?'

'Oh I suppose so, Coutts,' he would say with a heavy sigh and rather reluctantly hand the tickets over.

I played in the last of the Victory Internationals, which was against England at Murrayfield, and it was a marvellous experience – we won 27-0 and you could really feel the crowd pressing in around the pitch. Whenever we scored the whole place went berserk; you could actually feel the noise throbbing through you.

The first cap international after the war was on January 1 1947. We hadn't played France since 1933 because there had been a fall-out over the issue of France fielding professionals, and this was the hand of friendship after fighting together in the war. So we all ploughed over to Paris for January 1 and I was a reserve, which meant I didn't even have to strip off; but I had my bag-pipes so I was able to lead the team onto the field. We had a lovely dinner that night in the Eiffel Tower and enjoyed the hospitality immensely – so much so that I was a bit worried by the end of the evening that a few of the boys might fall over the edge.

That was a great occasion because things had been so grim for so long and it was just wonderful to be in this magnificent city, playing rugby and enjoying life. It was sad because you would find yourself thinking of all the players who were no longer with us that might have there, and you could argue that I would never have been capped had so-and-so not been killed in the war. But that was the life we had and I was thrilled to be involved; I actually should have been in the Palestine with my regiment but the army insisted I stay behind because I had a chance of being capped.

Scotland captain Doug Keller introduces HRH The Duke of Edinburgh to his teammates before the Calcutta Cup clash at Twickenham, 19 March 1949. *Press Association*

One of my favourite recollections is of Gordon Watt of Edinburgh Academicals, who was one of my army buddies. He was also in the Scottish side, and he took me aside before the England match at Twickenham and said, 'We're all being lined up to meet the King, then the whistle goes and we're off. But I've got false teeth and I don't want to meet the King with my teeth out.' So I said, 'You stand early on in the line and after you've met the King take your teeth out, wrap them in a handkerchief and pass them down the line to the touch-judge.' It wasn't the most sophisticated plan in the world, but he was happy enough with it and when it came off without a hitch, he was very pleased.

RUSSELL BRUCE

I won eight caps for Scotland and played in the six Victory Internationals and despite the number of players we lost during hostilities, we gave a very good account of ourselves. We won five of the matches – against the New Zealand Army, Wales in both Swansea and Edinburgh, Ireland and England at Murrayfield and only lost to England at Twickenham. I scored four tries during those games, so was very satisfied with how it had all gone.

I won my first official cap in 1947 when the Five Nations began again and captained the team later that season when we played England at Twickenham in the last game of the Championship – and I moved in from centre for that game to play at fly-half. That then became my new position and although I didn't play for Scotland in 1948, I was back in the team for the 1949 Championship and played all the games at fly-half. We won our opening game down in Colombes, which was a fantastic result against a good French team and Doug Elliot scored a try, as did Peter Kininmonth on his debut; we beat Wales in Edinburgh for our other victory that season, and I remember Doug Smith scoring a wonderful try on the wing in that game. My final two caps came against Ireland and England and although we lost both, which was a disappointing way to finish my Scotland career, I am so thrilled that I was given the opportunity to play in that blue jersey for all those matches, especially when you think about all the poor chaps who we had lost in the war. But for those of us who made it through, it really was a wonderful experience.

CHAPTER TWO

THE FICKLE FIFTIES

V INCE LOMBARDI, *the doyen of American Football coaches in the 1950s and 1960s, once characterised the true spirit of sporting triumph as 'being knocked to your knees and then coming back; that's real glory.' He was also famed for saying that: 'confidence is contagious; so is lack of confidence.' If ever there were two phrases that encapsulated the fluctuating fortunes of the Scotland rugby team during the 1950s, it would be hard to look beyond Lombardi's concise analyses. It was a decade when several players carved their names in Scottish rugby history, when some extraordinary victories were posted, and when formidable opposition were cowed by the men in blue; but it also saw many bleak years, years when supporters would wonder if they would ever see the thistle in glorious flourish again.*

Central to the team's endeavours was the great Border warrior, Douglas Elliot. He had made his Scotland debut in the non-cap 1946 Victory International against the touring New Zealand Army, delivering a mighty performance that contributed significantly to Scotland's victory, the only one to be posted by any country against the touring Kiwis. He was blessed with pace, stamina, the hands of a three-quarter and the strength of a prop, and became the outstanding Scottish rugby player of the immediate post-war years.

Having claimed victories away to France and at home against Wales in 1949, the 1950 season saw wins at home against France and England countered by defeats in Swansea and Dublin. In 1951, Murrayfield bore witness to one of the all-time great Scotland performances and one in which Elliot and Peter Kininmonth established themselves forever in Scottish rugby lore. Wales arrived in Edinburgh for the game on 3 February as 1950 Grand Slam champions and on the back of an impressive 23-5 victory over England on the opening weekend of the 1951 Championship. Their team contained 11 players who had toured New Zealand and Australia with Karl Mullen's Lions the previous summer, while Scotland had suffered a 15-12 defeat to France in Colombes on the opening weekend, had a young and inexperienced team – with none of the backs older than 22 – and in number eight Kininmonth the only Lion in the squad (Elliot had been unable to tour due to farming commitments). The result, it seemed, was a foregone conclusion.

In the build-up to the match, Elliot made the decision that he and Robert Taylor would abandon the usual back-row system of playing left and right flanks. Instead, Elliot would play exclusively on the open-side – he wanted to hunt the Welsh

---

Opposite: Arthur Dorward gets the ball away during the Calcutta Cup match at Murrayfield, 17 March 1956. *The Scotsman Publications Ltd. www.scran.ac.uk*

backline from every scrum and lineout, aiming to stifle their creativity and disrupt their freedom at every turn with a relentless campaign of terror. He had studied their play and had identified one of the keys to their attack, remarking with ominous simplicity: 'I know which way Glyn Davies sidesteps.'

Such was the effectiveness of Elliot's assault on the Welsh stand-off that John Gwilliam, the captain, moved centre Lewis Jones into the pivotal role to try and combat the maelstrom that Elliot was unleashing on Davies. It had little effect. As the Welsh sought to launch their attacks from further afield they found their efforts closed out in midfield by Donald Scott and Donald Sloan, who were taking a lead from their talismanic flanker's defensive efforts. As the final quarter of the game approached, Scotland were leading 3-0. A wild defensive clearance kick from the Welsh was gathered by Kininmonth, who let fly with a speculative drop-goal. He caught it perfectly. As the ball sailed high between the posts, the men in blue seemed to grow visibly. With Elliot and Kininmonth at their lead, Scotland overwhelmed their visitors in the closing minutes, scoring one try through prop James Dawson and a brace more through wing Bob Gordon, who was making his debut.

Such was the dominance of this performance and so resounding was Elliot's impact on the game that Glyn Davies never pulled on the red jersey again and it looked as if Scotland were about to embark on an historic run. How cruelly this proved to be the case.

Between that glorious February day and the corresponding fixture in 1955, Scotland suffered 17 consecutive defeats, scoring just eleven tries, six conversions, and four penalties in five years for a paltry total of 54 points, and endured humiliation at the hands of the Springboks in 1952 in the 'Murrayfield Massacre', going down 44-0. One of the reasons for this catastrophic demise in fortunes has been attributed to there being little or no consistency in selection between Tests during this terrible run, making it nigh on impossible for the team to develop any momentum. In 1953 alone, 30 different players were selected over four matches, and 39 new caps were awarded over only three seasons.

Throughout these years, however, Douglas Elliot remained consistently brilliant and often seemed to be the only man capable of dragging Scotland through the mire to victory. During the 1954 encounter with the All Blacks his colossal efforts almost single-handedly held the New Zealanders to a 3-0 final score-line.

After years of fighting an almost thankless battle for the Scottish cause, Elliot finally hung up his boots in 1954 – meaning that he was not part of the national team's revival, which began with victory over Wales at Murrayfield in 1955.

Winger Arthur Smith was Scotland's star in this match, finishing off a fine performance with a virtuoso solo try from a counter-attack started deep inside his own half, cementing a long-overdue 14-8 victory.

That Welsh success was backed up by a 12-3 victory over Ireland, also at Murrayfield, and after such a long period of despair, it was somewhat astonishing that the team should be travelling to Twickenham looking to secure the Triple Crown; however, the dream comeback was not to be and they lost 9-6, despite prop Tom Elliot's claims to have scored a try which referee Cyril Joynson disallowed.

In the context of previous disappointments this was a minor set-back. The black cloud which had hung over Murrayfield for five years had at last lifted. In 1956 Scotland ended a six year run of defeats to France by beating them 12-0 at Murrayfield. The rest of the decade saw mixed results with five victories – over France and Wales (twice each) and Australia – two draws against England, and nine losses.

After such a deep and depressing trough, these performances were building blocks for the future. As Lombardi also famously said when paraphrasing Confucius: 'the greatest accomplishment is not in never falling, but in rising again after you fall.' Once again, he might have been talking directly about the fortunes of the Scottish rugby team during that turbulent decade.

DONALD SCOTT (Langholm, London Scottish, Watsonians)
10 Caps: 1950-53

In March 1949, when I was coming to the end of my final year at Jordanhill College, I received a telegram from the SRU at about midnight on the Thursday night telling me to come to London the next day because I'd probably be playing for Scotland versus England on Saturday. Talk about amateurish.

So I had to go to college first thing on Friday morning and show them this request. I was supposed to be taking part in a gymnastics display as part of my course, but they reluctantly gave their blessing and off I went to the station.

On the way to catch my train I remember thinking, *This bag is awful heavy.* When I got on the rain and looked inside I realised that the guys at college had put one of these stones that you paint white and put on the side of the drive in my bag. So I left that in the Waldorf Hotel in London having carried it there from the train station – I can't think why I didn't leave it on the train.

When I got there I was promptly told that Graham Jackson had given himself a fitness test – he'd run down a line and got someone to come and tackle him – and had declared himself fit.

Well, he lasted ten minutes the next day – he had ligament damage in his knee and should never have played. He never played for Scotland again.

So that was my first experience – sitting in the stand watching as the team battled on with fourteen men. I remember one of the selectors pointedly informing me that I should be out there, and me just having to shrug my shoulders and agree. I felt like telling him in no uncertain terms that it wasn't my fault I wasn't playing – but I was quite young, so I just kept quiet. It was all pretty disheartening.

The next year Scotland beat France at home but then lost 12-0 in Wales. Meanwhile, I had gone off to do my National Service so hadn't had a pair of boots on for five weeks. I was sitting in the NAAFI having a cup of coffee with a mate, and he was reading the paper. He said, 'You're interested in Scottish rugby aren't you? Well, they're making a change to the Scotland team for Saturday. They've dropped DA Sloan and picked a guy called . . . good God, this is you . . . DM Scott!'

And that was the first I heard of it. I was posted down in Winchester and the letter would go from Murrayfield to my parents' house in Langholm. They must have put it to one side thinking it wasn't that important.

It was quite difficult in those days because you had to get a visa and a passport to go across to southern Ireland and I had nothing like that. I wasn't allowed to be photographed in my army uniform but all my other kit had been sent home. I managed to get hold of a dark shirt which still looked quite military – but that seemed to be okay and I got over there and played.

DWC Smith, this big Aberdonian, was on the wing. Before the match, he came out onto the pitch for training wearing running spikes. I said, 'What are you doing with those on? You'll cause real damage if you stand on someone.'

He said, 'I'm kind of slow compared to some of you guys so I need all the help I can get.'

He was sprinting up and down the pitch with spikes on and, of course, nobody would go anywhere near him.

We were thrashed 21-0 in the rain that day – the ground was really wet and I found it hard to keep my footing.

Derek Hepburn looks on as the ball goes loose against Wales at Murrayfield in February 1949. *The Scotsman Publications Ltd. www.scran.ac.uk*

However, I managed to keep my place for the next game against England, when Tommy Gray popped over a conversion at the very end for a 13-11 victory. I still maintain that Donald Sloan and I scored half a try each in that match. We chased after this ball and I'm pretty sure I scored, and he might say the same. When we were trotting back towards the halfway line, I put my hand on his shoulder and said something along the lines of, 'Great, we made it. We can win this game.' And it came out later that the people watching thought that was me congratulating him, so he got the credit.

SCOTTISH RUGBY UNION.

Telegrams:- "Scrum, Edinburgh"
Telephone:-.CEN 4874.

10 Coates Crescent,
Edinburgh, 3.
March 1951.

Dear Sir,

SCOTLAND V ENGLAND.

You have been chosen to play for Scotland against England at Twickenham on Saturday 17th March 1951. Please let me know at once by the accompanying card if you are able to play.

Bring white shorts, plain dark blue stockings, towel and soap. You will use jersey No. 4 which was provided for you against Ireland.

I annex a note of the arrangements and shall be glad to know where and when you will meet the official party, also whether you will require Hotel accommodation.

Yours truly,

Secretary, S.R.U.

Annexation referred to:-

Thu.15th March. Train leaves Edinburgh, Waverley, at 10 a.m. for Kings Cross. Railway tickets provided. Lunch and tea aboard. Arrive Kings Cross at 5.46 p.m. Proceed by 'bus to Russell Hotel, Russell Square. Dinner 7 p.m.

Fri. 16th March. Run-about at Richmond. 'Bus leaves Russell Hotel at 2.30 p.m. returning with party. Tea at Hotel. Dinner 7/-

Sat. 17th March. 'Bus leaves Hotel for Hampton Court at 10.30 a.m. Lunch at the Mitre Hotel at 12.45. 'Bus leaves Hotel for Twickenham at 1.45 p.m. Kick-Off 3 p.m. As there will be a Dinner in the evening, bring Dinner Jacket or Kilt. Mayfair Hotel

Sun. 18th March. 'Bus leaves Russell Hotel for Kings Cross Station in time to catch the 10 a.m. train to Edinburgh Waverley. Lunch and tea aboard. Arrive Edinburgh 6.40 p.m.

If you wish 2 tickets for Match, remit £1:10/- by return.

Donald Scott's letter from the SRU informing him of his selection to play against England at Twickenham in 1951. Note the charge for two tickets to the match.

In 1951 we beat Wales 19-0 at Murrayfield. Their team had eleven players who toured with the British Lions in New Zealand the previous summer, and they had thumped England a fortnight earlier.

The game was played in front of a record crowd at that time. They stopped letting people in, then hundreds more surged through a gap in the railings and climbed over the walls and turnstiles. The game was delayed for a little bit, and lots of supporters were brought in and sat on the grass in front of the schoolboys' enclosure, which meant that opposite the West Stand you had the touchline and then supporters only a couple of feet back. It was quite intimidating – you felt like you were in a real cauldron.

The first-half had been pretty tight and we were piling on the pressure at the start of the second-half but only leading 3-0 when their fullback, Gerwyn Williams, sent a clearance kick in my direction.

I was standing there ready to gather it when I heard Peter Kininmonth's voice saying, 'My ball!'

Scotland flanker Robert Taylor tries to shake off three Wales tacklers as Douglas Elliot looks on. *Press Association*

Well, he was my captain and he was bigger than me, so I decided to leave it to him. He caught the ball, pivoted and sent over the most perfectly struck drop-goal I had ever seen, from 25 yards out close to the touchline.

I think he'd played in the back division at school – so might have dropped a few goals back then – but he was 6′ 4″ and had moved into the forwards. His kick was the turning point and we went on to beat them 19-0.

I got a bit of a laugh afterwards because someone asked me what I would have done if Kininmonth hadn't been there. I said, 'Quite simple, I would have caught the ball, skipped past the Welsh defence with a couple of sidesteps and scored behind the posts. The conversion would have made it five points . . . Kininmonth only got three points for his drop-goal!'

Later in the match, I went through the middle and as I got closer and closer to the try-line I could sense this shadow coming up on my left shoulder. I was

Pupils from the Edinburgh Academy in the school boys' enclosure cheer on as Scotland record a famous victory over the Welsh.

very tense because the last thing you wanted in those days was to be tackled in possession when you were in the clear. So with about three or four steps to go, I flicked it to Bob Gordon who was on my right. For years afterwards I always said I gave him the pass with five yards to go, and he insisted that he got it 25 yards out. In the end we had to compromise.

That was a great victory – one of the best we've ever had. We played really well. Then, somehow, were beaten in our next game, against Ireland. They lost their fullback, AW Norton, to a late tackle from Doug Elliot and that seemed to fire them up. They played with fourteen men and we just couldn't score. It was a huge disappointment because we should have beaten them.

The reason results and performances fluctuated so dramatically from match to match was because it was all so terribly amateurish. There was no plan about what we were going to do. Probably the best captain we had was Doug Elliot, but even he said very little. He would just tell us to get out there, do our very, very best, and not make any silly bloody mistakes – because he felt that the desire to do well must just be within you.

I remember coming away from games thinking we didn't do badly but we

Douglas Elliot on his farm

didn't really do enough to win. I think winning was more important to some of us than others. I felt absolutely sick when we lost games we could have won, but I think some others felt that if we had put up a good show then that was okay.

A lot of rugby at that time was about getting the ball out to the wing as quickly as possible. Even if there was a great big gap in front of you, you were meant to get it straight out to the wing and give everyone a feel of the ball.

Well, international players – or even district and club players – should know exactly what is happening and be able to make up their own mind about whether to kick, pass or try to make a break when the ball comes to them. Perhaps if we'd had a good coach, they'd have picked out the strength of one or two players and come up with a way of playing that suited our game. But we didn't have that – only committee guys who had played 25 years earlier and were a bit out of touch.

Losing 44-0 to South Africa in November 1951 highlighted these shortcomings.

When I played in any match there were three things I thought the man opposite might do: they would run at me and try to beat me, they would run at me and pass the ball to change the angle of attack, or they would kick the ball.

Well, the South Africans did all that, but they also did something I had never seen before: they ran into you. They looked at you and said: *come and take me.*

Now, in those days back-row forwards in British rugby used to corner-flag when their team lost the ball, they would run back diagonally towards the faraway corner. So when these guys hit us in the middle of the pitch, there was a big gap between the collision point and our cover defence, and they exploited that because after they hit us they turned and popped the ball, and they had three brilliant back-row forwards – led by the great Hennie Muller – who were coming in their slipstream and taking the ball on at pace.

South Africa scored nine tries against us and seven were scored by the forwards, which was really unusual in those days.

You watch rugby now and it is all about contact, and laying the ball off in different ways – and that was the first time I saw that approach. We tackled all day, but when we got our opponents down the ball just wasn't there.

I remember, in the last minute of the game, I was totally knackered and found myself chasing their winger, a guy called Paul Johnstone. I got to him just as he was going over in the corner and forced him into touch.

Now, I'm not a religious man, but I said at that point, 'Dear Lord, get the referee to blow his whistle.' And he did. I got up on my feet thinking I couldn't have gone on, I was absolutely bushed. There is nothing more tiring in a game than having to tackle, tackle, tackle.

It was a pretty miserable experience. The only comfort I can take is that I thought I did pretty well within the context of such a heavy defeat, and I was the only back reselected for the next game.

Apart from that match, we were never really out of the frame. We lost games we should have won, because we weren't in a winning habit. I would love to have seen a team picked by the players as opposed to the selectors, because there were guys who got caps who I don't think should have been anywhere near the Scotland team, and guys who weren't capped who should have been.

For example, I played for the South of Scotland against almost the same South African team, and we only lost 13-3. Admittedly it was played at Hawick where visiting teams never got an easy ride, and there was a bit of snow on the ground which they wouldn't have liked, but there were some very good players in the South of Scotland at the time who maybe should have had a chance to play for their country.

When we went to Ireland in 1952, Doug Elliot said to me that there was going to be a meeting the next morning at which one of the selectors was going to tell us we were being flown home, and was going to ask if anyone didn't want to go by air. He then said, 'You'll tell them that you don't like flying.'

I said, 'Why am I going to do that, Dougie? I'm quite keen to get home.'

'No, you tell them you're not going to fly.'

Now, I was a great pal of Dougie's and he was a bit older than me so I usually did what I was told. But on this occasion I thought to myself: *I'm not going to bother too much with that.*

Sure enough, at the meeting this guy stood up and said that they were breaking with tradition and we were going to be flown home. 'Anybody not keen on flying?'

I just sat there, determined to say nothing. But then I got this bang between my shoulder blades – it was Doug.

So he and I put our hands up, along with two other guys who were staying on to play another game on the Monday.

I said to Dougie afterwards, 'What was all that about?'

'Let's face it,' he said. 'We'll all go to the dinner tonight and we'll be late to our beds and they're all going to have to be out at the airport at half past eight in the morning.'

'So?'

'Well, they'll not feel great, whereas you and I don't need to get up in the morning.'

'But the ferry is pretty early, too.'

'No,' he said. 'They don't run ferries on a Sunday. We're staying at the SRU's expense until Monday.'

So we had a free day in Dublin, and he had a couple of Border pals I didn't know about who were staying over until the Monday too. We had a great party.

Angus Cameron gets away from two Irish tacklers at Murrayfield, 1951. *Press Association*

KEN SCOTLAND (Royal Signals, Heriot's FP, Cambridge University, London Scottish, Leicester, Aberdeenshire)
27 Caps: 1957-65

There was no real sporting pedigree of any distinction in my family but I was born within a stone-throw of Goldenacre, and from a very young age I have memories of playing there with either a cricket ball or a rugby ball. All my interests at that stage were sports related.

It seems as if I was at Goldenacre every Saturday watching Heriot's play, but they used to still play a lot of big games at Inverleith, and I remember going along there to watch those matches too. However, I think the key moment as far as my early rugby development was concerned came in 1946 when my father took me to watch Scotland beat the New Zealand Army at Murrayfield. From then on I wanted to play for Scotland. It really concentrated the mind – that became my central focus in life.

Years later, when I made it into the Scotland team, I was happy to discover that the vast majority of the team had a similar sort of mindset. Over the years I think that has been the defining thing about the way Scotland play, and it has helped us punch above our weight for so long.

People often talk about youngsters being disheartened by Scotland not winning games, but I grew up during the era when Scotland had lost 44-0 to South Africa in 1951, in a run of 17 defeats in a row between 1951 and 1955, and it never dimmed my ambitions. But I suppose life was simpler in those days. There were no alternatives. We didn't have computer games, we didn't even have televisions.

Jim Greenwood puts in a big hit on Sean McDermott after the Irish scrum-half strays offside at a scrum at Murrayfield in February 1955. *The Scotsman Publications Ltd. www.scran.ac.uk*

While my ambition from a very young age was to play for Scotland, as I got older and started playing for the 1st XV at Heriot's School it became more and more apparent that this was not a foregone conclusion. I was playing stand-off and with players like Iain Laughland at Merchiston, Gregor Sharpe at Daniel Stewart's College and Gordon Waddell at Fettes, all coming through at around about the same time, I knew that I was going to have my work cut out. I was still very ambitious, but it wasn't clear if it was going to be achievable.

From school I went straight into National Service, and I joined the Royal

Signals specifically to play rugby because they had the best reputation for providing sporting opportunities. In those days there were three National Trials in a season and in 1956 I played in the first two at stand-off, but wasn't selected for the third. Then, in my second year in the army, I wasn't selected for the first Trial but got a letter on the Thursday before the second Trial informing me that I had been selected as a reserve fullback for that match – with *fullback* underlined.

The Trial was at Hawick and Micky Grant of Harlequins had been selected as fullback for the Whites, but he dropped out and I must have played well enough in his place to merit selection ahead of Robin Chisholm of Melrose, who had played the previous season and had been in the Blues team. And Micky Grant was selected at stand-off, which shows how up in the air selection was in those days.

I continued to play for the army at stand-off, and by the time I had finished my National Service I had played six games at fullback in my whole life – it just so happens that those matches had been two National Trials and four full internationals. From then on I played almost all my first class rugby at fullback.

The crowd invade the pitch at Murrayfield after Scotland defeat Ireland in 1955. *Getty Images*

England won the Grand Slam that year with the best back division I have seen. I could still name them now: Rob Challis, Peter Jackson, Jeff Butterfield, Phil Davies, Peter Thompson, Ricky Bartlett and Dickie Jeeps. Butterfield and Davies, in particular, were a couple of top-class players. They had both played in the centre for the Lions in South Africa in 1955.

Their back-row – Robbins, Ashcroft and Higgins – were pretty formidable also. At that time the forwards didn't do much with the ball in hand, their job was to get possession and give it to the backs, but that back-row were all ball-players. We had a good back-row – Ken Smith, Jim Greenwood and Adam Robson – but they didn't add as much in an attacking sense.

After the army I went to Cambridge and played the worst game of my life at fullback in the freshers' trial so I started my time there as third choice. I didn't play in the internationals that season until Robin Chisholm was injured against Ireland and I came in for the last game of the season against England.

Up to that point I hadn't ever trained specifically for rugby, but at Cambridge everything was about the build-up up to the Varsity Match. It was very concentrated. We played two games a week against sides like Cardiff, Northampton, Leicester, London Scottish and Richmond. Over an eight week period we would play almost all the top English sides and a few of the big Welsh teams. So when I got back into the Scotland side in 1959, I was fit and I was playing a high standard of rugby week-in and week-out. In rugby that is the crux of the matter – if you are playing at a high standard then you can take almost anything that happens on the pitch in your stride.

Ken Scotland in his Cambridge livery.

DAVID ROLLO (Howe of Fife)
40 Caps: 1959-68

I broke my nose after ten minutes in my first game, against England in 1959. Peter Jackson was on the wing for them, I went to tackle him from behind and my nose hit the back of his head. I was knocked out and when I came round they couldn't get the bleeding to stop, so I had to go off for ten minutes. A lot of Howe of Fife supporters had come all the way down to Twickenham to see me play – the club had cancelled its game against Harris that weekend – and I think they got a bigger fright than I did, having gone all that way to see me okay it looked as if I was only going to be on the field for ten minutes. Eventually they managed to get me back on the field by plugging me up with cotton wool – which I then had to spend a long and fairly agonising time pulling back out of my nose after the game.

France versus Scotland at Colombes, 1959. *Getty Images*

CHAPTER THREE

CHANGING FORTUNES

A S THE FIFTIES *gave way to the sixties, there was plenty of cause for optimism. In Arthur Smith and Ken Scotland, Scotland now had two of the most gifted backs the game has ever produced; in Gordon Waddell they had a fine tactician at stand-off; and in the pack, the likes of David Rollo, Norman Bruce, and Hugh McLeod provided an iron core.*

There can rarely have been a greater international debut than the one made by Arthur Smith in 1955. To have an international known simply as 'Arthur Smith's match' says it all. For 17 Tests, Scotland had stuttered and stalled, stagnant in attack and pedestrian in defence, bogged down by bad-fortune and their own limitations. That was until Wales came to town on a bright spring day in February 1955 and the winger's jersey was handed to 22 year old Arthur Smith, the Galloway-born mathematics wunderkind. His electric pace and balanced running lit up the afternoon with its verve and poise, his impulsive daring and audacious adventure utterly confounding the Welsh defence whenever he went on the attack. Late in the game he gathered the ball deep in his own 25 and set off up field. His pace and angles were breathtaking, his swerves and changes of direction entrancing; as he stepped and wound his way around and through the Welsh defence, the Murrayfield roar broke the air asunder and as he crossed the try line at the far end of the pitch it rose to a crescendo that hadn't been heard for years. It was a moment of virtuoso brilliance, an act of inspiration that stirred Scotland to a 14-8 victory and the team's first steps out of rugby purgatory.

Smith was slight in build, like a greyhound; brute strength was never an attribute that he possessed, but wit and guile were the weapons with which he augmented his frightening pace. He was the master of the swerve and the sidestep and a fine exponent of cross and chip kicks, which he used expertly to unpick defences that threatened to close down his running space. Having achieved a first-class degree in mathematics and a PhD from Cambridge, he was capped 33 times without ever being dropped and went on to captain Scotland on 15 occasions as well as skippering the 1962 Lions in South Africa, where he finished the tour as the top try-scorer.

Ken Scotland made his debut at fullback against France in Colombes in 1957 and scored all of his side's points as Scotland recorded their first win on French soil since 1949. As a debut, it was something of a baptism of fire as he had played virtually all of his previous rugby at stand-off and this was only his third-ever game

---

Opposite: Scotland captain Arthur Smith leads his team out before Scotland play Wales in 1958. *Press Association*

at fullback, with the previous two having been the National Trial matches. To watch him perform, one would never have known of his inexperience; indeed, he looked like he had been born for the role.

It was astonishing then that when the new star of Scottish rugby left the army to study at Cambridge, he was unable to get into the university team during his first year. He was third-choice fullback. Despite this rather remarkable setback, however, the 1959 Lions recognised his undoubted merits and picked him for their tour to New Zealand, Australia and Canada. Upon the conclusion of the tour, the New Zealand press named him as one of the five most influential players in the Lions squad, with the New Zealand Rugby Almanac *calling him the player 'most likely to win a match for his side'. His unpredictable surges into the attacking line were pioneering for a fullback, and his sense of timing, both in running and passing, were unrivalled. Indeed, Arthur Smith called him 'the best passer of a ball I have ever played with'. His kicking style too, was revolutionary. He abandoned the traditional straight-on toe kick at goal for an around-the-corner instep kick, and applied the spiral punt to devastating effect. For all that he joked that he could kick for goal with either his toe or his instep and 'could miss equally well with either', he was, more often than not, a deadeye shot and a pin-up for the developing fortunes of both Scottish and Lions rugby. When the great Munster, Ireland and Lions fullback Tom Kiernan won his 50th cap he was asked to name the greatest player of his time. Without a moment's hesitation he said, 'Ken Scotland. It was a privilege to be on the same field as he was.'*

Perhaps less celebrated than either Smith or Scotland, Gordon Waddell (son of 1925 Grand Slam hero, Herbert) was the guiding light at stand-off, the general who stamped his authority on games with a purposeful and patient control. Scotland performed well during this period but despite the exquisite talents of Arthur Smith and Ken Scotland out wide and the rising quality of the pack, they rarely dominated teams as they should have. Perhaps it was the lack of a hard-edge in the team, the lack of a grizzled warrior like Douglas Elliot who had always taken the game to the opposition and who had constantly put his body on the line for the cause. In 1964 a figure reminiscent of Elliot finally appeared. He was a chemistry teacher who played for Melrose; his name was Jim Telfer.

The emergence of a new generation of ambitious and self-confident Scottish players brought fresh impetus to the team's performances. During Telfer and Peter Brown's first season, Scotland drew 0-0 with New Zealand at Murrayfield, won the Calcutta Cup, defeated France at Murrayfield and Ireland at Lansdowne Road and shared the Championship with Wales. It was Scotland's most successful season in decades.

Following a 3-3 draw with England at Twickenham in 1965 they beat South Africa 8-5 at Murrayfield. Then, in 1966, they defeated Ireland at Lansdowne Road and England and Australia at Murrayfield, while also drawing there with France.

Before the decade had ended, the team had recorded memorable wins against

France, Wales, Australia and South Africa and had notable representation on the Lions tours of 1966 to New Zealand, Australia and Canada and 1968 to South Africa. Despite a relatively weak and unstructured domestic game and a run of seven straight defeats from December 1967 until November 1968, there seemed no threat of a return to the dark days of the 1950s. The team was too full of talent and, in players like Telfer, too bloody-minded to accept such poor standards. They lost matches, certainly, but then the quality of other teams operating at that time was very high. The New Zealanders were as ferocious as ever; Wales had luminaries in the shape of Alun Pask, Gareth Edwards, Barry John and Gerald Davies; Ireland had the likes of Mike Gibson, Willie John McBride, Tom Kiernan, and Ray McLoughlin; John Pullin, Bob Taylor, Keith Savage and Bob Hiller were stars for England; and across the Channel the French side was overflowing with maestros such as Pierre Villepreux, Walter Spanghero, Christian Carrere, Jean Trillo, Lilian Camberabero and Jo Maso.

But Scotland could hold its own among such dazzling company. Even when the magicians Smith and Scotland retired, in new caps Colin Telfer, Chris Rea, Sandy Hinshelwood and John Frame they were able to strike a balance between control, pace and flair, and when the backs combined with the grunt and gristle of the likes of Jim Telfer, Sandy Carmichael, Alastair McHarg, Peter 'PC' Brown and Rodger Arneil, they were truly a sight to behold.

A view from the south terrace during Scotland's victory over Wales at Murrayfield in 1961. *Press Association*

DAVID ROLLO

When I first played for Scotland I had number eight on my back. Then, against France in 1960 the selectors swapped me to tight-head and Hughie MacLeod moved to loose-head, so I played with number ten on my back. In 1961, they changed the numbering system, so against France I played number three. And in 1964, Brian Neill was captain, and he played tight-head prop, so I moved back over to loose-head, which meant I wore number one. I don't think there are many players who can say they have started international matches wearing those four different numbers on their jersey.

Arthur Smith attacks the French back-line at Colombes in 1961. *Press Association*

KEN SCOTLAND

The game had been pretty stagnant from the 1930s, through the war, and into the 1950s. There had been very little, if any innovation. The forwards got the ball and gave it to the backs. The first time I can remember forwards doing moves was in 1960, when DJ Hopwood, the South African number eight, started picking the ball up at the base of the scrum, and around that time the French had started peeling round the tail of the line-out as well. Also, Oxford had a great pair of half-backs in Mike Smith, who was England's last cricket and rugby double internationalist, and Onllwyn Brace, and they started initiating moves.

So the game was evolving a bit, and I was fortunate to be a part of that because in my first year in the Cambridge team Gordon Waddell – who was a really good tactical player and with whom I had a good understanding – was at stand-off. We started developing ploys with the fullback coming into the line. We just wanted to do something the opposition wasn't expecting. In those days each player drew his man and there was no such thing as drift defence, so a fullback coming into the line automatically created a two-on-one until the opposition figured us out. We also used the blindside a lot more than was previously fashionable.

Gordon Waddell passes the ball out of contact against the French in 1962. *The Scotsman Publications Ltd. www.scran.ac.uk*

We played with a leather ball, and throughout my whole rugby career there was never any suggestion of a spin pass, and miss moves were not thought up until well after I stopped playing.

After I left Cambridge, I spent two years working in the Midlands during which time I played for Leicester. It was a very different environment to what I was used to. It was highly competitive; at Cambridge everything you did was geared towards one match, whereas at Leicester you were playing big matches almost every week. And because of where I was living I couldn't train with the team for two years, so I was really dependent on playing tough games every week, and playing each match as if my life depended on it, because that really was the only way I was going to be able to keep match fit.

Then, in 1963, I got a job back in Edinburgh and I was looking forward to playing for Heriot's, but on my first day in the office I was told that I was being sent up to Aberdeen to work.

The two big clubs in Aberdeen at that time were Gordonians, who had a good pack and Ian MacRae at scrum-half, and Aberdeen Grammar, who were a young side with a good fixture list. But because I wasn't a former pupil of either Robert Gordons or Aberdeen Grammar School I had to join Aberdeenshire – which was more of a junior side. That was the end of me getting hard games every Saturday. Our best fixture was against Dundee High, who played good rugby but were not a big club in those days.

Peter Brown shows off his athleticism at training. *The Scotsman Publications Ltd.* *www.scran.ac.uk*

I was dropped for Stuart Wilson in 1964, and he played very well that season – but, as often happens, his second season did not live up to expectations, and I got back into the side for our trip to Paris in what must have been the slowest back division Scotland has ever fielded. Unfortunately I didn't play very well in that match and I knew at the time that I hadn't played well enough to keep my place.

After that I played a lot for the North and Midlands, and I enjoyed my time with Aberdeenshire but it was a lot of travelling. I seemed to be playing in Dundee every other week and I was the only married man in the side, so I was the only one wanting to get straight home. Also the injuries were taking longer and longer to get over. When that begins to happen, you know your time on the field is coming to an end. But I didn't have any regrets when I eventually retired. How could I? I had realised my childhood dream and played in some fantastic teams for Scotland and the Lions and at club and university level.

GEORGE STEVENSON (Hawick)
24 Caps: 1956-65

I played in the famous match against Wales in 1963 when there were 111 line-outs. The Welsh scrum-half, Clive Rowlands, just kicked to touch every time he got the ball. I think that was one of the first times I played on the wing for Scotland and in those days the winger put the ball in at the line-out. I touched the ball more that day than I had ever touched it in any match before, but it was only to throw the ball in after Rowlands had kicked to touch again. Wales won 6-3. What a dreadful game. They changed the rules after that, making it illegal to kick direct to touch unless you were in your own 22.

JIM TELFER (Melrose)
25 Caps: 1964-1970

My first game for Scotland was as a flanker against France in 1964. I had been a second-row forward at the school and I had never played in the back-row for Melrose or the South, so I played my first international match in a position I had never played before. I remember Leslie Allan showing me the angles to attack the stand-off at. He'd played a bit at stand-off for Scotland so he knew where the flanker should be coming from.

I played two or three games at flanker with Oliver Grant at number eight. Then eventually I was moved to number eight, where I had never played before.

Getting to the ground on match-day in France was always exciting. You used to be sitting on the bus deep in your own thoughts, and then you'd spot the police outriders kicking the cars out of the way. Only a few players would be looking out the front to start with, but by the time you got into the ground everyone was watching to see what the outriders were doing to the cars in front of them. The Irish were the worst. When you were heading to Lansdowne Road, you'd be flying up these streets the wrong way and the players would be glued to the action in front. I think it was a good thing, it certainly got the adrenaline pumping.

You must remember that players at that time weren't used to going away very often. Most people had never been to Paris, and you didn't see French club sides playing in Britain. The crowd was certainly a big factor in helping the home team – no doubt about that.

Jim Telfer in the thick of the action.

DAVID ROLLO

Against France in 1964, I was reserve prop in attendance, which meant I stayed with the team right up to the morning of the match, but once the players were on the park there were no replacements. So at lunch on Saturday, I had a full three-course meal – normally I just had a mushroom omelette – and afterwards Charlie Drummond said, 'David, you're not playing, you'd be as well coming next door with the committee for a pint of beer.'

So I had one pint of beer, then I had a second, and I was halfway through my third when I happened to look up and see John Law coming through the doors looking rather flustered. After a quick word with Charlie I was told that I was wanted over in the hotel. When I got there they told me Cameron Boyle was ill and that I was playing . . . I nearly fell to the floor.

But if you know you're fit then you can get through things like that. You might have a slow start but once you get going you're alright. I had a good game, we won, and I enjoyed it. But I was sorry for Cameron Boyle; I think that was his last cap.

Hughie McLeod. *The Scotsman Publications Ltd. www.scran.ac.uk*

JIM TELFER

I was a great admirer of Hughie McLeod. I think he was the best loose-head prop Scotland has ever had, better than Ian MacLauchlan, David Sole and Tom Smith. I remember playing with him for the South when I was just coming through. I'd be about 20 and he'd be about 30. We came out this scrum, charged across the park and hit the centre. I was the back-row and I was meant to be there before anyone else, but Hughie raced past me and got to the ball first. It was an eye-opener for me. I remember just thinking, 'This boy is different.' His attitude to everything was just different. He didn't drink, he didn't smoke – he went out training while everyone else was at home or in the pub. He was ahead of his time. I think Derrick Grant took a lot from him and he certainly inspired my attitude towards training and doing everything you can to improve your own game.

When Davie Rollo got to forty caps they dropped him, apparently because the SRU didn't want him to go past Hughie.

PETER BROWN (West of Scotland and Gala)
27 Caps: 1964-73

My first cap was against France in 1964, when David Rollo was brought in as a last minute replacement for Cameron Boyle. The interesting thing about that match was that we had a hush-hush meeting at 9am on the Friday, because the International Rugby Board rules stated that no team was to meet more than 24 hours before the kick-off. Now, other teams were doing it; Wales, for example, were already meeting up at Port Talbot on the Sunday before the match for scrummaging practice, but not announcing their team until after that practice so it wasn't officially a team meeting. But in Scotland, at least up until that point, we prided ourselves on not compromising when it came to following the rules.

Anyway, we all gathered at the Braid Hills Hotel in Edinburgh, met some of the team members for the first time, then got on the bus and went to Boroughmuir for a secret practice with nobody else present. We then went back to the hotel and had some lunch before getting on the bus again to go back to Boroughmuir for the official practice.

It was a hoot, and the thing is, in a funny sort of way, it brought the team together. A lot of very good players got their first caps that day against France – Stuart Wilson, Jim Telfer, Billy Hunter and me – and we won 10-0.

It's fascinating now to think that back then all we did was come together, have a run-around on the Friday morning, have another run-around for the press on the Friday afternoon, a team-talk with selectors present on the Saturday, and then go out and play.

There were no sophisticated line-out codes or anything like that. The big thing we practiced in those days was *the wheel*: with the ball being struck to the feet of the left-hand second-row in the scrum and the right-hand second-row pulling with his right hand on the prop in front of him and shouting 'away', so that we wheeled the scrum and came out with our heads up, the line in front of us and the ball at our feet. Now any brave man that went down on it did well, but he also thought twice about doing it next time.

JIM TELFER

There is a tendency to think that the game was not taken that seriously back then, but the truth of it is that we took it very seriously. We used to prepare as best we could by the standards of the time. We'd meet the night before, train at Boroughmuir, we stayed at the Braids and go down on Saturday morning to practice our line-outs in the park down the road from the hotel, and the backs would bugger about doing their thing – it was pretty well organised. We were trying to be as professional about it as possible.

Latterly, when I became captain, we asked for Sunday sessions at Murrayfield the week before the match. That was the first time that had ever been done.

PETER BROWN

Two weeks after my debut we played New Zealand at Murrayfield. Had they beaten us they would have achieved the Grand Slam, but they could only manage a 0-0 draw. They were a wonderful team, full of greats like Don Clarke,

Macfarlane Herewini, Wilson Whineray, Ken Gray, Colin Meads, Kel Tremain and Brian Lochore. I can still vividly remember Brian Neill's team-talk beforehand, he sat there and quietly went over our strengths then said it was 'absolutely essential' that they didn't get loose ball which would allow them to break free – those were his exact words 'absolutely essential' – and that's how we played the game. It wasn't rocket science – it was a clear and uncomplicated message which left us in no doubt as to what was required. We didn't plan to beat them – the whole approach to the game was about holding the All Blacks, and we were good enough. I have to say, the conditions were not good, which was great for getting in about them.

By the second-half they were struggling. They kept on putting the ball up in the air and, instead of kicking for touch, Stuart Wilson, at fullback, started attacking, just as Ken Scotland used to do. We actually came closer to scoring that day than the All Blacks did.

Scotland batter the All Blacks to a 0-0 draw at Murrayfield. *The Scotsman Publications Ltd. www.scran.ac.uk*

Earlier in the tour, when the All Blacks had played a combined Glasgow-Edinburgh side, and had stayed in the Marine Hotel in Troon, they asked for a physio to do the massages for the players. Well, my father was a physio in Troon so he went along and their wee stand-off needed a lot of treatment so my father brought him to his surgery, and while he was there – under the lamp – I went in and had a chat with him. We chatted rugby for a while and I told him that I had been a reserve in the game and that I could have been playing but that the selectors didn't like Glasgow players too much at the time.

My Dad must have done a good job because when the All Blacks came back to Scotland in January for the Test match they asked for him again, and at the dinner after the match my father was there, as was Kirton, who was still injured. I went over and re-introduced myself. He said, 'What you doing here?'

I said, 'Well actually I was playing number four against you today.'

He couldn't believe it.

Now, fast-forward to 1967, and New Zealand are back again and again they took Father as a physio. After the match Jim Telfer blew his top. He thought it was ridiculous that the father of one of the Scottish squad was in the New Zealand dressing-room helping them while there was nobody in the Scottish dressing-room. So pretty soon after that my Dad became Scotland's physio.

JIM TELFER

My second match was the 0-0 draw against New Zealand, which was a huge result. They were all over us. I was quite well known for putting my body on the line – not being very constructive but just killing the ball – and there was one occasion they were driving towards the line and the ball squirted out the side of the ruck and I dived on it. I just held it, held it and held it – then Meads kicked me and he nearly got sent off. That prevented the try which would have won them the game.

PETER BROWN

So we had beaten France, drawn with the All Blacks and we then went to Wales and stayed in the Esplanade Hotel in Penarth, which was the great Baa Baas hotel. I was sharing a room with Billy Hunter from Hawick. I'm a plukey faced 22 year old absolutely horrified at the speed with which 30 year old WJ Hunter can pull his safety razor over his cheeks as he shaves. And at half past two in the morning of the international the selectors returned to the hotel from the committee dinner, pissed out their brains, and they went into the players' rooms and tipped them all out of their beds saying, 'What are you boys doing sleeping? Wake up – you're playing an international today!'

But I wouldn't say that was why we lost that game. The biggest problem of my ten years in the Scottish team was the excellence of the Welsh. Do you know, in my first nine caps I played against all the top rugby nations in the world and the only ones we didn't beat were New Zealand, who we drew with, and Wales, who beat us 11-3 and probably should have won by more.

Murrayfield in the 1960s. *Getty Images*

JIM TELFER

Beating England in 1964 was perhaps just as big a result as the draw with New Zealand. Hughie McLeod played ten times against England and never won. We hadn't beaten them since 1950, but we actually won quite comfortably that day, scoring three tries. I made the pass for two tries and scored the third – and the crowd ran onto the field to celebrate, which was the first time that had happened – and I thought I had cracked it. I was dropped the following year so I soon found out that international rugby wasn't always that easy.

PETER BROWN

When we won the Calcutta Cup at Murrayfield in 1964, Dougie Jackson had been picked on the wing but when he arrived in Edinburgh he was ruled out with an injury. On Friday afternoon we went for a team run in front of the press, and George Stevenson from Hawick was there spectating. Afterwards, as we came off the field, he walked over and shook hands with Brian Neill. He said, 'Hello Brian, I'm playing tomorrow.' He hadn't even bothered to get stripped to come and practice with us – that's typical Stevie.

The match was the same day as the Grand National and there was a horse running called Team Spirit. We all had a bet on it, and guess what won the Grand National in 1964? That's right – Team Spirit at 18 to 1.

We only discovered afterwards that it was the first time in 13 years that Scotland had beaten England. I didn't appreciate that Hughie MacLeod and Kenny Scotland never played in a victory over England – the coverage in the press wasn't the same in those days.

Ken Scotland chases a high ball against England at Twickenham in 1963. *The Scotsman Publications Ltd. www.scran.ac.uk*

At the end of the 1965 game against England at Twickenham we were leading 3-0 and all over them. Then David Whyte, on the right wing, got the ball, came infield and kicked; they picked it up and fed it to their left winger, AW Hancock, who nobody had ever heard of before. He starts running – down the touchline, infield, back out to the touchline – is he in touch, is he not? – Iain Laughland misses him and he collapses over the line in the corner – they miss the conversion and it finishes 3-3.

The touch-judge on that side was a Scotsman called Doctor David Haultain, and he emigrated to Australia later that year. I think he was going to go anyway, but when he comes back to visit every year he plays a round of golf at

Muirfield, and we always say to him, 'You should be okay this time – nobody remembers.'

JIM TELFER

We toured Canada that summer and although there were no official capped Test matches, we won all five of our matches which was a great way to finish the season. I thought that it would set us up perfectly for the following year, but 1965 didn't quite go according to plan.

We had four internationals out of the Melrose club that season – David Chisholm, Eck Hastie, Frank Laidlaw and myself; we played ten internationals together and were never beaten – and I am the only player to have played against all three of the big southern hemisphere sides for Scotland and never been beaten, so I'm pretty proud of that. But we lost the first three games of the Five Nations to France, Wales and Ireland and on the back of those results I was then dropped.

Mike Campbell-Lamerton was the captain during that tough 1965 season and he was a wonderful guy, a real genuine bloke who put his heart and soul into everything he did. He was a great hulking man who was very effective at using his size. He was named captain of the 1966 Lions but was torn to pieces by the media and was replaced as captain half-way through the tour, which was a terrible thing to happen to such a good man.

Mike Campbell-Lamerton and Peter Stagg. *The Scotsman Publications Ltd. www.scran.ac.uk*

DAVID ROLLO

I remember playing England on a very hot day in 1965. Norman Suddon and I were the props and it was a great game to play in – with a lot of running rugby. There were scales in the dressing room, and I weighed myself before and after the match – I had gone from 14st 7lb to just under 14st. After we had finished we discovered we were both playing with number one on our jersey, so whichever one of us was meant to be at loose-head must have got a rave review – it would have looked like we were doing the job of two men.

JIM TELFER

It became known as 'Hancock's Game' because we were leading 3-0 when Andy Hancock, the English wing, took a pass from their stand-off, Mike Weston, and charged 70 yards up field dodging tackles from all over the place to score. Luckily the cover defence forced him in at the corner and they missed the kick, so it ended 3-3.

I was sitting up in the stands because I was a reserve and just had to watch the whole game, which was pretty tough – although not as tough as having to do it a month later when we beat the Springboks 8-5 and I was still out of favour.

But I was back in the team for the 1966 Five Nations and we opened our Championship by drawing 3-3 with France at Murrayfield. We then lost 11-5 to Wales in Cardiff but we turned things around by beating Ireland and England.

I was selected to tour with the Lions that summer to Australia, New Zealand and Canada, which was a fantastic honour, but when I came back I was injured

Peter Stagg rises high against the French lineout at Murrayfield in 1966. *The Scotsman Publications Ltd. www.scran.ac.uk*

for the autumn win against the Wallabies at Murrayfield as well as the opening game of the 1967 Five Nations, which Scotland won in France – so it was disappointing to miss out on all those famous wins.

JOHN FRAME (Highland RFC, Edinburgh University and Gala)
23 Caps: 1967-1973

They used to say in the seventies that it was harder to get out of the Scottish team than get in. When I was first selected in 1967 I was a fresh-faced 21 year old student at Edinburgh University and I was about to face New Zealand, the best team on the planet. I was up against the great Ian MacRae and Bill Davis in the centre. We played fly-half and left and right centre, while they played first five-eighths, second five-eighths and centre, so half the time I was marking one and half the time I was marking the other. Earlier in the tour, Danny Hearn had broken his neck on Ian MacRae's hip bone whilst playing for London and the Home Counties against the All Blacks. It had been a horrible accident, nobody's fault, but I suppose it would have added to the trepidation at the back of my mind that I was going up against this great powerful New Zealander. We lost 14-3; they scored two tries and Colin Meads was sent off for almost taking Davie Chisholm's head off with a wild kick – I remember it all vividly.

Colin Meads heads disconsolately for the changing-room after his sending-off. *The Scotsman Publications Ltd. www.scran.ac.uk*

It was obviously pretty exciting. The New Zealand team came with this terrifying reputation, especially Meads, and they all looked like they had been hewn out of granite. My mother sat in the stand and panicked every time the ball came near me because she knew all about the All Blacks.

I'm very sentimental and I remember having dinner in the McRobert Pavilion after the game. The New Zealanders, as they always are, were very gracious in victory, and I was sitting opposite David Rollo, having probably had a drop too much to drink. I remember sitting there musing about the whole experience: as a 21 year old from Inverness, to be winning my first cap against the mighty All Blacks in front of however many thousand people, it was kind of emotional. Davie had this lovely manner about him. He said, 'Aye, it's a great thing to play for your country.' That was me, I collapsed in a well of emotion.

Sandy Hinshelwood in action against the All Blacks. *The Scotsman Publications Ltd. www.scran.ac.uk*

Davie could be as fierce as he wanted to be, but he did his talking through his strength in the front-row. Several years later, during our centenary season, Gala were asked to go to Howe of Fife for an exhibition match, I think it was to open their new stand, and Davie was brought out of retirement to play the game. Gala were winning quite comfortably and it was a great day – beautiful weather and the ball was being thrown around by both sides.

But Gala had this young prop – who I won't name so as to spare his blushes – and he had obviously decided that he was going to make his reputation against this old-stager from Fife. So he was pushing and pulling, and ducking and bucking. And Davie just stood there like the man mountain he was.

Then, at half-time, a very embarrassed and shy Mr Rollo came up to me and said, 'Hey John, can I have a word with your young prop?'

I said, 'Be my guest.'

And with the crowd all craning to see what was going on, he asked the boys to pack down, and he said, 'Now son, what you're trying to do is this, but you should be doing that. Drop your left shoulder here, and get your right foot back there.' At half-time he was giving this boy a coaching lesson.

That was typical of Davie; while others might see psychological warfare in that, he genuinely wanted to help this boy who was getting it all wrong. He was a different breed.

The Scottish and Irish teams used to stay in the same hotel in Dublin when they played in the Five Nations, and I remember Tom Kiernan saying in his after-dinner speech in 1968 that he really thought it was time that the two teams had separate hotels.

Jim Telfer is caught around the neck against Wales in 1969. *The Scotsman Publications Ltd.*
www.scran.ac.uk

'The reason I say this,' he explained. 'Is that doing my rounds last night as a good captain should always do, I came through the reception at about 11.30pm and saw that man Syd Millar there, and his pal Davie Rollo, in their green and blue blazers, walking through the reception with their arms around each others' shoulders, singing: Take me back to the old Transvaal.'

That was them having had a couple of pints of Guinness together on the Friday night before the international, and then singing a song they had learned together on the 1962 Lions tour.

JIM TELFER

I was fit again after the win in France and came back into the team for our game at Murrayfield against Wales. They were a great side with guys like Barry John, Gerald Davies, John Taylor and Alun Pask but we played some super stuff and I scored a try in our 11-5 win. The rest of the Championship was a little disappointing after such a good start: we lost to Ireland at Murrayfield 3-5 after Tom Kiernan converted Noel Murphy's try and then fell 27-14 to England at Twickenham.

I had a great summer that year, touring South Africa with the Scottish Borders Club, but when the season started again I injured my knee playing against Kelso for Melrose and was ruled out until the final game of the 1968 Championship against England. Fortunately I did enough in that game to be selected for a return trip to South Africa, this time with the Lions, which was fairly remarkable considering how long I had been out for and the fact that Scotland had endured a terrible Championship when they didn't win a game.

The 1968-69 season started very well for us. I was selected as captain to face Australia at Murrayfield in November and we won 9-3. That win lifted our confidence for the impending Championship as it was our first victory in eight Tests and set us up well for our opening match of the 1969 Five Nations against France.

I can't remember much about the matches I played in because it was such a long time ago, but that is one of the games about which I do still have a vivid memory. I was captain of the team and it was at Colombes, which is the stadium where Eric Liddell won his 400 metres gold medal, and to get to the pitch you had to come through this wet tunnel with water dripping down on you, and then you came up right into the middle of the stadium. It was like being a lion being released into the Coliseum. You looked around and realised you were suddenly the focus of this huge hostile crowd.

We were warming up when this guy they called the White Corsican, Jean Salut – a blond-haired flanker who was the coming man of French rugby before

Jim Telfer and Budge Rogers in Twickenham tunnel before Telfer leads his men into battle, 1969. *Press Association*

Jean Pierre Rives arrived on the scene – injured his ankle as he was coming up the steps and had to call off. The French being the French didn't have a back-row to bring in for him, so they more or less reshuffled their whole pack. They brought Jean Iraçabal in at loose-head prop, moved the original loose-head selection, Jean-Michel Esponda, to tight-head, the original tight-head, Michel Lasserre, into the second-row, the original second-row, Benoit Dauga, to number eight where Walter Spanghero was meant to be playing, and then shuffled Spanghero over to Salut's position on the flank. So that was a bit of drama before the game had even started.

They completely outplayed us but it was significant that Gordon Connell got injured halfway through the first-half and Ian McRae came on as the first ever replacement in international rugby. He was our saviour because he was a far more nuggety type of player. The French got a scrum about twenty meters out and McRae hassled his opposite number, snatched the ball out the side of the scrum and fed me, and all I had to do was run over Pierre Villepreux to score the try. That took us 6-3 ahead.

Jim Telfer talks to his team during training at Myreside in Edinburgh. *The Scotsman Publications Ltd. www.scran.ac.uk*

For the next hour the French played some beautiful open rugby without ever scoring a try. They were twice over the line but didn't get the ball down.

One of their favourite ploys at that time was to run a switch behind their line with Jo Maso, who was a wonderful player, their danger man, but we managed to cover him and survive a late onslaught and it was a great victory.

NORMAN SUDDON (Hawick)
13 Caps: 1965-1970

We got a licking that day but still managed to come away with a 6-3 win. The French had plenty of flair but they just couldn't get over the line. They did everything but score. Having said that, we defended well – we stopped them dead in their tracks. They kept coming at us and coming at us, but we had the bit between our teeth. It was a great victory. Larry Lamb from England was the referee and he got escorted off the pitch after that game to save him from the wrath of the crowd – but it was a fair result. The French might have dominated the game but we stopped them scoring, and that's what rugby is all about – doing the business when your back is up against the wall.

JIM TELFER

Norman Mair wrote in his article on the Monday morning that the Scottish team wouldn't need to fly home, because they could walk over the Channel.

You can imagine how the referee was hassled. He had a police escort from the field.

As years go by people start to assume that we played very well that day, but we actually held on for sixty minutes.

CHRIS REA (West of Scotland and Headingley)
13 Caps: 1968 -1971

Having beaten Australia 9-3 at Murrayfield in November 1968 in my first cap and then beating France away in my first Five Nations match in 1969, I felt as if I was on a roll – but reality was soon to catch up with me. We were stuffed by Wales 3-17 at Murrayfield and I got a very bad dislocated shoulder against Ireland, which put me out for the rest of the season.

It was very frosty at Murrayfield and the pitch was fine but immediately off the turf it was rock hard. I smother tackled Mike Gibson on the far side of the field, opposite the main stand, and as I hit the ground and my shoulder came out. It was excruciating. Their hooker was a guy called Ken Kennedy, who was a surgeon, and he came across and said he would put it straight back in, there and then. Sandy Carmichael, thinking Kennedy was up to some skulduggery, charged across and shouted, 'No, leave him alone.'

And that was catastrophic for me, because by the time they got the stretcher out and got me into the changing room, I was frozen, and the medic on duty was Sir John Bruce, who was the Queen's physician, who probably hadn't put a shoulder in since his university days. There were three people standing on

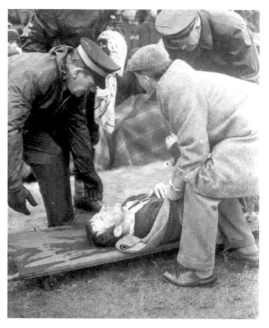

Chris Rea lies on a stretcher with a dislocated shoulder during the Ireland match. *The Scotsman Publications Ltd. www.scran.ac.uk*

my chest as they tried to get it back in. I've never known pain like it, and I still have problems with it today. But dear old Sandy thought he was doing me a favour.

JIM TELFER

I picked up the most bizarre injury in that Ireland game. I was standing out in the backs as a lineout was taking place and was next to the referee, Merion Joseph. As the ball went into play he raised his arm and caught me in the eye with his elbow. I was concussed and had to go off and then spent the night in hospital. I was replaced by Peter Stagg who was this big lump at 6' 10" and as he was getting ready to go on he sat on me – which was just what I needed.

That summer we went on tour to Argentina. It is interesting how you are often coloured in your opinion of countries and of people because of one experience, and I still can't get away from what I learned forty years ago about Argentina and their attitude to the game. I still have a jaundiced – and perhaps unfair – view of Argentinean players and Argentina as a place because we were treated so badly on that trip.

The place was a mess as far as I could see and the players were cheats. I know I shouldn't look at it like that, because they have produced some very good players.

When people ask me what was the hardest tour I ever went on, I always tell them it was that trip to Argentina, without any question of a doubt.

We went with 21 players and we went in September so we were very well prepared. I was captain and coach as well, while the committee men Lex Govan and George Crerar were joint managers. What they used to do was have a selection meeting where I would come down to meet them and they would say, 'This is the team, Jim.'

Well, I didn't accept that, and I got the team I wanted eventually.

They were nice enough guys, it's just that was what went on at that time. They were steeped in rugby but they liked a good time, so they let me run the playing side and they ran the off-field side.

I was left with terrible memories of all the bullet marks along the side of the hotel that we stayed in. It was just after Juan Peron had promised the poor people everything, and they all flocked to the cities. I have never been in a country that was so wasted by capitalism, as far as I could see. There were the very, very rich and the very, very poor; and huge slums on the road in from the airport in places like Rosario and Buenos Aires.

I've been back a couple of times since and it was just the same. I was there last in 2001. The poverty there just stuck with me. There were huge potholes in the road and cars that gave out fumes and fumes of rubbish – then women with fur coats and huge barbed wire fences around polo grounds. The difference between rich and poor was so stark.

All the people we met were rich, of course. There were a lot of Scots people out there who had made a fortune in banking and shipping and farming . . . typical Scots. The club rugby was very, very strong, and it was centred around the school system.

On the field we were on our own. There was no communication between us and Britain. Ken Oliver twisted his ankle at the first training session, so we asked for Tom Elliot to come out – he'd trained with the squad because Ken had been a doubt before we left, and had come down to London just before we flew out – but they wouldn't allow it. I thought at the time that it was the IRB but I found out many years later that it was the SRU who had decided we should just get on with it. So Rodger Arneil and I played in all six games. We won all the provincial matches but in the first game against the national side we lost Ian

Rodger Arneil.

Murchie in the opening minutes when he was short-armed by a guy called Alessandro Travaglini. Ian's feet were off the ground – and he was never the same player again.

We'd never really been in a country where everything you did was booed. The crowd couldn't see any good play in the Scottish performance at all, and it was a culture shock for us.

I had never seen grown men cry after a game until that tour. It was just so blatantly unfair, the decisions against us, we'd had to play with fourteen men, because it wasn't a cap international – it wasn't until 1981 that the IRB ruled that their member unions were permitted to award caps against countries who were then outside board membership, as Argentina were at the time – and Travaglini scored two tries, which just added insult to injury.

We then went to Rosario, which is a huge place with a population of around three million, and there was these national strikes going on. We had to walk to the game in twos and threes because the buses had been commandeered by the strikers and they were burning them. Before we left for the match, we went up onto the hotel roof in Rosario and we were looking around pointing out fires to each other – it was the buses being burned. This was before the game. The atmosphere was very hostile.

We decided that in the forwards we were going to have a pitched battle in the second match. We decided that if one of our guys got picked on we were all going to go in to make sure we were never second best – and they couldn't send off eight forwards.

We had this shortened line-out move, where we were to throw the ball over the top and the scrum-half ran round to collect it. But their scrum-half stood behind the line-out exactly where the ball was meant to go, which was completely illegal. So we pointed it out to the referee and the referee just shrugged. The crowd abuse was awful as well. Peter Stagg was easily identifiable because of his size and so the Argentineans would always kick the ball to him at kick-offs and this roar would just pound around the ground as the Argentine players charged at him, shouting abuse in Spanish. Our fullback, Colin Blaikie, would take all our place-kicks and he had to try and do it while the crowd threw coins at him – they were bouncing all around him and ricocheting off his head and arms and legs. It was unbelievable, a real bear-pit.

McLauchlan and Carmichael were taking the scrums so low that Frank Laidlaw was hooking the ball with his head. Sometimes, when the front-row collapsed, our second-row would kick through on the top of the oppositions' heads. It was brutal, brutal stuff. But we never gave an inch, and that to me was the best performance by a Scottish team in my time as a player – but it was out in Argentina so very few people ever saw it.

IAN McLAUCHLAN (Jordanhill)
43 Caps: 1969-79

That tour to Argentina was absolutely brutal. But the thing I liked about the Argentineans was that you could hit them as hard as you liked and they would never bother. They would dish it out, but they'd take it as well – and they'd never complain because as far as they were concerned it was all part of the game.

For a lot of guys on that tour they went out as boys and came back as men. Even guys as experienced as Alistair McHarg got quite a shock because the Argentineans didn't mess about. Alessandro Travaglini basically finished Ian Murchie's international career with a close-line tackle in the first match.

On tours you usually come up against an international or two during the midweek games, so you can get an idea of what they are like. But the Argentineans took all their internationalists away and to get around the amateur laws their whole squad happened to go on holiday to a place called Mar del Plata – a couple of hundred miles south of Buenos Aires – together for six weeks.

So we were playing these sides and beating them fairly easily – albeit at a physical cost – but when the Pumas came out the tunnel for that first match you would have thought someone had tied a bit of elastic to their backs and then let it go. They came out of the tunnel with their legs and arms pumping and their eyes bulging. The place was filled to bursting, and all you could hear was the ground reverberating to the words: *Pumas, Pumas*. And they were all huge. Our guys weren't small, but these guys were built like brick shit-houses.

NORMAN SUDDON

I didn't play in the matches against the Argentinean national team because Sandy Carmichael and Ian McLauchlan were in the side, but I watched the games and, take it from somebody who was in a ringside seat, they were brutal. Scotland got a licking in the first match. Murchie got his shoulder out and they were all really beaten up. We lost pretty heavily, 20-3.

We then went to Rosario to play the second game, and there was this bus strike which meant they stopped any buses out after 10am and burned them – so the game was put off to the next day. On the day of the match they had women with live pumas on chains on the pitch before the game. It was a culture shock – really hostile. The committee men were on the gin and tonics and were rolling about singing but Creamy [Jim Telfer], the captain, took control. He got the players through into a room by themselves and he said that it was going to be *one for all and all for one*. At the first scrum it was a case of hit anything within range – and we won the match in the end. All because Creamy decided we were going to fight fire with fire. I take my hat off to him, he turned it around.

JIM TELFER

Ian McLauchlan was the toughest guy I saw on a rugby field. He brought a hardness to the Scottish forward game which started about 1968-69 and went through the seventies. I'm sure that tour to Argentina gave him a valuable insight into what was needed in international rugby. It taught a lot of our forwards about how to look after themselves on a rugby field and about the kind of aggression you need to win international matches – and it was no surprise to me that so many of them went on to be great, great players for both Scotland and the Lions.

IAN McLAUCHLAN

The Argentinean guy I was playing against was an Olympic rower: he was a strong, strong boy. And there was a bit of jiggery-pokery going on early doors, so I smacked the hooker then turned to him and said, 'You're next.'

This guy spoke pretty good English, and he said, 'No, no, I don't play like that.'

I said, 'Great – I do.'

It was an Argentinean referee and on Wednesday he could speak perfect English but by Saturday he couldn't speak any. At the end of tour reception, Creamy called him a cheat and then went on about them being a dirty team and warned that if they didn't stop all that then they wouldn't be able to get any games in the future. He went on for about ten minutes – getting more and more worked up. Then the translator got up and spoke for about 30 seconds with everyone smiling and nodding. I was sitting next to the Argentinean team doctor, who spoke very good English, and afterwards he turned to shake my hand with a big smile.

I said, 'He obviously hasn't repeated our captain word for word.'

And the doctor said, 'No, he just told us how good we are.'

We came back from Argentina and in our next match beat South Africa 6-3, which was pretty special. They were a very good side, with a great back-row, where they had Jan Ellis, Tommy Bedford and Piet Greyling, who was a brilliant player – a real dog, his face was never more than two inches off the turf.

But because of the Apartheid thing they were never able to relax and enjoy being here. The management wouldn't let them put on a pair of jeans and go to a party, they had to get the blazers on and as soon as they did that they became a target.

The Scottish forwards train in the snow on Murrayfield's back pitches. *The Scotsman Publications Ltd. www.scran.ac.uk*

I took a couple of their players to a party in Edinburgh and because they had their blazers on a guy who had obviously had a few beers started giving them a bit of a stick as soon as we got there. Straight away they said they had to leave, they couldn't stay there in case there was trouble.

So it definitely wasn't a happy tour for them, but for Scotland it was still a big, big result. We played very well that day.

JOHN FRAME

I remember a stand-up shouting match at the Braid Hills Hotel before the South Africa match at Murrayfield in 1969. Peter Stagg, one of our second-rows, was a huge man who was a delightfully erudite and well-educated chap who had a very English accent, and he had submitted his expenses to the secretary and had included in it a copy of *Playboy*, which at that time was ten-and-sixpence. Peter had received his cheque from the SRU for his air flight, but with a red line through the copy of *Playboy* on his expenses form. And to the great amusement of the Scottish team, and to the embarrassment of the dowager ladies who used to live as permanent residents at the Braid Hills Hotel, Staggy and John Law had it out in the main reception area of the hotel. Staggy was

Peter Stagg.

launching forth, using a number of thoroughly unrepeatable expletives to describe John Law's approach to frugality, and explaining that while John Law may have a preconceived idea of what *Playboy* was all about he clearly had never taken the trouble to look at it, otherwise he would know that it was full of sophisticated and educational articles. Staggy pronounced vociferously that if Law was not going to entertain his ten-and-sixpence then he would never play in the blue jersey again. I think the management eventually managed to sort that one out, but from then on Staggy was regarded as a folk hero because he had the temerity to stand up to the great, ever-forceful secretary John Law.

JIM TELFER

The last game that I played in a Scotland shirt came in the autumn of 1969, not long after our return from Argentina. It was a controversial fixture against the Springboks right at the height of the anti-Apartheid demonstrations. Their players were under a huge amount of pressure off the pitch and it was reflected in their performances on it. They had some of the all-time greats in their team, guys like their captain Tommy Bedford, Frik du Preez, Piet Greyling, Hannes Maria and Henry de Villiers, but the outside influences were clearly getting to them. The atmosphere at the ground was very aggressive, bordering on evil, and whole areas of the crowd were sectioned off and the noise throughout the whole match was incredible. We recorded a famous victory, but the day really belonged

Ian Smith is congratulated on his try against the Springboks in 1969, while in the background the south terrace has been kept clear by the police. *Newsquest*

to Ian Smith. He scored a penalty but then gathered the ball deep in our half and went on this sweeping run that arced along the pitch and then just sliced right through the defence to score out wide – it was a moment of pure magic. Although it was heart-wrenching never to play for Scotland again, looking back, it was as good a result to finish your career with as you could ask for.

An anti-Apartheid demonstrator makes it onto the pitch and is pursued by the police. *Newsquest*

CHAPTER FOUR

FRUSTRATED GENIUS

THE 1970s, MUCH *like the 1950s, was a decade of two extremes. Between 3 February 1973 and 10 January 1976, Scotland went unbeaten at Murrayfield for eight matches, collecting the scalps of Australia and of all their Five Nations opponents, including, on two occasions, the mighty masters of the game from Wales; the closing years of the decade, however, saw consistently poor performances and between 1977 and 1979 Scotland drew two matches and won only one.*

But, despite these latter woes, the 1970s was a decade scattered with star-dust.

Mention the names Leslie, Lawson, Morgan, Hay and McHarg to Scottish fans, journalists and coaches of a certain age and you will invariably see a smile break across their faces. Add the names Irvine, Renwick, McGeechan, Broon, McLauchlan and Carmichael and you'll have them purring like Cheshire Cats. Those were the days. Even in defeat, even during the long period when Scotland went thirteen games without a win, those players could light up any match with moments of absolute, sublime genius, frightening aggression and savage bravery.

These men were giants of the Scottish game, recognised the world over from Auckland to Cape Town and from Paris to Buenos Aires for their excellence on the field of play. While the decade may belong to Wales' golden generation and the mighty achievements of the '71 Lions in New Zealand and the '74 Lions in South Africa, the seventies will always be looked upon with genuine affection by Scottish rugby supporters. Results could have been a lot better, but statistics only tell a small part of the story of this decade.

Made up of players with an astonishing assortment of differing skill sets, on their day Scotland were a match for anyone. In Ian McGeechan they had a gliding tactician operating outside the calm control of Colin Telfer; in the athletic Alastair McHarg and the colossal Gordon 'Broon frae Troon' Brown, arguably Scotland's finest ever forward, they had the exuberant engine and powerhouse of the team; in David Leslie they had the ferocious and uncompromising spirit of the ultimate competitor, balanced by the serene goal-kicking PC Brown at number eight; in Sandy Carmichael and Ian 'the Mighty Mouse' McLauchlan they had granite hard power and technical supremacy at the coal-face where, more often than not, the fate of games are decided – and in the Mouse in particular, they had a fierce and obdurate firebrand of a leader.

Around this core were an array of other players who gave their all for the Scottish cause, who did the unseen and unwelcome work that was necessary to create the quick ball, the momentum and the chinks in the opposition defence that allowed

Opposite: Sandy Carmichael, Gordon Brown and Ian McLauchlan ready themselves for a lineout throw.

players in the wider channels to weave their magic. Scrum-halves Alan Lawson and Dougie Morgan pushed the forwards on, darted and probed and were the driving spark for the rest of the backs; Nairn McEwan was a foraging force in the back-row; Chris Rae, John Frame and later Alastair Cranston were mighty presences in midfield; and out wide the electric pace of Billy Steele was complemented beautifully on the other wing by the barrel-chested power of Bruce Hay.

And in Jim Renwick and Andy Irvine they had players of true, unadulterated, genius. The finest two players that Scotland has ever had? Few who saw them in full-flight would argue otherwise.

Irvine and Renwick, the ultimate entertainers in the Scottish jersey, were irrepressible in every way both on and off the field and were at the heart of this great era of magnificent players; their majestic flair was mesmerising to watch, awe-inspiring and at times perplexing – for often their vision of the game was so ahead of their teammates that they seemed to be playing the match on their own. Their genius was based on a deep understanding of how rugby should be played, of the different nuances of the game and its infinite variety, but also in a recognition that no matter the level at which it was played, it remained a game and one that should be played for pleasure – both for the player and the spectator.

Irvine's style of play was characterised by an almost recalcitrant attitude to anything approaching preordained tactics, by his unstinting flair and luminous brilliance and his instinct to run, to always run, to attack from anywhere – and from deeper the better.

Irvine had a few weaknesses, particularly in defence or under a swirling high-ball, but with a broken field before him he was one of the stars of his generation; collecting the ball in space, he would open up his long stride and as the defence pushed up to meet him there would be a subtle change of direction, a swerve, a shift in balance, and he would be gone. The defence, beguiled by his nimble feints, would be left floundering in his wake, left to raise their heads from the turf and stare, breathless, at his brilliance.

Some would argue that Irvine lost more games for Scotland than he won, but the manner in which he could change the face of a game, the excitement that would grip the crowd when his hands touched the ball and which would rise to fever-pitch as he fizzed and flickered, darted and weaved his way to the try-line with an almost otherworldly grace, etched his place in Scottish hearts forever.

If Telfer and McGeechan were the calm and controlling midfield generals, Renwick was the impish artisan outside them, a purveyor of bold adventure in attack and – like McGeechan – heroic defiance in defence. A mischievous Puck with ball in hand he could conjure space from nowhere with a shimmy, a step, a lacerating angle or a sleight of hand and then he would put on the afterburners, accelerating into the line, through it and beyond. There was artistry in every moment of his play and a desire, like Irvine, to attack and to enjoy the game he was playing at all times. Small in stature, he looked – with his thick moustache and balding crown *wreathed by dark curls – like a swashbuckling character from a Dumas classic.*

But despite their outstanding talents, neither of these great players won anything of note for Scotland. During the peak of their careers they challenged for two Triple Crowns, but were undone on both occasions at Twickenham and neither took part in the triumphs of 1984.

The decade was indeed one of mixed fortunes for the Scotland team, but it also saw the most consistently excellent years of British rugby and oversaw subtle but fundamental changes in the game itself. In 1971 Bill Dickinson came in as 'advisor to the captain', the first move towards a legitimate coach at international level, and Scotland led the way in the British domestic game by establishing competitive leagues around the country.

As the 1970s came to a close and the careers of Renwick and Irvine began to enter the twilight years, France rode into town for the 1980 Five Nations fixture. If ever there was a game that summed up the rolling fortunes of these two players and of the national team during the previous decade, it was this one.

During a wretched afternoon, Irvine missed seven kicks at goal, one of which was directly in front of the posts. For over an hour it seemed that the great hero was at last fallen, the magic having finally deserted him. But then, as the clock ticked around into the final quarter, everything changed. Who knows what the catalyst was. The spirit of any other player would have been broken by the disasters he had experienced kicking for goal; but not Irvine. Just as Mohammad Ali had gone to the ropes in Kinshasa, pounded mercilessly by George Foreman for eight rounds, battered and bested until the crowds feared for his life, Irvine, like Ali, pulled himself up and out and began to dance. Mustering from who knew where a masterclass of running, passing and kicking, Irvine dragged Scotland back into the game. In the final quarter of the match he scored two tries, a conversion and two penalties to turn a 4-14 deficit into a 22-14 victory and ended the run of thirteen matches without a win. And alongside him was his old friend Renwick. A golden age it was indeed; gilded by genius but also tinged with frustration.

PETER BROWN

I missed the start of the 1970 Championship against France, but I was fit again for the Wales game.

When the letter arrived telling me I was back in the team, I thought I better phone my brother Gordon – who we had all assumed would keep his place in the second-row – to commiserate.

He always knew the team first, but when he answered the phone on this occasion I could tell immediately that he didn't know, so I said, 'Great news, I'm back in.'

He said, 'Terrific, who's dropped?'

I said, 'You are.'

Then, in the game, I tweaked my thigh chasing the kick-off at the start of the second-half, and of all the great things Gordon did, that is what he ended up in the *Guinness Book of Records* for: being the first brother to replace a brother in an international match.

JOHN FRAME

We were going to Wales for the second match of the 1970 Championship, and we used to gather at the North British Hotel on the Thursday at lunchtime, where a bus would collect us and take us to the airport so we could fly down to Cardiff. The secretary, John Law, who was by nature a very lovely but frugal Presbyterian – he epitomised all

Peter and Gordon Brown relax at the Braid Hills Hotel in Edinburgh in March 1970. *The Scotsman Publications Ltd. www.scran.ac.uk*

the qualities which has made Scotland famous throughout the world – and on this particular occasion I had been at a lecture in the morning and had to arrive slightly late. When I got to the NB I saw George Thomson, a Watsonian who was one of the selectors, and explained the situation. I must have looked sufficiently pitiful to prompt George to say that he was sure that nobody would mind if I went into the restaurant and had some lunch with the out-of-town players.

George got it badly wrong because the secretary minded, and I remember George being rubbished in the corner by John Law and being told that he was completely out of order for giving a player permission to have lunch. I suppose in those days it was better that we starved.

PETER BROWN

The only game Scotland won in the Championship that season was the last match at home against England, 14-5. By then I was the recognised goal-kicker and in those days you weren't allowed on the pitch at Murrayfield before an international, so I asked Frank Laidlaw, the captain, if I could take the kick-off to get a practice shot at goal.

The idea was that I would kick it dead, they would drop-out and always at the first line-out the referee would penalise one team or the other and it was a toss-up as to which one. So I converted the kick-off, Bob Hiller dropped out, ball into touch, line-out to Scotland, penalty to Scotland, and I kicked the goal.

PC Brown prepares to get the game under way with a long kick-off. *The Scotsman Publications Ltd. www.scran.ac.uk*

So everything went to plan and straight away we were thinking: *this is going to be our day.*

We introduced the tap penalty move to world rugby in that game. Nobody remembers that except us. We wanted to do something different and Ian McLauchlan came up with this idea at the team meeting. I'll always remember the stir it caused when Scotland were awarded a penalty just outside their own 22, and Mr McLauchlan walked forward to the ball and then turned his back on the opposition. The crowd were aghast as Alastair McHarg, my brother Gordon and I all ran forward in different directions, and the ball was passed to Gordon at the beginning of a move, I think, which ended with John Frame being tackled into touch close to the English line. Up until that point, when awarded a penalty you either kicked for touch, or you kicked for goal, or you sent a Garryowen up in the air.

Around this time, we also began going behind the wee stand they used to have on the back pitches at Murrayfield, where people couldn't see us, to practice illegal taking out at the line-out and obstruction. We decided we would never come off the field and complain about what the referee had allowed the opposition to do to us – we would get our retaliation in first. That was a small but important change in culture, and it worked. There is nothing like empowering players.

JOHN FRAME

We toured Australia at the end of the 1970 season, and that wasn't a particularly enjoyable tour. Frank Laidlaw was captain and he was a nice enough guy but a very, very intense character. Creamy was there as a coach. It was the first tour when there was a frowning approach towards alcohol, and we used to have these illicit drinking sessions which would end with guys hiding under beds and in wardrobes for fear of being caught drinking. Frank was terrified that we would be let down by not being fit, so we trained for three hours in the blazing sunshine the day before the Test. We took the field absolutely knackered.

For some reason, the only thing the Australians could organise when you visited their town was a reception by the local town council. And it became a standing joke that whenever you saw a guy with a Waratahs tie on, they would take the first opportunity to show you the tie and then go on to drone on about how they played for the Waratahs. So we developed this signalling system, so that if you were getting really bothered you would put your hand up and scratch the back of your head, and one of your team-mates would come across and rescue you. But it would become self-defeating because the whole room would be signalling at once. The second emergency signal was to take your hanky out and cough loudly into it – and it would be a like a flu epidemic sweeping the room. It would be excruciating – there were just so many of these functions.

We lost the Test match fairly heavily. We fielded Jock Turner at fullback, which was a suicidal waste of talent, and we had never played together as a back division in that shape before. It just didn't work. We lost 23-3, and you might say we were lucky to get away with that. To be honest, it was the end of a fairly unsatisfactory trip.

Scotland versus the Barbarians at Murrayfield, 1970. *The Scotsman Publications Ltd.* *www.scran.ac.uk*

CHRIS REA

We went to France at the beginning of the 1971 season, led 8-3 at half-time, and were playing really well. Jock Turner was at fly-half and was causing all sorts of problems with his size and strength, running at their fly-half. Then Ian Smith, at fullback, was injured, and they brought Brian Simmers on as a replacement, and instead of making a straight swap, for some extraordinary reason they put him at fly-half and moved Jock to fullback. Brian was lightweight, and he had played a lot of games for Glasgow Accies at fullback, so it was crazy – making two changes when one would have been more than enough. We ended up losing 13-8.

Our next game, against Wales at Murrayfield, was considered at the time to be one of the great matches of that decade. It was so fast and the lead changed hands eight times. I scored a try in the last ten minutes to make it 18-14 and Peter Brown missed the conversion from in front of the posts. That was crucial, because if he had kicked it they would have had to score twice and they wouldn't have come back.

I've never known noise like it. I was in the centre with John Frame, while Jock Turner was at stand-off, and we had to shout right into each others' ears but you still couldn't pick up what each other was saying. That was one of the reasons why we lost that last try. It was our throw-in at a line-out in our own 25 and Billy Steele got the wrong call, he couldn't hear in that incredible noise level. They wanted the ball to the front, but he threw to Delme Thomas at the back.

Then we immediately made another costly mistake when the Welsh sent the ball rightwards. We had agreed that in defence the wings would stay out no matter what, so when I saw JPR Williams coming into the line I started moving over from John Dawes to cover him, when, to my horror, Alistair Biggar came in off his wing to make the tackle, leaving Ian Smith scrambling across to get to Gerald Davies.

Gerald scored, and then, of course, John Taylor added two points from the touchline, with what was described as 'the greatest conversion since St Paul's.' I've never been so heartbroken. We were all just devastated. But looking back at it we were privileged to be involved in one of the greatest matches of that decade. And Wales at that time were the best side in the world, so to have almost beaten them was a great testament to a Scottish side which didn't have a lot of success at that time – although I always felt the side was a lot stronger than our results suggested.

JOHN FRAME

There always was an issue of slight inferiority. The Welsh were the first to kit their guys out in tracksuits, while we used to turn up looking like something out of the army and navy store, in this selection of weird and wonderful alternative outfits. I'm not sure how much difference these things made when we got on the pitch, but there is no question that if you make a team feel like a team by treating them with a degree of respect, then it is beneficial.

Some of the guys involved with the Scottish team at the time really did take the ultimate amateur view. The Irish, by all accounts, were pretty much the same.

PETER BROWN

At the end of that season came our famous win at Twickenham. Because it was the centenary season since the first international between Scotland and England at Raeburn Place in Edinburgh, we were scheduled to play two matches against England, at Twickenham and then Murrayfield, to celebrate. On the Friday night before the Twickenham match we went to the theatre to see Fiona Richmond in *Pyjama Tops*, which was highly controversial because it was one of the first erotic theatre shows in London. We had the two front rows in the theatre and it was absolutely magnificent. Its called *Pyjama Tops* because the male lead has a problem with his manhood and there's all these girls trying to encourage him, then he comes down in the final act and says he's done it – at last he's done it.

'Which female?' he's asked.

'I don't know. It was dark. All I know is that she had on a pyjama top.'

And at that the five females in the play start to come down the staircase. Each of them with her panties on but no top, meaning it's not her. Then the *au pair*

The teams merge for the Centenary Match photograph. *Press Association*

comes down the stair to great fanfare, with nothing on the bottom half and all she's got on her top half is . . . a Scottish international rugby jersey.

Now, that was almost an impossibility in those days because the guys who played for Scotland could hardly get hold of a jersey. To this day we don't know where she got it from.

CHRIS REA

Gordon Brown's great story, which I think was slightly apocryphal but based on a certain amount of truth, was about the captain's team-talk before that Twickenham match, which happened to be delivered by his brother Peter.

PC was going completely over the top, listing all the great Scottish victories over England, at Bannockburn and so on. Then at the climax of his speech he looked up at us and said, 'Remember Culloden.'

There was a pause before Gordon piped up, 'Peter, I don't think we did very well in that one.'

And not to be outdone, PC responded immediately, 'I said remember Culloden, and that's what I effin' well meant – because after Culloden they didn't have to get changed and have dinner with the bastards.'

We hadn't won at Twickenham since Wilson Shaw's match in 1938, but we had a feeling of real confidence before that match. We probably should have beaten both France and Wales that year, and although we had lost fairly heavily against Ireland we knew we had a really strong side.

It wasn't a great match but there were some exceptional moments of play. The English three-quarter line was huge, with Janion, Wardlow, Spencer and Duckham all close to the fourteen stone mark, which was very big in those days, and they scored a fantastic try with the ball sweeping across the field and back again before Hiller eventually touched down, and they led for most of the match.

We were 15-8 down when Duncy Paterson scored a try to make it 15-11, then with time running out we won a ruck and the ball went to PC, who was in the stand-off position for some reason. He lobbed this pass which I just managed to catch above my head. With John Spencer, the English captain, coming across I ordinarily would have passed to Steven Turk, who was on the left wing after replacing John Frame, and we would almost certainly have scored. But it would have been out on the touchline and I knew three points was no use to us – so I just went for it, as straight as I could. I was clattered by Spencer and a couple of others on the line, but managed to get the ball over.

It left PC with a hell of a difficult kick, halfway out to the touchline, and given that he had missed one in front of the posts against Wales earlier that season I wasn't overly confident. He just did his usual routine: turned his back on the ball, walked away, blew his nose, swung round and ran at it. I turned away, I couldn't watch . . . then there was this crescendo of noise which meant he had scored, because in those days you didn't applaud misses.

I saw it later on TV and the ball never looked as if it was going anywhere near the posts until the very last moment when it veered in . . . it was just totally bizarre.

That was the famous occasion, when Peter came running back and shoved away his brother Gordon, because he thought he was going to kiss him.

I always say I feel a bit like Stan Mortensen, who scored a hat-trick for Blackpool in that magnificent FA Cup final against Bolton Wanderers in 1953, and it became known as Stanley Matthews' Final. Nobody ever remembers Mortensen; and Scots will always remember who kicked that winning conversion but not who got the try.

My opposite number that day was John Spencer, with whom I'd played alongside at Headingley that season. I went into the English changing room afterwards, they were very gracious and I hope I was not too triumphalist. They had a beer for me and I sat with them and had a chat, but it was like a morgue and there was only one place I wanted to be – we had a fantastic night after that game from what I can remember.

It was a terrific moment but you don't really appreciate what you have achieved until long after the event. There have only been four winning Scottish sides at Twickenham to date – in 1926, 1938, 1971 and 1983. So we were part of something really special that afternoon.

JOHN FRAME

After we won that first centenary match at Twickenham, John Spencer stood up at the dinner and said that there was one thing the RFU forgot to mention to the SRU and that was that the game the following week was actually the centenary game and we were playing for the Calcutta Cup then and that they intended to win. And there was a collective rumble around the room.

That first game at Twickenham saw Fran Cotton win his first cap, and he said afterwards to Ian McLauchlan that the way McLauchlan had played was not the way he thought rugby should be played, and McLauchlan's great reply was that Cotton had seven days to get used to it.

CHRIS REA

We were treated to another fantastic team talk the following week. Bill Dickinson had been brought in earlier that season as adviser to the captain – we were not allowed to call him a coach – and he was a real character. And because

Duncan Paterson moves the ball away from the scrum against Wales. *The Scotsman Publications Ltd. www.scran.ac.uk*

it was the centenary match we got new shirts with a rose and a thistle side-by-side on the left breast. Well, Dickinson came into the changing room, marched up to PC, and poked his finger into his chest. He said, 'Right lads, see that badge? The thistle intertwined with a rose. You know what happens when a thistle gets intertwined with a rose? I'll tell you, the thistle effin' strangles the rose. Now we want you to go out and do exactly that to those bastards today.'

That was our team-talk – fantastic.

We were presented to the Prince of Wales and that was done early so we actually started the game at five minutes to three, with people still coming into the ground. We kicked off, they tried to run the ball but it was dropped in the centre, and John Frame pounced on it to score which was the quickest ever international try at that time, PC kicked the conversion, they kicked off, we kicked back, they were penalised, PC kicked the goal, so we were 8-0 up and it still wasn't three o'clock.

The forwards were superb against a huge English pack that day and we ended up winning comfortably, 26-6.

JOHN FRAME

When England came up to Murrayfield for the second match, this guy John Reason – who was regarded as being the doyen of the English rugby writers – said that England had lost the first game because they hadn't used their superior back division, which obviously didn't please us too much because we didn't think they were superior to us at all. I scored two tries in that match; the first

Police hold back the crowd after Scotland defeat England in the Centenary match at Murrayfield. *The Scotsman Publications Ltd. www.scran.ac.uk*

came about because Jock Turner banged the kick-off deep into the corner and Jeremy Janion, their winger, tried to run it back, then panicked when he realised that the whole Scotland team were closing in on him and he chucked the ball inside. John Spencer dropped it under the posts and I capitalised . . . and that all came about because they were intent on believing that they had this superior back division.

Everyone is always very admiring of the fact that I scored after just ten seconds, and I have to explain to them that all I did was run 50 yards, and there is no great achievement in running 50 yards in ten seconds.

JIM RENWICK (Hawick)
51 Caps: 1972-1984

We used to stay up at the Braid Hills Hotel in Edinburgh from the Thursday before the game. What a place that was – you needed an O-grade in map reading to find your room – it was like a rabbit warren. It was a rickety old place with all these long winding corridors and it seemed compulsory that every room had squeaky beds and floorboards and windows that rattled in the wind. It

The Mouse leads the Centenary celebrations back in the changing room. *The Scotsman Publications Ltd. www.scran.ac.uk*

wasn't flash but they really looked after us well and the food was good. It was a great spot for us to get away as a team in the build up to the big match.

Things have really changed over the years. My first cap was against France at Murrayfield for our opening game of the 1972 Five Nations. On the Thursday night before the game there was none of this sports psychology and analysis of the opposition, or even sessions to go over our moves or discuss our tactics – we used to go to the pantomime! All these big lads shouting 'Oh no, he isn't!' and 'Look behind you!' as part of their preparation to take on the French. Changed days.

On the Friday we would go up to the stadium but we mainly just hung around having our photos taken and talking to the press – we weren't allowed on the pitch. A few years later they let the goal-kickers on to do some practice, but that was it, no one else was allowed to set foot on the grass. It was a tough day on the Friday because there was very little else on – you would just be kicking your heels and getting all worked up before the match. We'd have one or two team meetings but the rest of the time was free. We'd go into town for a walk around, or go and catch a game down at one of the clubs who were playing a touring team from France or Wales or Ireland, whoever was playing

Alan Lawson and Colin Telfer reading *The Scotsman* at the Braid Hills Hotel in Edinburgh in March 1972. *The Scotsman Publications Ltd. www.scran.ac.uk*

Scotland that weekend. Sometimes we'd play snooker or go bowling, but it was tough trying to find something meaningful to do to keep your mind off the game.

On the Friday night the hotel would be full of all these committee men as there was always a big dinner on the night before the game – and a lot of them would be looking really rough on the Saturday. We would be sitting in our rooms, unable to sleep, hearing every creak of the bed or the rattle of the window and just thinking about the game the next day. A lot of us couldn't sleep on those nights, so we would head down to the bar and have a few pints – just to settle the nerves and to help you sleep, nothing major. They wouldn't let you get away with it now, of course, but while it wasn't openly encouraged in those days they didn't really mind you doing it.

I used to enjoy the bus trip to the ground on the Saturday. You packed your bag just before leaving the hotel and Bill McLaren would be on the TV doing the build-up for the match, so you were really getting a feel for the occasion by that stage, and when you went through Edinburgh you would see all these folk in their kilts heading to ground, waving to you as you passed and you hoped they couldn't see how green you were. I used to be sick before games – not always, but mostly. The nervous tension always got to me, but in a good way – it made me sharp.

We used to do most of our warm-ups in the changing room because there wasn't really anywhere else. Now and again you'd need a bit more space and there was one year that I had a bit of a dodgy leg that needed a proper warm up, so I went out into the car park on the back pitches and was dodging around between all the cars.

PC Brown was captain for my first game. He was quiet and wasn't all about fire and brimstone in his talk before we took the field, but I liked his approach – he was completely confident in his own ability and that helped you feel confident too. And it wasn't hollow confidence either – he just went out there and did his thing and he was always superb.

I don't remember much about that first game – you're just living on your wits and although you know the game is going to be fast, faster than anything you've experienced before, you still can't prepare yourself for what it is actually like. It hits you and the whole thing seems to pass in a blur. There are a few things I remember though – Colin Telfer gathered a loose ball near our line and started a counter-attack, passing the ball to Arthur Brown who hared off up field. He managed to get the ball to Alastair Biggar who stood up the last of the defence and passed inside to me for a clear run to the line from 25 yards out. If ever there was a way to settle the nerves in your first cap, it was that!

JOHN FRAME

I scored against France when we won at Murrayfield in 1972, and it involved a set move from a scrum near the West Stand heading towards the old clock end. The idea was that Colin Telfer would flip me the ball, I would pull in the back-row and then pop it back to Colin to go through the gap and score under the posts. So we started the move and everything was going to plan, but these were the days when balls had laces and I had a snagged nail which caught on the lace, so I couldn't deliver it and I had to pull it back. I just carried on with the French pack trying to figure out who had the ball. Everyone was talking about how brilliant it was, but it was all down to that snagged nail.

PC Brown takes the ball at the line-out during the Scotland versus France match. *The Scotsman Publications Ltd. www.scran.ac.uk*

The final score, 1972. *The Scotsman Publications Ltd. www.scran.ac.uk*

IAN BARNES (Hawick)
7 Caps: 1972-1977

When I was called into the Scotland side for my first cap in February 1972 as a replacement for Alistair McHarg I was doing my CA apprenticeship in Edinburgh being paid £52 per month. I got the call at work on the Wednesday morning so I went down to see the senior partner. I said, 'I am in the Scotland team for Saturday'. He jumped out of his seat. 'That's great news, Ian! Great for you! Great for the firm! Have a seat! Have a sherry!' Halfway through the sherry I told him that I would need Thursday and Friday off to go down to Wales. 'That's no problem, Ian. No problem at all – just take a couple of days holiday'.

We trained at Murrayfield on the Thursday morning and flew down to Cardiff in the afternoon. We were staying in the Angel Hotel directly opposite the Arms Park. The place was jumping – mobbed with supporters – and the Welsh team were there as well so you kept bumping into them in the foyer and in the dining room. On the Saturday we just walked across to the ground for the game mingling with the early crowd – not particularly professional but symptomatic of the tremendous community of spirit that the game enjoyed then – and it fairly got the goose pimples going.

England look to pressurise a clearance kick, 1972. *The Scotsman Publications Ltd.*
www.scran.ac.uk

I don't remember much about the game. It was that great Welsh side of the early seventies with JPR Williams, Gerald Davies, Barry John, Gareth Edwards and these guys but we did reasonably well in the first half and were actually leading with twenty minutes to go but we got humped in the last quarter. Gareth Edwards scored a great try – the BBC kept showing it every week for years at the start of Sportscene – He came round the back of a lineout in our half and kicked ahead, the ball stuck in the mud and he beat Jim Renwick to the touch in the corner. He handed me off as he came round the corner – and it felt as though a horse had kicked me.

JIM RENWICK

I still marvel at the distances that Gareth Edwards could pass the ball – it was like a torpedo – which gave Barry John the space and time he needed to work his magic. It wasn't a great game from our point of view, but I was happy that I made it on the score sheet again with a penalty when PC was injured. We got things back on track the following week against England at Murrayfield and thumped them 23-9.

In December the All Blacks came to town and we were unlucky not to win, to be honest. We lost 9-14, but it was 9-10 going into extra time and a score from either side would have nicked it – unfortunately Sid Going intercepted an inside ball from Alistair McHarg and ran the length to score. It was disappointing to lose but they had a great side. I was up against Bruce Robertson and that was some education – he was a big lad who had great hands but he knew how to run and kick too. They had great balance across the park – size and skill in Bryan Williams on one wing, electricity in Grant Batty on the other; Sid Going was always busy at scrum-half; they had a huge pack and in the back-row they had some of the all-time greats in Grizz Wylie and Ian Kirkpatrick. They were bigger and fitter than us, but the key thing was that they just didn't make mistakes – their basic skills were flawless. Their forwards would grind you down in the first-half, literally squeezing the life out of you, and they would explode into life through the backs in the second-half. It was in that game that I realised that I needed to work on my pace more if I was ever going to live with these boys. That's the one truth in any sport, but especially in rugby – you can never have too much pace.

That game also saw first caps awarded to Ian McGeechan at fly-half and Andy Irvine at fullback. Geech was pretty small like me, but we linked well together and stood up strong in defence against the All Blacks, and I liked his approach to the game; I think he enjoyed playing alongside me, too. Andy wasn't even fully fit because he'd knackered his knee during the National Trial the week before, but he had been an unused replacement during the Five Nations and was desperate to play – and despite his knee being dodgy he still managed to kick six of our nine points and he made some fantastic breaks. He was great to have at fullback and it was a position that suited him well as it gave him licence to attack from anywhere and to hit the line wherever he saw some space opening up. He wasn't the best defensive fullback I ever played with, but he had the attitude of: *if you score three, I'll score four.* Some people criticised him for being too flash, but he had steel in him too – remember he was injured coming into that first game and then he took a blow to the head and had to get stitches in his mouth at halftime. He was really gutsy that day.

ANDY IRVINE (Heriot's FP)
51 Caps: 1972-1982

Jim Renwick is about as close as Scottish rugby has ever got to producing a genius. He had a tremendous side-step, he had a lot of pace, he was very quick off the mark, and he had great balance, he did actually have everything. He could dummy, he could swerve, he was a tremendous tackler, he was a tough boy with a very strong and powerful upper body from the swimming he did in his youth, he could kick goals, he could drop goals, he could control the game, and to be honest he could have played anywhere on the park if he put his mind to it. He played most of his career at centre but he could easily have played stand-off at the highest level, and if he'd wanted to he could also have played on the wing or at fullback quite easily.

He was only 5′ 9″, but even today, although the boys are a lot bigger and more physical, he would have been a great stand-off. He could have easily coped with the big hits and the power because he was tough and he was awfully strong.

It was great having someone like him playing in front of me in that first match – he and I had an understanding about the counter-attack, that it was the best form of attack there was because it is in open play like that where all the real holes and opportunities to score are. He was so comfortable out there and so confident and it just gave me the confidence to try things too. I think Geech really appreciated having someone like that playing outside him too – a steady influence in tricky situations, but also someone who was really enthusiastic about attacking when it was on, or who was able to make something out of nothing. That was especially the case towards the end of the seventies when John Rutherford came into the side – Jim and John together were a tremendous combination. Jim has got a brilliant rugby brain. He doesn't say all that much, but when he does talk people listen because they have a lot of respect for what he says. I've sat down with Jim and had beers on numerous occasions after games, and he's just a breath of fresh air to listen to – he's got a great analytical mind when it comes to rugby.

Jim Renwick displays the defensive power that went wirh his dazzling attacking prowess.
SNS Pix

JIM RENWICK

Who attacks who in rugby? Is the guy with the ball attacking the defence? Or is the defender attacking the guy with the ball? I think it comes down to the ability of the guy with the ball. The more strings you have to your bow – in terms of kicking with both feet, side-stepping, timing a pass and so on – the easier it is for you to be the attacker, because the other guy doesn't know what's coming. If you're limited with what you can do then you're going to struggle because you're just waiting to see what happens and hoping you get away with it. You're not making the decisions. The more options you've got the better the player you are. I'd like to think that when I had the ball I was always attacking.

IAN McGEECHAN (Headingley)
32 Caps: 1972-1979

My Dad was born and raised in Govan and his love of sport started and ended with Rangers; like any aspiring young lad he had dreams of playing professional football, but the war put an end to any ambitions he may have had. He didn't talk much about the war, as many of his generation tend not to, but he told my brother Neil he'd been very lucky to survive. There was one incident when a Messerschmitt strafed him and a pal in a jeep. He jumped out one side, his pal jumped out the other; his pal was killed and my Dad survived. He never underestimated how fortunate he was to be able to come back from the war. He met our mum in a military hospital and he devoted the rest of his life to his family; we came first and he gave us everything. He used to slip me a fiver after games when I started playing for Headingley so that I wouldn't feel embarrassed about not being able to buy a round. I found out after he died that it was a quarter of his weekly wage; it was an incredible sacrifice and it's something that I'll never forget.

His Scottishness was certainly not something that he particularly pushed, but it was always a part of him and we knew exactly where we came from.

I was always tremendously impressed with Ken Scotland when I was growing up because he was really the first attacking fullback; and in the late sixties, with players like David Chisholm and Eck Hastie and Jim Telfer around then as captain, there were some great games – Scotland played with quite a bit of fluidity and they would try and do things. Ken Scotland would run from his own line and there was a vibrancy – the players would look to see what was on and have a go and that's what I remember most about those players at that time.

Scotland had a lot of success over the years – from three Triple Crowns in the opening decade of the twentieth century, to the Grand Slam in 1925 and so on, and there really was a special sense around the Scotland jersey and playing at Murrayfield that inspired generations of fans and players – and watching guys like Ken Scotland, I was among them. It inspired you to try and emulate them, it made you want to wear that blue jersey more than anything.

I played in the National Trial as a stand-off and I remember being chased all day by Jim Telfer and Rodger Arneil as they tried to take my head off. It was some introduction to what would be a long career with Jim.

I was first capped against the All Blacks and it was the third time I had played them in four weeks because I had faced them playing for the Rest of the Scotland and the North of England.

The Mouse took over the captaincy in that first season and he was a real inspiration – a great leader who always led by example and always said the right thing.

Ian McCrae whips out a pass against the All Blacks at Murrayfield in December 1972. *The Scotsman Publications Ltd. www.scran.ac.uk*

Alastair McHarg takes the ball into the heart of the All Black pack. *The Scotsman Publications Ltd. www.scran.ac.uk*

IAN BARNES

They used to hold trial matches in December each year – purgatory – miserable freezing Saturday afternoons in a bleak empty Murrayfield, a couple of hundred spectators in the old West Stand and miles of empty terracing; there was no shape, no structure, no chance if you were in the Whites, you were cannon fodder for the Blues; it was eighty minutes of watching the clock on the south terracing dragging its way towards 3.20pm and a warm bath – and then being told that the selectors wanted another half hour. I must have played against McHarg in a dozen trials and I honestly cannot remember winning a single line-out. And Gordon Brown wasn't bad either! So I more or less spent the next five years sitting on the bench and in those days before tactical substitutions the only way you got on was if somebody was hurt.

I would have liked to have been playing but I was happy enough just to be there. Home international weekends were tremendous. A heavy session at Murrayfield on the Sunday – four, maybe five hours – and it was tough because we had all played league games on the Saturday. We'd meet again at Murrayfield on the Thursday for a full session – three, maybe four hours – and then up to the Braid Hills Hotel. Evening meal – prawn cocktail starter, scampi fish course, fillet steak fully garnished, toffee pudding, cheese and biscuits – down to the Canny Man for three or four pints. A run through at Murrayfield on the Friday morning. Back to the Braids for lunch – prawn cocktail starter, scampi fish course, fillet steak fully garnished, toffee pudding, cheese and biscuits. A walk along Princes Street on Friday afternoon then dinner at the Braids – prawn cocktail starter, scampi fish course, fillet steak fully garnished, toffee pudding, cheese and biscuits. Cinema at night – always a western, preferably John Wayne – and a couple of pints on the way home.

The replacements tended to be a bit peripheral on the Saturday in the build up and during the game but the Saturday nights were glorious. Bus from Murrayfield to the NB, a couple of pints with the punters in the downstairs bar, change into your DJ, champagne reception, then the Match Dinner in the NB ballroom with its spectacular view along Princes Street to the floodlit Scott Monument and the castle. Everybody that was anybody in Scottish rugby was there and it was cigars, white wine, red wine, vintage port, the works – and after the formalities we were joined by wives and girlfriends for a real shindig fraternising with the opposition.

We used to hire our DJs from Moss Bros in George Street and have them delivered straight to the NB. They had our measurements so we just needed to phone our order in. Steven Turk from Langholm was pulled into the squad for one game at short notice and phoned his order in late on the Saturday morning. There was some sort of a mix up and he ended up with a suit five sizes too big for him. He was like a scarecrow. He got into a panic and was going to skip the dinner but we persuaded him that we could smuggle him in and that once he got sat down nobody would notice – which would have been fine except that he was a very good singer and Hector Munro, who was on the committee, oblivious to his predicament, was so pleased to have a fellow Langholm man in the squad that he suggested to the president that he get Stephan up to sing, which he did. Excruciating for Steven – hilarious for everybody else – people were rolling about on the floor. But he carried it off – he sang King of the Road and brought the house down.

ANDY IRVINE

My first game in the Five Nations was Scotland's opening match against France in 1973 – which was also the first game to be played at the new Parc de Princes.

There was a hell of an atmosphere at that game, the crowd were just crazy – 50,000 mad Frenchmen with a sprinkling of Scottish supporters, bands that played throughout the game along with drums and firecrackers and trumpets all over the place. The crowd would build themselves up into a frenzy as kick-off approached and as you came out of the tunnel you could actually feel the air beating with the noise. The passion on show was just incredible – it was a brand new ground but instantly it was a fortress. I had never experienced anything like it in my life.

We started the game quite brightly while the French team seemed a little overawed by the occasion. At one point their centre, Jean Trillo, was clattered in a tackle and the crowd started a huge chant of 'Maso, Maso' – calling for Jo Maso, their star centre who had been omitted from the squad. For periods of the game we actually seemed more popular with the crowd than the home team because of the style we were playing – we ran the ball from our own line at one stage and swept all the way up field and the crowd went mad, loving the adventure – hooters were sounding and firecrackers were exploding, it was something else.

Despite their indifferent performance, France scored a neat try through their outside centre Claude Dourthe and although we scored a try through Alan Lawson, PC Brown kicked a couple of penalties and Geech struck a drop-goal, their fly-half Jean-Pierre Romeu kicked three penalties and a drop-goal and that was the difference – they edged us out 16-13.

Weekends in Paris were fantastic and the post-match dinner was always superb – six courses and unlimited amounts of the finest wine, port, brandy and liqueurs – and the crowds were always so welcoming when you went out after the match.

Fans invade the pitch at the final whistle of the Scotland versus Ireland match in 1973, while the players show the close bond between the teams. *The Scotsman Publications Ltd. www.scran.ac.uk*

IAN BARNES

I got on as a replacement for Nairn McEwan against France in 1974 for my second cap – and the SRU secretary, John Law, must have forgotten that I had already played because he sent me another cap. It arrived through the post direct from RW Forsyth packaged in a Playtex girdle box. He twigged his mistake some time later and asked for the cap back, but I denied all knowledge and kept on denying it every time I met him for over twenty years until he died. So I ended up with more caps than Jim Renwick, Colin Deans, Alan Tomes and Tony Stanger.

ANDY IRVINE

Ian McLauchlan's first game as captain was against Wales in the second match that year. He took over from PC Brown, even though Peter was still in the team. I liked Peter as captain, but the Mouse had this aura about him that just gave you confidence – he was so aggressive and he always led from the front. As we prepared to run out of the tunnel and onto that famous Murrayfield pitch, he pulled us all in tight and gave one of the most inspirational team-talks I have ever heard. It was real power and passion and it still sends a shiver up my spine to think about it.

We were heading out to play on our home ground against a team that Scotland hadn't beaten since 1967 and contained nine British Lions, all of who were true greats of the game. Before you go out into battle, those are the kind of words you need to hear – they burn away the apprehension and the fear and ignite a fire in your soul. With a guy like the Mouse leading you in the battle, you were ready to take on the world. We fizzed down that tunnel and we unleashed hell on them.

IAN McLAUCHLAN

That Welsh side was filled with guys like JPR Williams, Gerald Davies, Phil Bennett, Gareth Edwards in the backs, Mervyn Davies, John Taylor and Derek Quinnell in the pack, so we weren't expected to win.

We played them at Murrayfield and the tradition at that time was for the president and all the selectors to sit in on the team talk, and I went to the president beforehand and asked him if he would mind leaving the room at that point so that I didn't have to speak to anyone except the players.

He agreed but didn't brief his other selectors, and after he had wished us all the best he said they would now leave the room and you could see that the rest of them were pretty reluctant to go.

Alistair McHarg turned to me and said, 'You do realise that if we lose today, you'll never play for Scotland again.'

Fortunately we won 10-9. I just thought that you should be able to say certain things to players, and they were inhibiting that.

IAN McGEECHAN

Gerald Davies always used to say that he wished he had been a fly on the wall during the Mouse's team talk before that game. He said the way we came down the tunnel and the ferocity of our performance was incredible and you could see the Mouse's influence over the way we played and took the game to Wales.

IAN McLAUCHLAN

In our next match, against Ireland, I came off the field with a suspected broken leg and got put in a taxi on my own to the Royal Infirmary, because nobody wanted to miss the game. It didn't bother me, because being part of the international set-up was fabulous, and the fact that we were ten years behind everyone else was all part of it.

If you tore your shorts during a game and got given a new pair, then they

Ian McLauchlan, pictured with his son, on crutches after injuring his leg. Despite this, he captained Scotland in the Calcutta Cup a week later. *The Scotsman Publications Ltd. www.scran.ac.uk*

were waiting for you coming off the field so that they could get them back. You had to go home and get your mother to darn yours.

It turned out my leg wasn't broken, although the bone was cracked. We played England at Twickenham two weeks later for the Triple Crown, and the doctor said I was fit to play so I played. I played before and after that injury, so I didn't miss any games because of it. There were a lot of guys carrying knocks that day, but basically we underperformed and that is why we lost.

ANDY IRVINE

In retrospect, although we were happy to see that the Mouse was in the team, there was no way he should have played. They said that it was a cracked fibula – but no matter how you dress it up, it was a broken leg, and who can play rugby with a broken leg? I suppose it's a testament to the kind of guy he was – how hard he was – that he was able to make it through the match at all and I can't even begin to imagine the pain he was in when he was scrummaging. But the Mouse wasn't the only player in the pack injured – there were a whole raft of them carrying heavy knocks. We might have been a good enough team to take on England at Twickenham and win with one or two guys carrying slight knocks, but we weren't good enough – and I don't think there would ever be a team good enough – to win with a pack of forwards who only had two or three guys who were 100 per cent fit. In the changing room before we went out there were guys getting pain-killing injections and others that were literally being held together with tape and bandages. It was crazy. But caps weren't as readily available in those days as they are now – and nobody really knew when their last chance might be, so you played no matter what. If they picked you, you played. But looking back it was no surprise that we lost – going into the game with players in that kind of condition was only going to have one result. It's still enormously disappointing that we didn't win the Triple Crown that year because, fully fit, we were more than good enough to do it.

JIM RENWICK

The following year we lost narrowly down in Cardiff in the opening game of the '74 Five Nations. It was 6-0 to them in the end and their try was little bit dodgy – Terry Cobner scored after some great play from Gareth Edwards, Phil Bennett and Gerald Davis, but Cobner's grounding was suspect – in those days you had to release the ball when you were tackled to the ground, but Cobner didn't and then managed to get the ball down over the line and the ref gave it. It would have been a tough call either way, but in the end it swung theirs. It was pretty hard to take at the time because we had competed well throughout the game, but they had class all over the park and probably deserved to shade it in the end.

The following week we played a real ding-dong match against the English at Murrayfield where the lead changed hands four times in the last 20 minutes. Andy Irvine scored an incredible try in the last five minutes or so when he took the ball at pace down the blind-side and stepped past four defenders to score in the corner. I thought we had it sealed then.

Andy Irvine races down the wing to score against England at Murrayfield in 1974. *SNS Pix*

ANDY IRVINE

I was convinced that my try had won the game as there were only a few minutes left and then Colin Telfer gathered a loose ball on our 25 and kicked it clear – it went dead straight and landed right in Peter Rossborough's arms and he slotted a perfect drop-goal. I was standing under the posts as it sailed over and I was devastated – to lose a game like that was just agony.

But we still had time. The Mouse said to us as we ran back to half-way that we just needed to get into range to kick a drop-goal or win a penalty, anything. The way the game had gone I didn't think it was likely that the lead would swing back in our favour again, but you never knew. It had been a crazy 80 minutes. We kicked off and launched a last-ditch offensive. In a moment of pure madness from a player of pure genius, David Duckham played the ball from a blatantly offside position and we were awarded a penalty.

The pressure of the situation was huge. Well, at least it should have been. The kick was tricky – it was on the wrong side for me and around 40 yards out near the touchline, but I felt incredibly confident as I teed up the ball and as I readied myself to kick it I just had this sense that it was going to go over. I struck it perfectly and it sailed true. And the crowd erupted around us, rising to their feet before it had even gone between the posts.

JIM RENWICK

Some of the boys hoisted Andy on their shoulders and carried him off the pitch, which was a bit much I thought at the time, but sometimes when you've worked so hard in a game, you've won it and you've lost it and you've won it again . . . well . . . emotions run high. But it's not the Hawick way to go over the top about things. When I scored I used to make sure that I didn't show that I was smiling. I just tried to touch the ball down and run back without showing emotion. There's a few times I've been in the vicinity when Andy had scored a try and I've just turned and run back. I've not jumped up and down and waved my arms about. It's not that I'm not pleased, it's just not the way we did at Hawick.

IAN McLAUCHLAN

We never won in France while I was playing. The French were always trying to bully you, so we tried to give as good as we got – but that didn't always work. We played them at the Parc des Princes in 1975, and at the first line-out all hell broke loose. Everyone was in, giving it plenty, except Sandy Carmichael standing at the front, who had never flung a punch in his life, and Victor Boffelli at the back, who wasn't a fighter either. Eventually the referee gets control back and he pulls Sandy and Boffelli aside. He says, 'Any more of that and you're off,' then writes their numbers down.

Sandy was pretty upset because in those days you just didn't get sent off in internationals, so he says to me, 'That's it. I can't do my share of the fighting now.'

I thought, thank God for that. He would probably have hit *me*. Sandy is the bravest guy I know, he would do anything that needed done on the rugby field, except he wasn't interested in punching. And you can't say to him, 'Punch that guy,' – because he doesn't want to do it and he doesn't know how to do it. It is against his nature, it is totally out-with his normal pattern of behaviour. He would scrummage hard, he would tackle hard, he would go down on the ball, he would get trampled all over – but that side of it was totally alien to him. And that is where the French were maybe used to a tougher rugby culture than us. We were distracted by the fighting, whereas it fired them up. We never seemed to settle into our game in France.

ANDY IRVINE

In 1975, we lost in France 10-9, but we had beaten Ireland 20-13 the match before that, and then two weeks later played Wales at Murrayfield. That game really sticks in my mind.

In those days we didn't warm up on the pitch but we would go and have a wander around as soon as we arrived at the ground, to see how firm the playing surface was so that we could decide the best length of stud to wear. I remember walking out of the tunnel with the old east terracing facing us and it was crammed full. It was so busy that for a moment we thought we'd got the wrong kick-off time – that it was two o'clock instead of three o'clock.

Scotland fans at the Ireland game at Murrayfield in February 1975. *The Scotsman Publications Ltd. www.scran.ac.uk*

When you turned round the main stand was nearly empty, because that was all ticketed – but because everyone wanted to see the game they had packed themselves into the rest of the ground more than an hour before kick-off. By the time the game started there were 104,000 people in the ground altogether. And if you listen to some rumours there were plenty more on top of that who weren't officially counted. They changed the rules after that: from then on it was all ticketed.

That was a great Welsh team, with 14 of their starting XV being Lions at some point in their career. They went on to win the Championship that year, but not the Grand Slam because we beat them 12-10 that day.

JIM RENWICK

We went down to Twickenham at the end of the 1975 Championship chasing the Triple Crown.

Before the game we went to this hotel to try and get away from the media and all the fuss. Dod Burrell, the chairman of selectors, got us in this room and was laying it down about how big a chance this was for us because Triple Crowns don't come along very often. He was talking about everyone having their job to do and he was getting pretty heavy. Then, all of a sudden the speaker on the wall burst into life. It was Tony Orlando singing Tie a Yellow Ribbon Round the Old Oak Tree. 'I'm coming home, I've done my time . . .'

Dod charged up to the speaker, grabbed the wire leading up to it, yanked the whole thing off the wall and stamped all over it.

Then he says, 'That's what I want you boys to do to the English today. They're at it already, they know fine well that we're in here and they've put the speakers on to distract us.' He kept going on and on and on about it – getting more and more worked up.

Gordon Brown contests the line out ball with Chris Ralston at Twickenham in 1975. *Press Association*

Well, a minute later the speaker in the other corner started up. 'Now I've got to know what is and isn't mine . . .'

Alistair McHarg was sitting in that corner, and he just stood up and flicked the switch to turn it off.

I started laughing. I couldn't help it – it was funny – and within seconds the whole place had erupted.

Dod just threw up his arms and said, 'F**k it then, get on with it yourselves.' And he stormed out. That was the whole thing knackered.

We lost that game 7-6 after Dougie Morgan missed a penalty from in front of the posts in injury time.

ANDY IRVINE

1975 was very similar to 1973. We defeated Wales and Ireland and had to travel to Twickenham to try and win the Triple Crown. Most of Britain and Ireland felt that we had blown it in 1973 because we were a much better team than England and had beaten them in each of our four previous encounters. After the success at Murrayfield in 1974 things looked to have got back on track and as we headed down to London, England looked even less of a threat to our ambitions than they had two years before.

We had a superior backline that day as England were missing guys like Duckham, Preece and Evans and we hoped for fine weather so that we could really take our running game to them. It was almost a complete role reversal to the 2000 Calcutta Cup in Edinburgh. We were the favourites travelling to the away venue looking to take the spoils with a game of running adventure. The home team were looking for ways to slow us down and to make it an arm-wrestle in the forwards. Just as in 2000, in 1975 the heavens were well and truly open and the pitch was a quagmire.

After penalties from Dougie Morgan and Neil Bennett took us into half-time at 3-3, England stole the lead shortly after the game resumed. Peter Warfield punted the ball from our ten-yard line and it sailed over my head. I ran back expecting it to die on the sodden earth, but it bounced high and over my head again and skidded over our line. It was a foot race between me and Alan Morley and I swear to this day that I touched it down first, but the referee, Paddy D'Arcy, awarded Morley the try.

We tried to work our way back into their half to turn the game around. We were only 7-6 down and should have manufactured a way to score, but Dougie Morgan missed two penalty attempts and Ian McGeechan was wide with a drop-goal attempt. The win would have given us the Calcutta Cup, the Triple Crown and the share of the Championship title. Because of those errors we went home with nothing.

IAN BARNES

I got on again at Twickenham in 1975. I must have been on the bench about twenty times by then and I suppose I was getting a bit blasé about it because as I was going up to my seat in the stand an English boy, Peter Yarrington, who I knew from the Penguins, offered me a pandrop and I just I stuck it in my mouth and sat down. England kicked off – Dave Rollitt hit Nairn McEwan with a straight arm right from the kick off and broke his jaw – so I was on. I got such a fright that I swallowed the pandrop down the wrong way and choked. Colin Telfer who was sitting next to me started banging me on the back. Bill Dickinson, the coach, was going spare but eventually we got down the stairs and out of the stand. You had to go out the back to get into the dressing rooms but when we got there the corridor door was locked. Bill Dick lost the plot. There was a policeman hanging about so Bill borrowed his truncheon and broke a glass panel in the door – but he cut an artery in his wrist doing it and there was blood spurting everywhere. The policeman put a tourniquet on it and told me to hold it. We got into the dressing room just as they were bringing Splash [McEwan] in and he was in a hell of a state – blood coming out of every orifice. By this time, I was shot to bits. I needed a ticket from the English doctor to give to the touch judge to get onto the pitch but everybody was ignoring me, running around fussing over Splash and Bill Dick. The team manager, Dod Burrell, came in – and he went mental because I was still there. He grabbed the doctor, got the ticket and pushed me out the door. I sprinted down the corridor my studs scraping on the concrete floor . . . I turned right . . . and right again . . . then left and right again . . . I could hear the crowd roaring but I had missed the tunnel. It was like a rabbit warren. I came to some steps up into the stand, so I went up them to try to see where I was. People were sitting there wondering who was going to come on – and I was peeping over the top wondering how I was going to get there. I managed to get hold of a steward who showed me the way. Allan Morley scored a pretty dodgy try for England – Andy Irvine definitely touched the ball first. Minutes to go and they were leading 7-6 when we were given a penalty 35 metres out slap in front. I remember standing there thinking to myself, *This is the big time – the first Triple Crown since 1938 – and I am playing!* But Dougie Morgan missed the kick. Full time – back into the dressing room – the heads were down. Dougie's was about his ankles, absolutely inconsolable. Then Renwick looked up and said, 'Hell, Dougie, I could have back-heeled a chest of drawers over from there.'

COLIN TELFER (Hawick)
17 Caps: 1968-1976

It probably had something to do with the way we were playing at the time. Bill Dickinson was still coach and he played a forward-dominated game. We had a good front five with Carmichael, Madsen, McLauchlan, Brown and McHarg, but to my mind we didn't have a back-row which suited a wider game.

Nairn McEwan and these guys were good players but I always felt that there was no link between that power in the front-five and a more expansive game. With Jim Renwick and Andy Irvine there we had the capability in the backs to play a wider game. You've got to play to your strengths and the front-five were ours, but I don't think we gave the backs enough opportunities to cut loose. We did at times, but not enough for my liking.

JIM RENWICK

We had the ability, there were some good attacking players, but I suppose we were out the habit of scoring tries and when that happens it quite often becomes a monkey on your back. You've got to believe you can score and expect to score.

But you've got to remember that in those days you didn't score as many tries. If you got three tries in an international you were lucky, so maybe it isn't as bad a statistic as it seems. And the other side of it is that at least we were getting a few results, whereas later on in the seventies we were scoring tires but couldn't buy a win. I'd rather win 3-0 with a disputed penalty than score five tries but lose by a point.

JOHN FRAME

We went on tour to New Zealand in the summer of 1975 and I had a wonderful time. It was a peculiar tour for me to go on because, as my wife says, she thought I had given up by that point. I don't know why I was picked – but I had the interesting distinction of playing in every one of Scotland's winning games and never experienced defeat on that tour. New Zealand is an incredible place to tour. Unlike Australia, where there is a huge concentration on town councils and local dignitaries, the New Zealanders seem to have a better idea of what it is like for tourists. New Zealanders are great hosts, probably because rugby is everything over there.

ANDY IRVINE

We always had a great time after international matches, but the best times were always had on tour. We were at a civic reception during the 1975 Scotland tour of New Zealand and I remember Ian Barnes putting his false teeth in Billy Steele's cup of tea. Billy didn't notice at first but as he got to the bottom of his drink he spotted something lurking. He went to fish whatever it was out and when he realised that it was something pretty unpleasant he instinctively threw them in the air. They flew across the room and just missed the British High Commissioner to New Zealand's wife by a few inches.

ALAN TOMES (Hawick)
48 Caps: 1976-1987

We had started really well on the tour, beating Nelson Bay in the first match, scoring eight tries to win 51-6, but then we lost to Otago at the House of Pain in Dunedin, which was my first game for Scotland. We then went to Christchurch and lost to Canterbury and were completely outplayed by their forwards. We managed to get things back on track by beating Hawke's Bay 30-0 and followed that up by beating Wellington at Athletic Park, 36-25. We then went to Gisborne to play Poverty Bay and although we had won the last two matches, we had been getting a bit of a doing up front all tour, so Bill Dickinson gave the forwards a real roasting, and Duncan Madsen was on the receiving end of some really harsh words. In the changing room he was bouncing around trying to look as angry as he could when he kicked the door leading into the showers. Well, his foot went right through it and it was like a fish hook – the studs got caught and he couldn't get his boot back out. Just then the referee came in to give us the usual chat about behaving ourselves and not getting too rough – and Madsen was hopping around with his foot stuck in the door.

JIM RENWICK

I've got a picture of myself on the pitch before the Test match at Eden Park. It was taken the day before the game and it's fine, nice conditions to play the match – but the next day it was six inches deep. I didn't go out onto the pitch beforehand, but there were boys coming in saying that it was wet and that the water was lying on the surface. I thought to myself, 'These boys haven't seen Langholm on a bad day, it can't be any worse than that.' Then we get out there and . . . flipping hell . . . I'd never seen anything like it.

IAN BARNES

I have only missed Hawick Common Riding once in my life – for the 1975 Scotland tour of New Zealand – and it was almost worth it. We trained hard, we played well and we had a great time socially. We threw it away against Otago and had no luck whatsoever against Canterbury but we were in good shape and genuinely fancied our chances against a transitional New Zealand side in the Test match. Then the rains came – an inch an hour for four hours. The pitch in Auckland was under water – two inches in places – there is no way the game should have been played – but we were booked in to fly home the next day so we took a vote and decided to get on with it. We played into a gale of torrential rain in the first half and held them to 6 – 0 at half time. I remember saying to Jim, *We can win this!* Then when we lined up for the second half the wind had turned 180 degrees straight back into our faces.

ANDY IRVINE

The pitch was covered in these large lakes of water, puddles four or five inches deep. It was dangerous – too dangerous to play in my opinion. If anyone got caught face-down at the bottom of a ruck, or a collapsed maul or scrum, they were in real danger of drowning. But they couldn't reschedule the fixture so they decided to play on – but on the understanding that the ref might blow up if it looked like a player might be any sort of danger under a pile of bodies. It was a risk though, it's just in those kind of situations that the most terrible accidents can happen.

JIM RENWICK

It was a joke. Grant Batty tried to drop a goal, and the ball just died in the water. The game should never have been played, but we were flying home the next day and 50,000 folk had turned up to watch – so I suppose they didn't have a choice.

We were playing into a gale in the first-half and we were only 6-0 down at half-time, which wasn't bad considering. But the wind changed at half-time and we got beat 24-0. If the wind had stayed we might have done better, but that's rugby for you.

ANDY IRVINE

It continued to rain for the entire match and the wind was at the All Blacks' backs, absolutely beating down on us. It was terrible – especially for someone like me standing around at fullback trying to keep warm. I couldn't feel my hands or feet, my face was completely numb and I was shivering all over.

They scored a converted try by Hamish Macdonald and went in at halftime 6-0 ahead, which was pretty good going for us considering the conditions and the wind. We knew that we would have a chance in the second-half and would use the wind to our advantage. Suddenly it didn't seem such a bad idea to have played the game after all.

Well, someone high up obviously had other ideas because almost on the stroke of halftime the wind changed direction and started to blow right down the other end of the pitch, pummelling the icy rain and the gale-force winds right in our faces again. It was ridiculous. Fair play to the All Blacks though; most sides would have just kicked to the corner and mauled the ball for 40 minutes, but despite the conditions they threw it around a bit. I suppose they knew that there was little danger of us being able to kick the ball very far when we cleared our lines and it was going to take us a lot of effort to work our way up field if we kept the ball in hand. They scored three more tries – two through Bryan Williams and one through Duncan Robertson and Joe Karam finished the game with 100 per cent success from his four conversion attempts.

JIM RENWICK

The All Blacks were a good side. You're talking about Bryan Williams, Duncan Robertson, Sid Going, Ian Kirkpatrick, Andy Leslie and guys like that. They were good lads and they were good players. If I'm being honest, I don't think we were ever going to beat them. One of the things I noticed most of all was how hard they worked on organising their defence. They were all very vocal and everyone knew what they were doing and had something to add, it wasn't just the stand-off calling the shots. Their size, power, aggression, skill levels and body position were all things we could learn from too. But their all-round attitude was the big thing for me. Because it was so important to them, they all had a lot of knowledge about the game, and it was impressive how quickly they picked up on what you were trying to do. It was after that trip that I really started studying the game properly and really watched folk closely, because that was when it struck home how important it was to use every little thing to your advantage. From then on, at dinners after international matches, I always used to ask the opposition questions like, 'How do you defend that?' or 'Why don't you do it this way?' Some of them wouldn't say anything, but some would tell you. That's the way you learn, because everybody does it differently, or you might do the same thing but you go about it in a different way.

IAN BARNES

The Test rugby was really disappointing but it was a great six weeks and a real eye-opener for all of us in terms of work ethic and attitude – within the context of what was still very much an amateur game. I was sixteen stone when we went away and over eighteen when we got back – and I have never recovered. There were no dieticians then – we had the best of grub and we just ate and ate and ate. Norman Pender was late down for breakfast one morning and the bacon was finished – Norman was not pleased. 'Six million sheep in New Zealand,' he said, 'and this lot have run out of bacon?'

JIM RENWICK

Overall I think it was a good tour – hard but good. We would train in the morning and they were tough sessions. Dickinson was good at getting you working hard, and guys like McLauchlan, Carmichael and McHarg had been around a while and they set the standard. They were good players and they pushed us on a bit.

But we also got the chance to see New Zealand too. To be fair it was the amateur days and guys were taking time off their work. You got an allowance every day and that was enough to live off, but a lot of guys were losing pay by being there, so there had to be a balance between doing the hard work and having a bit of fun. That was the beauty about playing in those days – we would train hard in the mornings but we played golf, went jet boating, went canoeing, and did things like that in the afternoon. And there were a lot of free nights, so you got to know boys.

IAN BARNES

International rugby can be a fairly intimidating place and there was nowhere more intimidating than the Parc de Prince. It started with the bus journey to the ground, hitting 100mph along the peripherique with the police motor cyclists kicking the cars out of the way to let the bus through. The stadium itself was just a mass of concrete swinging out over the pitch so the crowd seemed to be right on top of you. The dressing rooms were like a luxury hotel – thick carpets, televisions, trouser presses, coffee machines, refrigerators, the works. Then when you hit the pitch, the noise was unbelievable – Basque bands, cockerels running about, jumping jacks going off. The place erupted when the French came out – and they seemed to be doped up to their eyebrows, all lathered up with a glazed look about them.

When I played there in 1977 France had a boy called Gerard Cholley playing tight head prop and he was a real scary guy. He looked like Moby Dick in a goldfish bowl. He was the French Army heavy weight boxing champion. If he had gone down a dark alley with King Kong, only one of them would have come out the other end – and it wouldn't have been the monkey! I was rooming with Jim Aitken. He said to me, 'I don't think this guy Cholley is as hard as everybody makes out – first scrum we will both hit him'. Now I was not too keen on this idea but I was not going to let Jim know that, so I just kept quiet.

Ron Wilson kicked off – not ten – scrum back. Aitken slipped his binding . . . I hit Cholley . . . Jim didn't . . . Cholley exploded . . . fists flying everywhere. I was trying to keep him away with little pokes. Eventually Merion

Joseph, the referee, got things settled down. Fouroux put the ball into the scrum, Romeau stuck in a diagonal kick and the ball went into touch just outside our 22. As we were running across to the line-out Cholley was kicking at my heels. When we got there I was at 4, Cholley was at 3 and he was right in my face, and it did not take Einstein to figure out what was coming next. Mike Biggar was leading the forwards and I was praying that he would not shout my number and at least give me a chance to cover up. At the time we were doing this tag from 6 to 4 where I stepped out of the line and the big South African, Donald MacDonald, jumped into my space. Biggar shouted it, I stepped out, big Donald jumped into my space and got it right on the chin – and disappeared off on a stretcher not to be seen again.

I spent the next hour and a half avoiding Cholley – and that is a fair old trick in front of 70,000 people without anybody noticing. It was wild, the French got away with murder – cheap shots off the ball, gouging, stamping on heads. It was outrageous and afterwards Dod Burrell, who had been an international referee himself, was raging and he collared Merion Joseph at the dinner; Joseph was pretty defensive – he said, 'But, Dod, how do you stop the French fighting?' And Dod hit him with the immortal line: 'Tell them the Germans are coming.'

Three iconic images from the
1976 Calcutta Cup match. The
Queen meets Ian McLauchlan
before the anthems; Alan
Lawson scores one of his two
tries; Andy Irvine grubbers the
ball through the English
defence. *The Scotsman
Publications Ltd.
www.scran.ac.uk* and *SNS Pix*

JIM RENWICK

In 1977, while the Lions were on tour in New Zealand, the SRU took what you would now call a development tour to the Far East. I don't know who it was at Murrayfield who decided it was a good idea to go on a rugby trip to Hong Kong, Thailand and Japan – but good on them, whoever it was.

Everyone says the rugby was easy, and it was, but it was perfect for our purposes. We took a lot of young guys like Colin Deans, Bill Gammell, John Rutherford and Roy Laidlaw, who were all just beginning to make their names as big time players. There were a few older heads as well, like Mike Biggar, who was the captain, Ian McLauchlan, Lewis Dick, Ian Barnes and myself.

Nairn McEwan was the player-coach, and with a good squad of boys and a good committee the tour went really well. Everybody had little jobs to do – Gordon Dixon was the team photographer, and he kept that job right through the trip even though he didn't have a camera. We played five games and won them all fairly easily, but it was tough because of the temperature and the humidity.

The tour manager was Tom Pearson, a school teacher from Fife. He was a good guy but very straight, and I remember we arrived at the airport in Bangkok we all had to be dressed immaculately in our number ones – which was a pair of tartan trousers, shirt, tie and blazer. Now, normally there would be somebody there from the St Andrews Society, or something like that, and they'd be playing the bagpipes – but not this time. We got off the plane and it was bloody hot, we were all sweating like pigs and looking round for the Thai rugby official, but we couldn't see anybody at all. Then this wee guy comes over, he's wearing a pair of flip-flops, shorts and a t-shirt, and on his t-shirt it says: *F**K WORK – GO FISHING.* It turned out he was our liaison officer and I don't think Tom Pearson liked that at all. From then on we all wanted to be in t-shirts and shorts all the time, but Tom liked us to be in our number ones.

EUAN KENNEDY (Watsonians)
4 Caps: 1983-84

Andy Irvine and Bruce Hay were both tied up with Lions duty, so I was selected to go on that Scotland tour to the Far East. They took me and Colin Mair as the fullbacks. It was the last tour for guys like Ian Barnes and Ian McLauchlan, but the first tour for guys like Bill Gammell, John Rutherford, Roy Laidlaw and Colin Deans.

The games themselves were fairly easy going but the humidity was just a killer. I remember that we were all instructed to take salt tablets on a regular basis because the medical thinking at the time was that we were losing salts through our sweat. But of course, it's not the salts that you're really sweating, it's fluids and we all overdosed on these tablets because we were taking between four and eight of them a day. I remember after the game in Thailand, which was against the full Thai international team who we beat by about 80 points to nil, Ian Barnes came back into the changing room and pulled off his shirt which he then rung out into a bucket; we used to get weighed after the games to try and judge how much water we had to take back on board to keep hydrated, and they realised that Barney had lost around 14lbs in that one game. Nowadays the players are instructed to drink about half a litre of water for every couple of pounds they lose during a game, so Barney would have had to drink a gallon of water if he was playing that game now – but on that tour he had a couple of glasses of water and then just moved onto the beers with the rest of us.

After we played Japan we went to this great closing dinner which was hosted by Princess Chichibu and at the end of the dinner she said that she would like each of the Scottish players to come up individually to receive a gift. So we all started to go up one by one to receive a little box which we opened when we got back to our tables – and they contained these beautiful silver Seiko digital watches that had been engraved on the back with our names and 'from the Japanese Rugby Football Union'. Now, these watches were still several years away from being available in the UK and we were just delighted with them, but the members of our management started getting incredibly tense when they realised what we were being given because they were worried that by accepting them we would be contravening our amateur status. In the end we all just kept quiet about it and nothing ever came of it.

IAN BARNES

The Scotland tour of the Far East in 1977 was my swansong. We played pretty well beating Japan 74-0 in Tokyo with Colin Mair getting into the *Guinness Book of Records* for scoring 30 odd points in an international – albeit a non cap one. Japan was interesting but for me the highlight of the trip came in Bangkok when Jim Renwick and I went for a walk in the red light area. We ended up in this club just as the floorshow was starting. A girl got up on the stage and started slicing a banana with, what the compere euphemistically referred to, as her 'lady garden' . . . then she put a candle out with it . . . and as a grand finale she got herself up in this harness thing and started shooting ping pong balls out of her 'lady garden' into a jam jar on the other side of the stage. Six out of six and Jim turned to me and said, 'Hell, Barney, just think how many goldfish she could win at the shows.'

And that was my international career. It was not much but I enjoyed it. Rugby was, of course, a simple game then. It had a heart and it had a soul. And it had a tremendous community of spirit. It was run by the people for the people. Professionalism and globalisation were always going to take their toll. But the change could surely have been managed better.

JIM RENWICK

They looked after us well in Hong Kong. We were guests of the Hong Kong Jockey Club at the Happy Valley racetrack, and we played a round at the Hong Kong Golf Club. We were guests of honour at a banquet at the Hilton Hotel. Everyone was in dinner jackets and bow-ties while we were in our number ones – again. No expense had been spared, they had The Young Generation dance troupe on the stage and everything was going well until they brought the starter out, which was sliced pineapple with a lotus leaf as decoration.

I was sitting next to Gerry McGuinness and before I'd even started he was coughing and spluttering with an empty plate in front of him. He's saying, 'My throat's on fire – I need water.'

'What's wrong with you?' I asked. I thought he was mucking about.

'It's that leaf, there's something wrong with it.'

I said, 'Gerry, you greedy bastard, you're not supposed to eat the leaf, it's part of the decoration – it's like eating the skewer as well as the kebab.'

By now you could see that his throat has swollen up and he was frothing at the mouth. We were shovelling ice-cream down his neck and the head waiter was running round in a panic because nobody had eaten the leaf before so he didn't know what was going to happen.

Gerry was alright the next day but he was in quite a lot of distress at the time. At the next court session we had him up on a charge of gluttony. Toomba [Alan Tomes] was judge and his punishment was that Gerry had to eat this big cake we had bought. We were just going to let him start then shove his face in it, but he ate the whole thing – no bother to Gerry!

ALAN TOMES

We'd get team-talks in the changing rooms before internationals and guys would be talking about this being the most important thing you'll ever do and all that sort of stuff. Then you'd catch Renwick's eye and you could see he was thinking, 'What a load of crap.' I'd have to stare at the floor so that nobody could see me smiling. Jim and I were very similar in that sense. We took the game seriously but we didn't take ourselves seriously.

I remember playing Wales in the late seventies and I was marking Jeff Wheel, who was a pretty tough character. Nairn McEwan was giving the team talk and he turned to me and said, 'Wheel is going to punch you, he's going to kick you and if you go down he's going to stand all over you. So what are you going to do about it?'

I said, 'Let him have all the ball he wants?'

It was the most inappropriate thing I could think of. I didn't like all this mouthing off about what I was going to do. I preferred to do my talking on the pitch.

Renwick and I had some great times playing for Scotland, even if we went through a long losing spell at the end of the seventies when we hardly won a game. After the games we used to go back to the North British Hotel, have a quick change and nip across the road to the Abbotsford for a pint. I remember one time we were getting a lot of stick because we were in the middle of that losing run and we had been beaten by France, again. One guy must have been in the band which the French used to always have, and he had his trumpet with him. He was taking the mickey, and asked if any of us could play his trumpet because we certainly couldn't play rugby. Of course Jim could, so he got up and did The Last Post – which was quite appropriate given our losing record.

JIM RENWICK

We played England at Murrayfield at the end of the 1978 Five Nations. Neither of us had won a game that season so it was a big match because nobody wants to end up whitewashed. But we didn't play very well that day and we lost 15-0.

I nearly scored in the corner but got pulled down just short. But I've no complaints about the result – we got what we deserved.

It was a pretty disappointing season really. We used three different stand-offs – Ron Wilson, Geech and Richard Breakey – which is an indication that things weren't quite right. It also meant we lacked continuity.

But we weren't that far away from getting results, and although we didn't win anything the next season either, we got two draws

Ian McGeechan leads his team out against England, 1977. *Press Association*

against England and Ireland, so I think we were moving in the right direction. And with John Rutherford coming in at stand-off we were beginning to get a bit more consistency. Another guy who made a difference was Keith Robertson, who gave us a bit more spark in the backs.

KEITH ROBERTSON (Melrose)
44 Caps – 1978-89

My first game for Scotland was against New Zealand in 1978. I'd only played once on the wing before, for the South against the Anglos, when I had a good game against Lewis Dick, who was in the Scotland team at that time, so two weeks later I was selected to play against Bryan Williams.

He was fifteen stone – four stone heavier than me – and probably the best winger in the world at that time. I was shitting myself.

It was a horrible, wet day so inevitably the first thing they did was send a high ball up. I was standing there waiting to be flattened, and I'll always remember gathering that kick and Mike Biggar coming in and blocking off Williams before he could get to me, and I've remained eternally grateful to Mike ever since. It was one of those sorts of moments in your life when you look back and think, 'If I'd made an arse of that then would that have been the end of my international career before it had even started?'

But I still had eighty more minutes to get through. Fortunately, Williams didn't cope very well with the conditions, he dropped three balls when he was one-on-one with me, and I know that if he had held onto any of those passes he could have just wiped me away because he had that capacity to simply run over the top of people.

I actually came off the field thinking I hadn't done very much. Everyone was saying congratulations, but I was just relieved that I had got through it. I was never going to back down, but I was playing out of position and at a completely different level to anything I had experienced before – and until you have done it you never know if you are going to be able to handle it.

I was never comfortable on the wing. I always felt exposed because I knew I wasn't fast enough against the real flyers.

In my last game I was against Patrice Lagisquet, who was nicknamed the Bayonne Express, and if you look at the video there is a moment when the whistle had gone but neither of us had heard it, and he just stood me up then went round me, and he would have scored in the corner. But because the whistle had gone I hadn't been made a fool of in my last Test, which is another moment I look back and am grateful about. I knew my limitations and I wasn't quite fast enough and wasn't quite big enough to play on the wing.

We could have drawn that game against New Zealand in 1978. Geech went for a drop-goal, Bruce Robertson charged it down and hacked it the length of the field to score between the posts. The final score was Scotland 9, New Zealand 18.

JIM RENWICK

We really weren't playing that badly and we weren't getting beaten by a lot. Nairn McEwan had taken over as coach from Bill Dickinson, and I felt sorry for him because he put a lot of work in and he didn't always get the breaks. We were maybe just a few players short of being able to win these games that we were losing by one or two points.

Gordon Brown and Andy Irvine relax at training.
SNS Pix

ANDY IRVINE

We had a really good pack for a long time during the seventies, built around Ian McLauchlan, Sandy Carmichael, Alistair McHarg and Gordon Brown. But by 1978 these guys were either finished or coming to the end of their careers and there was a bit of a gap before the next generation were ready to take their place. So, while we had a lot of very dangerous backs – with Jim Renwick, David Johnston, Bruce Hay and myself, plus John Rutherford and Roy Laidlaw coming through – we were always living off scraps.

Norman Pender, Colin Deans and Ian McLauchlan in February 1978. *The Scotsman Publications Ltd. www.scran.ac.uk*

We went thirteen games without a win between beating Ireland in 1977 and beating France in 1980, but it wasn't all doom and gloom, we were always competitive, and we had a couple of draws in there too – we drew 7-7 with England at Twickenham in 1979 which would be a huge result for Scotland today – so I don't think the public or the team really felt like we were completely detached from the rest.

IAN McGEECHAN

I had to retire because of a cartilage injury, but it wasn't like my career was cut short – I was 33, had played with some outstanding individuals with Scotland and the Lions. The '70s was a golden age of British rugby and every team you played was just filled with quality – and then to play with those players for the Lions was a tremendous honour.

Jim Renwick in the 1980 Calcutta Cup match, while being watched by the respective captains, Scotland's Mike Biggar and England's Bill Beaumont. *Newsquest*

JIM RENWICK

When we beat France in 1980, for our first win in three years, it was typical Andy Irvine. He didn't play that badly in the first-half, but his kicking at goal was terrible – he missed everything and the crowd were beginning to boo him, which was really unusual in those days. If you had been allowed subs he'd have been off.

I remember saying to him at half-time, 'Have you got your boots on the right feet?' And he looked down to check.

He said, 'You know Jim, if I could get a taxi home right now then I would.'

I said, 'Good idea, I'll pay for it.'

But then in the second-half he turned it around. He scored a try in the corner, kicked the conversion from the touchline, scored another try which I converted, and then he kicked two penalties. We were losing 14-4 at one point and ended up winning 22-14. He was unbelievable and it was a hell of a turnaround. But if anyone could play like that, it was him. When he turned it on he was something else. By the end of the game the crowd were all chanting, 'Irvine, Irvine, Irvine.'

That was Andy's style – he wouldn't let the fact everything was going wrong effect him. His attitude, as I've said, was always: *you score three and I'll score four.*

Andy Irvine crosses against France at Murrayfield in February 1980. *The Scotsman Publications Ltd. www.scran.ac.uk*

Crowds flood to greet Irvine when the final whistle sounds after Scotland beat France in 1980, while David Johnston and Didier Codorniou swap shirts in the background. *The Scotsman Publications Ltd. www.scran.ac.uk*

They were great days, the seventies and into the eighties. The game wasn't as predicable as it is nowadays, boys used to play off the cuff the whole time and we knew how to react to the game, how to adapt to situations and counter. Bill McLaren used to say to me that he enjoyed commentating on those days the best. With the Welsh guys around like Gareth Edwards, JJ, Gerald, JPR, Phil Bennett and Barry John you could understand why. And we had great players too. It was all about getting the upper hand on your opposite number and you would try every trick going to get it. There were a lot of mistakes, but when it worked . . .

We were good enough to win some cracking matches, but we fell away in others. Wanting to attack too much maybe . . . and mistakes, little mistakes cost us. But the will to win was always there. It never leaves you. Above all, you wanted to win.

CHAPTER FIVE

IN SEARCH OF GREATNESS

B Y THE END *of the 1970s a new generation of players were coming to the fore, establishing themselves in the Scotland team and creating a hard core that would remain together for a number of years. Jim Aitken was a robust prop capped in 1977, Colin Deans a dynamic hooker who made his debut against France in 1978 and by 1979 there was a new rock to replace Sandy Carmichael as the cornerstone of the scrum at tight-head prop in the shape of Iain 'the Bear' Milne. Alan Tomes, David Gray and Bill Cuthbertson shared the work in the engine room. Competition for the back-row was as fierce as ever, with John Beattie, Jim and Finlay Calder, David Leslie, Iain Paxton, Derek White and John Jeffrey all vying for the three starting jerseys, while in the backs Roy Laidlaw and John Rutherford were about to establish themselves as Scotland's greatest ever half-back partnership, and the axis from which Keith Robertson, David Johnston and Roger Baird alongside the old heads of Renwick, Irvine and Hay could be unleashed outside.*

This new generation were determined to build on the achievements of the greats that had gone before them, having learned one crucial lesson from their predecessors – no matter how lauded those players had become, how well-regarded and how respected, there was a spectre that haunted them all, an unpleasant whisper in their ears, a shadow over their achievements. For despite their talents, despite all their hard work and for all the blood and sweat that they had spilled in the Scottish jersey, each had a gaping hole in his CV – for they had failed to land a title of any sort. The team had blossomed only occasionally.

But these new players looked to these ageing masters and burned with a furious ambition to break the trend of underachievement. Men like Irvine and Renwick, coming to the ends of their careers, had deserved much more than that. The 1980s stretched ahead of the fledgling stars and they were determined to make it a decade that counted.

In the summer of 1980, Jim Telfer replaced Nairn McEwan as the national coach. Ruthless, hard and uncompromising as a player, Telfer employed identical attributes in his coaching. No team under his stewardship would finish second because of a lack of effort; every ounce would be squeezed from every man, nothing would be left on the training paddock or the field of play.

Opposite: David Leslie. *Press Association*

He was determined that Scotland should not just be entertainers; the result at the end of each match was the thing that mattered to him and he set about instilling a hardness in the squad, offering a coaching and playing structure like never before and selecting tours that would push the players to the limit.

In his first Championship in charge, Scotland beat Wales and Ireland at home and were seven and six points adrift in Paris and London respectively. Nearly men still, but things were beginning to change.

In the summer of 1981 Scotland toured New Zealand. Although the injury-ravaged tourists were blown away 40-15 in the second Test, they had run the All Blacks close the week before at Carisbrook, the notorious House of Pain in Dunedin, before eventually losing 11-4. This tour had a resounding impact on the squad and on Telfer. They trained incredibly hard, played against quality opposition around the country, winning five of the six provincial games they played, including a 23-12 victory over the mighty Canterbury, and grew together as a group.

In November that year Scotland welcomed Romania and Australia to Murrayfield. Both were defeated and the 24-15 result against the Wallabies really made the rugby world sit up and take notice. Telfer was shaping a unit of dogged fighters who were developing a will to win to go with the intermittent flashes of dazzle and spark for which they had grown famous.

Despite this, however, the Five Nations of 1982 did not begin with the bang that Telfer had hoped for. Scotland drew 9-9 in the Calcutta Cup match at Murrayfield and lost 21-12 to Ireland in Dublin. These were not the standards that Telfer had either set or was willing to accept from his charges.

The training sessions grew longer and their intensity increased to boiling point. He flogged and abused the players, ripped them apart, tore them to nothing; and then, as only he could, he built them up again.

France flew into Edinburgh for their 6 March meeting. They were Grand Slam champions and although they had lost their opening two matches against Wales in Cardiff and, shockingly, against Les Rosbifs in Paris, they were determined to make amends against Scotland and gain revenge for their loss at Murrayfield two years previously. They knew how Scotland would play – with no little courage or gusto, but with a shaky defence that would crumble when the pressure was applied. What they encountered out on the Murrayfield pitch that spring day was quite a different beast. Hard, disciplined and ruthless in everything they did. Scotland won 16-7.

And so the team turned its attention to Wales. Cardiff had been the graveyard of so many Scottish hopes in the past. For twenty years the thistle had confronted the dragon in Cardiff without success; but Telfer was not prepared to have his team lowered into the grave to just wait for the sound of the shovels. He focussed on defence, on hard, aggressive defence, defence that would make the stands shudder and shake. Rucking would be low and hard and wild like a stampede of bulls. If the shirt had not been rucked off the back of each and every Welsh forward, the job had not been done properly.

And when the time came to attack, his boys would go at it for all they were worth.

Colin Telfer had come in as assistant coach for the start of the Championship and he instilled an understanding in the players that in Test match rugby, players have to make their own luck, create their own chances, and when those openings appeared, they had to make them count, they had to pour every last ounce of energy into them, had to pour in their very soul.

Andy Irvine's men did not disappoint. In a moment to be replayed time and time again in montages of the greatest ever Five Nations tries, Roger Baird, with the impudence of youth, gathered a loose kick from Gareth Davies deep inside the Scottish half just before it went out of play. The Welsh defence had chased well and there was virtually no space for Baird to move. The ball would be carried or kicked out and Wales would have an attacking lineout from a super field position. But then Baird stepped. He pivoted and like a hare out of the traps he accelerated. As the covering defence met him on the half-way line, he slipped the ball to Iain Paxton who opened up his long lolloping stride. Paxton was felled at the Welsh 25 but he got the ball to Alan Tomes who in turn passed out of a final despairing tackle to Jim Calder who skidded over the try line.

Not only was it a fabulous try conjured from nothing, but it was also a catalyst. The Welsh, stung by a try the like of which their Golden Generation would have been proud, fought back with all they had, thundering into rucks and mauls and hitting as hard as they could in the tackle. But it was to no avail. The shackles were off. Attack, counter-attack, furious rucking, booming defence. It was all Scotland. They scored five tries in a 34-16 demolition of their old foes and it marked a special occasion for Jim Renwick for this, his 47th cap, was the first time he had tasted victory in a Test match away from home and he celebrated with a searing run which took him from deep within his own half to score under the posts.

Telfer's hand was beginning to show and it was a line in the sand from which this team never looked back. Scotland finished the Championship one point behind the winners, France.

In the summer of that year, Scotland toured Australia. There was no let up in the training regime; indeed, if anything, it was harder than ever. Telfer drove his men to the edge, beyond the edge. And on a hot and humid day in Brisbane, he drove them into the history books as the team recorded their first, and so far only, Test victory against one of the southern hemisphere's big three away from home. It was testament to the progress the team was making under Telfer. The building blocks were falling into place.

JOHN BEATTIE (Glasgow Academicals)
25 Caps: 1980-1987

I grew up in Malaysia and I spent my childhood running around barefoot in Borneo and Penang for 12 years. A lot of people look back and think their childhood wasn't that great, but I look back and know that mine was fantastic.

I spent it on beaches, swimming in crystal clear seas, seeing orang-utans and huge exotic birds, living in the sunshine, running around an estate all day in barely any clothing. It was wonderful. You learned about wildlife and the whole way of living was wild and it was free and it taught you independence

My father used to tell me about Scotland – what a great place it was and which Scot invented what. He would play pipe-band music on his wee gramophone and we would march up and down to its beat, pretending to be in this far away place. It was sentimentalised over there with big St Andrews nights and Burns suppers, all these ex-pats coming together to celebrate their roots. You don't find a prouder Scotsman than one who lives abroad.

I didn't start to play rugby until we moved back to Scotland and I went to school in Ayr. It was a game I loved immediately; it was rough and fast and the lifestyle I had enjoyed outside had toughened me. I was the misfit boy from Borneo and the only thing I could do was sport, so inevitably sport became a huge part of my life.

When I was growing up in Malaysia, my heroes had been guys like Colin Meads, Brian Lochore and Ian Kirkpatrick – I liked the tough, rough guys, not the glory boys like Andy Irvine or Jim Renwick. When I came back to Scotland, David Leslie became my new hero. I liked his overt aggression; he enjoyed it . . . and when I played, so did I. It wasn't violence – there is no place for that in the sport – but an appreciation of the physical nature of the game.

Scotland used to train at the Jordanhill ground in Glasgow and I once sneaked into a session and spent the whole time just watching him rucking; and I remember watching him play New Zealand at Murrayfield when he kept the entire All Blacks team at bay until he went off injured.

I once came up against him in the National Trial. I was in the Whites along with the Hastings brothers and by half-time we had managed to build a 20 point lead over the Blues. Iain Paxton went off injured and Leslie came on. He was supposed to slot straight into the Blues but he saw the way things were going, ordered me into the Blues, took my place in the Whites and ran right over me. That epitomised his attitude – he hated losing, just wouldn't accept it, especially from a young upstart like me. He had the strength of a prop, the athleticism of a back and the hands of John Rutherford. He could have been a centre, but he was built to be a back-row. He was loud, arrogant, and confident and the best role model I could have ever asked for.

I won my first cap against Ireland in Dublin in 1980. As a student you were plucked from anonymity to suddenly being in the eye of this storm. Ian McLauchlan is phoning you up to ask what kind of boots you would like, and you are saying you would like a pair of Adidas Rom because they are all the rage at the time, and he's saying, 'Do you not want something better than that?' The man from Adidas is putting cash inside your boots. The boots are taken away to have the white stripes painted over. It was a completely crazy time.

Then all of a sudden I was rooming with David Leslie, my hero, and he used to talk me through how I should sleep. He had a certain way that I should do it, lying in what he called *The King Position*: flat on my back with my arms outside the covers. Then in the middle of the night he was jumping out his bed and tackling things. I couldn't sleep a wink – I had to take a sleeping pill. Then it was up early in the morning, massive breakfast followed by a huge lunch with prawn cocktail, steak and chips – it's crazy when you think about it now.

Now I wasn't scared of Ireland because I had been there with the B team and beaten them. But it was a bizarre feeling – one minute you are watching these games on TV, the next you are in the middle of it.

I still think there are times when I played international games and didn't do as well as I should have because I wasn't really in the moment, I couldn't quite believe I was there. I remember a hush in one game, when someone shouted, 'Beattie, for f**k's sake, do something!'

NORRIE ROWAN (Boroughmuir)
13 Caps: 1980-88

We went on a short tour to France in the summer of 1980 when the Lions were away in South Africa. It was Jim Telfer's introduction to coaching the national team and we were his guinea pigs – so you can imagine what that was like.

I've got a scar on my face from a punch-up in the first match in Côte Basque. I was new to all that. I was waiting for the ref to blow his whistle, but in France they wait until everyone has finished knocking the living daylights out of each other and then they scrum down and off they go again.

Playing out there was a bit like being a gladiator in reverse. Instead of it being: 'Eat, drink and be merry, for tomorrow you die,' in France they kill you first and then afterwards they treat you like a superstar. All the restaurants and bars are free, free, free!

KEITH ROBERTSON

That trip to France was exactly what Jim Telfer wanted. He was determined to toughen us up – the French were knocking hell out of us on the pitch, and we were knocking hell out of each other in every session. Before the French Barbarians match in Agen he focused in on this chap, George Mackie.

He was saying, 'Stand up for yourself. You're too nice – stop being so bloody nice,' and he shoved him against the wall. But Mackie came back at him like a raging bull and drove him back against the opposite wall.

He knocked the wind out of him, but Jim was delighted. 'That's what I want to see. Now get out there and show these Frenchmen what you're made of.'

Andy Irvine kicks off against France in 1981. *The Scotsman Publications Ltd. www.scran.ac.uk*

JIM CALDER (Stewart's Melville FP)
27 Caps: 1981-85

The first time I played England, at Twickenham in 1981, I scored a try with only a few minutes to go when Steve Munro flipped the ball back inside and I dived over. That made it 17-16 to Scotland, so we just had to get through the next two or three minutes and we would have beaten them down there for the first time in ten years.

As you would expect, England had one last go. They sent the ball along the backline, but it was very scrappy and the final pass ended up behind Mike Slemen. However, he recovered the ball and did this loop right round all the backs and the forwards to the opposite touchline, before passing to Huw Davies. Suddenly, out of nowhere, Norrie Rowan, our prop, was chasing their fastest player and there was just no other defence. That would have been a big result for us. Full marks to Slemen, he was a lovely rugby player and he danced his way out of trouble, but it was really tough to swallow at the time.

ANDY IRVINE

Bruce Hay was one of the toughest guys I ever played with or against, but he used to get some stick about his pace. He scored this interception try against

Ireland in 1981 and was chased all the way to the line by Tony Ward, who wasn't the fastest thing on two legs either.

As Bruce ran back over the halfway line, Renwick said to him, 'Aye, that's the first time I've seen a try in slow motion and live at the same time. It's lucky it was only Tony that was chasing you.'

John Rutherford dashes past the last of the French cover to score at the Parc des Princes in 1981. *The Scotsman Publications Ltd. www.scran.ac.uk*

NORRIE ROWAN

We arrived in New Zealand in the summer of 1981 after an horrendous flight and stayed in this wee town called Taumarunui for this week-long training camp before playing King Country. We were staying in a travel lodge type hotel and every morning we would walk down to the local park carrying our boots, go through two or three hours of hell with Jim Telfer, walk back up, shower, change and when you came out the hotel after lunch there would be a row of cars waiting for you, with a liaison officer saying, 'Right, who's fishing? You're in that car. Who's shooting? You're in that car. Who's golfing? You're in that car.' They were all local farmers, and they'd take you off to do whatever you wanted, and invariably you'd end up back at the farmhouse having dinner, drinking beer and enjoying the chat, back to the hotel at night, straight to bed, up in the morning and off to training again.

JIM RENWICK

We went to a state reception at the parliament buildings in Wellington. I was just keeping out the road, hanging about at the buffet stand, dipping my prawns in the sauce, when this old boy comes across and says, 'How are you enjoying our beautiful country?'

'Aye, its fine,' I said. I couldn't really be bothered with this but I thought I better make some small talk, so I said, 'And what do you do?'

'I'm Robert Muldoon, the Prime Minister of New Zealand,' he says.

'Aye, and I'm the Provost of Gala,' I said back to him,

So off he went his own way and a bit later, when it was time for the speeches, up this guy gets and he was exactly who he had said he was. I was saying to the rest of the boys that we better get ready to do a runner because he might want the Provost of Gala to speak next and I hadn't prepared anything.

Iain Milne jumps for joy when he learns that he has been selected for his first cap in 1979. The Bear would go on become a cornerstone in the Scottish pack for more than a decade. *The Scotsman Publications Ltd. www.scran.ac.uk*

I thought we had a real chance in the Test series because the All Blacks maybe weren't as strong as they had been in the past. If we had taken a few chances earlier in the match then we might have done it. We had a good scrum and we kicked well. The difference was that when we had them under the cosh they held on, then at the start of the second-half they were putting a bit of pressure on us and we gave away an easy try when the ball came out the side of a scrum and Dave Loveridge pounced on it. That wrapped it up for them and that was maybe the difference between them and us – they did the damage when they got the chance.

We trained hard for the second Test right up to the day before the match and I felt we were just a wee bit burned out by the time we got there. If I'm being honest, I think we trained too hard on that trip. Boys were picking up injuries, pulling muscles and that sort of thing. We trained in the morning and afternoon, and then watched videos at night. Sometimes the videos were two or three years old so they weren't even relevant to what we were trying to do. But I suppose Jim Telfer just wanted us to be together and watching rugby and thinking about the game. That was just his way of doing it and I'm not saying he was wrong. I'm just saying that it's not the way I would have done it. A lot of the boys had taken time off their work so there should have been more of a balance between work and play.

He wanted to put up a good show – there's nothing wrong with that – and to be fair we didn't play too badly. We only just lost the first Test in Carisbrook, which was a good effort, so maybe he was right in some ways. But they put 40 points on us in the second Test, and I thought we did too much work in the week before that match. We were in the game right up until half-time, and it was only in the last twenty minutes that they ran away with it, and I think a lot of that was down to boys being dead on their feet.

I could see a lot of differences between that tour and the '75 one. The players didn't get out to see the country and meet folk. Things were changing, they were taking fat content measurements, and maybe it was the right idea because that was the way the game was going, but I don't think it had been properly thought through yet. At the end of the day you have to make sure the boys are ready to play on match days but we seemed to be carrying a lot of guys with knocks and pulled muscles. You've got to remember we were amateurs, and our bodies weren't used to that level of work. It was the hardest tour I had been on. With the Lions we trained hard but it wasn't as intense as that tour. The day we got to New Zealand we arrived and trained for an hour in the afternoon. In fact we even trained in Singapore in the heat when we stopped on the way over.

ANDY IRVINE

We created enough chances to win that first Test. John Rutherford was fantastic, he took the ball to the line whenever he could and had their defence at sixes and sevens; he made some great breaks, but we just weren't able to finish them off. That try by Loveridge was infuriating and typical of Scotland's fortunes over the years – we battle hard to stay in the game for the majority of the 80 minutes, but the opposition do something cheeky, or even just react quicker than we do at the very moment when there is a slight lapse in concentration, and they capitalise to score. It's maddening and heart-breaking all at the same time.

On the back of that score their spirits rose and they were soon crossing our line again with Stu Wilson flying in with a try.

But as captain I was extremely proud of the way the team fought back. We didn't go into our shells but instead continued to attack them and unleashed a flurry of adventurous running and slick handling that had them clawing on for dear life to the lead – we really had them rattled. Colin Deans went over for a try and we nearly scored through Renwick, Rutherford and Steve Munro – but as ever against the All Blacks it was a valiant effort that came to naught. Their players said afterwards that they were relieved to hear the final whistle because they thought we might have edged it, but that's easy to say in the aftermath of a close game – the reality of the situation was that they held on as they so often do and secured the win.

The second Test saw us lose 40-15, but it was much, much closer than that. They pushed into a 22-6 lead but then we came back at them with some fantastic play and Bruce Hay scored a scorcher of a try. I converted and then added a penalty and we were back in contention at 22-15. We were denied another score under their posts and then Steve Munro broke clear. If he hadn't been in bed with flu during the two days leading up to the Test he would have cruised in, but he was struggling and was caught by Bernie Fraser. Shortly after that Jim Calder seemed to have made amends for us when he touched down for a perfectly good try but we were brought back for a very dubiously called forward pass. The frustration at all these missed opportunities was growing too much and we imploded slightly towards the end. The All Blacks ran in three tries through Allan Hewson, Stu Wilson and Bruce Robertson, all of which were converted by Hewson and scoreboard took on a lop-sided look that in no way reflected the quality of our challenge or our play.

Colin Deans nails Tony Ward before the Irishman can do any damage at Murrayfield in 1981. *The Scotsman Publications Ltd. www.scran.ac.uk*

NORRIE ROWAN

I thought that that tour was fantastic, despite the Test results and the slogging that Jim Telfer gave us – the combination of hard work and such good times off the field bonded us and created a real team ethic while lacing the whole thing together with fun. Everything that followed stemmed from that tour.

JIM RENWICK

Australia toured Britain in the late autumn of 1981 on the back of series victories over both the All Blacks and France and we played them at Murrayfield in December. The conditions were fairly horrendous that day so it was mainly all kicking. Andy Irvine kicked five penalties to give us an 18-15 lead and shortly afterwards their fullback, Roger Gould, caught me with his boot as he took a mark and I had to go off to get some stitches. I was just back on the park when Rudd [John Rutherford] put a high kick up which David Johnston chased. I should have done the same, but I was still a wee bit groggy. Anyway, Gould and Johnston both missed it and the ball bounced over everyone's head into my hands and I scored under the posts. That's what they call good vision. I call it being lucky. It shows you that rugby isn't always a fair game – I didn't

Bill Cuthbertson gathers the ball, supported by Roy Laidlaw, during the Australia match at Murrayfield in December 1981. *The Scotsman Publications Ltd. www.scran.ac.uk*

deserve to score, I was in the wrong place, but that's why they call it the luck of the bounce – and I had played enough games for Scotland over the years when the luck of the bounce definitely went against us. After all those years of disappointment I began to wonder if we might be on the brink of something special.

ANDY IRVINE

The night before we played England at Murrayfield in 1982, Jim Telfer brought a video into the team-room at the Braid Hills Hotel, where we always stayed.

He said, 'Right boys, we're going to watch England's last game against Wales. I want you to have a look good at this and afterwards we'll have a good discussion about what we have learned.' So the lights went out and after five minutes we're all nodding off. Then, at the end of the match the lights came back on and Telfer said, 'Okay, we've seen the opposition, we're going out to play them tomorrow – anyone got any comments?'

Absolute silence.

'Jesus Christ, I can't believe this, we've been watching them for an hour and a half, has nobody got anything to say?'

Still silence.

Then, slowly, up goes Jim Renwick's hand.

Telfer says, 'I might have guessed: only a Border boy would show any interest. Yes, Jim – what's your point?'

'You couldn't open a window could you? It's roasting in here.'

Nobody would have the balls to do that except Renwick. The place just erupted. Even Telfer saw the funny side of it.

That was typical of Renwick. He was a pretty laid-back character no matter what the circumstances were. You get guys in the changing room who are banging their head off the wall and thumping their chest. Jim would look at them and you could tell he was thinking, 'What the heck are they doing?' But in his own quiet way he would build himself up, and when that whistle went he was a very determined individual. He was always as competitive as you could ever hope anyone to be, but maybe he was a wee bit unemotional about it all and some people might have got the impression that he was a bit cool, a bit laid back, and that his heart wasn't really in it, but nothing could have been further from the truth.

ROGER BAIRD (Kelso)
27 Caps: 1981-88

We stayed down at the St Pierre Hotel just outside Bristol before the Wales game in 1982 and did all our preparation there. Jim Telfer's team-talks were legendary, even at that stage. I'd had him in the B team, and it was worth getting picked just to hear what he was going to come out with next. On this occasion it was just after the SAS had swung in through the windows at Whitehall to end the Iranian siege – so that was the theme. We were going to be like the SAS. We were coming from Bristol, going into Cardiff, going to kick the shit out of them, and get the hell out of there – and it all went to plan.

It wasn't a bad Welsh side, they were coming to the end of their great spell, but there were still some fantastic players there – Gareth Davies, Ray Gravell, Elgan Rees. Fortunately, we got the bounce of the ball, and things just seemed to click for us that day.

JIM RENWICK

You've got to have a culture in the team where guys aren't scared to take a chance, and everyone is expecting the good runners to have a go. It's a self-fulfilling prophecy. If the team believe that they can run at the opposition and cause some problems then they are geared towards doing that, and even if it

Andy Irvine kicks for goal against France in 1982. *SNS Pix*

goes wrong then they are ready to tidy up, and when it works it's worth it. But if the team as a collective isn't thinking that way then you have no chance. It's not a risk moving it on your own try-line if everybody in the team knows that you're going to do that; but if you're the only guy thinking that way then it's a big risk.

Our game plan was based on a strong defence and patience, waiting for our moment to counter-attack. We knew it would come. In every game there are one or two chances that come your way and if you take them you can swing the match in your favour. So we knew we just had to bide our time and when the moment came, no matter when it was or where we were on the pitch, we would go for it. All-out. Because when those chances came, you had to make them count.

JIM CALDER

I knew I wasn't the quickest thing on two legs so I had to be thinking two steps ahead the whole time. I remember glancing across when Roger Baird fielded that ball from Gareth Davies and half expecting him to kick the ball into touch but I was also thinking that I might start edging my way up field, just in case. So I gave myself a head start. Colin Deans was on the other side of Alan Tomes – he was a sprinter and actually got there before me, but the way Toomba turned after he took the ball from Iain Paxton meant that I got the pass.

It's funny, I was in the Roseburn Bar recently with Donald Wilson, who runs Murray International Holdings, and played for Stew-Mel, Heriot's and Kelvinside in his day. He was chatting away and he said, 'The best try Scotland ever scored was when Roger Baird collected that kick from Gareth Davies at Cardiff Arms in 1982 and broke up the left touchline.' He talked his way through the whole build up, 'Roger passed inside to Packie who opened his legs and what a sight that was. Packie was crocked in the tackle but still managed to get the ball away to Alan Tomes.'

I was just sitting there enjoying the moment.

'It looked as if Toomba was going to score, but the Welsh had come blazing across the pitch and he was pulled down just short, so he threw the ball out to . . .'

And then his brow began to furrow, and he said, 'Who got the try?'

At first I thought he was joking, but he was being serious. I suppose because he was a winger he remembered all that open running rather than the wee guy who flopped over the line at the end.

JOHN BEATTIE

I broke my knee cap on the back pitch at Murrayfield just before the 1981 tour of New Zealand. It was the last ruck of the practice, I was dehydrated because I had been out the night before, I was badly underweight because I had been at the Hong Kong Sevens, I had a sore shoulder, and I was given the ball by Jim Telfer. I ran into Iain Milne and my left knee-cap just exploded. It came halfway up my thigh. I was rushed into hospital, operated on, and I was there for three weeks. It got badly infected so I was told that if the drugs didn't work I'd get my leg taken off. I remember lying in my hospital bed and Andy Irvine came in to see me with his tour blazer on; Iain Paxton had been given my blazer, and I just burst into tears.

After that I had a year watching, and I remember watching the 1982 Wales game on television at Glasgow Accies' clubhouse, thinking it was brilliant. But when Paxton ran up the wing . . . I died . . . every step he took . . . I died.

ROGER BAIRD

People say I was brave to run it back, but it was a percentage thing. I was right next to the touchline so the worst that was going to happen was that I was going to be put into touch. I think that score released the pressure on us a bit. It gave us a bit of confidence that we could compete with these guys and take it to them. The hard work ethic that Telfer had instilled was beginning to show dividends, not just in our ability to win ball up-front but in our belief that we were capable of dictating how the game was going to pan out.

It went on from there with fantastic scores from Jim Renwick, David Leslie, David Johnston, Lucky Jim Pollock and Derek White. I remember, we were walking back to the halfway line after the last of those scores and the young guns were getting pretty full of it – Renwick turned to us and for once he wasn't joking around. 'Just, watch what's going on here boys. This ain't over yet.' That was Jim's 47th cap and he still hadn't won away from home, so it meant a lot to him. When Jim gets serious you take notice.

Of course, we held on for one of the great wins in Scottish rugby history, 34-18. It really was a brilliant day. My folks were there and it was fantastic for them – in fact every rugby supporter over a certain age claims to have been there. There's a great story about a boy from Longniddry who was watching the game at home. He's a great supporter of Scottish rugby and when the game was over he said to his wife, 'I'm just going out for a pint of milk.' Seven hours later he phoned in and his wife is not surprisingly pretty keen to find out where he'd got to. He said, 'I'm in Cardiff – I just had to come.' He'd got in his car and driven all the way down for the night out!

A handful of us – Jim Renwick, Derek White, John Rutherford and myself – were going to Hong Kong the next day to play for Scottish Borderers in the Sevens, and we met Eddie Butler, the Welsh number eight, at the airport. He was playing for Crawshays Welsh, or something like that, and he said he had never been as glad to get out of Wales in his life. They got hell for that – absolute hell.

That match was a big watershed. It got rid of a lot of the baggage Scotland had been carrying around. Winning away from home was a big thing, and we weren't used to winning as emphatically as that, and we weren't used to winning playing that sort of good rugby.

JIM POLLOCK (Gosforth)
8 Caps: 1982-85

When I got called into the Scotland team for that Wales game, I thought it was a wind-up. I had played quite well for the Anglo-Scots two weeks before, but I had only been involved in one training session, and it never occurred to me that I might be involved in the Five Nations until the Thursday before the match, when the school secretary at Kenton Comprehensive ran across the field and said I had to ring this guy Ian McGregor immediately. I naturally thought it was a friend of mine taking the piss – but I rang the number and this very sombre voice said Keith Robertson had tonsillitis and I was taking his place.

I rolled up on the Friday not really knowing anyone's first name, never mind anything else. We went through the moves on the 17th fairway at St Pierre Hotel golf course, then pitched up against Wales and beat them quite convincingly and I scored a try. International rugby? A piece of cake!

I was very fortunate because the season after that I got my second cap when we went down to Twickenham and won there. So I had two victories out of two and those were Jim Renwick's first away wins after more than a decade in the Scotland squad. My next match was the draw against New Zealand, and then I played against England, Ireland and France during the Grand Slam season. So, in my first six games we won five and drew one against the All Blacks – I think I deserved the nickname Lucky Jim.

NORRIE ROWAN

In 1982, we went to Australia and it was a similar sort of trip to the New Zealand tour the year before. We had a training camp up the Gold Coast and then we played a game in a place called Mount Isa. They put on a barbeque for us, which we got taken to on this old school bus along a really bumpy road. Eventually we arrived in this valley which was packed with the whole town. There were bands singing and it was just fantastic. Jim Telfer says, 'Everyone back on the bus at ten o'clock.' This was at about seven o'clock, and by eight o'clock Jim Pollock is on the stage singing King of the Road. Creamy is going mad, 'Everyone back on the bus, now!' But it took him ages to track down all the players. Back at the team room, Jim is going mad. 'You're here to play rugby, you're no here to sing and dance. You're here to represent your country.' That was at nine o'clock.

JIM CALDER

While we were out in Australia there was a doubt about Iain Paxton so our brother John was brought out. He arrived on the Monday, played on the Tuesday and scored two tries – for one of them he plucked the ball off his toes, going at pace, and dived over – then in the next midweek game he scored another two tries, and suddenly he's got four tries in two games with the Test match getting closer and closer.

I remember there was John, Fin, myself and Jim Telfer standing around, with Packie lying there in his bed. Jim said, 'Just so you know – if Packie doesn't make Saturday then John, you are in.' Fin and I are looking at each other and shaking our heads in disbelief. John was getting great news and here are his two brothers shaking their heads and muttering under their breath. Fin hadn't been capped at that point and this was supposed to be his big chance, and here was Spawny John – as we call him because he always seems to land on his feet – coming in and stealing the show! But in the end Packie dragged himself from his sickbed and declared himself fit, so neither Fin nor John got to play. Fin's time would come later, but for John that was it.

Looking back on that period, you realise all the things that that Scottish side achieved – we won in Cardiff for the first time in 20 years, beat Australia in Brisbane, drew with New Zealand in 1983, we won the Grand Slam in 1984, eight of us toured with the Lions in 1983 – and I'm not sure we appreciated at the time just how special those successes were. Of course, there were no world rankings in those days and Scotland and Australia were much of a muchness in those days, so while we were obviously delighted to win over there we didn't feel as if we had turned the world on its head.

JIM RENWICK

I had made myself unavailable for the tour to Australia, so it was disappointing not to have been a part of that famous victory down there, but I'd had enough of touring by then. New Zealand in '81 was the final straw for me – it was getting too much like hard work. It had been exceptionally hard over there, and I was coming to the end of my career and I couldn't be bothered going through that again.

But the boys did well in 1982. They beat Australia 12-7 in the first Test and that was the first time they had won an international match in the southern hemisphere. I remember watching the game on the telly, and Toomba was shouting to the pack, 'Come on boys, Scotland have never won a Test in the southern hemisphere.' So he must have been pretty geared up because Toomba wasn't the type of guy that did a lot of talking unless he had something important to say.

Australia came back and gave us a bit of a doing the next week, but a win over there is some achievement so they did well.

KEITH ROBERTSON

To be honest, the fact that we had won down there was a bigger thing than the fact that we had beaten Australia. We had beaten Australia before at home, but no Scottish team had ever won in the southern hemisphere, so that was something new. Strangely, the match we won was in near perfect conditions, but the second game, when they got their own back on us, was played in a gale, which you would have thought would have suited Scotland better. But it was the end of a long, hard tour; a few players were carrying knocks, and we perhaps didn't have quite enough strength in depth to back up that first result.

ROGER BAIRD

There was outrage in Australia after we beat them because they had dropped Roger Gould and Paul McLean, who had been two stalwarts of their team for a long time, to bring in the Ella brothers – Glen and Mark – at stand-off and full-back respectively. They brought those old-stagers back for the second Test in Sydney a week later and absolutely stuffed us. Gould scored two tries and McLean kicked five penalties and three conversions and Michael O'Conner scored their third try. He was another great player. That was his last game for Australia before he switched to rugby league and he went on to become a major star in that sport as well, which was a huge achievement in those days because rugby league players looked upon guys from union as big softies.

    That defeat to us in Brisbane was perhaps a bit of a turning point for Australia because it forced them to have a long hard look at themselves. Certainly, when they came to Britain in 1984 and achieved the Grand Slam, they were magical. I was lucky enough to be in the South side which beat them at Mansfield Park the week before the Scotland Test and they clearly didn't fancy it in the mud that day – but when they got up to Murrayfield they were on a whole different level. Mark Ella was back at stand-off, Michael Lynagh was at inside centre, Andrew Slack at outside centre, David Campese on the wing, and Gould still at full-back.

KEITH ROBERTSON

The 1983 Five Nations was very disappointing by and large – having had a good season the year before, we lost to Ireland, France and Wales in the first three games and only really put in a good performance against England at Twickenham. That was obviously a famous victory and it remains the last time we won there. We played tremendously well throughout the whole match and Roy Laidlaw scored a great try off the back of a scrum which Peter Dods

Roy Laidlaw scores in the Calcutta Cup at Twickenham in March 1983. *The Scotsman Publications Ltd. www.scran.ac.uk*

converted to add to his two penalties. I dropped a goal and then big Tom Smith scored in the last minute to take the match out of England's reach at 22-12. About fifteen minutes before that Jim Renwick had a drop-goal attempt from about the ten-metre line and it was that bad I almost scored off it on the wing. Dusty Hare was scuttling back and the ball was bobbling round all over the place, and I almost got there in time. As I was running back I remember Jim muttering, 'That's effin' garbage'.

So when I scored the drop-goal, I ran past him and said, 'That's how you do it, Jim.' I was just joking around but I think he was a bit miffed at that.

Jim was always great value on the rugby pitch. He was very serious about his rugby but he was such a natural and he had that sort of character which meant he was always able to take a step back and see the funny side of things.

I remember one game down in Wales when he was flattened by Steve Fenwick, and when Fenwick pulled him back off the turf Jim said to him, 'Do that one more time, Fenwick, and that'll be the second time you've done it.'

But to play alongside Jim was wonderful – those dancing feet, the angles of running, his acceleration. He could see it all and to get those wins away from home as his career was winding down was no more than he deserved. It was just such a shame that he and Andy Irvine didn't really get a chance to share in the spoils the following year because of injury. They, more than anyone, deserved it.

CHAPTER SIX

THE SECOND SLAMMERS

FIFTY-NINE.
It was a number that haunted Scottish rugby. Fifty-nine. It was fifty-nine years since that first game at Murrayfield, since Herbert Waddell had struck that drop goal in the decider with England; fifty-nine years since Scotland had won its last Grand Slam.

It has been stated ad nauseam that Scottish sportsmen – and rugby players in particular – suffer from an inferiority complex. This can no doubt be debated forever, but it is interesting to note that many of Scotland's finest rugby performances have taken place in the season following a Lions tour when the players selected are given an opportunity to see first-hand what their rivals from England, Wales and Ireland are really made of. Training and playing together in such a close-knit and intense environment provides the ultimate platform for these players to test and measure themselves against their fellow tourists.

In 1983, the Scotland players who travelled to New Zealand in the famous red of the Lions had their eyes opened to the shortfall between them and their rivals. And the difference? Significant as it turned out. They were, in John Rutherford's words, 'fitter, better and mentally stronger than the best players from England, Wales and Ireland.'

For this group, any sense of inferiority was dispelled. But the 1983 Lions tour was something of a double-edged sword. For all that it boosted confidence within the Scottish ranks that they could more than compete with the players from the other Home Unions, it was a devastating experience for British and Irish rugby in general, with the tourists going down to a 4-0 whitewash for only the second time in their history. And it nearly broke Jim Telfer, who coached the side. For a while he considered giving up coaching altogether.

But something special had been building in the Scotland camp. Not only had a core of the squad gained invaluable experience on the Lions tour, but after Scotland had toured Australia and New Zealand in 1981 and 1982, there was an understanding of what it took to perform and win at the highest level. The victory in the first Test in Brisbane in 1982 built a confidence that the team took into its 25-25 draw with the All Blacks at Murrayfield in the autumn of 1983.

Opposite: Peter Dods kicks Scotland's first conversion of the Ireland match, 1984. *The Scotsman Publications Ltd. www.scran.ac.uk*

And so the spring of 1984 rolled in. Scotland had a strong and competitive squad filled with battle-hardened players. Jim Telfer continued to be assisted by Colin Telfer and had the inspirational prop Jim Aitken installed as his captain. Although injury had robbed the squad of two of their most celebrated players in Jim Renwick and Andy Irvine, there was still plenty of firepower elsewhere in the Scottish line-up. Roy Laidlaw and John Rutherford, who had both come through the Scotland B ranks under Jim Telfer, were forging a commanding partnership at half-back; the back-row of David Leslie, Iain Paxton and Jim Calder were ferocious, dogged and devastating; the front-row of Aitken, Colin Deans and Iain Milne were full of power and guile, while in the engine room behind them Alan Tomes and Bill Cuthbertson were the heart-beat of the team; in the midfield Euan Kennedy and David Johnston weaved magic to release Keith Robertson and Roger Baird, and Peter Dods was the points machine at fullback. Complementing these fifteen were John Beattie, Alastair Campbell, Gordon Hunter and Jim Pollock, who each came into the team as injuries and form dictated and were as tenacious, ambitious and excellent as any other player in the squad.

But there was pressure too; great pressure. Fifty-nine years of it.

JIM TELFER

That Lions tour really took a lot out of me. I was very disillusioned when we got back and I felt that maybe I wasn't cut out for coaching at that high a level. I seriously considered quitting rugby altogether. I also expected someone else to have come in to replace me, but they left the door open for my return and once I was back in a tracksuit again and back in the Scotland environment I felt reinvigorated. That was down to the players – the enthusiasm that was going around that squad was infectious and you couldn't help but be drawn into it.

Jim Aitken was the new captain, having taken over from Roy Laidlaw at the end of the 1983 season, and I thought he was very good – he was excellent at looking after the other players, encouraging them and so on and he led from the front in everything he did. And although the Lions tour had been tough on me, the players who went gained a lot from it and, ironically, David Leslie, who didn't tour, seemed to gain even more.

David Leslie. *Getty Images*

KEITH ROBERTSON

We'd had nine players away with the Lions in New Zealand during the summer of 1983 and when they came back I remember John Rutherford at the first session saying, 'We know these guys and we have absolutely nothing to fear. We should be looking to win the Championship this year.' And I think that was the beginning of the belief developing which led to the Grand Slam in 1984.

EUAN KENNEDY

I didn't get capped until I was 29, so I really served my apprenticeship to international rugby. I played over 50 times for Edinburgh and represented Scotland B on many occasions and I did wonder at times if I would ever make it.

I had some great experiences with Scotland B over the years. Jim Telfer was in charge for several of the games and although I would never class myself in same core group as them, that team had players like Rutherford and Laidlaw who came up through the B ranks with Telfer and who went on to have such a lot of success with him over the years.

I remember my first game for Scotland B was against France down in Rheims in 1976, when I was 21. They always say that the step from club rugby to B rugby is intense, and it certainly was – particularly in somewhere like Rheims. They used to auction the B and Test games out around France, so they were well supported by the winning city, so you always got big crowds. I was playing fullback in that game and was taking the kicks and whenever you lined up a shot at goal all the brass bands would start up and play at their highest pitch to try and put you off. We lost that game narrowly, something like 13-7, which against France away from home was a pretty good result. I was in the changing room afterwards and asked Jim if I could go and swap my shirt; he said that I had played well and done my country proud, so of course I could. So off I went and swapped my shirt and didn't think very much else about it. A few weeks later, however, I got a letter through from the SRU with a bill for £15 for my shirt. I wrote back and said that I had been given permission to swap it, but that obviously didn't cut very much with the secretary because I was invoiced again. I was a student at the time and £15 was a lot of money for me, so I did what most players in that situation would have done and ignored the bills. But they kept on coming and at the start of the following season I received another letter stating that unless I paid my bill the whole situation might have a negative bearing on my international selection. Now, I can't imagine that the international coaches would have really decided not to select someone if they thought they were the best player in their respective position in the county just because they hadn't paid a £15 bill, but I didn't want to risk it and finally paid up. But it was a classic example of the SRU's mindset that they couldn't ever let anything like that go.

In 1979 David Johnston joined Watsonians and I moved from fullback to centre. I had tried to persevere at fullback and was playing some pretty decent rugby but I couldn't get in the Edinburgh team at the time because Andy Irvine and Bruce Hay were both playing there for their clubs and were ahead of me. So my chances of getting into the district setup and then onwards to international honours was looking increasingly unlikely unless I looked at a different position.

So I made the move in '79 at the same time that David joined and when we started playing together things just clicked. We played inside and outside centre, which is very much the norm now, but back then centres would often play left and right – which I struggled with a bit because I was new to centre and didn't always know the right defensive lines to take if I found myself in the outside centre position. But David and I worked on just playing inside and outside centre – I was the big player inside and he was just lightening quick outside and it worked brilliantly. I certainly found it difficult in later years when I was picked for Scotland Trials and played with a centre who only played left and right, because I would often find myself exposed in the wider channels. I played once with Jim Renwick and I was never going to argue with him over the style that he wanted to play, but I struggled when I had to play outside him.

They made me captain of Scotland B in 1983 against France in Ayr and that was kind of like the rugby equivalent of a pirate's black spot because very few players who were given the B captaincy went on to play in a Test match; it was kind of an old wives tale in rugby circles, but it certainly crossed my mind that they were saying I had gone as far as I could with that appointment. But we won that game and they obviously thought I had done enough to move on up the following season.

In 1983 I captained Edinburgh against the All Blacks in the Wednesday game about ten days before they played Scotland. We lost but despite the fact they had a pretty much full-strength team with guys like Stu Wilson, Wayne Smith, Bernie Fraser, Robbie Deans and Murray Mexted playing we pushed them pretty close and if we had perhaps kicked more of our goals we could have put them under some serious pressure. It was the most physical district game I had played up to that point, but the team had stood up well.

On the Saturday Watsonians played Heriot's at Goldenacre and we won, which was a great result for the club, and the next day the Scotland squad all met up for training. It emerged that Keith Robertson had been injured playing for his club the previous day and there were all these whispers going around that I would definitely be in as his replacement – but you can never tell what the coaches and selectors are thinking, so I had to just get on with things as normal. Before we headed out Jim Telfer sat us all down in the changing room and told us that Keith had indeed been injured and that I would be starting against the

All Blacks the following week. It was a wonderful way to find out I was going to win my first cap – normally you get a letter through the post and you don't have anyone around to tell, but I was there with my peers, with guys who I had been playing club, district and B rugby with for years, and there were some lovely words said by them at the time.

It was an incredible week getting ready for that match – knowing I was going to be starting and that I was going to be playing in a packed Murrayfield against the best team in the world. I had been involved with squad sessions before but never in the build up to a Test match – the Thursday meet and quite a hard session that day, then the run-through for the press on the Friday, staying at the Braid Hills Hotel and then going to the game on the Saturday. The Friday session is very light and just for the benefit of the press, so all the ground-work for the Test match is laid during that one session on the Thursday, which would be unthinkable now – and was also nothing compared to the preparation that the All Blacks had been doing because they were in the middle of a long tour. But we were very lucky at the same time because the players who had come back from the Lions tour were all quality players who had improved while they were away and they were all confident that we could do something against the All Blacks – and that belief in itself gave you belief.

The trip to Murrayfield is a wonderful thing – seeing all the fans making their way there and you have these police outriders guiding the coach through town. And there was a certain point on the way that we would reach and all the players would start singing Flower of Scotland – and we would reach the final chorus just as we arrived at the ground.

JOHN BEATTIE

There was a TV strike so it wasn't being televised. Jim Telfer had been on the Lions tour that summer and it hadn't gone well, a lot of the English players hadn't believed in what he was doing so hadn't carried out his instructions on the pitch, and he

John Beattie reaches the ball under pressure from New Zealand's Murray Mexted, as Jim Calder follows up in support. *Getty Images*

was determined to make amends for that disappointment. We were determined to help him out.

This was him moulding the team that would win the Grand Slam the next year. I remember being in a team meeting, we were in white jerseys that day, and it was decided that anything went. The basic plan was to stand on them as much as we could. I remember being in one ruck when it felt like you had fallen off your horse coming over Beechers Brook in the Grand National. It has never left me: that image of white jerseys going right over the top of me. There were a couple of rucks where we blew the All Blacks' pack apart. The idea was that because there was a TV strike, anything went.

EUAN KENNEDY

Because of the TV technicians strike the game wasn't televised in the UK at all – but I was able to get a copy of the New Zealand broadcast, which is a great memento although it's a shame that it was commentated on by the Kiwi pundits rather than Bill McLaren.

Players always warn you that the step-up, in terms of pace, physicality and intensity – as well as a reduction in the time you have to think and make decisions – goes up significantly from club to district level and again from district level to B level, which it does. But the step-up from B to Test rugby is just incredible.

We wore white jerseys and shorts and blue socks for that match and within about a minute of the kick off I had my hands on the ball and took it into contact and Bill Cuthbertson thought he would help me out and bound onto me as I took the tackle – but in doing so he completely unbalanced me and I ended up on the other side of the ruck . . . which is the last place you want to be against the All Blacks, especially in the first few minutes when everyone's really fired up. Their entire pack poured into the ruck and danced all over me, raking me out the back. I was absolutely covered in welts and stud marks and as I got up I noticed this red patch just below the thistle on my shirt – and because we were playing in white it really stood out. But by the time we went in at half-time the entire left side of my shirt and the leg of my shorts were covered in blood, just saturated. There were no blood replacements in those days so I had to ask the ref if I could go and see the doctor at half-time. Donald Macleod, the SRU surgeon, pulled off my shirt to reveal one particularly bad stud mark that ran from my collarbone and down my chest . . . and we both looked in horror at my left nipple, which had been severed and was literally hanging on by a couple of threads. Fortunately because of all the adrenaline pumping around my system I couldn't really feel it, so he put in two or three stitches to put things back into place, bandaged me up and got me a new shirt before sending me out for the second-half. As I left the medical room to go down the tunnel, Donald called after me, 'Welcome to international rugby!'

I was eventually able to identify the culprit when I got the video from New Zealand – it was Mark Shaw, their flanker, who I actually met up with several years later playing in the World Rugby Classics tournament in Bermuda; I have a photo at home of the two us out there, with him pointing at my nipple and leering eerily at it.

That first cap was an incredibly emotional moment – especially as it was at home. But as time went on and I began to think more and more about the game I realised how frustratingly close we had come to beating the All Blacks, something that Scotland have still never managed to do. I can still remember vividly the performance of our forwards that day – they were just incredible; it was one of the finest rucking performances Scotland have ever had, they completely out-rucked the All Blacks pack and every time they went into contact you could have thrown a blanket over them.

JIM POLLOCK

We trained as usual on the back pitches at Murrayfield the day before that match, and tried to get this set move to work. Jim and Colin Telfer, the coaches, had done their homework on the All Blacks and knew they came up flat in defence, so they devised this move where we took the lineout – I think Bill Cuthbertson won it – and moved it out to David Johnston, and he kicked it over them for me to race up the touchline and score. But there was a gale force wind and David Johnston was kicking it here, there, everywhere, and I was running around like a blue arsed fly for two or three hours chasing this ball. I was absolutely knackered. Jim Telfer was losing the plot – he wanted to scrap the whole thing because if it didn't work in training then it wasn't going to work in the game – but David was adamant that he could pull it off, and things were getting a bit heated between the pair of them. Fortunately, on the day, it all went to plan – which almost made it all worth while. That try pulled us level but the conversion was from wide on the right and unfortunately Peter Dods couldn't kick the points, so we had to settle for an honourable draw – which I think we more than deserved.

I think I helped create a bit of history that day because it was the first international match in which touch-judges were allowed to intervene, and I was involved in the incident when that happened for the first time. I was playing against this guy called Bernie Fraser. It was 25-all when they got a scrum on the 25 yard line and the scrum-half came left towards us; Bernie had already scored twice and I didn't want him getting another one so I drifted out and tackled him into touch even though he didn't have the ball. The match carried on and they got a penalty about ten yards out, but in the meantime Bernie had been kicking the shit out of me in front of the stand. He managed to break my nose but as a result of that the touch-judge, a Scottish official called Brian Anderson, intervened and the penalty was reversed because of foul play. Because of that incident, I think I have a name-check in Stu Wilson and Bernie Fraser's book, *Ebony and Ivory*, which, as you can imagine, isn't particularly favourable.

EUAN KENNEDY

That game was really the foundation to the Grand Slam season a few months later and I can only say how fortunate I realise I am that I got to experience that when someone like Jim Renwick missed out on it all because he was injured. I felt hugely humbled by the whole thing and so proud to have been there; it meant so much to me, but I can only imagine how much it would have meant to Jim to have been part of it after all his caps and his years of playing for Scotland . . . it was very tough that that experience was taken away from him because of injury and given to me.

Jim Renwick, David Johnston and I were completely contrasting types of centre. I was much more physical than they were – I liked to line up players in defence and hit them as hard as I could so that they would think twice about coming my way again, but Jim and David were quicker and they could beat a man on a sixpence. I think that's why David and I worked so well together, our styles complimented one another. He used to say that I would make all his tackles for him and maybe sometimes that would be the case, but the pace he possessed was something that I could only dream of.

JIM TELFER

One of the cornerstones of 1984 was that the players were able to accept constructive criticism from me and from each other and then acted upon it. That was the key and it was the same in 1990. Both squads were full of characters and strong-minded individuals who made sure that they lifted the efforts of all those around them. They demanded the best out of each other and that fitted well with my approach to coaching – it was the same with the Lions in 1997 and the Scotland team in 1999. I'm the first to hold my hands up and say that my style didn't fit every player, but every now and then you would get a squad of like-minded individuals that would all be on the same wave-length and you knew that you could achieve something special with them.

JIM CALDER

There really was this innate belief that developed within the squad, an understanding that we were a special group of players and that we were on the verge of achieving something extraordinary.

You would look around the team and see class everywhere. John Rutherford and Roy Laidlaw were the best halfbacks in the Championship, we were solid and strong in the midfield and in players like Colin Deans and the Bear you had grit and awesome power.

Then you would look at guys like David Leslie; he was a real eccentric off the pitch – he used to wear gloves in bed and sit in the changing room until the last minute before training reading a book, looking as if the last thing he wanted to do was play rugby. But when it came to the build-up to an international he was a different animal altogether, absolutely ferocious. He was eccentric in every way but he was also the ultimate warrior that you would want beside you in the trenches – he would do everything he could, push his body to the very limit, to get a win.

JIM TELFER

Scotland always have the best chance of winning a Grand Slam or a Championship when we play France and England at home and Wales and Ireland – and now Italy – on the road. It was the same in '84. We went down to Cardiff for the first game and they had picked Richard Moriarty, a great big fella, at the back of the lineout to try and dominate David Leslie. But because of his size, he was slow and David just had the run of the game over him. Colin Deans would throw long at the lineout and David would just drop back to gather it, his pace taking him away from Moriarty at the tail.

The Bear takes the ball on against the Welsh at the Arms Park. *Getty Images*

We scored two great forwards' tries in that game – the first off a set-move from a free kick when David Leslie charged onto the ball at pace then offloaded to Iain Paxton to score, and the second was from a series of drives from a lineout that saw Jim Aitken dive over.

EUAN KENNEDY

Playing my first Five Nations game at the Arms Park was wonderful – although it wasn't as daunting a venue as it might have been because I had watched the great game down there two years previously when Scotland had run riot and laid-to-rest their Cardiff hoodoo. Wales were going through a bit of a transitional period at the time and the majority of our team had been there and done it in '82, so we were very confident going down there. I played against Robert Ackerman, who ended up going to rugby league shortly afterwards and had played for the Lions, and I just remember him sledging me through the entire match. Because I was 30 at the time and it was only my second cap he kept calling me granddad all game; we would line up against each other and he would ask how my old, tired legs were feeling, or we would tackle one another and he would push me into the ground as he got up and say, 'Oh, you're doing well granddad, keep it up.' The whole experience was just amazing, playing in front of that passionate Welsh crowd and then to get the win away from home in our opening game was a great way to start the Championship. Funnily enough though, my wife missed me running out before the game – she had been caught in the wine bar with various other wives and was having a great time and they all missed the anthems and the kick-off – and she then further compounded her faults by taping *Dallas* over the recording of the game. I didn't get around to sitting down to watch the game until the following Thursday and had to fast-forward through an hour of *Dallas*, which she had recorded on the Wednesday night, before getting the last 20 minutes of the match.

JIM TELFER

The Calcutta Cup up at Murrayfield was the 100th game between Scotland and England and they came into the match on the back of a great win over New Zealand in the autumn. It was the classic clash of the English maul versus the Scottish ruck and on the day it was the ruck that won-out. Our players – especially our forwards – were faster and fitter and in the end that was the big difference.

We concentrated on putting a lot of pressure of Dusty Hare, their fullback, because it was a pretty filthy day and Roy and John were punting kicks to him all day while our outside backs chased him down. It obviously rattled him because he ended up missing six kicks out of eight at goal.

We scored a super harum-scarum try in the first-half with a long ball over the lineout that Iain Paxton hacked on and then David Johnston dribbled it a bit further, controlled it and scored. The second was one of the all time great Scottish scores – Jim Calder wrestled the ball from Dusty Hare, set up a quick ruck and the ball was fed to John Rutherford who picked it off his bootstraps, drew Clive Woodward and dropped a lovely ball out to Euan Kennedy who shot home to score. We ended up winning 18-6.

Scottish fans celebrate the 18-6 result in the Calcutta Cup at Murrayfield. *The Scotsman Publications Ltd. www.scran.ac.uk*

EUAN KENNEDY

I experienced all the highs and lows of rugby in one game in the Calcutta Cup by scoring a try and then ripping all my knee ligaments to pieces. The try was a wonderful moment, although if David Johnston had been playing outside John Rutherford when he gave that pass it would never have happened. John did a great job of taking the ball off his boots, but he then compensated with his pass and it flew about eight feet in the air. Luckily I'm 6′5″ so I was able to take it and go through, but even then it was close.

My knee injury occurred when England were running a move through Les Cusworth, their fly-half, and he gave a scissors pass to John Carlton, their open-side winger; I was in the process of diving to tackle Les Cusworth as he gave the pass to Carlton and because I'm as tall as I am, when I'm horizontal in the air I cover quite a lot of space. I actually managed to tackle them both because I took Cusworth down and Carlton ran smack into my knee and tripped over . . . and my knee just disintegrated on impact.

There's a photo of me just after I scored against England and my fists are clenched in celebration and I'm just roaring with delight – that moment typified everything that it meant for me to play for Scotland because in that moment everything I had dreamt about for that day had come true. I had scored the winning try against England in front of a packed Murrayfield crowd. David Leslie talked about that same photo in the book that came out after that season and he said that, for him, that photo typified what it meant to all of the team and to Scotland when we won the Grand Slam in 1984.

The players erupt in Dublin. *Getty Images*

JIM TELFER

There was a month between that game and our next fixture over in Dublin and I flew down to see Ireland play England at Twickenham. It wasn't a great game and the Irish lost 12-9. They changed quite a few players in time for our match after that.

The night before the game I decided to use some reverse psychology on the players. I showed them a video – not of us beating Wales or England, but of the

Aitken and Colin Deans in victory mood at the final whistle goes in Ireland. *Press Association*

e joy of the moment. Jim Telfer celebrates as Scotland seal the Triple Crown. *Getty Images*

South losing to the All Blacks. Ten of our team had played that match and it had been refereed by Fred Howard, who was taking charge of our match with the Irish the next day. I wanted to keep their feet on the ground by showing them that defeat and I wanted them to get a sense of the kind of interpretations that Howard had of the rules. It's the kind of thing that only works with honest players. In '84, that was exactly what we had.

KEITH ROBERTSON

We won the Triple Crown by beating Ireland at Lansdowne Road. They had shared the Championship with France the previous year, and gave us a real fight. Their captain, Willie Duggan, won the toss and let us play with the wind – a real swirler – which was actually what we had been hoping for.

The first-half was an absolute dream. Roy Laidlaw scored two tries in the same corner – one from a lineout peel down the blindside and one that was just raw pace off the back of a scrum. There are still Scottish supporters that carry a banner in that corner that says 'Laidlaw's Corner'. We also won a penalty try

Keith Robertson, Roy Laidlaw and Peter Dods return to Edinburgh after winning the Triple Crown. *The Scotsman Publications Ltd. www.scran.ac.uk*

from a scrum when it was wheeled and the ref said that Duggan had illegally prevented us from scoring. We went in at half-time 22-0 up and the second-half was much of the same. Gordon Hunter came on at scrum-half for Roy and made a fantastic break – I ran a scissors angle off him and he gave me a great pass in space that put me in under the posts. And then we scored another cracking try as Roger Baird made a break up the touchline and fed Peter Dods on his outside to score in the corner. We won 32-9.

The Irish boys put up a real fight all through the game and afterwards they came over and said they had a party arranged for us back at the hotel. It was a great night. There was a big banner proclaiming us as Triple Crown champions and we didn't put our hands in our pocket all night.

It was strange because we hadn't even thought about the Grand Slam at that stage, it had been so long since we had won anything that all we were thinking about was the Triple Crown, and it wasn't until the next day that we started thinking about the France game.

I think a lot of players would agree that the Grand Slam was almost an anti-climax after the Triple Crown, which seems a strange thing to say given the magnitude of what we achieved and the atmosphere in the ground that day. It was just that until that stage, winning the Triple Crown had been our entire focus.

JIM CALDER

The French had looked strong all season and there was a big doubt about Roy Laidlaw playing because he had been concussed against Ireland, and his replacement, Gordon Hunter, had got his cheekbone depressed when he knocked heads with a supporter as he ran off the pitch at the end of the match. So they were talking about bringing back Dougie Morgan or Alan Lawson, I think. In the end Roy was fit.

In the build-up to the game France had been wracking up the points at will and Peter Wheeler, the English hooker, had called them 'unbeatable'.

They started well and were running us a bit ragged – their scrum-half Jerome Gallion ran in a try from the back of their scrum and we were 3-6 down at half-time.

David Leslie did two things that really had a huge impact in that game. First, he took out Gallion, who was the heart of that French team, with a phenomenal tackle off the tail of a line-out which was only just on the legal side – and Gallion had to be taken off.

Then, with the French leading 12-9 midway through the second-half and really putting pressure on us, I remember lying on the deck in a ruck and seeing the blond hair of Jean-Pierre Rives being scraped back by Leslie's boot. He wasn't kicking but he was scraping away. Of course, the French were incensed; and all that the referee saw was Phillipe Dintrans, their hooker, come charging in and taking out Leslie, so we got the penalty.

The French were up in arms – everyone talks about French indiscipline but on that occasion they lost the rag for a good reason – and the referee marched them another ten yards back, to put Peter Dods within range for a penalty. All of a sudden we were back in it. We should have been penalised and back on our own line defending, instead we were kicking a penalty and the French had worked themselves into a state of agitation which festered for the rest of the game, and really upset their rhythm.

David had been saying to me the night before that he couldn't stand Rives, that he was nowhere near as good as people said he was. It was obviously a big thing in his mind. That was typical of Leslie. He had not only talked about it – he did it.

EUAN KENNEDY

David Leslie was not someone you wanted to get in the way of 48 hours before a game, let alone two hours before. He was so focussed . . . furiously focussed . . . the most focussed individual I have ever come across, and he would be the first guy that any player in that team would put on the team-sheet to go into battle with. He had a terrible accident a few years ago when he fell off the roof of his house and although he still struggles a bit with his speech these days, he has done really well to recover as well as he has. It's that focus and drive of his. We had the 25-year reunion for the team in 2009 and David got up to make a speech, which was extremely brave of him. And that was just like him – he would always do the unexpected and he would always challenge himself to overcome any adversity.

JIM CALDER

The whole match was incredibly brutal – especially in the scrums. The French have always prided themselves on their scrummaging and if they don't dominate you there it gets under their skin. Well, our front-row were strong, really strong, and loved to scrum. In the Bear we had one of the greatest tight-heads the game has ever seen. He was the cornerstone of that whole pack and the French couldn't shift him, he was just a block of concrete. Eventually they knew that the only way to have any chance of getting into the ascendency was to start throwing cheap shots. From the back of the scrum you could hear these punches coming in from the French, you could hear them connecting with the Bear's face and around his head . . . but he didn't retaliate, didn't throw one punch back. He just took the hits and then he got angry. And he exacted his revenge in the most powerful and effective way that he could – he scrummaged them into the ground. He pounded into them on the hit and drove on and on, shrugging away the punches until the French had no choice but to give up hitting him because they had to do everything they could just to keep their scrum intact; and the Bear just kept on crushing them, milling them into the ground. It was frightening and awe-inspiring at the same time. I have never seen anything like it.

Jim Calder scores the Grand Slam clinching try. *The Scotsman Publications Ltd.* *www.scran.ac.uk*

JIM TELFER

The turning point, of course, was Jim Calder's try. John Rutherford had put a high ball up on Serge Blanco, their superstar fullback, just a few minutes before and as he took it he was caught by our forwards and driven back downfield. The French cleared the ball desperately and gave us a line-out just a few yards from their line. Colin Deans threw the ball in to Paxton who was going to tap it down to Jim Calder, but Jean-Luc Joinel got to the ball first and deflected it – and it fell straight into Jim's hands just as he had been expecting it to! Everyone says that that try was a fluke, but with the exception of the wrong hand getting to the ball to begin with it worked like a dream. Peter Dods kicked the conversion and then added a penalty, his fifth of the day, to extend our lead – that last kick was particularly impressive as he could only see out of one eye, the other having completely swollen shut.

When the final whistle went it was a strange feeling – I experienced more elation the week before when we claimed the Triple Crown. It wasn't until much later that our achievement sunk in. It had been fifty-nine years since our last Grand Slam and this was only the second one to ever be recorded by Scotland.

A small drink to celebrate . . . Colin Deans, Jim Calder, Roger Baird and Roy Laidlaw prepare to get the Grand Slam party started. *Getty Images*

JOHN RUTHERFORD (Selkirk)
42 Caps: 1979-1987

When I look back now on that whole era, I realise now how lucky I am to have been a part of something so special. And as a group we were incredibly lucky that all the various strands came together as they did because that team was made up of combinations that worked well together rather than being a team of superstars.

When I was first capped in 1979 it was as much to do with luck as anything else. I was probably third in line but there were a few injuries so I got in. Again luck had played a part a couple of years earlier when the SRU had taken a bit of a punt and selected me for the tour to the Far East; not only was it a great trip to be a part of, but it was also when my partnership with Roy Laidlaw really started.

There are incredible similarities between us. We both played for unfashionable clubs at that time. Roy is the middle of three brothers, and so am I. We both have parents who came from Glasgow and settled down in the Borders. Our birthdays are only a day apart. And, of course, we got on well – which was the really important thing. When you play in a team that are up against it all the time you quickly have to learn to stand up, so when I moved on to playing for the South and then for Scotland it was so much easier. Suddenly I was surrounded by great payers, I was getting the ball when and how I wanted it, and I was only expected to do my own job.

It is one of those things, just as it was with the entire team throughout the early eighties – the whole was better than the sum of the parts. If you split Roy and I up I don't think either of us were anywhere as near as effective. He got to know my play well – he knew what I would be looking to do in any situation; and I got to know his play – how far he could pass it, what side he was stronger on, that sort of stuff.

For me, the win in Cardiff in 1982 was the beginning of the long road towards the Grand Slam. During that period I never thought we would lose at home, regardless of who we were playing. Looking back at the results, we did a few times, but that belief was there – and as long as you keep your feet on the ground and continue to prepare properly, that confidence is a great thing to have. Combining that with the confidence that we gained from beginning to win on the road, particularly that season, there was a big swing psychologically for that team – we feared no one – and there is no doubt that it helped us with the final push when we played France for the Grand Slam. It was a special, special time.

JIM TELFER

After a while it really came home to roost how special a moment it was and it remains perhaps my greatest achievement as a coach – greater even than the triumphs of 1990 or even those of the '97 Lions.

7

THE NEW BREED

A S HAD SO *often been the case in Scottish rugby, after the great high of the 1984 Grand Slam, there came an almost inevitable low. In May the team travelled to Bucharest and suffered a 28-22 loss to Romania. In the autumn they were hammered 12-37 by the great Wallaby side containing the sublime Mark Ella, Nick Farr-Jones, Michael Lynagh and the peerless David Campese, who were themselves writing history that year with their memorable Grand Slam tour.*

In 1985, in a campaign that proved to be a polar opposite to the previous season, Scotland went through the Five Nations without registering a single victory.

There was a realisation throughout Scottish rugby that the time had come for a new broom to sweep through the squad. In 1985, Derek Grant was made head coach, with Ian McGeechan appointed as his assistant.

From a playing point of view, six new caps were selected for the opening 1986 Five Nations fixture with France at Murrayfield. And what a selection of players it was. In the history of Scottish rugby, could there ever have been a higher standard of debutants winning their first caps in one game? Of the six, three would go on to captain their country with distinction, four would play Test rugby for the Lions and two of those would captain Lions tours. Those six new caps were Jeremy Campbell-Lamerton, Matt Duncan, Scott Hastings, Gavin Hastings, David Sole and Finlay Calder – who came into the team as a direct replacement for his twin brother, Jim. A new broom and new breed of player. Physically powerful, dynamic, charismatic, tenacious and ferociously ambitious.

After the white-wash of 1985, 1986 was quite a different campaign. In a thrilling opening encounter, the new players made an immediate impact. Despite the French scoring from a quick throw-in after Gavin Hastings' kick-off went directly into touch, the fullback more than made amends by steering his side to victory and his name into the record books by kicking six penalties to edge Scotland home 18-17, his efforts in front of goal eclipsing the previous Scottish record of seventeen points in a single match which had been jointly held by Andy Irvine and Peter Dods.

The team then suffered a blip in fortunes when they travelled down to Cardiff where, despite scoring three tries through Matt Duncan, Gavin Hastings and John Jeffrey, they were pipped 22-15 by Wales.

Two weeks later, however, England were welcomed to Murrayfield on 15 February for one of the most extraordinary Calcutta Cup performances ever posted by a Scottish

---

Opposite: Gavin Hastings. *Getty Images*

side. The visitors arrived in Edinburgh riding high on the back of strong wins over Wales and Ireland and their team was full of stars, with players such as Peter Winterbottom, Paul Rendall, Maurice Colclough and Wade Dooley in the pack, Nigel Melville and Rob Andrew at half-back and Jamie Salmon and Simon Halliday in the centre. The first-half was a close-run battle and thanks once again to Gavin Hastings' boot, Scotland went into halftime with a 12-6 lead. When they emerged for the second-half, Scotland were rampant. They tore into the English ranks, splitting them at will out wide and demolishing them in the close exchanges. Rutherford and Laidlaw displayed a master-class in how to conduct and control a game. Laidlaw scurried around the fringes and marshalled his forwards with aplomb while Rutherford stepped and danced and fizzed passes to his outside backs. One glittering run from the fly-half completely bewitched the oncoming defence as he stepped and shimmied and accelerated to the line for one of the great Calcutta Cup tries. Rutherford's score was followed by another from the electric Matt Duncan and the annihilation was sealed by Scott Hastings' first Test try, while his brother finished the match with three conversions and five penalties to his name for a 33-6 victory.

Four weeks later, Ireland were beaten in a tight encounter at Lansdowne Road, 10-9, thanks to a try from Laidlaw and two Gavin Hastings penalties to round off the Championship in style.

At the end of March, the squad returned to Bucharest to make amends for the previous summer's disappointment and saw away their hosts with ease to record a 33-18 win.

In 1987, the Calcutta Cup match at Twickenham was postponed until the end of the tournament because of bad weather, and by the time the team travelled to London, they had beaten Ireland and Wales at Murrayfield and fallen just six points shy of France at the Parc des Princes. Arriving in London at the beginning of April, Scotland's preparations were marred by Scott Hastings' withdrawal with a fractured cheekbone. In an effort to increase the speed of the pack, Grant selected five players who, at the time, were all playing number eight for their respective clubs: Iain Paxton, Derek White, John Beattie, John Jeffrey and Finlay Calder. On paper it was a wonderfully aggressive and athletic back-five behind Sole, Deans and Milne, but it proved, in reality, to contain one major flaw: there were no players of any notable height to operate and control the middle of the lineout. The 1987 battle for the Calcutta Cup was effectively settled along Twickenham's tramlines, with Nigel Redman and Steve Bainbridge absolutely massacring the Scottish lineout and laying a perfect platform for their own backline to attack. England went on to win 21-12, reclaiming the Calcutta Cup and burying Scotland's Triple Crown hopes.

To compound matters, the game saw a devastating knee injury suffered by John Beattie. Tackled by Gary Pearce after taking a quick tap-penalty, Beattie's knee ligaments buckled under the impact from the Northampton prop's shoulder. Carried from the field of play he was never to wear the blue of Scotland again. It was a bitter and tragic blow for both Beattie and the team, especially as it meant he would miss the inaugural Rugby World Cup later that year.

Every sport has its ultimate prize. The Jules Rimet Trophy, which was eventually superseded by the FIFA World Cup Trophy; the Claret Jug; Wimbledon's Gentlemen's Singles Trophy; the Vince Lombardi Trophy; the Larry O'Brien NBA Championship Trophy; the Ashes; the World Series Commissioner's Trophy . . . the list goes on. And at last rugby had its own. A little 38cm trophy in gilded silver supported by two cast scroll handles, inscribed with the words International Rugby Football Board *and below that* The Webb Ellis Cup. *16 nations would contest for it and the coveted title of world champions between 22 May and 20 June 1987 in the rugby hotbed of New Zealand.*

Despite the loss of Beattie, Scotland looked like a formidable force as they flew to the Antipodes for this landmark tournament. But their prospects were undermined by an injury to Scott Hastings that kept him out of the first match, and by another career-ending knee injury. In the week following the conclusion of the 1987 Five Nations, John Rutherford, Iwan Tukalo, Matt Duncan and Iain Paxton were invited to play in an exhibition game in Bermuda, despite an SRU decree that all players should rest before the start of the tournament. Rutherford, one of the most senior players in the team, its tactical controller and one of the most talented players ever to pull on the number ten shirt for Scotland, injured his knee during this North Atlantic soujorn. He had an operation to try and fix it when he returned home and hoped that it would hold up throughout the tournament. It didn't. The first game of Scotland's World Cup was against France and less than fifteen minutes were played before Rutherford was forced off, with his knee in pieces. Like Beattie, he was never to return.

It was widely accepted that the clash with France would decide the outcome of Pool 4 as the other nations grouped with Scotland were Zimbabwe and Romania. Despite the early loss of Rutherford, Scotland were leading 13-6 at halftime. But second-half scores from Philippe Sella and Serge Blanco pushed France into the lead until Matt Duncan slashed down the wing in injury time to draw the match 20-20. Gavin Hastings had a kick from the touchline to win the game, but the angle, the distance and the Christchurch wind conspired against him and the ball went wide. Despite the match being drawn, France were handed the initiative in the pool as they had outscored Scotland in the try-count.

Both Scotland and France strolled to wins in their remaining pool matches – 60-21 against Zimbabwe and 55-28 against Romania in Scotland's case – and the result in Christchurch pushed Scotland into a quarter-final with the eventual champions, New Zealand. They were swept aside by tries from fullback John Gallagher and lock Gary Whetton, both of which were converted by Grant Fox, along with six Fox penalties, the match finishing 30-3 and sealing Scotland's exit from the tournament.

Scotland gained revenge over their Auld Allies for what befell them at the 1987

World Cup, winning 23-12 at Murrayfield in the 1988 Five Nations, thanks largely to a mighty all-round contribution from Gavin Hastings, but that was their only win in that year's championship. There was plenty of evidence inside these performances, however, to indicate that once again the cycle of Scottish rugby was beginning to turn and a new generation of players was coming to the fore to replace the old guard

Ian McGeechan was promoted to the role of head coach in 1988, replacing Derek Grant. Roy Laidlaw's career was coming to an end and he was soon succeeded by another young scrum-half from his hometown club, Jed-Forest. Gary Armstrong, a stocky farmer's son blessed with a sharp snipe and the strength of a number eight cultivated on his father's farm was some replacement indeed. Over the next decade he would fight fierce duels with the likes of Melrose's Bryan Redpath and Dundee High School's Andy Nicol for the Scotland number nine shirt, but when fit and on form he was considered vital to any Scotland success.

Outside Armstrong, Rutherford's successor had emerged in Melrose's Craig Chalmers, who was first capped in 1989 when he was just 20 years old, making him the youngest-ever Scotland cap at the time.

And out wide another youngster had pushed himself into contention for international recognition. Tony Stanger was a gangly centre from Hawick who had only recently converted himself into a winger. Another new face – quite literally – was that of centre Sean Lineen, son of All Black great Terry, who arrived to play for Boroughmuir in October of 1988 and who, thanks to his Scottish grandfather, was eligible to play for Scotland – a feat that he realised in January 1989 against Wales at Murrayfield.

Around this new blood there was a gnarled and experienced back-row of Derek White, Finlay Calder and John Jeffrey. David Sole and the Bear were the pillars at the front of the scrum and there were fresh legs in the boiler room in shape of Damien Cronin and Chris Gray. In the backs the Hastings brother carried size, pace, skill and confidence enough for thirty Scotland teams.

In 1989, Wales were thumped 23-7 at Murrayfield, England were battered to a 12-12 stalemate at Twickenham and Ireland were undone 37-21 at Murrayfield. The only disappointment occurred in Paris, where the team suffered a 19-3 defeat at the Parc des Princes; Fiji and Romania were swept aside 38-17 and 32-0 at Murrayfield in the autumn, with the new wing sensation, Tony Stanger, scoring two and three tries in his first two Test matches.

It was quite a turnaround. And whispers were beginning again. 1989 bore remarkable similarities to 1983; would it, or could it, serve as a similar springboard to something special as it had done six years earlier?

NORRIE ROWAN

In the summer of 1984, we went to Romania – what a reward that was for the boys who had just won Scotland's first Grand Slam in 59 years!

A pal of mine from school, Rob Cunningham, who had toured there with Bath the previous year, told me to take over stockings, perfume, soap, cigarettes and what have you, to barter with. Well, they confiscated my bag at the airport and I had to kick up a real fuss to get it back. They just wanted the stuff for themselves, and it took some serious diplomacy from Brian Meek, the journalist, to persuade them to give it back to me.

I remember after about three days I wanted my washing done, so I gave the chambermaid a bar of soap . . . she jumped in the bed and lifted up her skirt! If it hadn't been for her moustache I might have been tempted.

The only decent meal we got was the lunch before the Test match. We'd been starved for three weeks then all of a sudden there were Chateaubriand steaks and all the food we wanted – which was obviously the last thing we needed before a game.

We lost the Test match 28-22 and there must have been a thousand people at the reception that night, all going bananas. We went back in 1986, and we beat them and there were barely 50 folk at the function that night. It was all politics. They saw rugby as a way of promoting their politics and if they got beat nobody wanted to be associated with it.

EUAN KENNEDY

I made it back from my knee injury in time for the Romania tour, which was Jim Renwick's last tour and the Test match where he equalled Scotland's record number of caps. But it was a tough place to go, the poverty was just awful.

People had jobs but often the jobs they had were so menial. You would be travelling down a dual carriageway and you would see gangs of 20 people trimming the grass verges with hand sheers.

Deodorant was unheard of and soap was a luxury item out there and we would give the hotel chambermaids bars of soap and it was like we had given them a bar of gold. It was a real eye-opening tour and history has obviously shown what a terrible regime they had in power there at the time.

I remember we went down to Constanta on the Black Sea to play a game. I was sharing with Tom Smith, who was about 6'8"; I was 6'5" and we were in this tiny wee room like a rabbit hutch. We were about 14 floors up, so I went out onto the balcony to get a bit more space and to look out over the sea-front and I suddenly saw a pair of feet bobbing up and down from above me – it was Sean McGaughey doing pull-ups on his balcony on the outside of the hotel.

Colin Deans practices his hooking as Ian Hunter feeds him the ball. *Press Association*

JOHN BEATTIE

We had our own food and I remember leaving used chocolate wrappers lying around and when we walked away the waitresses would be licking the foil – and I remember thinking: *this is real poverty.*

It was baking hot. We had been given one of the earliest versions of Gatorade, but they had mixed up the wrong concentration so it was almost all salt with a bit of liquid. You took a couple of quick gulps and suddenly your whole mouth was sticking together. You couldn't separate your tongue from the roof of your mouth so you couldn't breathe.

EUAN KENNEDY

I was involved in four pretty momentous games; unfortunately my fourth and last Test match was momentous for the wrong reason because it saw us come up against one of the all time great sides in the 1984 touring Australian team. They had some of the very best players ever to emerge from that country – guys like their captain Andrew Slack and Michael Lynagh in the centre, Mark Ella and Nick Farr-Jones at half-back and obviously Campese out wide . . . they were an outstanding team. With Ella leading the attacking line and really revolutionising it with that flat, flat alignment they used and with runners changing direction at the last minute and hitting the line straight, it was so hard to defend against and in the end they just embarrassed us. The Home Union backlines in those days all used to get the ball in their hands and then arc out so that they were almost running at a 45 degree angle. This meant that the defending stand-off would call the drift and the entire backline would drift across the field, tracking the attack and usually giving the defensive line a man overlap so that they had cover for the attacking fullback or blindside winger coming into the line. But the Australians were very much like the French and the All Blacks – they took the ball straight, cutting against the defence, making it difficult to defend against using a drift system, but then they combined it by passing the ball late and right on the gain-line . . . it was like nothing any of us had encountered before and they just cut us to ribbons.

I had been out for four or five weeks in the lead-up to that game with another knee problem and played a game for Edinburgh the week before they picked the Scotland squad and obviously played well enough to win selection. But I never felt that I was as fit as I needed to be for that level of Test match rugby and unfortunately that proved to be the case.

Looking back, I always had a great admiration for both Colin Telfer and Jim Telfer as my Scotland coaches, but it is Ian McGeechan that I remember most fondly as a backs coach. I was picked for the Blues team in the National Trial in 1980 and in those days if you got in the Blues team you were almost certainly a shoe-in for the Test side. But in the first half of that trial I played possibly some of the worst rugby of my career, it was awful. At half time I was moved into the Whites team and although I played a bit better it still wasn't great – and I stuck out like a sore thumb because my shorts and socks were the same colour as the Blues team, but I was now wearing a white jersey. I was absolutely devastated after that because I knew I'd blown it. The next day we had another training

Jim Calder sports a ripe black-eye following a Scotland training session. *The Scotsman Publications Ltd. www.scran.ac.uk*

session and before we started Geech took me aside and just told me not to worry about the previous day's performance, that it was done and all that I could do now was focus on the next training session – and that even if nothing came of the trial that time around, I just had to keep on playing the way I had during the season and my time would come again. I didn't make it into the Test team then, but I took his words with me and I kept working and in the end I made it. It wasn't a long international career, for all that it was a long time coming, but every moment was wonderful. It is good to look back and talk about the good times but it was even better experiencing them. How would I describe my rugby career? 16 seasons, brilliant memories, great laughs and lots and lots of friends . . . lifelong friends. What a game.

JIM POLLOCK

The last game I played for Scotland was in Paris in 1985, when I was called up as a late replacement for Roger Baird. It wasn't a great game, it was quite a dour affair which we lost 11-3, and as you can imagine the changing room was a pretty depressing place afterwards.

Then this chap came in and said he owned a nightclub in Paris and if anyone wanted to go he had some tickets available. So the tickets were snatched out of his hands and thrown on the floor, and I casually picked them up. We went to the after-match function, which was the classic French dinner, with everything in French. It was dreadful, but by the end the mood had lightened a bit and I said to a few of the boys that I had these tickets, so off we tootled.

We found this place and I couldn't believe it, there was these really expensive cars parked outside and everyone was dressed in fur coats. Of course, we're all in our dinner jackets. So I went to the front of the queue and said something like, 'Ecosse – tickets.' And we were immediately ushered through the door.

I went to the bar and ordered two whiskies, a vodka and a gin and tonic. Bang, bang, bang, bang, the drinks were laid down: two bottles of whisky, a bottle of vodka and a bottle of gin. I tried to pay but the barman managed to explain that the first drinks were all free, so I decided to throw a bottle of champagne in as well.

About two hours later, after we had played all sorts of drinking games, and Serge Blanco had come in – with a white dinner suit on and all the women in the nightclub falling all over him – I decided it was time to leave. God knows what happened to everyone else.

So, I'm outside lying on top of a Porsche when this blue van with a flashing light on top of it comes round the corner and these four guys in blue suits jump out, pick me up and throw me in the back. It was one of those sobering moments when you think: *I'm in big trouble here.*

I couldn't explain where the hotel was or anything like that, but I happened to have the invitation for the dinner in my pocket so I showed them that – they just seemed to ignore me. The van was tootling along at about ten miles an hour when suddenly the backdoor opened and one of the policemen kicked me in the backside, propelling me out of the van.

So I'm rolling along the street, my dinner suit is wrecked all the way down the left side, and as I turn around to call them all the names under the sun I notice my hotel to the right.

Somehow I made it through the foyer and to my room. I opened the door, and walk in – and there is absolutely nothing there. No wardrobe, no TV, no bed, no chair . . . absolutely nothing. I ended up sleeping on the carpet floor in my ruined dinner suit.

When I woke up the next morning my suitcase was outside the door – but the furniture was still gone. Who took it? Well, nobody was coughing up to that the next day.

John Jeffrey makes a break from the back of the scrum against Ireland at Murrayfield in February 1985. *The Scotsman Publications Ltd. www.scran.ac.uk*

GAVIN HASTINGS (Cambridge University, Watsonians, London Scottish)
61 Caps:1986-95

I left school at 18 and wasn't capped until I was 24, so that was a reasonably long apprenticeship – maybe that was why I hit the ground running. Mind you, that first match against France couldn't have got off to a worse start.

Colin Deans joins Scotland's new caps before the France match in 1986 – Scott Hastings, Finlay Calder, David Sole, Matt Duncan, Jeremy Campbell-Lamerton and Gavin Hastings. *Getty Images*

I tried to land my kick-off on a sixpence but I went a bit too far and landed it just in touch. I thought, 'Oh God, that's not a great start, the boys aren't going to be too happy with me putting the kick out.' I turned and started jogging back towards the posts, ready for them to scrum down on the halfway line, then all of a sudden I heard this big roar, so I turned round and I saw half a dozen Frenchmen running towards me. It was a case of: eeny, meeny, miny, moe; and I picked one of them but he didn't have the ball and Pierre Berbizier scored. At that point I thought, 'Oh-oh, the rest of Scotland are not going to be very happy with me.'

You can't see the try on TV. They out-foxed the camera men as well.

I don't remember what was said behind the posts, Colin Deans was the captain and he was probably wondering why they had picked this silly bugger at fullback, but at least I had plenty of time to redeem myself. If you're going to lose a golf hole it might as well be the first one, because you've then got seventeen more opportunities to win it back.

Scott Hastings and Gavin Hastings. *The Scotsman Publications Ltd. www.scran.ac.uk*

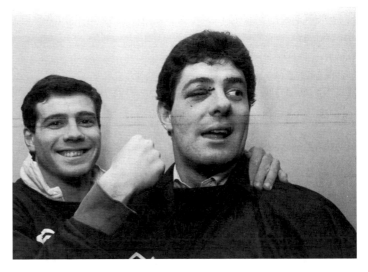

SCOTT HASTINGS (Watsonians)
65 Caps: 1986-1997

I was under the posts saying, 'What happened? What happened?' I looked at John Beattie, and he said, 'I don't have the foggiest idea,' or something a little a bit more colourful than that. It was a rude awakening to international rugby.

GAVIN HASTINGS

Fortunately things got a wee bit better, and in a funny sort of way it probably did me quite a lot of good. That's what international rugby is all about – expect the unexpected.

I have never watched that game again, so I have no idea how many kicks at goal I had, but I would wager that I had at least ten opportunities – and I missed two or three that I was really cross about – so it wasn't my best kicking performance of all time.

I remember lining up my first penalty opportunity and thinking, 'This is the biggest kick of my life.' And I was really chuffed to get that one over – because you never know if you are going to be able to do it until you are in that position. There are a lot of people who have been put in that position and not managed to live with the pressure.

I have no idea if it was any good as a game of rugby or not, but looking at the statistics I would expect it was a really boring match. I don't suppose it really matters.

Two weeks later, we went down to Wales. In those days Cardiff, with that old horse-shoe of a stadium, was an amazing place to play. It was a brilliant atmosphere – fantastic singing – and perhaps we were a bit over-awed by suddenly playing in somebody else's backyard. It was a game we probably should have won, but Scott had a try disallowed early on and Paul Thorburn had his kicking boots on that day.

It was wet and horrible, and we were playing with these Mitre balls which were crap – you couldn't kick for toffee. But with them leading 16-15, Thorburn lined up this penalty from about ten metres inside his own half. I thought there was no chance – that he was just wasting a bit of time. Then this ball came through the posts like a torpedo. I think it bounced off my chest because it was going so fast and I wasn't actually sure if it was going to duck under the bar or scrape just over. I've never seen a bigger kick. I could hardly see him – he was miles away. The ball just sneaked in through the corner of the post and the crossbar – it could not have been closer. He kicked another penalty after that, and that took the game beyond us, 22-15.

David Bryson, Alister Campbell, Derek Turnbull, Gavin Hastings, Alan Tait and Andrew Ker sport Stetsons on their return home from the Canada tour in May 1985. *The Scotsman Publications Ltd. www.scran.ac.uk*

JOHN BEATTIE

A key game in my life was in 1986 when we beat England by a record score. I'd read a book – New Zealand half-back Dave Loveridge's autobiography – and he talked about how the All Blacks had thought the 1983 Lions weren't very fit so had decided to speed the game up. Now, the only way to do that was at the line-out, so they had extra ball-boys making sure that they were always able to get the ball back into play as quickly as possible.

Well, we were very fit because there had been a really deep frost that winter which meant lots of club games were called off and we were training through at Murrayfield together every weekend. Meanwhile England had this huge pack, which didn't move around the park very well at all. So we got the SRU to supply a lot of extra ball boys. Colin Deans was very fit and very fast, so every time the ball went out he ran to the spot and the ball-boys got the ball to him straightaway, he did this code which was designed so that rather than standing there shouting numbers and letters it depended on the way he was holding the ball, and he would throw it in. You could see the English struggling – it was just faster than anything they were used to.

Also, on the Thursday, during a team meeting, the phone went and it was Jim Calder for Finlay. He said that he knew I didn't get on very well with Maurice Colclough so at the first line-out I should start punching him – and those genuinely were our tactics: speed the game up, start a fight, and shout abuse at them the whole time.

Now with tactics like that it was never going to be very precise, but the mayhem suited us because we were very fit and everything was happening at 100 miles an hour.

JOHN JEFFREY (Kelso)
40 Caps: 1984-1991

On the day before the game, Jim Calder phoned up to remind us that Maurice Colclough had been shit-scared of John Beattie on the previous Lions tour – which you can understand, because John was crazy.

That night we went to see *The Terminator* and we all loved it when Arnie came out with that immortal line, 'F**k you, asshole'.

So we were talking about it all after the film and we thought it would be a brilliant idea for us to turn to the English boys at the first lineout, make pistols with our hands and say, 'F**k you, asshole' . . . and John Beattie would deck Maurice Colclough.

John Jeffrey and Alister Campbell contest the line-out with Donal Lenihan and Phil Orr during the Ireland match at Murrayfield, 1985. *Getty Images*

Things kick-off after John Beattie starts a fight with Wade Dooley during the 1986 Calcutta Cup clash at Murreyfield. *Newsquest*

So we got to the first lineout and that was exactly what we did; but instead of decking Colclough, John decked Wade Dooley. It was the most ridiculous case of mistaken identity I'd ever seen. And unfortunate too, because it was never a good idea to upset big Wade and a massive scrap broke out.

But it worked in a way because all through the rest of the game Wade was on the lookout for John trying to hit him again and Colclough was scuttling around with one eye over his shoulder waiting for John to do something crazy or just attack him out of the blue – and the rest of us could just get on with things because all their attention was on John and getting ready to hit him should he start anything else. Arnie would have loved it.

JOHN BEATTIE

People always talk about the physical aspect I brought to the game, but that's not something I really focussed on. I always thought of rugby as a

Irish scrum half, Robbie McGrath receives the full attention of Colin Deans, Iain Milne and John Beattie as Roy Laidlaw looks on. *Newsquest*

game of chess, and that's what really fascinated me about it as a sport. When I played I came up with different back-row moves, some of which led to tries – those were the most satisfying parts for me, thinking my way through a game, plotting strategies to beat the opposition; it certainly wasn't all physical.

I've always found the whole Scottish-English thing a bit funny because I always think a border is just something someone drew when they stole a bit of land. It doesn't mean you hate the people on the other side. As an international player, you kind of pretend to – but you never do.

That game in 1986 was particularly special for me because there is a bit in Bill McLaren's commentary when he says, 'What a game John Beattie is having,' and that will stick with me for the rest of my life. People talk about luck in those wins, but that was the start of players like the Hastings coming through, Matt Duncan, Fin Calder and JJ – dynamic and powerful, a whole new mindset and style of Scottish player.

GAVIN HASTINGS

We finished joint top of the table with France that year, having scraped past Ireland 10-9 in our last game. That match probably should have finished as a

Roy Laidlaw. *Getty Images*

12-12 draw, but I missed a conversion after Roy Laidlaw scored yet another try at Lansdowne Road, then we conceded a penalty in the dying moments, but Michael Kiernan missed a fairly straight-forward kick. So we scraped through but were pretty lucky because we hadn't played all that well.

All in all, it was a pretty good season. We had a really good team spirit in that squad, and the fact that some of us were younger and were only just breaking into the team I think helped. It was a breath of fresh air for some of the more established guys, like Roy Laidlaw and Colin Deans.

ROGER BAIRD

I have this unfortunate record of having played 27 times on the wing for Scotland and never scored a try . . . but I actually scored a try against Romania when we went there in the summer of 1986, believe it or not. It was one of the most bizarre things ever. Laurie Prideaux was the touch-judge and Roger Quittenton was the referee – a couple of Englishmen – and I got the ball on the left-hand side, beat my man, ran in, touched down and thought, 'Great, that's that bogey put to bed.'

I looked round and there was Prideaux with his flag up. I couldn't understand it, because I wasn't anywhere near being out of play. I think he must have had *an episode* because we got photographs the next day and I was miles away from touch. I suppose that was the moment that best illustrates that it just wasn't meant to be.

I suppose it did play on my mind a bit. As a winger, not scoring in 27 Test matches . . . well . . . it's not great. I should point out that I did score for the Lions, and I was top all-time try scorer for the South, and since the old districts have now been disbanded I probably still hold that record. But for Scotland, the longer it went on the more of a burden it probably became. It certainly didn't do your confidence much good.

NORRIE ROWAN

Because Romania had lost, the dinner after our game there in 1986 was pretty low key and didn't last long, but afterwards we were invited down to the British Embassy for drinks. And when the guys got back to the hotel, everyone was blootered. That was the season when Scottish & Newcastle brewers started to move into sponsoring Scottish rugby, and I always remember Iain Milne had the chairman of S&N round the neck, leaning practically all his weight on him, completely pissed, and waving round this ceramic beer stein full of wine and singing songs. The look of terror on this wee guy's face was classic.

The guys ended up back in one of the rooms and there was a bit of damage, so the hotel manager insisted on us paying the bill of £900 in cash – which would buy a house in Romania at that time.

There had been a bit of a rift between the players and the committee. The committee were saying that we were all in it together, but when the bill was sent out for the damage to the room it was divvied up amongst the players and not the committee. They said they weren't there, but neither were some of the players – it seemed to me like they only wanted to be part of the squad when it suited them.

ROGER BAIRD

There had been a bit of trouble at the dinner after the last home international in 1986 Five Nations. Somebody had thrown a tomato and it had hit the head of the Royal Bank on the head. They were SRU's chief sponsor so the committee were pretty unhappy, so Dod Burrell, the president of the SRU, told us that there would be big trouble if there was anything less than exemplary behaviour at the dinner after the Romania game.

Well, we went to the dinner and you have to remember that this was Romania in the time of Ceauşescu. There was no food and no drink. It was just a hellish, awful affair. But afterwards things got a bit out of control and there was some wrecking done at the hotel that night. The next morning we're all sitting on this bus looking into this hotel which had a big glass façade and we can see Dod Burrell and Bill Hogg negotiating with the hotel staff. When

A great combination on paper, Iain Paxton, John Jeffrey, John Beattie, Finlay Calder, and Derek White were all playing number eight for their clubs and their combined selection against England was dynamic and athletic – but was lacking, crucially, in height. *The Scotsman Publications Ltd. www.scran.ac.uk*

Dod got on the bus he was shaking with rage, and you could hear a pin drop. He said, 'You've let yourselves down, you've let your clubs down, but most of all you've let your country down.' Nobody dared look up . . . except Roy Laidlaw, who still hadn't sobered up. He put his hand up and said, 'Aye Dod, but at least we behaved at the dinner.'

It was not a nice place to visit. We had folk trying to jump on the bus to claim asylum, there was queues for food everywhere. It was serious depression.

GAVIN HASTINGS

In 1987 we were due to play England first up at Twickenham, but there was snow and the game was postponed, and if we had played them then I'm sure we would have smashed them – probably by as much as we did the year before – but we then played them in the last game of the season. So we won our two home games against Ireland and Wales, and went down there with a chance of the Triple Crown, but we played appallingly and lost.

It was the comfortably the worst game I had played in for Scotland so far, which was frustrating because we had played quite well that season up to that point.

Scott Hastings races in for Scotland's second try against France at Parc des Princes in Paris, March 1987. *The Scotsman Publications Ltd. www.scran.ac.uk*

Marcus Rose was at fullback. He used to catch the ball and dribble it five yards into touch, and the whole of Twickenham would roar. It was just the most negative brand of rugby you have ever seen. I don't quite know how we contrived to lose that game.

I remember the following day we went to the FA Cup final. Charlie Nicholas was playing for Arsenal and he scored two goals on the most beautiful day you could imagine. It had pissed it down at Twickenham the day before, so I suppose the gods had conspired against us.

DAVID SOLE (Bath and Edinburgh Academicals)
44 Caps: 1986-1992

The first World Cup was a huge success. It was very much uncharted territory, but the New Zealanders were so passionate about it, and their team swept everyone aside, so there was a real buzz the length and breadth of the country.

For Scotland, it was really tough. We had a nightmare journey out there, which didn't help. We flew from London to LA in blazers and ties, where we picked up the US and Canadian teams then flew to Hawaii to refuel, then from Hawaii down to Auckland. But as we were about to land in Auckland the captain came on the tannoy and explained that we would have to take another loop and hope that visibility had improved. We did this twice before the decision was made to divert to Christchurch. We landed there but weren't allowed off the plane. Then the captain announced that the fog had cleared in Auckland so we could go back there, but unfortunately the flight engineer's tachograph was up so we had to wait for a relief crew. We were on the ground in Christchurch for five hours before we flew back up to Auckland. When we landed we were all pretty tired after 36 hours in transit, and it was decided that it would be a good idea if we went out for a jog.

Everyone was worn-out and pissed-off, the last thing they wanted to do was go out jogging. We headed up to this local park and we had a game of touch, which turned into a game of what you might call 'Samoan touch'. There were t-shirts getting ripped off as tempers flared, and if nobody came to blows then quite a few came damn close. Eventually we stumbled back to the hotel with bleeding noses and ripped t-shirts to get ready for dinner.

The next morning the Irish, who were staying in the same hotel as us but playing in a different group, asked if we were interested in getting together with them for some live scrummaging. That sounded fine, so after we had done our own training, we met up. It was all pretty gentle to start off with, it was still less than 24 hours since we had got off the plane and we eased our way into it – and then, all of a sudden, the Irish decided to they wanted to really go for it, but they didn't tell us beforehand.

Iwan Tukalo, Keith Robertson, Gavin Hastings and Roger Baird launch Scotland's 1987 World Cup kit. *The Scotsman Publications Ltd. www.scran.ac.uk*

The next scrum . . . BANG . . . they piled into us. Of course, it all kicked off. From that moment onwards it was like an international: the Scottish pack and the Irish pack were kicking lumps out of each other on some back pitch in Auckland. You think about how the players are wrapped in cotton wool now, and you shake your head in disbelief at the way it was.

GAVIN HASTINGS

Those first few sessions we had of the tour were ridiculous. We had just come off a killer journey and boys were firing into each other playing touch and again when we had the session against Ireland.

The World Cup was a whole new concept for everyone and no-one wanted to feel that they were underprepared, so they went into the training sessions hammer and tongs – an approach that would be unthinkable these days. The session we had with the Irish lasted three hours and in the last few minutes my brother pulled his hamstring. That was effectively his World Cup over after that – he missed the France game, ran around for a few minutes against Romania which aggravated the injury, and he missed the rest of the tournament. Compared with how players are looked after – and look after themselves – these days, we were in the dark ages.

Rugby was pretty low key in those days. Apart from a few weeks during the Five Nations, it was always relegated to deep inside the sports pages. We all had full-time jobs and enjoyed our rugby at the weekend before getting a few beers down our necks, and if you were lucky then four or five time a year you played in front of a big crowd at an international match – so, arriving in New Zealand was amazing because the streets were awash with bunting.

Andy Dalton, the All Blacks captain, seemed to be on the television every half hour appearing in commercials, and I remember we composed this letter which was sent to a guy called Russ Thomas, who was the chairman of the World Cup, pointing out that this seemed to be a contravention of the amateur regulations. The way they got round it was that they would have a slogan on the bottom of the screen saying: 'Andy Dalton – Farmer'. They just overlooked the fact that he was the All Blacks captain as well. You could see professionalism beginning to sneak in through the back door.

The squad having a laugh during a training session, 1987. *The Scotsman Publications Ltd. www.scran.ac.uk*

FINLAY CALDER

I remember when we got the plane to fly from Auckland down to Christchurch for the first match against France, the Scots were in the number ones – white shirts, blue blazers, ties – and we're thinking we look pretty smart. Then on came the French and they sat down beside us and they're all in Gucci suits, listening to Walkmans, and I remember just thinking to myself, 'Who pays for all this?'

GAVIN HASTINGS

Walking out onto Lancaster Park for the opening match with France was awe-inspiring. We really knew that we were part of something special with this first

John Rutherford in full-flight – a sight that Scotland missed during the World Cup. *Getty Images*

World Cup and we were there in this great bear-pit that was ringing with noise – bagpipes trilling on the air and it was wonderful to see and hear such a lot of support so far away from home.

That match saw come classic gamesmanship from France – a couple of players were down injured in the field of play and while they were being attended to, Blanco took a quick tap-kick and snuck up the touchline and ended up scoring under the posts.

You could argue that the French were just cannier than we were – they had shown that when they had played us at Murrayfield the season before and scored from that quick lineout after my kick-off went out on the full and all our boys were trooping back for the scrum on halfway. But that try at Lancaster Park got our blood boiling and we fairly roared back at them after that.

In the end it came down to my kick to convert Matt Duncan's try, which went just wide. That was disappointing, but it happens. What it meant was that unless one of the other teams in our pool caused a major upset, we were heading for a quarter-final with New Zealand, which was ominous.

FINLAY CALDER

We then travelled to Wellington to play Zimbabwe at Athletic Park. We put a full-strength team out and ran them ragged, winning 60-21, and scored 11 tries

John Jeffrey races away from the Zimbabwe defence in Wellington. *Getty Images*

in the process. Gav picked up another record – he seemed to collect them for fun – by kicking eight conversions to add to the try he scored. We went down to Dunedin to play Romania eight days later and put out much the same team as the previous two Tests. We won 55-28 but we were in pieces by then. Squad rotation was unheard of, but we really should have been smarter about how we used the players we had at our disposal. Zimbabwe were never going to be a threat to our chances, but I think after the France game the coaches didn't want to take anything for granted. We secured qualification through to the quarters, but the team was being held together with sticking tape at that stage.

DAVID SOLE

We were in a killer group with France and Romania – who were a pretty good side in those days. They had a team built around their army and police, so they were a pretty tough outfit who we'd lost to in 1984.

John Rutherford had hurt his knee playing in a tournament in Bermuda a few weeks before the World Cup and although he travelled he wasn't really fit, and he was carried off within minutes of the start of first game against France, so that didn't help. We picked up a lot of injuries and I remember on the Thursday training session before the quarter-final in Christchurch there was only three fit forwards training: myself, Fin Calder and Colin Deans. So how we managed to put a competitive team on the park was a miracle.

Obviously we knew the lay-out of the games before we arrived in New Zealand, but we didn't manage it very well. We should have rested a few players for the Zimbabwe game, but they chose not to take a risk and we ended up beating them by 50 odd points. We basically tried to play the same team in four matches within the space of fourteen days. Roger Baird and Jeremy Richardson were in the 25-man squad but didn't get a game – which was senseless.

KEITH ROBERTSON

By the time we got to the quarter-finals, we were just patching guys up to get them out on the park, which is always going to end in disaster against a team like New Zealand. I had a broken finger, Iain Paxton was struggling with a shoulder injury, Alan Tait had a dead-leg. Meanwhile, New Zealand had been pretty smart in their team selections during the group stage so they were fighting fit and ready to go, and we were just holding onto their coat-tails.

We all believed beforehand that we had a chance if we played to the best of our ability and took what opportunities might come our way, but once we got on the park we were just trying to fight off wave after wave.

I'll always remember John Gallagher scoring between the posts and when he turned round to jog back to the halfway line I was closest to him. He said, 'Well, enjoy your flight home.' That still makes my blood boil. It didn't need to be said. He should have been magnanimous in victory.

But people forget that if it hadn't been for the ingenuity of the French in our pool match against them, when Blanco took a quick penalty when players were receiving medical attention and scored beneath the posts, we would have ended up top of our group and going into the easier half of the draw against Fiji in the quarter-finals and Australia in the semis. To this day I still feel hard done by, but I suppose he was just quicker-witted than us so fair play to him. We even had a chance to win it at the death when Matt Duncan scored in the corner, but Gavin's conversion went wide – so we ended up drawing and they finished ahead of us on points difference.

GAVIN HASTINGS

That All Black team was something else. They had cruised through their pool, beating Italy, Fiji and Argentina and scoring 190 points in those three games; no one was going to stop them getting their hands on that cup. They were physically bigger, faster and more skilled than any other team in the world, everything about them was already professional in anything but name. They were awesome. I remember Derrick Grant saying in the press conference after they had knocked us out of the tournament that he had come to learn that in

New Zealand 'they simply breed a different kind of player.' It was then that I decided that I would stay on and play a season in Auckland – I wanted to learn all I could from those types of players; and the lessons that I learned playing with guys like Grant Fox and Sean Fitzpatrick changed the way I played and approached the game forever afterwards.

It was disappointing to be going home at the quarter-final stage but it had been a wonderful experience to be part of that first World Cup. We could all see how it was going to change the game and open it to audiences around the world. It was a special time to be involved.

NORRIE ROWAN

The management used to allow us to have parties after the games when on tour, so we would send the dirt-trackers out to all the hairdressers and department stores with invitations for our parties. When we went to the first World Cup the tournament was sponsored by Steinlager, and when the liaison officers had a meeting halfway through the tournament to see how things were going they worked out that the Scottish team had drunk more Steinlager than all the other teams put together. That was because we used to have these parties and we would do a deal with the hotel manager that if he gave us free wine as well as

Norrie Rowan, David Sole, Iain Paxton, Scott Hastings and Derek Wylie ply a stuffed koala with lager as they set off on the McEwans-sponsored Australian tour in September 1988. *The Scotsman Publications Ltd. www.scran.ac.uk*

free beer, we'd make up the cost by giving him the beer we were getting from the sponsors. So we had hundreds of women coming to these parties where there was free wine and free beer. All the other teams started leaving their hotels to come and party with us. We didn't win the World Cup but we had the best parties.

At the airport, before flying home, we met up with the Irish team. We had a vote to see who would want to go back to New Zealand, and only two of the Irish boys said they would return, but every one of the Scottish boys wanted to go back.

JOHN JEFFREY

We had a good win against the French in '88, but the rest of the campaign was a wash-out and not particularly memorable – except for one incident. After the Calcutta Cup match, which was an awful, drab affair that we lost 9-6 at Murrayfield, we had a fairly massive night out – as you always did in those days. I remember all the tables had a load of booze on them that was virtually all gone by the time they even said grace. Four of our players were in bed before the end of the dinner. In retrospect, I wish I had been one of them.

After the dinner the captain used to take the cup out with them and you'd fill it with drinks all night and offer it around to punters to drink from. You'd get some pretty nasty mixes of drinks in there so it's not surprising that my memory of the whole night is fairly hazy. But I do remember bits and pieces. Dean Richards and I decided to fill the cup with whisky and then poured it over Brian Moore's head. He started chasing us and we ran out of the pub and into a taxi, still with the cup. We went to another two or three pubs and then came back. I don't remember an awful lot after that.

The battered Calcutta Cup after its adventures on the streets of Edinburgh.
Press Association

NORRIE ROWAN

It was the Englishman . . . he couldn't catch it. There was nothing malicious, they were just passing it around like a rugby ball, but because they kept on dropping it, it just got really bent. The last time I saw it the doorman at Buster Browns had a broom handle through the lugs of the cup and was trying to wedge it back into shape. They were just passing it back and forward and it was dropped. It wasn't disrespect, it was just drunken antics.

JOHN JEFFREY

After a while I sobered up a bit and I remember looking at it and thinking: *this is a bit of a mess.* We headed back to our hotel eventually and handed it in at reception. When I woke up the next day all I could remember was the thing lying there behind the reception, battered to pieces.

Both Deano and I were banned by the RFU and SRU – although he got away with it more than I did. He was banned for a week while I was banned for five months! It's a chapter of my life that I am not terribly proud about, but I'm still annoyed about how long my ban was compared to his.

SEAN LINEEN (Boroughmuir)
29 Caps: 1989-1992

I arrived in Edinburgh in October 1988, just to play a bit of rugby for Boroughmuir and have a bit of fun, and by February 1989 I was playing for Scotland. My first taste of it was for Edinburgh against Australia that November. They asked me to play in that match and of course no Kiwi is ever going to turn down a chance to play against the Aussies, and from there I made it into the Probables team at the National Trial. I played really badly in that game but for some reason the selectors decided to go with me anyway.

I remember getting the letter from SRU secretary Bill Hogg saying I had been selected to play for Scotland against Wales. I was staying in a flat in Blair Street at the time, and I was so excited I ran down the road to tell my

Sean Lineen in a kilt on Calton Hill, Edinburgh, in October 1988. *The Scotsman Publications Ltd. www.scran.ac.uk*

mate, it was pouring with rain and I slipped on a big pile of dog shit and nearly wiped myself out – that would have been a novel way of getting in the record books for the shortest international career in the history of rugby!

I qualified because my grandfather had been born in Stornoway, although I wasn't sure if that was the case at the time and I had to phone my mum up to check. A few years after I was capped I went up there to present the rugby club with a jersey and meet my grandfather's brother. Finlay Calder and David Sole had told me that they only spoke Gaelic up there, and being a thick Kiwi I believed them. So they gave me a couple of phrases to use. I remember getting off the plane and they had the whole entourage out to meet me – radio, TV, everything – it was a big story in the Outer Hebrides. So I hopped off the plane and greeted them all by saying 'Cala hara', which I thought was some sort of friendly salutation but apparently in Gaelic really means 'Up your arse.' They got me a good one there.

Damian Cronin on his way to scoring Scotland's first try against Ireland at Murrayfield in March 1989. *The Scotsman Publications Ltd. www.scran.ac.uk*

Chris Gray and Kenny Milne were also making their debuts that day, so that was the final pieces in the jigsaw for the 1990 Grand Slam being put in place. Only Gavin Hastings, who was injured, was missing.

The thing that got me most playing in that first game against Wales at Murrayfield was the crowd – the noise was unbelievable. I'd never heard anything like it before. We won that game fairly easily, 23-7. Then we drew with England at Twickenham.

I'll always remember Finlay giving Andy Robinson such a hard time that day. I was at the back of the line-out so I saw and heard it all. He patted him on the head and gave him abuse at every line-out. 'You're too small, what are you doing here, you're too small. Oh, here comes the ball, I'll get that. You can't reach it. You've lost it again. You're too small.' Then JJ got in on the act, and it was a real torrent of verbal abuse. Robinson just lost it. He was chasing them instead of the game. JJ and Finlay were pretty clever at that sort of stuff.

That was the game when Geoff Cooke, the English coach, said we were a bunch of scavengers, and a lot of people got very upset at this. Derrick Grant said, 'Well, scavengers feed off shit,' and Norrie Rowan, who was never slow to see a commercial opportunity, made a whole load of t-shirts with those words emblazoned on the front, which he put on sale in his pub, and they sold out.

The Ireland game in 1989 was a cracker. We beat them convincingly in the end, 37-21, and played really well, with Iwan Tukalo scoring a hat-trick in that game – the little bugger never passed the ball.

So we went over to France looking to win the Championship – but we got absolutely slaughtered 19-3. I remember Gary Armstrong saying that he learned a big lesson about scrum-half play that day against Pierre Berbizier, who stood on his toes and got in his way all afternoon. He just didn't let him play. I suppose that was a wake-up call, that we still had a lot to learn.

David Sole ploughs through the Irish ranks in search of the ball. *The Scotsman Publications Ltd. www.scran.ac.uk*

I'd staved my fingers quite badly in a club game the week before the match, and I'd had to keep them in ice for about four days in a row before the match because I couldn't move them. On the day of the game I had them taped up and Jim Telfer was doing his usual sort of team-talk, giving us a hard time and getting us worked up. He had us punching the wall, and for me it was absolute agony.

We went out there and looked at the French players and they were on a different planet. They were staring at us with their eyes bulging – snorting and spitting – the whole works.

There was a fight and I came flying in and smacked Laurent Rodriguez, their number eight, on the back of the head, only succeeding in hurting myself. It was

Bloodied warrior – JJ in action in 1989. *Getty Images*

like a fly glancing him on his head; he turned round and looked but I was on the other side so he saw Derek White and planted him instead.

NORRIE ROWAN

Romania played Scotland exactly a week before their revolution started. They had no money, so they had flown over with their national airline to Heathrow and got a rickety old bus from London up to Edinburgh. After the match they came to the Carlton Hotel for dinner but once dinner was over they had no money to go for a drink. I owned the Tron Tavern at the time, so I threw a party for the teams with a free bar.

They had all this securitate with them, who were covering the doors of the pub because they knew all the boys wanted to defect. I didn't know much about what was going on, to be honest, but I was approached about helping get one of them – Christian Raducanu – out, and that's how I ended up getting involved. I opened the back door, he ran down to the Cowgate, confronted a policeman, and said he wanted political asylum.

He played a couple of seasons at Boroughmuir and I helped him out with a bit of work. I remember on his first day I gave him £20 and he started crying.

He said, 'In Romania this is a month's wages.' He went down to play at Sale and then Leeds, and he brought his wife over and had a second kid in Yorkshire. He's now a multi-millionaire.

TONY STANGER (Hawick, the Borders, Edinburgh Reivers, Leeds Tykes, Grenoble)
52 Caps: 1989-1998

I won my first cap against Fiji in 1989, which was obviously a very memorable game for me as it was my first game and I scored two tries, but it was also momentous because it was the first time that Flower of Scotland was played as our national anthem before a game. It used to be God Save the Queen, but it was changed that year and Flower of Scotland has been our anthem ever since.

Gary Armstrong clears the ball against England in 1989. *Getty Images*

IAN McGEECHAN

Billy Steele brought Flower of Scotland to rugby. It became the tour song on the '74 Lions tour. We sung it before every game and every Test match and it was the last thing we would sing before we got off the bus – and we wouldn't get off the bus until we'd finished it. And we then sang it live on television after the tour and gradually the players in Scotland began to sing it themselves on the field until it became the thing that we sung before the matches at Murrayfield. I can still remember the first time it was sung before an international and I realised how far it had come. I remember it being sung and thinking about Billy and how he had started all that – and it was a very powerful, emotional song that a lot of people had shared, not just Scots.

CHAPTER EIGHT

MARCH into HISTORY

AFTER *leading the Lions to victory over Australia in 1989, Ian McGeechan's mind went into overdrive. The key personnel in the series victory had, by and large, been English. Despite early clashes of culture between players from England and Scotland, the two dominant countries that had made up the Lions squad, McGeechan and his cohorts had managed to create a successful amalgam between the Scottish quick-ruck play and the thundering juggernaut of the English maul, which had allowed the Lions to take the game to the Australian forwards before unleashing the wit and guile of their fast and powerful backs.*

Lessons about his charges had been learnt and McGeechan would, in due course, rack his brain for a game-plan to take on the English; but first there were three other games to be played, and each, as ever in the long history of the Championship, presented as difficult an assignment to overcome as any other.

Towards the end of 1988, a group of senior players had travelled down to Selkirk for a meeting with Jim Telfer to see if they could encourage him out of retirement. Iain Milne, Iain Paxton and Finlay Calder had taken it upon themselves to stir the passionate rugby flames that still burned so brightly in Telfer, knowing that the Melrose man could get results and performances out of the Scotland forwards like no other. There would be pain to endure in training – much of it; there would be endless torrents of abuse to shoulder, savage impatience and anger to bear; but there would also be spine-chilling inspiration, an endless pursuit for technical perfection, and a desire to win that would be instilled in the core of every player. These hardened campaigners knew that if this Scotland team was to follow in the footsteps of the '84 immortals and savour the sweet taste of Championship success, then the silver-haired task-master, who had been there and done it all before, was the final piece of the jigsaw that they needed.

So by 1989 Telfer was back; the furious Border bull unleashed once again. The effect that he had on the Scottish pack was profound, even if it wasn't, at first, all that apparent.

Having sat out the first round of matches, Scotland started their campaign with something of a whimper, scraping past a limited Irish side 13-10 at Lansdowne Road, having been 7-0 down at half-time and 10-6 down before Derek White stole the show and the result for the visiting team with the second of his two tries, the first of which had been converted by Craig Chalmers.

Next they welcomed a hefty French outfit to Murrayfield who were reeling from an English battering the previous week. After French flanker Alain Carminati was dismissed for stamping on John Jeffrey's head, Scotland went on to deliver a

---

Opposite: David Sole marches his team into battle. *Getty Images*

knock-out blow to the defending champions, with Gavin Hastings and Craig Chalmers scoring three penalties between them, Finlay Calder and Iwan Tukalo scoring a try apiece and Chalmers adding two conversions for a 21-0 victory.

Another narrow win in Cardiff, by 13-9, saw Damien Cronin cross for Scotland, and his try was complemented by three Chalmers penalties. It was, like the Irish game, gritty but unspectacular.

And so it came down to one game. Winner takes all.

Now McGeechan and Telfer, with their assistants Dougie Morgan and Derrick Grant, had to find a way to stop those English heroes that McGeechan had cherished so dearly just a few months before; they had to find a way to counter the awesome power of Mike Teague, Wade Dooley and Paul Ackford, the ferocious competitiveness of Brian Moore, the calm control of Rob Andrew, the sublime genius of Jeremy Guscott, and the scorching speed of Rory Underwood.

The back-row of Teague, Peter Winterbottom and Mick 'the Munch' Skinner growled with muscle and menace. In the front-row, Moore packed down with two of the most powerful scrummagers ever to wear the red rose – Jeff Probyn and Paul 'the Judge' Rendall. Behind them Dooley and Ackford had been imperious in the lineout, freeing the electric English backs to tear through the opposition ranks at will. The power, control and relentless attacking play of the 1990 English team had swept all before them in the Championship. Guscott and Will Carling had been at the epicentre, Underwood the arch-finisher with four touchdowns. The team had scored 11 tries and conceded only two. Scotland had scored five and conceded two but in none of their victories had they displayed the dominance that England had shown in the previous rounds. Carling's men had had Irish eyes crying with a 23-0 demolition at Twickenham; they had sacked the proud bastion of the Parc des Princes, hammering the French 26-7; and had doused the fire of the Welsh dragon 34-6 at Twickenham. All that were left were the Scots. Bloody-minded, certainly, and with a back-row that could bend the letters of the law to breaking point, but ultimately lucky to have found themselves in a Grand Slam play-off. The Championship, the Triple Crown, the Calcutta Cup and the Grand Slam were England's for the taking. Surely nothing could stand in the way of their destiny . . .

FINLAY CALDER

We had a great team coming together towards the end of the eighties and there was a steely determination throughout the squad that we wanted to be the very best that we could possibly be. But we also knew our limitations. We knew that at our best we could compete with any team in the world, but we were also aware that we lacked depth – should we lose players in certain positions to injury, we would probably begin to struggle. So we had to maximise our potential with the resources that we had. To do that, we needed to have the best-drilled pack around. That meant that we needed Jim Telfer back in harness.

I asked Jim to meet with me at the Philipburn Hotel just outside Selkirk and I brought Iain Milne and Iain Paxton with me. They knew him better than anyone else in the squad and I knew that they all respected and trusted each other. It was quite a tricky meeting and I didn't actually think that Jim would come back because he was so involved with his job as the headmaster of Hawick High School. It had also been his life's work putting the '84 squad together and I wasn't sure if he wanted to commit himself to trying to do that again.

JIM TELFER

Fin and I had a very strong bond that went back many years and when he phoned and asked that I meet him and a few other players in Selkirk, there was no way that I felt that I could say no. Bob Munro, the convener of selectors, had also telephoned me and warned me about what they were coming to talk to me about, but even though I knew that they were going to ask me to come back to coach the Scotland forwards, I still hadn't made up my mind by the time I met them. I was fully committed to Hawick High School and I wasn't sure if I was willing to make any compromises with my job. But I had a very positive meeting with the director of education at the Borders Regional Council, and I eventually decided that I would give it another go – as so often happened with Scotland, the lure of being involved again was too strong to resist.

Scotland played Australia at Murrayfield in my first game back and David Campese took us to pieces. But we were able to blood Gary Armstrong in that game and over the next few matches we also gave caps to Craig Chalmers, Chris Gray, Kenny Milne, Tony Stanger and Sean Lineen. The 1989 Five Nations was positive for us and we beat Wales and Ireland – scoring a record 37 points against the Irish – and drew with England, and on the back of those performances more Scots were selected for the Lions tour to Australia than for any other tour before or since. Fin was named as captain and he was joined by David Sole, Gavin and Scott Hastings, JJ, Derek White, Craig Chalmers, Gary Armstrong and Peter Dods – and only Gary, JJ and Peter failed to play a Test match. That's a major core of any team and they came back much improved as players.

FINLAY CALDER

Jim has always had a fascination – some would say an obsession – with the way the All Blacks played. Scotland have not always had the personnel to emulate that style, but in 1990, just as in 1984, we had the players to do it – a big man at tight-head and seven quick and hard-working forwards. The Lions tour was seminal for all of us – training and playing with our Home Union rivals we realised – as the '83 Scottish Lions did – that the Scottish players were fitter and trained harder than anyone else.

DEREK WHITE (London Scottish)
42 Caps: 1982-1992

I think the time spent on the Lions tour made a huge difference to our psyche. The six weeks we spent with the English boys dispelled some of the mystique about them. For one thing, the Scottish guys soon learned that we had by far the superior fitness over them and a better work ethic, too. Dean Richards used to tell Roger Uttley when the forwards had done enough training, not the other way around. There wasn't a cat's chance in hell that any of the Scottish boys would have turned around and suggested anything like that to Jim Telfer! Jim and I never saw eye-to-eye, but there is no doubting the discipline that he instilled in us or the improvement he made in our technical ability.

JOHN JEFFREY

We boys in the back-row used to take a hell of a lot of stick from Jim Telfer. It was his dominion. There was no hiding from him. Luckily for Fin and me, he used to give the most flak to Derek White, but when he turned on you it wasn't a good place to be. There was one game against Ireland in 1989 when Brendan Mullan came back on a switch and cut right through the three of us. You should have heard Jim afterwards. He said that we were an embarrassment and that if we didn't sort ourselves out he could take three guys off the street and could train them to be an international back-row. If any other coach said that you would roll your eyes and say, 'whatever', but it is a mark of the man that I believe he could actually have done it.

KENNY MILNE (Heriot's)
39 Caps: 1989-1995

Jim Telfer's bollockings were something else. He gave Derek White a hard time, there's no doubt about that, but he used to destroy me. I'm not convinced that it was necessarily the right psychological approach to have taken with me. I might have been a better player had I been encouraged more than barracked the whole time. But Telfer's approach did work in one respect – I was determined to do everything I could to avoid giving him an excuse to bollock me, so I was focussed on perfecting every facet of my game.

JIM TELFER

I was keen for Fin to continue as Scotland captain after the Lions tour, but he didn't want the job. He recommended that we give the captaincy to David Sole – which we eventually did, but not before a lot of debate as many of us

Helped by his desperation to avoid the ire of Jim Telfer, Kenny Milne worked tirelessly on his lineout throwing. *Getty Images*

wondered whether it should instead go to Gavin Hastings. David and Gavin are very different, and not just in the obvious difference between their positions on the field, but in personality. Gavin is brash and confident while David is more thoughtful and reserved. But they were both strong personalities and when David retired in 1992 it was a natural move to hand the captaincy to Gavin – which he was also given for the Lions tour to New Zealand in 1993. David led the team very well – he was quiet but strong and led from the front.

IAN McGEECHAN

As captain David Sole was no tub-thumper but he carried so much respect among the players that he had no need to be.

FINLAY CALDER

I always felt that my role as captaincy was just a caretaker one. I strongly believe that the man to captain any side should be the best player in the team – and for me, in 1989, it was David Sole. There was a hardness to him, an edge, and that is what you needed in the team for Scotland to compete. It was an attitude that Derek White, Damien Cronin, JJ and myself also had and I think that's why we did so well despite not being as big as guys playing for teams like England and

France. That edge we brought to things definitely helped the Lions in Australia – when you combined our attitude to fitness and the aggression we brought to the game with the skills of guys like Guscott and the power of guys like Dean Richards and Mike Teague, it was a potent recipe.

JIM TELFER

Our first game of the Five Nations was against Ireland in Dublin. We had to go there without Ian McGeechan because he had flu, which wasn't ideal – especially as I was suddenly in charge of the team, which was not something I had prepared for at all. It wasn't a great game, but Derek White scored two tries – although one was a bit dodgy as it came from a forward pass. It's interesting that we scored from a forward pass in Ireland in '84 and that Roy Laidlaw scored a brace then too. The main difference was Sean Lineen, though. He brought a different element to our attack that had been missing before – he used to hit the line short off Craig Chalmers and run straight. Very simple, but what a difference it makes to opening up space and catching out defenders on the inside. It's just something that New Zealand-reared players do so well and so naturally – it was the same with John Leslie when he came on the scene in 1998. It was Sean's pass to Derek White that was fractionally forward and we

Finlay Calder races away with the ball against Ireland. *Getty Images*

were lucky that the referee missed it, but we deserved to score off the move purely because of the angle Sean took – a flat, tight ball off the back of the lineout that got us in behind the Irish defence and then the offload to Derek.

TONY STANGER

I suppose I was lucky coming through the Hawick system. I grew up watching Hawick win championship after championship, and we won it again in my first year in the Hawick side; then I came into a settled Scotland side which was having an unusual amount of success; so I always had this expectation that we would win games.

I scored two tries against Fiji in my first game then three tries against Romania in my second, which was a great start – but with no disrespect to those countries you knew that at that time they were ranked much lower than Scotland in the pecking order. It was a really good way to settle into the team and get used to the pressure of international rugby, but my first game in the Five Nations was against Ireland away and it was a huge wake-up call. I was against Keith Crossan, who I have always had a huge amount of respect for as a player, his technical abilities and understanding of his job as a winger really did open my eyes. It was a different type of game as well, a lot of pressure and not so much ball. You were getting hit harder in the tackle than anything I had experienced before, you had no time to make decisions. I learned a lot in that game.

KENNY MILNE

Sean Lineen and Derek White played really well out in Dublin and Chic Chalmers' kicking saw us home, but people tend to forget the shift that Paul Burnell put in in that game. We were in real trouble at one stage in Dublin, 7-0 down and the home crowd really pushing their team on, but Paul's play – something that most people would totally miss – was instrumental to us edging past them to win.

Derek White and I had formulated a tactic to give him an edge on our attacking scrum ball. As Gary Armstrong fed the ball in, I would hook it as hard as I could so that it would fire straight through the second-row and into Derek's hands. As I say, we were struggling badly at one stage, but we held in there and managed to win a scrum close to their line. We crashed into the scrum and Paul Burnell got his side up just as I struck the ball hard into Derek's hands. Those fractional seconds and the angle of the scrum made all the difference. Derek was gone before the Irish back-row even knew that the ball had left Gary's hands, and Derek's acceleration took him to the line.

Derek scored, but it was really all down to Paul. The effort he put in to get his side of the scrum up was huge and without it Derek would never have made it.

FINLAY CALDER

I remember coming off the pitch after the game and just feeling relieved that we had managed to win – to get a result on the road is as good a start to a Championship as you can get and we had won without playing particularly well, so we knew there was more to come.

KENNY MILNE

We had a move called 'JJ Watsonian' which worked off the back of a scrum and involved JJ, Gary and Gavin. In the week before the France game Jim said that we had to rename the move because it came out clearly on the TV during the Ireland game. I said, 'Simple: we're playing France so we'll just rename it *Jé Jé Watsonian*.' I got a good clout over the head from Jim for that one.

Sean Lineen straightens the line against the French as Scotland cruise to victory. *Getty Images*

FINLAY CALDER

We had France at home in the next game and we absolutely steamrollered them after Carminati did what we all longed to do and kicked JJ in the head. It happened a few minutes into the second-half and we were only three points to the good at the time. It was a decisive moment. We had been dominating much of the game but hadn't converted that dominance into points but when Carminati was sent off by Fred Howard you could see their heads dropping and that was when we stepped up a gear.

We peppered Blanco with kicks all afternoon and he had a fairly torrid time of it. When they went down to 14 men they really began to be stretched and we ran them ragged. Our defence was strong and we controlled the ball well in the elements and I felt that we were comfortable all the way through.

KENNY MILNE

We headed down to Cardiff for our third game and I remember thinking that we were going to be on the receiving end of a serious backlash. Wales had been thumped 34-6 at Twickenham and in the aftermath of that game their coach, John Ryan, had quit. He was replaced at the helm by Ron Waldron who was the head coach at Neath, who were a super side. Neath were quite like us – they played a fast, loose game with athletic forwards, so it was set up to be a really fast-paced game.

FINLAY CALDER

But they left out the key ingredient. As Jim Telfer knew from his studies of the All Blacks, to be able to get away with a fairly light forward pack, you need to have one or two immovable cornerstones. We had Paul Burnell at tight-head and Damien Cronin at lock. Waldron went light-weight all the way through his pack and Brian Williams, his loose-head, was only a shade under 14st and he was completely gobbled up by Paul. We destroyed them in the scrums and it was a bit disappointing that we didn't translate that dominance on the scoreboard. Del Boy crashed over for a try and Craig Chalmers kicked three penalties to seal the win – it was tight, but Cardiff has always been a hard place for Scotland to go and win so there were no complaints.

GAVIN HASTINGS

That was a very strange year. We went over to Dublin first up and sneaked a win, then came back to Scotland and beat a fourteen man France team fairly

Gary Armstrong gets the ball away from the wreckage that the Scottish forwards have made of the Welsh at the breakdown. *Getty Images*

handsomely after the early sending off of Alain Carminati, then went to Wales and won. So we weren't playing particularly great rugby, but we were winning our games and all of a sudden we were going into the last weekend with three wins and a real chance of a Grand Slam. It just kind of crept up on us.

The whole build-up to the Grand Slam showdown was just magical. We had missed the first weekend and played every weekend since then, whereas England had missed the penultimate weekend – so they had a whole month to think about coming up to Murrayfield, and there is no question in my mind that that played into our hands. We had the momentum.

It never crossed my mind that we were going to lose that game. I was totally comfortable with our ability. We hadn't played particularly well up to that point so we were due a big performance.

IAN McGEECHAN

In the lead-up we deliberately kept things low-key – it was important that we didn't give the English players anything to feed off; instead we let them talk up their Grand Slam hopes and used that ourselves to fire up our players. For Jim Telfer, Derrick Grant, Dougie Morgan and me, the game really lasted two weeks.

I bought a new VCR for the analysis – one with four heads so that I could get clear, still images. From that I was able to get a feel for the way England played, analyse the patterns of their game. I could see that they blew teams away early on. They dominated physically and their lineout was superb – from that dominance they were able to get the ball out to Carling and Guscott in the midfield, backed up by the back-row. I would stay up until one or two in the morning trying to work out a way to beat them. In the end it was a cold, calculated strategy mapped out on A4 paper then filed in plastic folders and labelled, then boxed and labelled again.

TONY STANGER

From a personal point of view, that game was about rugby, it was about beating the fifteen men out there on the pitch, not the whole nation or avenging something that happened hundreds of years ago – it wasn't a grudge match. The downside of the media sometimes is looking for the sensational angle and reading something into a situation which quite simply doesn't exist.

Ian McGeechan looking calm in the build up to the Grand Slam showdown. *Getty Images*

The beauty of it was that it was a winner-takes-all situation, and the way England were playing made them the overwhelming favourites. While we naturally didn't like that because they were coming up to our patch – we also acknowledged they had played great rugby that season and scored some fantastic tries. So we knew we were going to have to go some to beat them but we felt we were capable of causing an upset.

There was a lot of hype in the media about this match being nothing more than a formality for England, and you did hear stories about them ordering t-shirts with *Grand Slam Champions* printed on the front, but you never know if that was true. But I don't remember any direct quotes from the England players saying that they were the best team and it was just a matter of turning up to get the job done.

People made the connection afterwards between them not kicking penalties and that being a sign of overconfidence, but I don't buy that. They made the call on the pitch and there is nothing wrong with being confident in your own ability.

KENNY MILNE

We were sitting in the changing room after training and Jim Telfer sat us all down. He said that we had to prepare ourselves as best we could before the England game, that there would be no drinking and that we had to do all we could to ready ourselves for the challenge that lay ahead. 'This is a once in a lifetime opportunity,' he said. 'We're playing for the Calcutta Cup, the Triple Crown, the Championship and the Grand Slam.'

'Well,' I said, 'we're bound to win one of them.'

JIM TELFER

The media attention was incredible in those final few days before the match – there were headlines everywhere, even in the tabloids, which was a rare thing for rugby coverage at the time, and the build up was all over the radio and on the TV. It was a huge moment for Scotland to be in that position again and there was a level of expectation higher than ever before because of what had happened in 1984. And the English media were all over it as well, although in a slightly more arrogant way. They had played some incredible rugby that year and when they had won their last Grand Slam in 1980, Bill Beaumont had led them up to Edinburgh and skelped us with five tries to seal the Championship. The English newspapers had a carbon copy of the scenario all mapped out. And the key that day was that their players believed the same thing. They thought that all they had to do was show up, bully us off the park and let their backs run riot.

SEAN LINEEN

It was typical of England – they decided early not to kick their penalties and to go for tries – they just thought they were going to turn up and win. They made it so easy, they gave us all the ammunition we needed – and the guys were well up for it. There was a brilliant team talk by Geech on the morning of the game, but I think the guys knew all week that we were going to win it.

IAN McGEECHAN

In my speech to the team before the game I talked about how they would be playing not just for the fans who were in the stadium and not just for those who were watching the game around the country; they were also playing for all those Scots throughout the world whose lives had taken them away from the land of their birth and for whom the blue jersey still meant so much – because the jersey was a symbol of their home and their roots and who they were and to win would make them prouder than anyone else in Scotland. I was thinking about my dad when I said that because his heart had always been in Scotland.

DAVID SOLE

From the moment England beat Wales all the build-up had been about the fact that they were going to pick up their first Grand Slam in ten years. It was becoming a bit irritating that this was a foregone conclusion. Nobody was writing or talking about us, it was all about England, so I was determined that we would make a statement early on that if they wanted their Grand Slam then they were going to have to get past us first, and during the build-up to the game I put quite a bit of thought into what we could do to show that we were playing for the big prize as well.

We had a training session on the Wednesday before the match, which went incredibly well . . . everyone was so fired up. Afterwards I got a few of the guys together and said I had this idea about making a statement of intent, and Fin said he was against it because he remembered walking out at Sydney Football Stadium for the first Test against Australia on the 1989 Lions tour and getting absolutely stuffed. Big Gav piped up that he thought it was a great idea, and that we should have a piper leading us out, and all wear kilts which we'd whip off Bucks Fizz style.

And Fin said, 'Where are we going to put our claymores?'

To which Gavin replied, 'Now you're just being stupid.'

So I bounced it around some more of the guys and the general consensus was that it wasn't a bad idea, and then, in the last few minutes before the game when I was making my final pitch to the players, I basically said, *we're walking out there and we're not going to hold back: this is our time.* It was something a bit different.

A lot of us knew a lot of the English players very, very well, because we had been on the Lions tour the previous summer. That had been a squad which had fought its way through some pretty tough moments – we were stuffed in the first Test, we were 18-4 down in the midweek game against ACT, and we had to dig really deep to turn things around. It had brought us together as a group and when you go through those sorts of things with those sorts of players there is a huge amount of respect and affinity there. But, on the other hand you hit your friends the hardest. Sure we respected them as men, but we wanted to get one over on them because if we didn't they would get one over on us.

IAN McGEECHAN

The famous walk out was done so the home support would understand we were there for real; that it was our Grand Slam as well. And when the team walked out, that was exactly the message that was delivered. The noise of the crowd shook the whole ground.

TONY STANGER

I think everyone was pretty honest with themselves, saying we could win the game, but it wasn't until that walk onto the pitch that we realised just how big an opportunity it was.

I didn't know we were going to walk out until just before it happened. It had obviously been discussed at some level, but it wasn't something that I needed to know about until it was happening. Normally everyone fired out of the tunnel at 100 miles an hour because they were bursting to get going – so this was completely different and it could have gone either way. And fortunately for us it just set the whole thing up, it hooked into the mood of the crowd: hopeful rather than expectant. But the reaction of the crowd did catch me out, then we had the anthems which calmed us down but there was the same sort euphoria for the kick-off – and then we were into it. Everything remotely positive, be it a Scottish tackle or an English knock-on, was met with this huge surge from the crowd. I think every player would agree that a crucial component of the success we achieved that day was the passion of the crowd.

SEAN LINEEN

When we walked out the noise was unbelievable. It was real lump in the throat stuff. And when the crowd sang Flower of Scotland – well, that was just frightening.

Assisted by Gavin Hastings, Craig Chalmers lines up a kick for goal. Getty Images

Crowds are not that great in modern day rugby. There are moments, but I think people expect more from professionals and there isn't that same blind devotion. The crowd can be the 16th man, and in Scotland, in games like that, we really need to have that 16th man on our side all the time.

FINLAY CALDER

I knew so many of the English boys so well after the Lions tour and they were just a fantastic bunch of players. Jerry Guscott was just effortlessly brilliant, Underwood had speed that defied belief and the pack were all enormous – except for Brian Moore. But what Brian lacked physically, he made up for mentally. I'm so glad that people now see in Brian Moore the man which I have known all this time. He's an extraordinary human being. I've never seen a man as driven about anything and everything in my life. He's just a compulsive winner. We're a funny nation because if he was Scottish we would have been so proud of him, but because he wore an English jersey he became this figure of hate. He had a lot of Scottish traits – not particularly big, thrawn, bad tempered and with this phenomenal desire to win. With the Lions I quickly recognised that this guy knew a lot more about rugby than me, so I put him in charge of the forwards and he revelled in the role, because it was recognition for him, and he had the respect of his peers. The contact in international rugby is unbelievable. It's like a cartoon, you see stars, and to think clearly through all that muddle takes some doing – but a few guys have the ability to do that, and Brian is one of them. And England didn't need Brian to be big because, as I say, every other player in their pack was a monster. They had cruised through the Championship, dominating everyone physically and then whipping the ball out to those electric and clever backs. What a team.

IAN McGEECHAN

I knew that if we could keep the ball away from England and keep it in play that we could nullify their efforts to establish those early patterns of play; and we did it – in the first 15 minutes of the game, England didn't touch the ball. The video analysis meant that we knew how England would play and we just had to be there first, knocking them backwards at every phase of play. There was a system but they never assumed we might have thought things out and planned how we were going to play, so they all claimed that it was just chaos – but it was organised, planned out meticulously and then executed by the players.

DEREK WHITE

Mike Teague tells a story about Mick Skinner in the build up to that game. He had been swanning around all week telling everyone in the team, in the

Micky Skinner and Mike Teague battle for the ball with Finlay Calder and Derek Turnbull. *Getty Images*

management, in the press, just how easy it was going to be – they were going to stroll to the Grand Slam. They were the best English team yet.

The game was only minutes old when Fin took a quick tap and launched himself into the heart of the English pack. He was met by a juddering hit from Skinner, but Fin kept his feet, kept pumping his legs and moments later the rest of our pack were in behind him, powering on through Skinner and the rest of the English forwards. We won a penalty and as Skinner was getting to his feet, his shirt covered in stud marks, Teague turned to him and said, 'Still think this is going to be easy?'

TONY STANGER

The game plan at that time did not involve a huge amount of rugby being played, it was about kicking and putting them under pressure, and I suppose that febrile atmosphere suited our style of game.

JOHN JEFFREY

There was – and has been ever since – a lot made about how Fin and I used to spend our lives offside on a rugby pitch. The English boys made a lot of noise about it during the build-up to the game and Carling was moaning about it throughout the match.

Maybe they were right, but the way I see it, the laws of the game are fairly flexible. You push it to the limit until you're caught – and the ref can only penalise you if he sees you.

In many ways I think it was a more honest time – you put your body on the line to slow up the ball or to try and pinch or disrupt it and in turn you got your dues for doing so from the boots of the opposition pack. But I knew what I was doing out there and I deserved the shoeing. It was all part and parcel of the game.

KENNY MILNE

The English forwards were massive; I mean real man-mountains. And they loved to scrummage. The pressure and weight that came on in every scrum was just phenomenal, it felt as if your eyes were going to burst from the sockets, that you were going to rupture every vein in your body. Every time we went in Jeff Probyn would be boring in on me so that I couldn't hook, or piling so much pressure down on Soley – devouring him – that I couldn't see the ball coming in. Every scrum was a fight for our very rugby survival and Soley was really struggling. I was quite big for a hooker in those days, so Paul Burnell and I worked to take as much pressure as we could off Soley. I would focus on scrummaging against Probyn with Soley, leaving Paul to take on the Judge and Moore. But for all our efforts we were starting to give away one free kick or penalty per scrum and this was still only in the first quarter of the match, when we were at our freshest. We knew that if we crumbled up front, that would be it. Every set-piece was a challenge both physically and psychologically. If one broke, so would the other, and the game would be England's.

David struggled in the scrum, but he held in there. Just. Everyone remembers Stanger's try, Gavin and Chic Chalmers kicking, the back-row, Scotty Hastings' tackle on Underwood. No one remembers the shift that the front-row put in, but for me, that was the key.

FINLAY CALDER

The crucial error England made was that Dean Richards was fit bit not selected. At that point we began to think we had a chance. People don't realise how strong he was. He had calves like I had never seen in either a professional or an amateur. If he'd had a bad temper then he would have been a real bad man, but he didn't have that edge to him. I used to always reckon that if Dean Richards was playing and Rob Andrew was playing then we had no chance. If it was one or the other we had a half chance, but both of them could strangle the game in their own way – Dean with his strength, Rob with his right boot.

But they didn't pick Dean, they went for Mike Teague at number eight instead. Mike was a wonderful player, as hard as they come and had been voted man of the series for the Lions, but he wasn't a number eight. We knew that. But more importantly, Mike knew that too. The technical aspect of playing number eight detracted from what he was so very good at – which was pulverising the opposition in the tackle and taking the ball at pace from a playmaker, not picking from the back of a scrum and implementing play himself.

Dean would have been a different story at eight. He would have strangled the life out of us, as he did several times over the following years.

When we scored our try it was from an error at the back of the England scrum by Teague. I don't think Dean would have made that mistake.

The ball was turned over and we were handed a golden opportunity to attack off the resultant scrum.

TONY STANGER

I didn't play well against Wales and I went through serious hell thinking that I would be dropped for the Grand Slam game. I wanted to try and get myself back on track, so I made myself available for Hawick for their big game against Stewart's Melville. It seemed a good idea at the time to get back up on the horse, but Alex Brewster landed on me during the match and my collar bone shot out. I had been selected again for the Scotland team, but now there was a chance that I might miss the game because of the injury rather than my form during the Wales match. They called in Roger Baird as cover – so he nearly got two Grand Slams to his name – and put me through the mill with some contact work to see if the shoulder was OK. It was pretty painful but I tried to hide how sore it was when I was hitting rucking shields and tackle bags – and then Ian McGeechan made me do some live tackling on Dougie Morgan. It was painful but it didn't restrict me too much, so I was cleared to play. The next day, of course, I woke up and my shoulder was agony. It was OK so long as I didn't have to put my hands above my head. And I just figured, what are the chances that I'm going to have to do that . . .

GARY ARMSTRONG (Jed-Forest, Newcastle Falcons)
51 Caps: 1988-1999

That turnover from Mike Teague's knock-on set us up in a cracking part of the field to launch an attack from first phase – slightly to the right of the posts, around forty yards out from the try-line. A position like that gives you plenty of room to attack on either side of the scrum and as a result it puts doubt in the mind of the defending players – they don't know if you're going to whip around one side or the other, flood the blindside or move the ball open.

We had called a move earlier in the game when I would get the ball from the back of the scrum, carry it forward to commit the English back-row and then release Gav as he came into the line from fullback. When we ran it, I passed the ball to Gav too early and didn't commit the back-row at all so they just smashed him. One of the things I remember most about that match is the bollocking I got from Gav for that. When we got that turnover ball and the scrum was ours, we called the move again. I took the pass from JJ, who was playing at number eight after Derek White had gone off injured, and took off. I could sense Gav coming up on my outside and could see Mike Teague and Rob Andrew covering across. I knew that I had to hold on, hold on, hold on... and just as they had to check to tackle me I passed. It wasn't the best pass I've ever given and Gav did well to catch it. That piece of skill he showed to juggle the ball, fix Rory Underwood and then put in a chip kick as he was ushered into touch was class.

TONY STANGER

Without it ever being discussed, I think everyone appreciated that the next score was going to be crucial. It was absolutely on a knife edge. And the timing could not have been better for us, or worse for England. We started the second-half but our kick-off didn't go ten which gave England a scrum on the halfway – but they knocked on at the base which gave us the chance to have a go – and the rest, as they say, is history.

It was a planned moved which we had worked on a lot which we called Fiji, and the kick at the end was always an option. It just so happened that Gav came across in front of me towards the touchline and his chip forward was inch perfect.

Once the play is in motion you act instinctively, then you jump around a bit excitedly, then you realise you have 35 minutes to knuckle down and hold onto the game. It can't have been much of a spectacle as a rugby match, with us hanging in there, tackling and tackling, but when there is that much at stake the excitement can be all consuming.

GAVIN HASTINGS

You only ever see Tony Stanger's famous try in that match from the movement of the scrum, so people forget that it came about right at the start of the second-half after I kicked off and the ball went straight into touch – just like it had on my debut against France. We came back, scrummed at halfway and Mike Teague knocked it on at the base, so we were given the put-in and we scored from that.

It was a set move called Fiji which we had worked on for years in practice, and there it was – it just worked. I was bundled into touch after putting in the kick ahead, so I didn't ever see Tony touch it down – and of course some people still argue that he didn't touch it down at all. You wonder in these days of television replays whether it would have been given, but it would have taken a brave man to disallow that score.

TONY STANGER

It was definitely a try. I remember being given a try against Australia in 1996 when I was tackled over the touchline and didn't get the ball down but the

Tony Stanger celebrates his try with Chris Gray. *Press Association*

referee gave the score. I was very aware at the time that it shouldn't have been a score, so you instinctively know when a try should be given and when it shouldn't – and I instinctively knew at the time that it was definitely a try.

I'll never complain about people wanting to talk to me about that moment. I remember Brian Hegarty dropped a ball in 1978 and Gallion scored the try which gave France victory at Murrayfield. He was playing out of position on the wing, but nobody at Mansfield Park ever let him forget it. It was a shame, because he was a great player for Hawick, he worked hard and played four times for Scotland that year, but that is the incident which will always be attached to him. So I'm not going to complain about scoring the try which won the Grand Slam always being attached to me. It is a very positive thing to be associated with. I still get people coming up to speak to me about that match now, 20 years on – and it is amazing the number of people who tell me they were at the game, I'd never have thought Murrayfield could hold that sort of capacity. I think almost every rugby supporter in Scotland was there, and a few more.

As a player, nothing else has come close to that sort of atmosphere.

FINLAY CALDER

We had the element of surprise, we had the home advantage and that gave us inner-belief. It was a good side full of good people. There wasn't a position where we were carrying a passenger – everybody was there on merit.

Right from the off Ian McGeechan recognised that if we got involved in a roly-poly match we were in trouble, so he said we had to raise the pace of the game and not allow them to settle. So we took quick line-outs, took two-man line-outs and did all those sorts of things. Our performance that day was a classic example of the whole being worth more than the sum of the parts. The day just surged its way through and took everything with it.

I can't recall a shred of nastiness in that game; maybe there was the odd slightly late incident, but there was an enormous respect between the two groups which had toured together with the Lions the previous year.

I remember one point, when Will Carling stepped inside and came back at the forwards, and about five of us got him. He was inside our 22 and we just picked him up and took him about 20 metres back. That was a big psychological moment, as was Scott's tackle on Rory Underwood. Rory was lightening quick and he went searing through the middle, but out of nowhere Scott caught him up.

People don't realise how good a tackler Scott was, he was absolutely fearless. I once saw him in Hong Kong, when he tackled three guys in quick succession then ran the length of the field to score, and then got straight back on his feet ready to go again. That was in 1989, when he was at the height of his fitness. He was a phenomenal specimen for an amateur. The two of them – Gavin and Scott – were away ahead of their time in terms of physique.

They were also supremely confident people, and rightly so. I got my first cap on the same day as them in 1986, and while everyone was psyching themselves up that pair were flicking the ball off their biceps to each other. An awful lot of people are driven on by the fear of failure, but I don't think the prospect of failure ever entered their heads. They just believed they were as good as or better than anyone else on the park – and that's a great thing to have as long as you have the ability back it up, which they did.

It was unbelievable noise, all game. Everything we did was met with immense support. They were willing us over the line, and I think that eventually wore the English down. And when the final whistle went the whole place just went crazy – the crowd swarmed the pitch and we were just hugging each other. From a personal point of view I was also delighted that I had matched my twin in winning a Grand Slam.

Mike Teague is a very, very close friend of mine, and he said to me afterwards that he knew we were going to win after the first ruck, when he was caught on the ground and studded to bits by eight snarling Scotsmen. He also said that, in a funny sort of way, he was glad that we had won, which was a fine compliment.

And, in fact, that game also did the most extraordinary amount of good for English rugby because they went away after that and regrouped, and they came back stronger and more determined to succeed than they ever would have otherwise.

Grand Slam champions. David Sole is enveloped by Chris Gray and Finlay Calder. *Getty Images*

TONY STANGER

Winning in 1990 was so special not because it was England that we beat but because it was a *great* England team. They proved that by winning back-to-back Grand Slams over the next two seasons. It was a great achievement for us because it was such a big challenge.

SEAN LINEEN

That Scotland side was definitely the best team I ever played in and continuity was a key factor. During the Grand Slam season the only change to the side was against England when Derek White got injured and Derek Turnbull came on.

But that team and that success wasn't because of the system – it was despite the system. It was luck that brought that group of players together at that time. We had half a dozen genuine world class players – the three back-row boys, David Sole, Gary Armstrong and Gavin Hastings, while Scott Hastings wasn't far away – and the rest of the side was made up of very good players, and the coaching team was pretty useful as well.

The back-row used to have this whisky club, but despite what he says JJ was never a good whisky drinker – you'd think he would be, with the nose he's got. Anyway, I remember one night before a fitness test up at Glenalmond when the three of them drank this bottle of whisky. The next morning we were set this shuttle running test and, as far as I'm aware, Derek White still holds the record for the lowest number of lengths. You were meant to sprint the 100 metres, have a 20 second rest and do it again. He did one, was halfway back and had to charge off into the trees to be sick.

But they were three fantastic rugby players, and I think the whole team had a great team spirit. There were so many strong personalities in that group, and we had a hell of a lot of fun.

David Sole is carried from the field amid a sea of Scotland supporters. *Press Association*

INCHES FROM GREATNESS

W ITH THE *Grand Slam sealed for the second time in six years, Scotland returned to the Antipodes in the summer of 1990 for a tour of New Zealand that included six matches against the top provincial sides and two Test matches against the All Blacks.*

There is little doubt that this Scotland squad was one of the finest ever to come together. Their legacy had been secured by their success in the Five Nations, but if they wanted to truly stamp their mark on the record books, a victory over New Zealand away from home would seal their place in history as the greatest-ever Scottish side.

The players and the management knew that winning in New Zealand would boost confidence to a level previously unknown to a Scotland team. From there they could carry their progress into the autumn Test against Australia at Murrayfield, the 1991 Five Nations, the one-off Test in August against Romania in Bucharest and then into the World Cup, where the majority of their games would be held at Murrayfield.

After the Grand Slam success, the team knew that they could be on the verge of immortality. The players were there, the coaching structure that was in place was supreme, and the fixture list laid out before them seemed tailor-made to give them every advantage and opportunity to prove how good they really were.

Rugby, like all contact sports, is a game of the finest margins, a game where the team that wins the small battles and rides their luck can tip the balance of power in their favour, no matter how narrowly, to emerge victorious. It is a game of inches. And in the end, that's exactly what it came down to.

FINLAY CALDER

I'm a lucky man. I've had a lifetime of great experiences, but out of them all, three in particular stick out above the rest. One is pretty obvious, two are less so.

The first one was with the Lions in 1989 when we were in the changing room before we went out to play the second Test at Ballymore. Obviously we had played badly and been absolutely humbled in the first Test so we'd made a lot of changes, and there was such desperation in the changing room it was palpable. It was indescribable – very, very tense.

David Sole in solemn mood. *www.sporting-heroes.net*

Then there was this slightly surreal moment when Dean Richards came up to me – he might have been the hammer of the Scots but he's just a lovely, gentle person – and he said, 'You know Finlay, I don't really like all this noise, would it be alright if I went and stood outside?'

I said, 'Of course, of course.' There was no point in him standing there feeling awkward. And if he wasn't man-of-the-match that day then he was dash close to it.

That second Test in Ballymore has been pumped up as the years go by, but I have to say we were pretty pumped up at the time – and you could see in the Australians' eyes that they maybe weren't frightened but they were pretty intimidated by us.

If you are going into a difficult situation then you want to know exactly where people stand, and that was one of two occasions in my international career when I just knew we were going to win because of the personalities we had in the changing room – that was one, and it was same when Scotland played Canterbury in 1990.

New Zealand have always been pretty cute with the schedule they give touring teams, they fly you up and down the country to wear you out, then the week before the first Test they'll give you Canterbury – who have a spectacular record against touring sides.

So it was one of those occasions where you think, 'Well, this is going to pretty rough, so let's get our retaliation in first.' We knew there was no way out, we just had to go forward and take on whatever came across your path, and it was as brutal a match of rugby as I ever played in. There was absolutely no nonsense and no prisoners taken. It was a great game.

We beat them reasonably comfortably in the end, and earned the total respect of what had been a fairly partisan crowd. In the bar afterwards, their captain stood up and said, 'Great game of rugby lads. Play like that next week and you'll beat the All Blacks.' And I wish we had paid more attention to him because I don't think we really believed we had a chance until after the first Test.

My third abiding memory was playing for the Stewart's Melville FPs 2nd XV with my brother Jim, right at the end of our playing days. It was on the back pitches at Inverleith against Watsonians and by this stage they were way ahead of us as a club in terms of ambition and professionalism.

Jim and I must have been 35 or 36 years old, and during the warm-up I remember hearing at least three Antipodean voices amongst the Watsonian boys. Now, there was a few things that got us going in those days and that was one of them.

It was a phenomenal game for second team rugby which we won in the end by something like 35 points to 33, and it was undoubtedly one of the most satisfying afternoons of my rugby life. Jim and I sat in the changing room afterwards and we were absolutely shattered, but we had just managed to pull out the stops one last time. I know it doesn't sound as dramatic as the more obvious achievements, but I remember feeling that night that there was still fight in the old dogs yet.

JIM TELFER

It was hard not going on the tour to New Zealand, but I had too many commitments to fulfil with Hawick High School. I was confident that there would be little or no interruption in the coaching set-up caused by my absence – with Ian, Dougie and Derrick we had a super four-man coaching panel who were all on the same wavelength and they kept me up-to-date with how things were progressing throughout the tour. New Zealand is a wonderful place to tour – the hardest of rugby playgrounds – and it was a real testament to the quality of our team that they went unbeaten in the provincial matches and came so close to winning in the Test matches. But the players learnt valuable lessons out there that we would take into the World Cup the following year.

DODDIE WEIR (Melrose, Newcastle Falcons)
61 Caps: 1990-2000

When I was younger I was very, very slim. I could hide behind a goalpost and the only thing you'd see were my ears. My first love was always horses and it was at the Duke of Buccleuch pony club that I met a chap called Sandy Fairbairn. I used to play rugby for Stewart's Melville on a Saturday and then Sandy asked if I would come down and play for the Melrose minis on a Sunday, and I thought that sounded great so I signed up. That caused a bit of consternation at home because both my father and brother are big Gala men so playing for Melrose was just not the done thing, but I was able to get away with it because I was playing for Stew-Mel school on the Saturday, which was when Gala minis played. And from the minis I just graduated through the Melrose team until I was playing my senior rugby for them.

That Melrose team was fantastic and was coached by Jim Telfer, and playing senior rugby in that sort of environment brought me on hugely. Jim was the best coach I ever worked under – he's a great, great man and his record speaks for itself. He's done everything in rugby – from winning titles with Melrose, to Grand Slams with Scotland and coaching a winning Lions tour. His passion for rugby is unrivalled; there would be no difference in his attitude or approach to training and preparing for games, whether it was with Melrose or with Scotland or the Lions – he was always the same.

My Scotland career started with Scottish Schools and we went on tour to

New Zealand in 1988, which was a great trip. We were coached by Rob Moffat and I remember him telling me and Richie Gray after the first game that if we played like that again we would be going home. We were billeted out to families and it was a super time, travelling around the country and seeing what a big part rugby played in people's lives.

I was selected for the senior Scotland tour to New Zealand in 1990 and was part of Brewster's Breezers midweek team. Alex Brewster led by example both on and off the field and the whole tour was a hell of an experience. I was this 19 year old skinny lad and suddenly I was on tour with these guys who had just won the Grand Slam, travelling first class and staying in five-star hotels; it was an amazing difference to the schools trip I had been on two years earlier.

JOHN ALLAN (Edinburgh Academicals, Natal)
9 Caps: 1990-1991 [and 13 Caps for South Africa: 1993-1996]

My family emigrated to South Africa when I was seven, but my father was always keen to ensure I never forgot my Scottish heritage and he used to get me to read *The Broons* and *Oor Wullie*, which he had posted over every week. We used to sit and watch Five Nations rugby together and listen to Bill McLaren, and I would imagine fulfilling my father's dream of one day running out in that blue Scotland strip.

I decided to come back to Scotland the day I was selected for a South Africa XV to play an international XV and the game was called off because of the anti-Apartheid sanctions. I knew that if I was to achieve my goal of playing international rugby, I would have to follow my roots back home to Scotland. I wanted to play the best teams in the world at the 1991 World Cup and I figured that I would need to play at least two years of domestic rugby in Scotland before I would have a chance of being selected, so I arrived in Edinburgh in time for the 1989-90 season.

The first game I played in was down at Hawick where Edinburgh Accies hadn't won for 25 years. The Scottish selectors were present to watch Jim Hay, the Hawick hooker, and a few others. I knew they were present but I was more interested in impressing Bill McLaren, my boyhood hero, who was also there. We won the game and we did very well in the scrums and lineouts and before I had even really settled in Edinburgh I was called up to the Scottish squad sessions. Thinking back, every athlete has to be ready for that moment – right time, right place – and I know how fortunate I was that it worked out so well.

To this day I talk about the first time I heard Flower of Scotland sung at Murrayfield as a player – on the Grand Slam day in 1990. On that day, even as a reserve, I felt that I came of age and really inherited the Scottish passion which is still with me today. I learnt that day that a nation's pride is far more important than talent or individuals and I was so proud to have been born in Scotland and to be there representing them on the international stage.

My first cap was against New Zealand on the summer tour and it was daunting not because I was playing the All Blacks; I had no fear of them thanks to my South African upbringing. It was daunting because I was replacing the Grand Slam hooker, Kenny Milne, and would be scrumming with his brother, the Bear. I had no doubt that the brothers were upset that I had come into the team, and that was natural, but they treated me with respect and we all recognised that as a small nation we had to stay united if we were to be victorious.

The night before the game there was protestors outside my room chanting: *Allan hooks for Apartheid* – fortunately I'm a heavy sleeper but I was told that some of the boys chased them away.

SEAN LINEEN

We played really well in the provincial games on that 1990 tour and beat West Coast, Nelson Bays/Marlborough, Southland, Manawatu and Canterbury, which was massive, and drew with Wellington. That Canterbury game was really vicious. We just didn't lie down and the forwards were outstanding.

We shouldn't have been as far away from winning the first Test as we were. Iwan Tukalo had a shocker. It wasn't necessarily his fault, but every try they scored was on his wing, and he was dropped for the second Test. He just had a bad day, with bounces of the ball and that sort of stuff, and we lost some silly tries there. I scored a try from a move that we had worked on a hell of a lot, so that was a high for me and we scored another two through Chris Gray and Soley.

SCOTT HASTINGS

Sean Lineen and I had very quickly struck a great rapport with each other. In and around Edinburgh the teams used to meet up in the bars and socialise with each other, so it was always great fun – and here was this guy, Lineen, who wanted to play and party as well. There was this common understanding there that we were playing this game for fun, but we would take it very, very seriously when it came to the big games.

We understood each other, we knew each others' angles and we loved to test each other. We were probably regarded more as a defensive pairing than an attacking unit, but when we were out in New Zealand in 1990, after winning the Grand Slam, we decided that the back-row of Finlay Calder, Derek White and John Jeffrey were getting too much of the ball. And we decided that not enough teams were having a real go at the All Black midfield – we particularly wanted to have a run at Smokin' Joe Stanley. That was a turning point because we played some good rugby on that tour and we scored some damn good tries. I put Lineen in for a score under the posts down in Dunedin, and as he ran back into position I high-fived him, and my hand is still stinging now – we were both so pumped up. I also remember the line from the stadium announcer was: *And the New Zealander scores against New Zealand.*

We didn't quite get the scalp in the end, but we came pretty close, and that second Test still irks with me because it was there for the taking.

John Gallagher looks to power through Gavin Hastings' tackle in 1987 – three years later the All Blacks were pushed to the limit to secure their Test victories. *Getty Images*

DAVID SOLE

The rugby that we played in the Test series was, without doubt, the finest that I ever experienced with a Scotland team. We really pushed on from the Grand Slam, which was rare for a Scottish side to do – to follow success up with continued improvement. The fact that we played so well made it all the harder that we fell short when a famous result was almost within our grasp.

SEAN LINEEN

After the first Test, it began to dawn on us that we were actually capable of beating the All Blacks. I remember David Sole's wife, Jane, had called the next day to say that she could see from the looks on our faces before the match that we didn't think we could win it. So for the second Test in Auckland, the guys were ready for it, and we should have beaten them, there is no doubt in my mind about that. We scored two tries to their one, and I think most people would agree that Mike Brewer was offside when he tackled Gav and won the penalty that Grant Fox kicked to make it 18-18. Fox then added another penalty to scrape a 21-18 victory for New Zealand.

But we're not the only team that will feel they have let a golden opportunity slip against the All Blacks in New Zealand. They have this handy knack of getting away with things.

JOHN ALLAN

After I returned to South Africa and was picked for the Springboks in 1993, one of the major differences that I noticed between playing for Scotland and playing for the Boks was the belief against the world's best. I remember when Scotland were beating Buck Shelford's legendary All Blacks team by 10 points in the first Test in 1990, one of our players said he couldn't believe that we were winning. I told him that that's what we were supposed to be doing; of course, we eventually lost that game. When I played for South Africa and we got into a similar situation, my teammates would be saying: *let's beat them by 20 points or more.* Losing for Scotland was bad but not life threatening; losing for South Africa was – and still is – a national disaster.

GAVIN HASTINGS

The two most frustrating parts of that game were the try that David Sole scored which was disallowed because the referee couldn't see him grounding it under a pile of bodies, and the penalty that Mike Brewer won from an offside position was a shocker. We were that close to making history and it still hurts. It was inches. Centimetres. If they had a video referee back then, Soley would have been awarded the try. And then Brewer won that penalty that should never have been given and they drew level. Foxy held his nerve – as he so often did – and that was us. Defeated by the All Blacks yet again. But we had played well and deserved so much more.

TONY STANGER

The good thing was that we had this expectation that we were going to win. It wasn't arrogance, it was just recognising that we were all surrounded by good players and that we were beating some good teams. We took that self-belief to New Zealand in the summer of 1990. It was the end of that 1987 World Cup winning team; we lost the first Test, but then lost the second Test by just a whisker against the best team in the world. As a young man you didn't appreciate just how special it was to be part of a Scotland team capable of going to places like Auckland believing that if you played well you could beat the best team in the world in their own backyard, and then after learning a lot of lessons in the warm-up games and in the first Test we did almost do exactly that in the second Test. There had been some pretty dark days for Scottish rugby before that, and I was part of a few pretty harrowing defeats later in my career – like losing by 58 points to South Africa in 1997, or losing to Italy in 1998 – but those few years around the start of the nineties were a real pinnacle in our history.

SEAN LINEEN

It was always fantastic to go away on tour with the boys – you build up such a sense of camaraderie and there is always tremendous craic and banter, especially in those days when you did proper tours with midweek games and the rest.

We had this thing on that tour whereby the guys who had not had sexual relations with a lady on that trip sat on the left-hand side of the bus, while the guys that had been with a woman sat on the right-hand side – and as you can imagine, the longer the tour went on, the more guys were gravitating towards the right-hand side of the bus. Near the end of the tour it was about half and half, and Ian McGeechan's wife had just come out. The next morning we all jumped on the bus to go training, and Geech was last on. All the boys were sitting there, waiting to see which side of the bus he was going to sit on. When he took his usual seat on the left there was a few boos. He sat there for a few moments – then shook his head, got up, and moved to the right-hand side. All the boys erupted.

Scott Hastings was in charge of getting the t-shirts sorted out for that tour. All the players and management had signed a plate and Scott had got them made up into t-shirts, but he had thought it would be funny to add a phantom name. Unfortunately he hadn't paid too much attention to where he had put this new name and when they came back from the printers we discovered that right underneath our team manager Duncy Paterson's name it said, 'A.S. Hole' – which we thought was really funny, until Duncy found out about it. We had to spend four hours sitting there changing Hole to Haley. It wasn't as much fun having people asking who A.S. Haley was.

JOHN ALLAN

My off-field memories are numerous and the part I enjoyed the most in my Scottish playing days was the ability the squad had to enjoy life away from rugby. In New Zealand we visited many areas and the players were great ambassadors to their nation, and they had fun doing it. It was a formula that I took with me when I came back to Durban to play for the Sharks – play hard on the field and enjoy life off the field. That's the key to rugby fulfillment.

DODDIE WEIR

I was selected to play against Argentina for my first cap in the autumn of 1990. They were not the team they are now but it was still a great achievement when we ended up winning 49-3. I was very tall and skinny – I was 6'6" and only 13 stone when I was first capped which would be unthinkable these days, but fortunately I was scrummaging behind the great Iain Milne, who more than made up for my lack of weight – I think each of his legs were probably about 13 stone. I'm not one to remember all the matches I played in or all the details, and although I know the date – 10 November 1990 – I can't remember very much about the match itself. With all the adrenaline pumping and playing at a speed that I'd never known before, the whole thing went by in a flash. I remember meeting Princess Anne before the game and she asked me how I was and how I was feeling and I just gave a gibbering non-answer back to her: 'I'm fine, yes, thank you, not bad, thank you, yes.'

There was always a big thing made of you in the squad after you'd won your first cap and there was a lot of major drinking which doesn't happen so much nowadays I'm sure, but it's a pity if it doesn't because it was a huge thing to win your first cap and it should be celebrated – and it makes you feel more at ease within the squad if you go and have a big drinking session with all your teammates, it makes you really feel like you belong.

I always took the attitude that I wouldn't be in the team, so it was always a pleasant surprise to be selected. Of course, there were times when I *wasn't* selected, so that attitude helped then too – and I didn't get in the Scotland team for the 1991 season because Mr Gray and Mr Cronin were in the team ahead of me, but having had that first taste of international rugby, all my focus was aimed on doing everything I could to experience it again.

GAVIN HASTINGS

There was a lot of expectation on the team as we went into the 1991 Five Nations. We had started the season with a resounding win against Argentina at Murrayfield in November, winning 49-3. But the odd years are always harder for Scotland in the tournament as we have to travel to Paris and London. We lost the opening match against France 15-9, then won well against Wales at Murrayfield before heading to England where we were overpowered 21-12 as they marched to the Grand Slam. We finished on a high by beating Ireland at home, but it was tough to see our old rivals assuming our Grand Slam crown and beginning to look ominously strong for the World Cup.

JOHN ALLAN

I popped my rib cage against Wales in the 1991 Five Nations and just about all that I can recall from that game was having to scrummage on through the pain. Every time there was a dropped ball my eyes would roll and I had to brace myself for the impact of the collision and then the pressure coming on, puffing away trying to get through it.

We had a fantastic time with the Irish boys after we played them and one of my fondest memories from my time with Scotland was after that match when both teams had been drinking together and ended up standing on the tables singing and celebrating our Celtic heritage.

SEAN LINEEN

Coming back from New Zealand, we were obviously incredibly disappointed not to have won a Test, but we had gone unbeaten in the provincial games and had continued to bond after the highs of the Grand Slam. The World Cup was fast approaching, so we had to concentrate on the positives that we gained in New Zealand and switch our focus to 1991 Five Nations and the World Cup.

We didn't do very well on the road that season, but the Parc des Princes and Twickenham are tough, tough places to go and win, no matter who you are, and we won our home matches comfortably.

As part of our build-up to the World Cup we then travelled out to Bucharest to play Romania... and got cuffed – just like the 1984 Grand Slam team. Romania was a difficult place to go at the best of times and keep spirits high, but to lose there made it doubly tough. At the dinner David Sole, as captain, was up at the top table and you could see he was not enjoying himself. At our table there was Finlay Calder, Derek White, JJ, Damian Cronin, young Graham Shiel and myself, plus six Romanian guys. So each of us took it in turn to go up and down a drink with Soley, and by the time he had to make his speech he had skulled six glasses of red wine and was pretty pissed.

He got through it, but when he sat back down Damian Cronin said, 'I've never liked these blazers.' And he grabbed the breast pocket and ripped it clean off. Derek White burst out laughing, so I grabbed his pocket and ripped it off. The next fifteen minutes were spent ripping clothes off each other. You could see Bob Munro, the convenor of selectors, and the other committee guys looking at us then shaking their heads in disgust. We ended up walking out of the dinner, looking like refugees from some Monty Python comedy sketch, and getting a taxi back to the hotel where we had a great night.

At the airport the next morning Bob Munro gave us the biggest dressing down. We'd all been around a bit so we were just nodding and shaking our heads at the appropriate moments, and saying, 'Yes Bob; no Bob; three bags full Bob.'

But poor Graham Shiel, the new lad, was petrified. He thought he was never going to play for Scotland again. And, of course, Bob knew that we were lost causes, but he was determined to give this youngster the fright of his life by giving him a proper dressing down. All the while the rest of us were standing behind Bob pulling faces. I don't think Graham knew whether to laugh or cry.

JOHN ALLAN

I remember taking double portions of food in Romania knowing that they would take half for themselves if we didn't watch out. I earned a bit of status for myself on that tour – not for my on-field exploits – but for getting our squad, plus all the media guys, into a nightclub for free. We ended up having a very memorable night which cemented my place as part of the Entertainment Committee – and which I reckon probably helped my future squad selection.

GAVIN HASTNGS

Despite the hiccup in Romania, as a squad, we were nicely settled for the World Cup. The main core of players had been together for a number of years and we had been through some real highs and lows together – which added experience and steel to the group. All our pool games were to be played at Murrayfield and we knew that we were better than the other teams in our pool – Ireland, Japan and Zimbabwe – so we had every chance to do well.

JIM TELFER

We based ourselves in St Andrews in the build up to the tournament. As we had all of our games at home we decided that St Andrews would be a good spot to get away from all the hype building up in Edinburgh. It worked really well. We had great facilities at Madras College to train at and the players were able to get away from rugby by playing golf or walking along the West Sands, and they were able to go out for drinks in the evening in the knowledge that it wouldn't get out of hand.

FINLAY CALDER

The management of our squad was a world away from '87. We played a strong team for our opening game against Japan and won 47-9 and then rotated things for the Zimbabwe game, which we won 51-12. That rotation was the key to our success in that tournament because everyone got a chance to play and everyone wanted to perform when they got a chance. We were ruthless whenever we took to the field, no matter who was wearing the jersey.

SEAN LINEEN

The pool came down to a Scotland-Ireland play-off at Murrayfield. There was a real Irish invasion in Edinburgh for the match and the atmosphere was incredible.

It was a pretty tight game, but the turning point came when Chic Chalmers put up a high ball on Jim Staples and as he caught it Fin Calder almost knocked him out of the stadium. Fair play to Staples, he took the hit pretty well and played on, but we could see he was shaken and a few minutes later we put another ball up. We put another great chase on and the volume of the crowd just rose up and up as the ball started to come down on Staples. We were right in his face as he took it – or tried to take it – and the ball ricocheted off his shoulder and straight into Graham Shiel's arms, who scored under the sticks. We also scored a couple of tidy tries through Gary Armstrong and Scotty Hastings and Gav and Chic kicked solidly. We went on to win 24-15. We finished undefeated in the pool stages and were through to the quarter-finals to play one of the real surprise packages of the World Cup, Western Samoa, who had shocked Wales and Argentina and had given Australia a real scare before losing 9-3.

JIM TELFER

Nobody expected us to face Western Samoa in the quarter-final before the tournament – everyone thought it would be Wales. The Samoans had played some fantastic rugby throughout the tournament and their victory against Wales had been well deserved. We didn't know an awful lot about them, but Ian McGeechan was meticulous with his video analysis and we soon concocted a game plan for taking them on. They were very powerful physically and were confident in their own abilities, but we knew that if we could match their physicality, absorb their hits and look to nullify that area of their game, then they would be there for the taking.

Iwan Tukalo leaves Pat Lam in his wake as he makes a break against Western Samoa and looks to chip the last line of defence. *Getty Images*

GAVIN HASTINGS

The best we played during the 1991 World Cup was against Western Samoa. I think we would have beaten anyone in the world that day. They were a good side, they had already beaten Wales, and if you look at all the guys who were playing for them that day, they were a wonderful side. Frank Bunce, Steve Bachop, Pat Lam, Peter Fatialofa – these guys were all playing provincial rugby in New Zealand, so they were playing a far higher standard of rugby week-in and week-out than anyone in the Scotland set-up was. So we knew that we had to be at our very best if we were to have any chance and in the end we gave them an absolute doing, 28-6. Jim Telfer got his tactics spot on that day, he suggested I take the ball up short during the first ten minutes and because they were all looking out wide for the big hits, we were able to gain the yardage through the middle.

So, that was a very positive performance leading into the semi-final against England, which I still say to this day was the toughest game of rugby I was ever involved in – both physically and mentally. I got an absolute shoeing all game. The first time England got the ball, Rob Andrew sent it up in the air and when I caught it the English forwards just trampled right over the top of me.

Fin Calder bursts up the blind-side and into the clear in the quarter-final. *Getty Images*

FINLAY CALDER

The semi-final was a pretty dour affair as a spectacle, but it was tense and tight, just as knock-out games tend to be. We had won the Grand Slam game the year before by playing fast and loose and taking our opportunities when they arose, but the writing for England's performance was on the wall when we played them at Twickenham in the 1991 Five Nations. They had learned lessons for 1991 and tightened their whole game up, controlling everything through their forwards and Rob Andrew. It may not have been pretty, but it was a master-class in power-play and employing the necessary tactics to win in a tournament like the World Cup.

GAVIN HASTINGS

If I could change one thing about my rugby career it would be that infamous missed kick from in front of the posts when the scores were level at 6-6 – but it's just one of those things that I can't do anything about. There was a penalty awarded and Micky Skinner hit me bloody hard, I was down and the physio was on giving me treatment just before the kick was taken, so I suppose if one of us had thought about it a bit more, it might have been sensible to step aside and let Chic have a go – but it is easy to say that with the benefit of hindsight.

At the end of the day, I'm glad it's me rather than anyone else – because I know I can live with it. It's an annoyance in my life in that it gets brought up every now and then – nothing more, nothing less. It missed by a couple in inches. The slightest change in the angle of my boot when I struck the ball and it would have gone over. But when you're a goal-kicker, that is sometimes all the difference there is.

After the game it was an important hour in the changing room, and I was able to put things in perspective. Yes, our World Cup dream was over – but I didn't mean to miss it, I didn't want to miss it and I played a pretty good game apart from that. It allowed me to put the whole rugby thing into perspective – no one had died, no one had been seriously injured and no one had lost a job, so I was able to move on, and I think I had moved on by the time I left the changing room. Basically, there was hee-haw I could do about it.

Scotland look on dejectedly as the English players celebrate their passage through to the World Cup final. *Getty Images*

TONY STANGER

Scotland will probably never have a better chance to go all the way. We played all our pool games, the quarter-final and the semi-final at Murrayfield, with a team that had shown over the previous eighteen months or so that they could beat teams like England and hold their own against the All Blacks.

It was a high pressure environment. Because of 1990, England knew what could happen and they played a very smart tactical game.

People talk about Gavin's kick, but I honestly can't remember much about it – what I do recall is that at the time we didn't feel like it was a kick to win the game. It wasn't in the dying minutes, and if he had kicked it the whole contest of the game would have changed and who knows what would have happened.

It was two good teams nullifying each other. Because of what was at stake there wasn't much risk taking going on. It was a game of chess.

Scott Hastings kicks through against the All Blacks. *Getty Images*

It was a good opportunity, but let's not take anything away from England – the reason why 1990 was special for Scots was because England had so many fantastic players in their squad and we didn't beat them for the next ten games. We deserved to win the game in 1990 but I'm not sure you could say that about the semi-final in 1991.

JOHN ALLAN

I think the 1991 World Cup saw some of the best performances Scottish rugby has ever seen. The victories against Ireland and Western Samoa were thoroughly convincing and Scotland had a genuine chance to win a World Cup.

We played well against England but we didn't capitalise on our pressure and the rub of the green went against us; after the Grand Slam the previous year it was just not meant to be.

SEAN LINEEN

After we lost to England in the semi-final, we went down to Cardiff to play the All Blacks in the 3rd/4th place play-off. Three nights before the game we all decided to have a night out, but Jim Telfer got wind of it, so after dinner he stayed down in the foyer waiting to nab us on the way out. John Allan was the first ready, and he came strolling down the big stairs into the foyer with a Hawaiian shirt and pair of loud trousers on. Telfer let rip. We all sneaked down the fire escape, but John was too scared to go out after that.

The night after that we went out to a show which wasn't very good. So most of us left and we ended up going to a bar and getting absolutely wasted, and at about midnight the cast from a couple of other shows turned up – including 18 gorgeous women from a dancing troupe – so we sat at the kerbside tables with them until the small hours of the morning.

All of a sudden there was a shout of 'stop thief'. A guy had stolen a hand-bag and was legging it down the road; at least he was until David Sole jumped up and hit him with one of the best tackles I've ever seen. It was an absolute cracker. That was two days before we played the All Blacks – there is no way we should have been out.

But the guys worked really hard, which meant we felt we were allowed to play hard sometimes too. I would say the Scottish guys were among the fittest in the world at that time, because we had to be given the style of rugby we played.

Doddie Weir rises above the All Black jumpers to secure the ball for Scotland in the 3rd/4th place play-off game. *Press Association*

JIM TELFER

It was hard for the players to pick themselves up mentally and physically after the semi-final defeat to play the All Blacks in Cardiff. It felt as if the tournament was already over and that it was just a dead rubber – which it was. Both teams were hurting, but as defending champions, the All Blacks were hurting all the more and there was no way that they were going to suffer further ignominy by being beaten by us. In the end it was quite a tight game – Walter Little scored the only try of the match near the end to give them the win, but I was very proud of the manner in which the players performed. Gavin had one barnstorming run in front of the main Arms Park grandstand when he ran straight over their giant prop, Richard Loe.

JOHN ALLAN

We did Scotland proud even at the final dinner after-party where we joined the fellow semi losers, New Zealand, to play a game with beer bottles called 'Seven Dwarfs off to work'. It was a classic amateur rugby moment – both teams kicking back and having a good time together after a fairly brutal match and consoling one another after the disappointments of being knocked out of the World Cup. They were great days.

DODDIE WEIR

There was a bit of a fuss made after the final because a few the Scotland players turned up at Twickenham wearing Australia shirts. It was just a bit of fun and it got blown out of all proportion. I, of course, certainly wasn't one of them and was purely there to support the spirit of rugby . . .

JOHN ALLAN

After the World Cup I went back to South Africa to marry my fiancée, Claire, and would have returned to Scotland had a job in computer programming come through there. At the time I was playing rugby all year round with Scotland and Edinburgh Accies and then heading to play for Natal when the Scottish season was over. It went on for three years and it wasn't sustainable so I decided that wherever a job came up, that would be my final destination – and it happened to be South Africa.

Becoming a Springbok had been a dream of mine growing up; every boy at school idolises the Boks and becomes an imaginary one whenever they step foot on a practice field. The ironic part is that despite having nine caps for Scotland

and having just played in the World Cup, it took me an extra year to make the Boks because some small-minded people in South Africa labeled me a *Veraaier* – a traitor – because I had played for Scotland. So in 1992 when I was at my peak and had helped Natal to the Currie Cup, and the media thought I was a certainty because of my knowledge of international rugby and the UK, which was South Africa's first tour destination after isolation, I wasn't selected. When I made the squad in 1993, it was the culmination of hard work, belief and most importantly passion – which I inherited from my Scotland playing days. I have some fantastic memories and very good friends to this day from my time in Scotland, who I still keep in contact with. I owe my Springbok rugby career to Scotland and for that I will be forever grateful – I am fortunate to have two hearts: my Scottish one which gives me my passion and my South African one which has created my character.

JIM TELFER

The squad started to break up after the World Cup – JJ and Fin retired and Chris Gray was never selected again. John Allen returned to South Africa, Derek White retired after the 1992 Five Nations and then following the summer tour to Australia that year Sean Lineen and David Sole hung up their boots. It is always sad when a great era comes to end, but these things are part of life and although you are sad to see them pass, the next chapter is always an exciting prospect.

CHAPTER TEN

THE ROAD TO THE RAINBOW WORLD CUP

FOLLOWING *Australia's triumph in the 1991 World Cup, Scotland turned their attentions to rebuilding – both figuratively and literally.*

After claiming a powerful win over Scotland on the opening weekend of the 1992 Five Nations, England marched irresistibly through the rest of the tournament to claim a back-to-back Grand Slam. Although they lost to Wales in Cardiff, Scotland posted wins against Ireland at Lansdowne Road and France at Murrayfield and then travelled Down Under in June for two Tests against the world champions in Sydney and Brisbane, which were lost 27-12 and 37-13 respectively.

New players such as Andy Nicol, Rob Wainwright, Peter Wright and Kenny Logan were blooded that season and construction began on the redevelopment of Murrayfield Stadium, converting it into an all-seated amphitheatre to match any sports arena in the world. The new North and South stands were opened for Ireland's visit in the 1993 Five Nations, which Scotland won 15-3, but it was a mixed tournament for Scotland that year as they lost to France and England away from home, but backed up the Ireland victory by defeating Wales comfortably 20-0 at Murrayfield.

At the conclusion of the tournament, Ian McGeechan stepped down as head coach. Jim Telfer took up a new role as director of rugby and Richie Dixon and David Johnston were appointed as Scotland coaches. Their first season in charge was a baptism of fire. It began with a 51-15 humbling by the All Blacks at Murrayfield and continued through the Five Nations, where the best result was a 6-6 draw with Ireland, and into the summer tour to Argentina when the two Test matches in Buenos Aires were lost 16-15 and 19-17.

Mercurial. It is an oft used word in sporting parlance, used to describe a player capable of match-winning genius one moment, of catastrophe the next. The Oxford English Dictionary defines the term as 'volatile, lively and unpredictable; likely to do the unexpected'. In the lexicon of Scottish rugby that term would simply have a name inscribed in its entry: Gregor Townsend.

Townsend was never a steady controller at stand-off in the mould of Colin Telfer or even his teammate in the Scotland squad, Craig Chalmers. His game was one of

Opposite: The 'Toony Flip'. *Getty Images*

adventure. There are a handful of Scottish internationalists who will forever hold a place in the hearts of the Murrayfield faithful for their acts of creative daring, for their sparks of genius, for their ability to turn a game on its head with a moment of inspired genius that no one else could have imagined, let alone realised, in the heat of a Test match battle. David Bedell-Sivright, Bill Maclagan, GPS MacPherson, Herbert Waddell, Douglas Elliot, Ken Scotland, Arthur Smith, Andy Irvine, Jim Renwick and Gregor Townsend. Geniuses all. But like any genius, not without their flaws. For to conjure space or to throw a match-winning pass, to shimmy and break, to commit to an interception or to kick for glory, one must take risks. And risks, by their very nature, sometimes lead to disaster.

But if Townsend was the maverick genius in the Scotland three-quarter line of the mid-1990s, he had a steady anchor backing him all the way. Gavin Hastings was recognised the world over as one of the finest fullbacks ever to play the game. Physically intimidating, powerful, fast and as canny as a fox, he possessed great courage, tactical awareness, classic skills and a siege-gun boot. His place-kicking for goal was exceptional, even if the miss against England in the 1991 World Cup will haunt the rest of his days, and as he entered his swansong years he was still Scotland's number one place-kicker. But even if the legs were tiring and his body less able to absolutely consume an opponent in the tackle as it had before, his brain was as sharp as ever.

If ever there was a match in which these two greats of the Scottish game combined, it was in Paris during the 1995 Five Nations. From the outside, that season was looking bleak for Scotland. But for all their trials, Dixon and Johnston had been able to continue the blooding of new players. Between 1993 and the autumn Test against South Africa in 1994, Townsend, Derek Stark, Bryan Redpath, Peter Walton and Craig Joiner had all gained Test match experience. In the January match against Canada at Murrayfield and the Five Nations of 1995, Stewart Campbell, David Hilton and Eric Peters would also gain Test recognition as the squad began to take its shape in preparation for the third World Cup, which was to be held in South Africa that summer.

With the World Cup looming round the corner, it was vital that Scotland generated some momentum during the 1995 Five Nations. They started strongly against Ireland and then travelled to France, where Scotland had failed to record a win for 26 years and there seemed little prospect of that winning streak coming to an end any time soon. Despite their progress against Canada and Ireland, Scotland were written-off before the first kick of the game had even been struck. France were formidable and were looking to stamp their authority on Scotland, who would also contest Pool D with them in South Africa. But in Paris in the springtime, the most wonderful things can happen. It was during this game that Gregor Townsend truly made his mark on Scottish rugby with a display of daring and accomplished skill and for a moment that he will be forever remembered – his famous 'Toony Flip' – a sublime pass out the back of his hand to Gavin Hastings as he was being tackled, releasing the ageing warhorse at fullback for a clear sprint to the posts for what would prove to be the clinching score. The whole performance from the team had been outstanding that day but in that one phase of play Townsend had displayed the type of weapon that he had at his disposal; it was a phenomenal piece of supreme rugby skill that left Scotland delirious and sent shockwaves through the rugby world. In that moment, Townsend had announced himself on the international stage; although he was playing outside centre at the time, he was widely regarded as the heir apparent to the great John Rutherford and a figure who bore all the enigmatic traits and creative majesty of Andy Irvine.

As a team, Scotland were incomparable to the one that had been playing during the previous two seasons. As French Federation president Bernard Lapasset stated in the aftermath of the Paris match, 'Rugby is not for the country that is stronger and richer. It is for the country that shows the greater courage, discipline and teamwork for 80 minutes.'

Two weeks later, Wales were blown away in Edinburgh 26-13 and on 18 March the team flew south to Twickenham for the final match of the Five Nations and another winner-takes-all play-off. But with England as powerful and claustrophobic as ever, Scotland's Grand Slam dream came unstuck against the metronomic boot of Rob Andrew, who scored seven penalties and a drop-goal to secure a 24-12 victory and a third unbeaten English campaign since 1991.

Devastatingly, a few weeks later Townsend ruptured the posterior cruciate ligament in his knee playing for Gala against Hawick and was ruled out of the World Cup. But despite this set-back, the rest of the squad was in positive shape as they prepared for South Africa – which would prove to be the most extraordinary World Cup yet.

Scotland cruised to an 89-0 victory over Ivory Coat in their first match in Rustenberg; they then took on Tonga in Pretoria and won 41-5 before playing France for the pool, also in Pretoria. In a bitterly fought contest, they were defeated thanks to an injury-time try by Emile Ntamack, which sent Scotland into a quarter-final with New Zealand.

The All Blacks were a team of superstars who had set the tournament alight with thumping wins over Ireland, Wales and Japan. Every one of the players in their squad was world class and in 20 year old sensation Jonah Lomu they had a supernova. Despite giving a good account of themselves with Doddie Weir scoring two tries and Scott Hastings one, Scotland were defeated 48-30 and were out of the tournament. As the sun set on Loftus Versfeld, so too did it set on the career of Gavin Hastings. He was carried from the field on the shoulders of Doddie Weir and Rob Wainwright, beaten but not bowed and with the words of his old Auckland University teammate Sean Fitzpatrick playing in his ears, the ultimate compliment that a New Zealand captain can give: 'His heart may be Scottish, but his soul is that of an All Black.'

ROB WAINWRIGHT (Edinburgh Academicals, West Hartlepool, Watsonians, London Scottish, Caledonia Reds, Glasgow Caledonians)
37 Caps: 1992-1998

There were a number of Glenalmond boys from my era who went on to represent Scotland with distinction – myself, David Sole, Iain Morrison and David Leslie. All of them were influential on my international career. David Sole was an inspiration in the early nineties during my few seasons at Edinburgh Accies and then for one season with Scotland. Iain Morrison was ahead of me at school and he came into the Scotland set-up after me, but it was great having him around the Scotland squad and he was a fantastic player. David Leslie possibly had the biggest influence. How do you even begin to describe David Leslie? He was the coach of the Anglo-Scots and I learned a lot from him at the time. He was incredibly intense and I liked that intensity – in short doses. The Anglo-Scots played four games a year and we were a bloody good side, well trained and organised. It is one of the many downsides of the way professionalism has gone in Scotland because the demise of the Anglo-Scots as a serious team has cut-off a great source of players, when we need all the talent we can find.

I was at Cambridge University for six years and I think I probably started to get noticed after playing well in the Varsity matches. I played for the B team against Italy in 1989 and then dropped off the radar for a couple of years before playing in the National Trial in January 1992. In those interim years it had basically been a case of waiting for JJ and Finlay to retire, but I have to say that I felt very sorry for Graham Marshall, who was a bloody good player, but had been very much the understudy for both JJ and Finlay for several years. When they retired it looked as if it was Graham's time, but he suffered a career-ending injury early in 1992 and so I rose one vital notch in the pecking order.

I had a good game in the Trial match at number eight and was capped later in the season off the bench against Ireland in the Five Nations. In those days you didn't have substitutions, only replacements, and Neil Edwards very kindly left the pitch with about three minutes to go so that I could get on. I was moved into the second-row and I don't think I actually did anything in those couple of minutes but run around a bit, but it was still a great thing to win that first cap and to be a part of a victory at Lansdowne Road.

We played France in the third game of the tournament and Ian Smith was injured, so I started at open-side flanker. I don't remember an awful lot about the game except that it rained a lot and the ball was like a bar of soap – although again I hardly touched it – I just ran around like a blue-arsed fly.

The summer tour to Australia in 1992 was the first time that I consolidated my place in the team. I was still pretty new to the whole set-up and just tried to keep my head down and work hard. It was an amazing experience, though there was a bit of tension on the tour between the captain and the coach which could be a little uncomfortable for the rest of the party. David Sole and Richie Dixon publicly clashed with one another now and again throughout the tour – on the training pitch, in meetings – and it wasn't good at all. I remember thinking that all that sort of stuff should have been handled privately between them backstage, but it all came back to haunt me six years later when I was captain and had a very similar experience. David was annoyed about the changes made in the coaching style with Richie replacing Jim Telfer, while conversely in Australia in 1998, I was annoyed about Jim coming in to replace Richie – and we had one or two public spats which I wish had never happened.

As I came into the Scotland set-up, a lot of the elder statesmen in the team were either gone or were coming to the end of their careers. Derek White, Derek Turnbull and David Sole were still there, but everyone else was pretty young. We went out to Australia on tour in 1992 and it was one of those tours with a lot of young guys trying to make their mark – although I never had the feeling that any of us really believed that we would win a Test match. It is the perennial problem in Scottish rugby and I suppose that much of that belief stems from the raw fact that historically we very rarely win against the southern hemisphere teams, and had only once done it away from home against one of the big three, in 1982. Even when we went ahead against Australia on that tour I don't think that many of us felt that we would be able to hold on to secure the win – and it was a self-fulfilling prophecy.

PETER WRIGHT (Boroughmuir)
21 Caps: 1992-1996

My first cap was against Australia in Sydney in 1992. They had big screens at either end of the stadium and it was the only time that I played in a Test with them showing replays of the action during the game.

We kicked off and obviously I was pretty pumped up for my first Test match – playing against the world champions in their own back yard. Tim Gavin collected the ball, made a couple of yards and was tackled. Now, nobody believes me, but it was purely an accident when I kicked him in the head as he went down.

At the time, I was thinking to myself, *I'm going to get sent-off here in the first minute of my first cap.* But fortunately the referee didn't see it and gave a scrum to Australia. I was looking from side to side to see if the touch judges were flagging, and they weren't – which was fantastic. I was thinking, *Got away with that one!*

Then, as their physio ran on, I looked up and spotted the big screen showing the replay, with my foot clipping Tim Gavin's head. The crowd were howling.

The referee sauntered up to me and said, 'Lucky I can't penalise for something being shown as a replay.'

Later in the match, I had given away a penalty and was standing there holding the ball. Nick Farr-Jones – who had just been voted Australia's most eligible bachelor and was a national hero after leading Australia to World Cup glory in 1991 – came up to get the ball and just as he went to take it I dropped it in front of him. They showed that on the replay about five times, and the crowd were going nuts. I wasn't a popular guy at all that day. It was like pantomime – with me as the villain.

Before the second Test, Bob Dwyer, the Australian coach, said the only way Scotland could win the ball in contact was illegally, and Colin Hawke, the New Zealand referee, penalised us off the park. That was David Sole's last game and he scored a try which was the last ever four-pointer in international rugby; he got up at the after match function and absolutely destroyed the referee. Usually it is all platitudes and votes of thanks, but he said he couldn't believe the referee had been taken in by the comments Australia had made and called it pathetic. I thought it was quite refreshing to see someone stand up and say what they really thought.

I was the first Scottish player to be yellow-carded in an international. It was the Scotland versus England game at Twickenham in 1993, the referee was a wee red haired Irishman called Brian Stirling, and basically Will Carling had come right over the top of a pile of bodies so I went in and rucked him out the back. The referee blew the whistle and pulled Gavin, the captain, and myself aside. He said to Gavin, 'Look, I'm going to yellow card number three for dangerous use of the boot on number twelve.'

And Gav, tongue in cheek, replied, 'A yellow card? He should get a medal for stamping on that bastard!'

I came off after that game and Jim Telfer just shrugged his shoulders and said, 'Unlucky.' It was one of the few times when it was actually just good rucking, with my shoulders in front of my hips. To his credit, Will came and spoke to me at the dinner after the game and said he was on the wrong side and deserved what he got – but at that time referees were beginning to get strict about putting your feet on players. The good thing was that in those days it was just a warning and you didn't get ten minutes in the sin bin.

SEAN LINEEN

After games at Murrayfield we used to get changed and head to the Carlton Highland Hotel where we met the wives and girlfriends, who wanted to talk about anything but rugby while all you wanted to do was talk about rugby. You love your wife but with the best will in the world you want to have a beer with the guys you have just done battle with – so you would be champing at the bit to get down to the President's Reception and have a drink and a bit of chat with your mates.

Then they did away with the President's Reception because everyone was sick and tired of having to go through all the boring formalities – but we didn't tell the women that; we still had the President's Reception, but it was around at the Mitre Bar in the Royal Mile. The whole team would be there.

It ended up with the wives saying, 'It's getting earlier and earlier this President's Reception.'

The guys would be getting into the hotel, dumping their bags and saying, 'Right, I'm off to the President's Reception. It's a big one today – mustn't be late.'

GAVIN HASTINGS

When the All Blacks came to Edinburgh in November of 1993, they really showed the world that they had taken the game forward, yet again, to a level previously unknown in rugby union. They were all pace and power and intricate moves done at speed and with perfect precision. They had an incredible pack with Zinzan Brooke, Jamie Joseph, Ian Jones, Olo Brown, Craig Dowd and Sean Fitzpatrick and in the backs they had Va'aiga Tuigamala, Frank Bunce and Jeff Wilson. Wilson made his debut against us and scored a hat-trick of tries. The way they played was just frightening – they blew us off the park at every stage and all we could manage were a few penalties between me and Craig Chalmers as they romped to victory 51-15. It was a real statement of intent from them that they were building towards the World Cup two years later, looking to make amends for what happened in 1991. Their players said of that tournament that they had really just turned up expecting to win it and hadn't expected much of a challenge from anyone else – and they were fools to have had that attitude when they played Australia who had players like Lynagh, Farr-Jones, Horan and Campese. You could see that they were not going to make that mistake again and had really pushed on to develop a new style of play. They were terrifying.

ROB WAINWRIGHT

Jeff Wilson and the other three-quarters did all the damage against us, they were just unbelievable. Even when they were 30 or 40 points up, those guys were still grinding, looking for more. I was the sort of game you try to block out of your memory.

GREGOR TOWNSEND (Gala, Northampton, Brive, Castres, The Borders)
82 Caps: 1993-2003

The 1994 Five Nations was my first full year in the international set-up and we were going through a bit of a tough time. I was injured during the autumn internationals when we lost heavily to New Zealand, then I came in at centre against Wales and we were badly beaten again, so it hadn't been a good six months and we were getting heavily criticised.

I was moved to stand-off for the England game at Murrayfield, which was great because that is where I wanted to play, but I wasn't happy with my performance. We kicked a lot, which worked I suppose because we scored from a high ball, but I was playing well below my potential in terms of going through with breaks and making the sorts of decisions I would normally make.

We were losing by two points with not long to go so the call was that I was to kick a drop-goal whenever we got within range. I missed one but then got another chance and slotted it with less than a minute left on the clock, which looked like it had won the game for us. But then we lost the ball from the kick-off and England were set up for a drop-goal of their own, with Rob Andrew in the pocket. Two years previously I had been sitting in the crowd behind the posts when Gav missed that kick to go ahead and then Rob Andrew had kicked the drop-goal to win the World Cup semi-final, and now he was ready to do it again.

Well, I was determined to stop history repeating itself, so I sprinted out – I was onside – and I charged it down. And I felt far more elation then than when I kicked the drop-goal a few minutes earlier, especially when I saw Ian Jardine diving on the loose ball, because I knew in my heart we had won the game then – naïvely so, as it turns out.

Possession ended up coming out on the English side, which was strange, and then the referee gave them the penalty – which was doubly strange because surely if we had cheated on the ground the ball would have come out on our side.

The penalty was between the halfway line and the ten-metre line, John Callard kicked the goal and that was the last action of the game.

We were incredulous at the time, but we didn't have enough video evidence. Then two days later, *Reporting Scotland* came out with this story that England had blue sleeves on their jerseys and they had a tape of Rob Andrew's hands on the ball, trying to win it back after his kick was charged down.

At the time I was upset with the defeat, I wasn't too happy with my own performance, but I didn't have the history with Scotland versus England games that some of the senior players had, and I didn't realise it would be another six years before we would beat England again.

GAVIN HASTINGS

The rest of that season was pretty hard going. We drew with Ireland 6-all in a pretty dreadful match at Lansdowne Road and then lost to France at Murrayfield. We then went on tour to Argentina, which is a tough, tough place to go and we ended up losing both Test matches. The results were poor but we were able to give game-time to Craig Joiner, Kevin McKenzie and Andy Nicol, who all won their first caps, as well as to players like Gregor Townsend, Bryan Redpath and Kenny Logan who were still pretty new to the set-up, which was important for the continuing development of the team as you always need fresh impetus as well as building experience in your squad before a tournament like the World Cup.

The following season the Springboks came to Edinburgh and much like the All Blacks the previous year, you could see them trying to develop their game as the World Cup approached – which was a huge occasion for them because it was the first time they had been allowed to enter and it was being staged in their country. We were battered in that game and lost 34-10 and they scored some cracking tries through Japie Mulder, Joost van der Westhuizen, Rudi Straeuli and Chester Williams, although again it was a useful exercise for us because you need to test yourself against the very best and players like Iain Morrison, Graham Shiel and Kenny Logan were able to get further Test experience, which was vital. Their team was full of guys who would go on to be the core of the 1995 World Cup team and become household names around the world – guys like Andre Joubert, Pieter Hendriks, Pieter Muller, Hennie le Roux, Os du Randt, Mark Andrews, Ruben Kruger and, of course, Francois Pienaar.

1995 started much more positively with a good win over Canada at the end of January which was followed by another positive performance against Ireland at Murrayfield, which we won 26-13. Our second match of the Championship was against France in Paris, which had been a bit of a graveyard for Scottish teams for over a quarter of a century. Although we had played well against Ireland, no one really gave us much of a chance as we headed into that second fixture.

GREGOR TOWNSEND

I can remember virtually every minute of that day in Paris in 1995: the walk we took in our hotel grounds during the morning, which happened to be the beautiful Versailles Palace; the police motorcycle outriders taking us to the game, banging their fists on the cars in-front as we bombed right into the stadium; and the Parc des Princes atmosphere which was something different to anything I had ever experienced before, with the bands inside these enclosed concrete stands almost deafening you.

Going to Paris, you just knew it was going to be a game that tests everything:

your mental strength in that atmosphere, your focus and concentration because they are constantly going to be asking you questions, and your fitness because they are going to be running at you all day and you have to play better rugby and more rugby if you are to have a chance.

They scored in the opening minute and in a funny sort of the way that was the best thing that could have happened to us. It was the shock to the system we needed, we needed to start playing and we did, and managed to get ourselves into a 13-5 lead at half-time.

Then with a few minutes to go, and the scores tied 16-all, I was involved with a wayward kick which led to a French try which we didn't defend very well. So, from being in a position to get a draw or even a win, we were now looking at a defeat.

But we got possession back, got up to their halfway line, and then Chic sent the ball to me on a miss-one. I could feel the defence drifting over towards me and I knew I had to cut back inside. Gavin had been on my shoulder the whole game, running great lines. I knew if I could suck in both the centres – Philippe Sella and Thierry Lacroix – and get an offload away on my outside then there was a slight chance of putting Gavin into space. So my first job was to get my elbow free, I did that and managed to hold the contact for that half-second I required, but Gavin wasn't calling for it outside he wanted it inside, and as I went down I managed to turn the ball under my arm to get the pass away.

I'd never done that in a game situation before. I don't think that's because I'd not been able to do it, its just that no one had called for it. It's just a small adjustment, the skill itself is nothing special. It was all about Gavin grasping the opportunity. If he had gone outside he would have been closed down by their fullback, Jean-Luc Sadourny, but the angle beat everyone.

I think any try would have been great – we hadn't won there in 26 years – but scoring in the last minute with the captain – and not just any captain, but Gavin Hastings – scoring it. Well, you couldn't write a more dramatic script than that.

Gavin Hastings makes a break against England at Twickenham in the Grand Slam play-off in 1995. *www.sporting-heroes.net*

ROB WAINWRIGHT

That '95 game in Paris was incredibly exciting to be involved in because the lead changed hand so many times and then Gregor pulled off his Toony Flip and sent Gavin in and we were all jumping all over the place in celebration. But I remember that Gavin wouldn't look at any of us after he touched down because he knew he still had to take the kick to win the game – and he had some demons to quell there after 1991.

GAVIN HASTINGS

Most people will hopefully remember that about my career – rather than the missed penalty four years earlier. It was a source of huge personal pride and pleasure. People often talk about a moment when everything happens in slow motion. For me, that was the moment. I got this ball and the space just opened up, then suddenly these posts appeared as if by magic in front of me. It was silent all around me and I just remember running towards the posts – it was easy. I felt in complete control

If I look back at any game in which I was captain then that was the one which gives me the most satisfaction, because I firmly believe that the attitude I took into that match as captain was fundamental to us believing that we could win it.

It was my 13th game as captain and it was Scotland's 13th attempt to win there since 1969, and I quite like these little statistics, which give you a reason why you are going to win the match.

GREGOR TOWNSEND

We sang Flower of Scotland in the changing rooms straight after the match, then we went back out to the pitch and sang it to all the Scots who were still in the stadium, throwing our socks and shorts into the crowd. And then the dinner that night – well, it was one of the great amateur nights.

PETER WRIGHT

We were all sitting at the same table, which is the way the French always did it. As you can imagine, we were having a great time, when Gavin turned to Stewart Campbell and said, 'The first time I played over here one of the boys showed me a trick.' Then he picked up the knife which was really, really heavy and tapped the middle of this huge plate, which smashed into a hundred pieces. There was a silence for about three or four seconds, as we all looked at each other, then all at the same time it dawned on us that this was a good game and we all picked up our knives and started tapping plates which all shattered. We just scooped the plates up and threw them under the table. When the waiters turned up to serve the steaks there was nothing there to put the meat on. And things degenerated from there.

Gav asked if one of the guys could give him a French phrase to say during his speech, and Damian Cronin said he was happy to help out. Now, nobody in their right mind would ever trust anything Damian tells you, but Gav was on a high so he did. He got up and said whatever it was that Damian told him to say. The French all burst out laughing and the wee translator went bright red.

He said, 'Mr Hastings, are you sure you would like me to translate that?'

And Gav said, 'Absolutely,' – thinking he had said something really funny . . . which he had.

The wee translator starts speaking, but he's staring at his feet and looking really uncomfortable. 'Mr Hastings would just like to say that he was so happy with the victory today that after the game he went back to the hotel and had wild, passionate sex with his wife.' So the whole place just erupted again, and Gav being Gav, saw the funny side of it.

There was a live band and we were all chatting away, drinking and having a great time. Then one of the guys said, 'Where's Stewart Campbell?' We looked over to the band, and there was Stewart up there with his kilt on, playing with the band. And apart from the occasional dud note he did pretty well.

I remember going to the toilet a couple of times during the meal and at the back of the room was a table with the police escort riders who had cleared the way for us all weekend. They had bottles of whisky and wine on the table, which were getting emptier and emptier, but they still drove us back to the hotel. And then the party carried on with the wives of the players getting driven up and down the street by all these drunk policeman, doing wheelies and all that sort of stuff.

ROB WAINWRIGHT

That game and the night out afterwards really drew a line, in my opinion, under the amateur era. It was one of the all-time great amateur nights out; we drank the most incredible amount of champagne after the match, went to the dinner and then met up with all the wives and girlfriends and just had this amazing evening. All the police escorts we had were drinking away and were then giving the wives and girlfriends rides up and down the street on their bikes. Doddie got taken for a tour into town by one of the police escorts and at one point they were in this fairly dodgy-looking area and Doddie asked where they were. 'I do not know, we are lost,' came the reply. The policeman had to flash his lights at a passing taxi and managed to get directions back to the Ambassadeur Hotel where we were all staying.

The SRU's coffers were much healthier in those days because they weren't paying any players, so they would always pick up the bar tab afterwards. I remember going to the team hotel after the win in '99 and because all the money was going to the players and into the running of the professional teams, there was nothing like the same money going around for the post-match entertainment and the whole atmosphere was completely different.

The amateur era was a great, great time. It was a chance for us to escape from the mundanity of life and spend some time in the

Kenny Milne during the encounter at the Parc des Princes. *www.sporting-heroes.net*

limelight. The team-spirit was fantastic and we would always stay together after the matches, and the wives and girlfriends always got involved after our official dinners were over; everything just felt incredibly tight-knit – which all started to change when professionalism came in.

GAVIN HASTINGS

It took a while to come down from Cloud Nine after that match, but once we were home we knew we had to turn our attention to Wales, who were coming to Murrayfield two weeks later. Wales weren't at their strongest in those days, but they still had great players with guys like Ieuan Evans, Nigel Davies, Neil Jenkins and Robert Jones. Robert, who I knew very well from the Lions, scored a good try in that match and Neil Jenkins was metronomic with his kicking, as he always was, but we played some scintillating stuff and David Hilton and Eric Peters both scored tries which I converted and I kicked four penalties and we won 26-13.

That obviously set us up for a Grand Slam showdown with England. It was very similar to the 1991 showdown which had also been played at Twickenham. It was a game for the purists, as they say – not particularly exciting and although we tried to play a running game, they had learned their lesson against us in 1990 and made sure that they strangled the life out of proceedings whenever we met. As ever, they had a huge pack, absolutely monstrous, and with Dean Richards at the heart of it, they kept the game very tight and Rob Andrew's boot did the rest. It was disappointing to lose such an important game that way, but England were clever and did what needed to be done – they kept the ball with guys like Deano, Ben Clarke, Tim Rodber, Martin Johnson and Martin Bayfield, even though they had a fantastic set of backs – and they ground out the win. It wasn't very inspiring, but it was a demonstration of how to win crucial games clinically.

ROB WAINWRIGHT

We came unstuck against England in that last match, but we had been playing some fantastic rugby and been involved in some truly great games that season.

Scotland's captain Gavin Hastings evades Rob Andrew's tackle during the Five Nations decider match against England at Twickenham. England edged the encounter to win the Grand Slam. *Press Association*

When we went down to Twickenham I genuinely think that only three or four of us actually thought that we stood a chance of winning – because Scotland's record there is so appalling. Conversely, when you look back to that Paris game, it's interesting to note that some of the best games Scotland have ever played have been against France in the Parc des Princes or the Stade de France – the 1995 and 1999 games in particular – but often the return fixture is a pretty terrible affair. The latter point has much to do with the approach that the French have when they travel, but with the former, for whatever reason, Scottish teams tend to look to play an expansive, attacking game in France. Strangely though, they can't seem to replicate that same attacking intent when they go to Twickenham.

PETER WRIGHT

The first game of our 1995 World Cup campaign was against the Ivory Coast, up in Rustenberg near Sun City in the North West Province of South Africa. We won at a canter, 89-0, and afterwards we went out for a beer. So we went into this bar and the guy behind the counter said that we had to hand over our guns, which would be put in the gun room. We said we didn't have any guns and he thought we were mad because we had gone out in Rustenberg without a gun. I was speaking to a girl in a nightclub later that night and I'd bought her a couple of drinks, she offered to buy me one back and when she opened up her purse there was a gun in it.

We got accused of wrecking a restaurant. I think the story had come from the French. We were training in Pretoria the day the story broke and afterwards we were all sitting at the front of a stand recovering from a particularly tough session. The press were behind us, and Dunc Paterson was behind them speaking to the *Pretoria Star* newspaper asking for a retraction and apology. He obviously wasn't getting very far, and all of a sudden he came out with immortal words, 'Well, if you don't put a retraction in I'm going to send my four biggest guys up there and then you'll find out what wrecking is all about.' You could see all the press guys' ears pricking up.

SCOTT HASTINGS

When we were staying in Rustenberg the management made sure that we experienced a side of the country that was a world away from our luxury hotel and playing and training facilities. We made trips out into the townships and it was one of the most incredible experiences of my life – we were all struck quite profoundly by the whole thing.

As we travelled around the country you could see the impact that the

Kenny Logan beats the tackle of the Ivory Coast's Patrick Pere. *Ross Kinnaird*

tournament was making – in terms of support for the team, from money coming in from around the world with the fans touring around the place and from government incentives as they pumped money in for the tournament. The legacy that the World Cup would leave on South Africa was plain to see and it was wonderful to know that the tournament could make a real difference to people's lives.

KENNY MILNE

South Africa was a very interesting place to go for the World Cup, but it was also fairly dodgy. We had armed guards with us all the time and we were told in no uncertain terms that there were areas that we were just not to go to. I thought that when the football World Cup was played in 2010 that there would be more incidents of people getting into trouble in the rough areas than there were, but the fact that there weren't was fantastic and you could see the good that tournaments like that can do.

DODDIE WEIR

South Africa was a great place to travel to, but there was still a risk of trouble so we always travelled everywhere with armed guards. But we still got out and about, did some safaris, went to Sun City, played a lot of golf and generally took both our rugby and our play seriously. That's the key to touring – you have to balance hard work with fun because the fun pulls you together as a team, it helps you bond as a group. As I say, South Africa was a great place to be but you had to keep your wits about you. There was one particularly memorable moment when our armed guards thought it would be amusing to arrest me for something or other after a night out. They bundled me in a car and drove me into downtown Pretoria – I'm sitting squeezed in the back of this car in handcuffs and my blazer next to these guys with guns and bullet-proof vests, getting taken through these seriously rough and dangerous parts of Pretoria. They thought it was a great laugh.

Bryan Redpath, Graham Shiel and Kenny Logan relax after training. *John Stillwell*

TONY STANGER

I played all my school rugby at centre. When I first got in the Hawick side it was on the wing and that went quite well and that's where I ended up making my mark in senior rugby – but I always felt my best position was centre. So, in the summer of 1994 I told the selectors that I wanted them to view me as a centre rather than a winger, and I went from being in the team to out of the squad of 50 which was named at the start of the season. The selectors phoned me up and asked me to play on the wing against South Africa in November and I did it – but realised that the only way I was going to be able to make the switch was if I put my foot down and said I wasn't available for selection on the wing no matter what. I didn't play in the 1995 Five Nations Championship, but then got back into the squad in the lead-up to the World Cup and played in the first game against the Ivory Coast as a centre. It was great to have made that switch within the space of twelve months. It was a tough thing to do, I had to stand my ground, but it was an important thing for me to do personally and is probably the rugby achievement of which I am most proud.

And what I do now as talent manager for the Scottish Institute of Sport is down to that one decision. I had to sit down and work out how I was going to achieve what I wanted to achieve; I realised there wasn't enough knowledge in rugby at that point so I needed to go back to university to study sports science, which then opened my eyes to a whole new world. I started looking at my own preparation, I stopped drinking, I worked hard on certain aspects of my game like kicking, I got in better shape investing my own time and money in working with different people . . . all the stuff that is laid on for players now.

It was the year before rugby went professional, so that first year at university my wife worked and gave me pocket money as a full-time student, but that was the only way I could get the information I thought I needed.

I recognised that people would give their left arm to play for Scotland, and that they might look at me as a selfish so-and-so. But it had always gnawed away at me, and it was something that I needed to do for my own peace of mind – and it was a tremendously positive thing for me to do.

When the game went professional I was no longer able to tell the selectors where I wanted to play. I was on a contract and when we toured New Zealand in 1996 I played on the wing. I maybe only got five of my 52 caps in the centre but those are the five that give me most satisfaction.

Rob Wainwright breaks through against the French in a thrilling first-half where Scotland dominated proceedings. *Press Association*

PETER WRIGHT

The French match was our big one. The referee in that game was a guy called Wayne Erickson, who was an Australian and an ex-prop. He set up a scrum and put his foot in to mark the distance apart he wanted between the two front-rows.

Well, he stood on my toe, and for some reason he had running spikes on, so it was absolutely agony. So he got a volley of abuse for that, and it was the one time I got away with it. He did apologise to be fair.

In that same game I remember rucking Thierry Lacroix and managing to take the strip off his back, which I thought was quite impressive. But as I was standing there admiring my handy-work, Marc Cecillon came right across the ruck and smacked me in the side of the jaw. I spent the rest of the game trying to get him back. If I'd known then what I know now – he's in prison for killing his wife – I maybe wouldn't have been quite so keen to make an enemy of him.

We had to win that game to play Ireland in the quarter-finals, whereas if we lost we were going to play New Zealand, so we knew what was at stake. We got ahead and were playing well, but then we let them back into it, and Lacroix, who had been struggling with his kicking in the tournament up to that point, couldn't miss. We lost a try in the second minute of injury time from a free-kick scrum. We had been pushing their scrum all over the park and this time we wheeled them and shoved them into touch. It collapsed and the referee gave them the free-kick, which they took quickly and Emile Ntamack scored in the corner.

I remember asking the referee after the game why he had given the free-kick, and he said, 'Because I did.' That was all he would say. And then they wonder why players have a massive dislike of referees. Why would we give away a free-kick when we were that much on top? It was ludicrous. And if he'd put his hand up and admitted he made a mistake you could have accepted that – everyone has a job to do and we all make mistakes, but the bigger person is the one who puts his hand up and takes responsibility.

GAVIN HASTINGS

If ever there was a game we contrived to lose, which we should have won at a canter, then that was it. There was a defining moment with about fifteen minutes to go, when we were attacking near their 22, and one of our boys put in a late tackle after the clearance kick had been made. The ball landed on the halfway line and when then we got marched back another ten yards because one of the forwards argued. Thierry Lacroix kicked the goal, so all of a sudden we had gone from really piling the pressure on them to conceding three points ten seconds later. The French might not have won the game until injury time, when Emile Ntamack scored that try and Lacroix kicked the conversion which made it 22-19 – but to me, that was the moment when we lost it.

I don't think we lost that semi-final in 1991 in the same way as we blew it against the French in 1995. Against England we were hanging on by our fingernails, but in 1995 we had started off so well, and just on that one lack of concentration we allowed the whole game to change.

We probably weren't as good a side in 1995 as we were in 1991, but we were pretty competitive and had we won that game against France we would have beaten Ireland in the quarter-finals easily – because we were a far better side than them – and we would have given South Africa a run for their money in the semis, especially the way the weather was. We probably just lacked one or two really good players to make us into an outstanding side, but we weren't a bad side by any stretch of the imagination.

BRYAN REDPATH (Melrose, Edinburgh Reivers, Narbonne, Sale Sharks)
60 Caps: 1993-2003

We were confident because we had won in Paris for the first time in years, and we were facing them again only a couple of months down the line. We had had two good wins in our opening games against the Ivory Coast and Tonga and had been playing some nice rugby. We knew that if we performed then we knew we could get a result – with the team we had and the style we were playing we felt that we were capable of beating anybody.

France lock Olivier Roumat races away with the ball as the encounter in Pretoria reaches its thrilling dénouement. *Getty Images*

But we killed ourselves in that game. We gave three consecutive penalties away in the second half, two of them for late tackles, which was just stupid.

I remember the stadium clock reading 84 minutes as the scrum packed down – and we were still in there. Then the scrum dropped and we were penalised; Ian Jardine went to tackle Abdel Benazzi and took a bang to his eye so he couldn't get up again. They cleared the ball and their backs threw out a miss pass, and Ntamack scored out wide and that was it – they created a simple overlap and their wing scored.

ROB WAINWRIGHT

It was the same as my first tour to Australia in 1992. We got ourselves into the lead but instead of pushing on and continuing to attack France to put them away for good, we sat back. It's a subconscious change of approach which is kind of inexplicable, but is one that has been suffered time and time again by Scottish teams.

BRYAN REDPATH

It was hard to take because we had built a good lead and had played pretty well – and I have good memories of the game, if not the result. But it's the old sporting cliché – it isn't over until it's over and France played right to the death and took their chance. Which left us to face the All Blacks.

SCOTT HASTINGS

If I have one regret about my time representing Scotland, it was that against the very best teams – the good England sides, France, Australia, New Zealand – we too often missed our chance because we let through soft tries. The thing about these teams was that they would never give away those sorts of scores, you had to work your backside off for everything you got, but we didn't always make sure the same was the case for them.

PETER WRIGHT

On the same day as we lost to France, Max Brito – who had played against us a few days earlier – broke his neck playing for the Ivory Coast against Tonga. It was a couple of hours before our game and I remember watching it. He went into a ruck and didn't get up again – but we didn't know how serious it was at that stage.

When we came off after our game we were pretty down and disappointed about the whole thing, then Duncy Paterson came in and told us how serious Brito's injury was. And it was a really strange thing because in a macabre sort of way it perked us up. We had lost a game of rugby which meant we were going to have to play the All Blacks instead of Ireland next, who we would really have fancied our chances against, but Max Brito wasn't going to walk again. It put everything into perspective. We had no right to feel sorry for ourselves when you thought about what that guy and his family and friends were going though.

KENNY MILNE

The France match was a real heartbreaker. We hadn't played very well against them in Paris earlier in the year and won; in the World Cup we played much better than them and lost. It is one of the cruel ironies of sport that these things happen. Right at the death it was never a free-kick to them after that scrum – we had the shunt on them and should have been rewarded for it. It was hard to stomach because we felt that we had deserved to win that match which would have taken us into a quarter-final with Ireland, and we hadn't lost to Ireland in years, so we would have been pretty comfortable with facing them and would have expected to progress through to the semi-final. As it was we got New Zealand in the quarters and they were a phenomenal side.

It was quite amusing in the build up to that match because all the focus was on Jonah Lomu. Gavin, being the man that he is, was going around all week saying that Lomu would be easy to tackle – all you had to do was tackle him low and the momentum of his run and his size would just fell him. Well, within a couple of minutes of the kick-off the ball went out to Lomu and he sets off on this run. Craig Joiner reckoned that it would be easier to tackle him from the side or from behind, so he gave Lomu his outside shoulder, which the big man duly took. What Craig hadn't accounted for was that Lomu was every bit as quick as he was big and as soon as he had made the break on the outside he was gone – Craig didn't get near him. So all that was left of our defence was Gavin. One on one. Gav ran up to meet Lomu, dipped his shoulder for the tackle . . . and was completely trampled over. Behind the posts Gav pulled us all into a circle and started saying, 'Don't worry lads, it's just a minor setback,' and so on, but all I could think was: *I thought Lomu was supposed to be easy to tackle!*

GAVIN HASTINGS

New Zealand had already established themselves as the team of the tournament by the time we met them in the quarter-final in Pretoria. They had demolished Ireland, Japan and Wales in their pool and had clocked up over 220 points in just three games, which was just unbelievable. Having played them in 1993, we

Despite Gavin Hastings' assurances that Jonah Lomu just needed to be tackled low, the giant winger rips through the Scottish defence yet again, leaving Graham Shiel and Iain Morrison in his wake. *Press Association*

had seen a glimpse of what was to come, but even that didn't really prepare us. We were a good side but their play was just from a different planet – the speed and the strength and the skill across every position. And in Jonah Lomu they really had something that no one had ever seen on a rugby pitch before – and he had only just turned 20 at the time.

We scored some good tries that day. My brother got one and Doddie Weir got two, and I pretty much kicked everything that I could to try and keep us in it, but they ran away with it in the end. I had decided to retire after the World Cup, so as they began to really rack up the scoreline, I knew that the final minutes of my international career were drawing to a close. It was an emotional time, but what a fabulous tournament it was to bow out from. We didn't recognise the impact that the World Cup would have on South Africa at the time, nor did we really appreciate until later the symbolism of Mandela wearing the Springbok jersey to the final, which had for so many decades been the

Doddie Weir and Rob Wainwright carry Gavin Hastings from the field as Scotland's captain says farewell to the international arena. *Getty Images*

ultimate image of Apartheid to much of the country. But looking back on it all, it really was an incredible thing to have been involved with and I am so proud that I was there to play a little part in it – even if it was just as a very peripheral figure amongst so many others at the tournament.

KENNY MILNE

That New Zealand game was Gavin's last match, but it was also mine and Iain Morrison's. Gav and I came onto the scene together on tour to Canada in 1985, so it was nice to go out together in 1995. I keep in touch with him and a lot of the other guys from that time and to celebrate our 40th birthdays, Gavin and I decided to run the London Marathon, which was a great thing to do together and shows the bond that playing rugby together can continue to hold through the rest of your life.

DODDIE WEIR

The final game against New Zealand is a big memory for me – I scored two tries and it was Daft Gav's last game. He was a great servant to Scottish rugby and had achieved so much for Scotland and Lions, so it was nice to be part of his last game.

ROB WAINWRIGHT

As an experience, the World Cup was just fantastic. You watch the film *Invictus* now and to think that we were part of that history is amazing, a real privilege.

SCOTT HASTINGS

The emotion that swept across the country when South Africa won their first World Cup match was extraordinary – and you suddenly realised what it meant to the country to be back from their international ban and to be playing, finally, in a World Cup. You could see the awareness of what the Springboks were achieving growing and growing throughout the tournament in every facet of society, not just the white communities, and by the end it was just unbelievable. And when Nelson Mandela appeared wearing the Springbok shirt, it was incredible. The way they won it – against the All Blacks, who had been far-and-away the best team in the tournament – showed the courage of their players, but it also showed how sporting performances can be carried on an emotional wave of support, and you could really see for the first time how rugby could change the face of a country. It really was amazing to part of the whole thing.

CHAPTER ELEVEN

11

A NEW DAWN

THERE *is an ancient Chinese curse: 'May you live in interesting times'.*
In Scotland in particular, 1995 will be remembered with delight tinged with
poignancy. The Toony Flip, the wonders of the Rainbow World Cup and Vernon Pugh's
announcement in Paris on 27 August that the game was now 'open'.

Some would say that rugby union had, in one way or another, been professional
for years. There is the apocryphal story of Barry John declaring that he had no
interest in playing for a professional rugby league team because he 'couldn't afford to'.
Others would argue that the advent of the World Cup in 1987 was the first true
step to professionalism, for an event that generated so much revenue could not
continue indefinitely without the entertainers on show eventually demanding their
share of the spoils. Indeed, one of the defences for the IRB declaring the game open
was to dispel the culture of shamateurism that was already prevalent in a number of
the leading rugby nations.

The various levels of professionalism in different countries before the game went fully
open can be discussed and debated at length. In Scotland, however, it is generally
accepted that the players prided themselves on adhering to their staunch amateur roots.
The SRU itself was draconian in enforcing its dogmatic stance on professionalism and
clamped down severely on any hint of money being earned by a player as a result of his
rugby status. Roy Laidlaw and John Rutherford were banned from rugby for three
years following the publication of their co-authored memoir, Rugby Partnership, *as*
was Colin Deans for publishing his autobiography, You're a Hooker, Then.

But while the SRU's defiance was, in many ways, a noble defence of the game's
amateur traditions, it also meant that the union was catastrophically underprepared
for the professional era when it at last arrived.

In 2007, Gill and Macmillan published Brendan Fanning's From There to
Here: Irish Rugby in the Professional Era, *a fascinating study of the transformation*
of a disorganised Irish Rugby Union – which was once brutally derided by its own
president Noel Henderson's observation that 'while the state of British sport may be
mostly serious but never hopeless, the state of Irish sport, though mostly hopeless, is
never serious' – into one of the most successful unions on the domestic, European and
international stage. Ulster, Munster and Leinster have dominated in Europe for over
a decade, each having lifted the Heineken Cup (twice in Munster's case) and
featured almost perennially in the knock-out stages of the competition. Leinster won
the Magners League in 2002 and 2008, Munster in 2003 and 2009, and Ulster in

---

Opposite: Gregor Townsend. *Press Association*

2006. Meanwhile, the Irish international team won the Triple Crown in 2004, 2006 and 2007 and the Grand Slam in 2009 and has established itself as one of the top five teams in the world.

There is no equivalent publication about Scottish rugby in the professional age. From the SRU's professionalisation of the four traditional districts, to their compression into two 'Super Districts', to their expansion to three professional teams with their reintroduction of the Borders, and then their reversion back to two with its closure, Scottish professional players have rarely had a moment to settle in a stable environmentt. Resources are stretched to the limit and the purse-strings are held tightly by Murrayfield; as a result, Edinburgh and Glasgow have flourished only in blips and have, in reality, achieved very little of any substance. Edinburgh qualified for the Heineken Cup quarter-finals in 2004, finished second in the Magners League in 2009 and have beaten of Toulouse, Stade Français, Castres, Leicester, Bath, Wasps, Cardiff Blues, the Ospreys, the Scarlets, Munster, Leinster and Ulster, but have often done so when their own hopes for qualification to the latter rounds of competitions have been snuffed out. Glasgow, too, have taken some mighty scalps, most notably Toulouse's at the Stade Ernest Wallon in 2009, and qualified for the Magners League's inaugural semi-finals in 2010. But there are still no titles, no trophies, no grand place in the history books.

It has been a tumultuous decade-and-a-half for Scottish rugby since Rupert Murdoch's News International Company signed the SANZAR (South Africa, New Zealand and Australia Rugby) nations on board for his Tri-Nations and Super 12 tournaments in 1995 – after which the other world unions jumped desperately, and on the whole blindly, aboard the professional ship as it set sail for a new dawn. Any potential tome on Scottish professional rugby would no doubt ponder the merits and deficiencies of the myriad decisions that were made under intensive time pressure by the SRU in 1995. Should the domestic leagues have gone professional, or was the professionalisation of the districts the correct way forward? Were the amalgamation of Edinburgh and the Borders into the Edinburgh Reivers, and Glasgow and Caledonia into Glasgow Caledonians the wisest utilisation of limited resources? Was the third team, the Borders, ever really given a proper chance to establish itself when it was resurrected in 2002, or should there have been a team set up in Stirling, Perth, Dundee or Aberdeen instead? And then there was the rebuilding of Murrayfield into the mighty stadium that it is to today – the cost of which plunged the union into debt to a tune of over £20 million, which it is still battling to overcome today. Should the SRU have taken on this rebuilding itself, or should it, as the IRFU have done with Lansdowne Road, have held out until the government stepped in to finance the redevelopment?

Throughout all these machinations, the SRU, its employees, its structure and its very role in the Scottish game have come under constant scrutiny, both within its own ranks and without. Serious questions about professionalism, player welfare, team and league structures and so on were asked in 1995 and have continued to be asked every year since then. They will continue to be asked until consistent success is established across the board, replicating the achievements made across the Irish Sea and in the other major unions around the world. For in the professional era, victories, titles, trophies, qualifications, rankings, performance-based business viability and the provision of entertainment for the paying fan is what the game is now about; indeed, they are the only barometers of success. It is no longer just about pulling on a jersey and giving your all for your teammates, your supporters and the badge on your chest. The essence of the game has changed and what it means to pull on a professional club or international jersey has a different edge to it than in days gone by. Whether that has been to the benefit of the greater good of the game is, and perhaps always will be, open to debate.

Interesting times, indeed.

GORDON BULLOCH (West of Scotland, Glasgow Caledonians, Glasgow Rugby)
75 Caps: 1997-2005

In 1996, we were sent letters which said we were being offered an SRU contract and that you were either a grade one, two or three player, which meant you had a salary of £20,000, £30,000 or £50,000. It was done en-masse; we all went in to negotiate together, so as soon as the senior players at that time were happy we all signed. That meant that there was no real succession planning for when the guys who had signed for £20,000 or £30,000 became senior players, and it ended up with some individuals who had won 30-odd caps still being on £20,000.

We would turn up on Monday morning for training and everyone had to wear a shirt and tie, because we didn't know what you did as a professional rugby player. We'd get changed and do two minute runs, because that's what athletes did – no one knew how to train professional rugby players to get fitter.

Nowadays the coaches are told how long they can have a player by the medics and by the strength and conditioning team. Back then you were run into the ground by the coach and then passed over to the medics and fitness guys after the coach was done with you. It has gradually evolved since then. Marty Hulme came in and started introducing specific training depending on your body shape, position and so on.

We were on a learning curve in terms of nutrition as well. At one stage during the 1999 World Cup, if we'd been served boiled chicken and red pasta sauce one more time, there would have been a riot. I remember one meal only eight out of the forty squad members turned up for dinner because we knew what we were going to get. Then you'd walk down the corridor in the hotel at half-past-nine at night, and there would be empty pizza boxes discarded outside all the rooms. It took a while to recognise that you have to entertain guys and give them some sort of quality of life. You can't expect guys to live and breathe rugby, rugby, rugby, just because you say they are rugby players.

Rebuilding Murrayfield: the old West Stand has been demolished and cleared to make way for its new incarnation – a project that plunged the SRU into millions of pounds of debt. *Scran*

ROWAN SHEPHERD (Melrose)
20 Caps: 1995-98

Some of the training sessions were very long. Because we were full-time we were expected to be on the training paddock more-or-less full-time – but if you look at the way the professional boys are handled these days, that's not the way it works. Training sessions are shorter and they are far more specific.

It could have been handled better in terms of introducing the players to the professional environment. We got bombarded with all the fitness and dietary advice, and there wasn't much support for what was really a huge change in lifestyle. I mean, one day we were amateurs then the next we signed a bit of paper and we were professionals with all that that entailed.

Nobody seemed to have worked out what it was going to be like, and more importantly what it needed to be like. We were training with the clubs, then we were coming in and training at Murrayfield, then we'd play district rugby, then some of us would go off and play international rugby, then we'd be back with the clubs. Everybody wanted a piece and it was pretty hard going as a player because you didn't know whether you were coming or going.

And it wasn't just the players who were having to learn on the hop. The coaching team – Jim Telfer, Dave McLean, Richie Dixon, David Johnston and so on – were searching for the right formula as well.

DODDIE WEIR

I used to ask Alan Tomes what he did to get so big and he said, 'Wait until you're 24 and the stones just come on'. That was the best news I'd ever heard – minimal training and I could eat what I wanted. I never used to enjoy training but that all changed when the game went professional and I signed for Newcastle Falcons. I was still pretty gangly when I went to Newcastle, but Steve Black took me under his wing and made training – even hard training – very enjoyable and he soon got me up to a decent fighting weight.

My experience of professionalism – along with various other guys like Gary Armstrong – was completely different to that experienced by guys who signed for Scottish sides. There was none of this stuff that the SRU insisted on like turning up for training in a jacket and tie. It was a lot more informal at Newcastle; we had one of the finest men on the planet in Blackey sorting out our training and the quality in our squad was also very high. We had 14 internationals in the starting 15 and some of them were real superstars. The first few years we mainly focussed on building our fitness in training. We all had skills and understood the game because we had all played international rugby, but that focus on fitness took us into the English Premiership and then helped make us champions the follow season. In later years we had to start focusing on honing our skills again as well as our fitness because other clubs caught us up, but it was all really well structured and organised, a totally different experience to that in Scotland.

When my contract expired at Newcastle – at the same time as Gary Armstrong's – we decided to sign for the Borders. We were Border boys through and through and wanted to do all we could to help the region. Tony Gilbert the coach was a hard, hard task-master and it was a completely different experience to being at Newcastle. We would train from 7.30 in the morning until 4.30 in the afternoon and have something like five training sessions a day which was way, way too much. It was so tedious, dull and draining and I soon realised that I was playing for all the wrong reasons – all the fun had gone out of it – so I decided to retire. Tony adopted the same attitude that the SRU had to training at the regions when the game went professional – they would slog the players to death on the training pitch and if the team lost on the Saturday, then it was the players' fault not the coach's. Tony came to the Borders with a big reputation in New Zealand and at various clubs, but he didn't try to adapt to suit his players. I liken it to a good golf coach. A good golf coach will come and analyse a player's swing and although it may have faults he won't try to make the player change his swing to emulate his own – rather, the coach will figure out ways to tweak the player's swing to improve it rather than trying to revolutionise the whole thing. From the outside looking in, that also seemed to be the case of what happened with Matt Williams when he became Scotland coach – he tried to completely change the way the Scottish players played the game instead of trying to help them improve the style they already had.

Doddie Weir towers over his teammates at a lineout at Lansdowne Road, 1997. *Press Association*

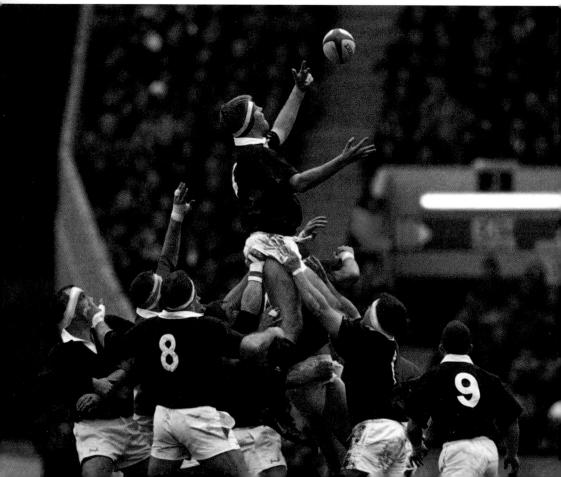

I thought it was a ridiculous decision for the SRU to close the Borders for a second time and amalgamate them with Glasgow. It just didn't make sense and I couldn't understand the reasons given for it. The SRU had put a lot of money into redeveloping the pitch at Gala and had signed a long-term deal to maintain it; the ground had superb parking, the facilities at the Border College that the team used for training were great, and there is a niche market in the Borders because rugby is the major sport there. I also heard that there were plans to merge with Gala Fairydean FC to make a main Borders sports centre for training and playing, which would have been brilliant, but the rugby team was dissolved before it had a chance to happen. The pitch, changing rooms and facilities in Glasgow were dreadful, parking was a nightmare and the interest level is mainly in football. Even though things have improved with Glasgow in the last couple of years, I still think it was crazy for us not to have a third team – especially when the facilities were already there and up and running.

GORDON BULLOCH

With the game going professional, people started properly analysing things so rather than just saying, 'These are our strengths, we'll play to them and hopefully we'll be good enough to beat the opposition,' they were also looking at the other teams and picking out their weaknesses.

In my first season we did alright line-outs wise, but then the following year everything suddenly started to change. Before you chucked the ball to either the front, the middle or sometimes the back – that's just what you did, nobody had thought of moving things around. But then teams started moving the target. I think the first real innovation we had was Eric Peters at five, taking two steps back and going up in the air – and we won ball all year that way, and it seemed revolutionary at the time. Then we got to the 1999 World Cup and South Africa won just about every single ball in our opening game, and that made you think again.

DONNIE MACFADYEN (Glasgow Warriors)
11 Caps: 2002-2006

I'm part of the first generation of Scottish players whose career was 100 per cent in the professional era. Having said that, when I first came into the Glasgow ranks, professional rugby was still a very new concept so what was considered as being professional in 1999, when I started, was night and day to what it is now. Now it seems like a properly professional sport, while back then it was essentially amateurs training slightly more than they normally would and getting paid for it – it used to be the thing that on a good day you would get home to watch two episodes of *Neighbours*, the lunchtime showing as well as the early evening one – whereas now it really is a full-time job, but it took a long time for that transition into full professionalism to take place.

The amount of analysis that goes in now as well as the strength and conditioning of players are the two things that I really noticed develop during my time at Glasgow and with Scotland. As far as the analysis went, when I first started it was all videos, so the picture wasn't necessarily all that brilliant and you had to stop the tape and rewind it and all that kind of thing – but now they have this programme called Sports Code, which tracks every facet of the game and training. Every player gets DVDs of their games and their training and the Sports Code programme calculates how far they run and so on. The programme breaks the game down and you get clips of every bit of play that you're involved in – and it's the same with the opposition players that you're coming up against that week, so you can study how they run and step and pass, or you can study lineout and back-row moves. It's a different world.

The players now all train with GPS trackers on so that the coaches and fitness guys can track the work that they're putting in at training, and they wear heart-monitors to make sure that they're always working as hard as they can – if the heart-rate is too low then the fitness guys know that player needs to increase his intensity; there are no hiding places any more. They've also recently introduced a kind of hovering drone with a camera at Scotland sessions so that the coaches can watch the movement and patterns and so on of the players from an aerial viewpoint, which is so much better than just standing on the side of the pitch.

That kind of analysis is great for the coaches because it gives them a much better understanding of what players are actually doing in training and in a game, and they can adapt their training methods to suit the player as opposed to just getting everyone to do one big squad session together.

Speaking to big Al Kellock at Glasgow, he told me that video analysis takes up the vast proportion of their time these days, especially in team meetings. As I say, it's more than a nine-to-five job for the players now. On a Monday for instance, they will be in at around 8.30 for speed work, lineouts, weights, then they'll have a meeting, then the decision-makers will meet, then the captain will meet with the coaches, then the whole team will meet up again and they will go through all the video footage. It's incredible how much it has changed.

ROWAN SHEPHERD

When I came into the side in November 1995, replacing Gavin Hastings after his World Cup heroics, we played Samoa at Murrayfield in our first Test match as professionals and drew 15-15. There wasn't a lot of rugby getting played at that time. I remember Toony was getting moved around so we didn't really have an idea about what kind of team we were trying to be. I think that because of the type of player he was and that he was now a professional, they figured he could play anywhere they wanted him and he would always play to his optimum, which was a ridiculous attitude to have. But then they seemed to see sense and he got a run of games at stand-off during the 1996 Six Nations – and things that season took off from there.

GREGOR TOWNSEND

While 1995 was a great year because we won in Paris, 1996 was even better. We had this young team – with Gavin Hastings, Kenny Milne, Craig Chalmers and Gary Armstrong all out the team – and we just had this great belief in ourselves. I was playing in my favourite position at stand-off, with Bryan Redpath, a good friend of mine, at scrum-half; and with guys like Rowan Shepherd, Craig Joiner and Kevin McKenzie coming into the side, there was just this great feeling. Everybody wrote us off, but we played a great brand of open rugby – which I think is the type of rugby Scotland need to play – and we were really successful.

ROWAN SHEPHERD

We went to Ireland first-up, and that was at a time when Ireland couldn't buy a win off Scotland. Naïveté was a good thing for us. Mike Dodds, Craig Joiner and myself were the back three, and we had decided we were just going to have a go. It was pouring with rain and we should never have been counter-attacking but it worked. I remember with five minutes to go there was a really positive feel, the crowd on the terraces had gone quiet, and I said to Scott Hastings, 'We've got this one.'

He snapped back, 'No we haven't, not until the final whistle goes.' He had been there and done it, and he gave us young bucks a bit of a reality check. But the photo on the front of *The Scotsman* the next Monday was of Scott jumping on top of me and punching the air at the final whistle. I wish I'd had the wherewithal to tell him to calm down because we had another game the next week.

Doddie Weir. *Press Association*

We played France next, and I think David Johnston and Richie Dixon must have been shitting themselves because we were playing against Emile Ntamack, Phillipe Saint-Andre and Jean-Luc Sadourny, so they brought in a psychologist called Richard Cox to speak to Craig Joiner, Mike Dodds and myself. He just said, 'Right, you're on the same wavelength, you're going to have a go, you're going to play France at their own game.'

And we just nodded our heads and said, 'Let's do it then.'

Knowing no better, we just let rip and had a go. Toony was on fire and everything we tried worked, and we won 19-14 in the end. I spoke to Saint-Andre about it recently and he said that he is still reeling from that match. It was his second match as captain and he was sure he was going to lead France to the Grand Slam that year, and Scotland was not a match they expected to have a problem with.

It was a great day at Murrayfield, with a typical Murrayfield crowd. We got awarded a scrum and they jumped up and down like we had just scored the try of the century. It was great fun.

ROB WAINWRIGHT

In 1996 we felt that we could beat anyone. It was the best season I had. Richie Dixon was under a huge amount of pressure from above and I don't really know where it started to go wrong for him.

The difference, psychologically, between the England game in 1995 and the

France game at Murrayfield in 1996 was stark – we knew right from the start of that 1996 match that we would win. We scored two tries in twenty minutes through Michael Dods; people talk about the Murrayfield roar and the noise that went up for those two tries and throughout the game was the best I'd ever heard it . . . it was indefinable.

GREGOR TOWNSEND

A lot of that was down to how we started the game. We called a 'miss-one-blind' from the kick-off. It's quite a gutsy call with a miss-one, and then the blindside winger coming outside the centres and being missed as well. We ended up making a huge break off it and that set the tone.

Rob Wainwright. *Press Association*

The whole game was pulsating. I remember Rob Wainwright catching a high ball in our 22 and running it out, and Shep was running at them all day.

In the lead up to Mike Dods' try, I remember Basil [Bryan Redpath] chipping forward and running past Laurent Cabannes, one of the great exponents of this open-type of rugby, as if he was at half pace. The French couldn't live with the speed we were going at.

We dropped the ball over the line three times that day, and with other missed opportunities we could have scored a few more than the five tries we got against France in 1999. I remember Jim Telfer saying after the game, 'Yeah you were good boys, but you should have won by 30 points.' And he was right.

Jean-Claude Skrela, the French coach, said, 'Scotland are now playing rugby just as we want to play the game. Now we have to go home and learn from what we have done today.'

ROWAN SHEPHERD

Next we went down to Wales and I had heard people talking about breathing out of their backside before but I didn't really understand what they meant until I played in that match. It was totally harum-scarum. They had clocked the style we wanted to play, with Townsend playing flat and Ian Jardine hitting up the middle to provide quick ball, so they slowed us down pretty effectively and it was harder to get round them. It was exciting from the point of view that it was erratic, not because it was great rugby – there were a lot of mistakes.

STEWART CAMPBELL (Dundee HSFP, Caledonian Reds, Glasgow Caledonians)
17 Caps: 1995-1998

It was the last time Scotland played at the old Cardiff Arms Park, with the old horse shoe stand sticking out above the pitch. I remember we had a line-out near to their line and we couldn't hear the codes, we were screaming in each others' ears but still couldn't hear a thing, because the Welsh were making so much noise and it was just bouncing down off the roof of the old stand.

When Arwel Thomas missed that last kick of the game, which would have got them the draw, we were all standing together under the posts but nobody celebrated. It was just a huge sense of relief because we should have won comfortably but ended up almost throwing it away.

ROWAN SHEPHERD

We were all a bit shell-shocked. We were three from three and were suddenly favourites to win the Grand Slam.

England had lost their first game to France in Paris and hadn't played particularly well against Wales in their last match, but they had recalled Dean Richards at number eight and he was the difference that day. He was like a honey pot at kick offs. He got under everything and slowed it down.

Because we were such a young team we maybe weren't aware of what we were involved in. I think the occasion slightly got the better of us. It was my fifth cap and a lot of the guys in the side were in the same sort of position – apart from Scott Hastings, the rest of us were all still trying to find our feet. If you look at the Scottish sides that won the Grand Slam in 1984 and 1990, there was a lot of experience there which helped them cope with the occasion as well as the rugby match.

It wasn't a great game. I think if we had got something out of Gregor's break-out from our 22 early in the second-half then that might have opened things up, but in the end it was a total anti-climax. England came up, strangled the game brilliantly and went away with the win, 9-18.

The English had Will Carling and Jeremy Guscott in the centre, and to this day I'm still amazed at how little they were used – but I suppose they just didn't fancy running at Jardine and Hastings because those two boys could tackle.

It was a disappointing end to the tournament and we not only missed out on the Grand Slam but also the title because of point-difference. It was then that the mistakes we made dropping the ball over the line against France really came back to haunt us.

ROB WAINWRIGHT

The Row 19 Whisky Club was founded on the plane out to New Zealand for our summer tour in 1996. Normally the seating was done alphabetically, which meant that I normally sat next to Jim Telfer, but on that flight row 19 was me, Doddie, Gary Armstrong and Ian Smith. We were in complete luxury on the top deck of a jumbo jet and all of us appreciated savouring the odd malt whisky. So we sat there, stretched out over these whiskies before getting some sleep, and a little whisky appreciation group, which has lasted many years, was born.

Richie Dixon and David Johnston developed the most amazing feeling in the squad while they were in charge. They rarely receive the plaudits that they deserve for their time in charge, but I want to go on record to say what a great job they did. Often their training sessions were led by the players. Great teams are not led by coaches but by the players and a strong core of leaders within that. That was a team in the truest sense of the word because it was so much more than the sum of its constituent parts. We all worked really well together and had a great bond; unfortunately the team started to be tinkered with in terms of personnel – partly due to injury – and that great feeling and bond seemed to die a little. It started when we went to New Zealand and our top-scorer from the Five Nations, Michael Dods, wasn't included because Jim Telfer, who was the tour manager, didn't think he was big enough for the professional era, which given Scotland's limited resources seemed a luxurious attaitude. As the tour rolled on, a distracting rift developed between the tour management and the players and coaches.

STEWART CAMPBELL

It was the tour from hell. The food was the main thing – our management phoned ahead to every hotel and all we got to eat was either boiled chicken or boiled salmon with rice – and tour morale just went through the floor. Then in one hotel we got an apple pie and we were all cheering, but they hadn't put any sugar in it so it tasted horrible. You felt like a machine – they completely overlooked the importance of the players being in a good place psychologically.

I was sharing with Barry Stewart and it was his 21st birthday. There was no party or anything like that – but we sneaked out to get a KFC for a treat. We climbed out the window of our room and when we came back we were like two little kids hiding behind cars with our party bags full of greasy chicken bits because we were sure Telfer would be keeping his eye out.

Don't get me wrong, I know you have to take in the right stuff, but when you are training that hard you can get away with eating a bit of the wrong stuff once in a while because you burn it off the next day. When you spend weeks on end being told you can't do this, and you can't do that, you end up rebelling against it.

We went from an amateur environment to going completely overboard, and I think they missed the boat from a mental wellbeing perspective – which is huge in rugby. There wasn't a fall-out, but there were a lot of disgruntled players.

It is strange because at the World Cup in South Africa in 1995 it was the same management set-up, but it was just a wee bit more flexible. Maybe they saw that trip as a way of imposing the new way of doing things, whereas the World Cup was not the place for mixing things up.

ROWAN SHEPHERD

It was the first professional tour so Jim Telfer was keen for it to be done properly and he had us on strict diets which included absolutely no alcohol. We were drinking hot chocolate in the pub and Jim was coming round checking our mugs. The media heard about it and it became a bit of an issue, but we understood the situation. I would say that the one lesson from the tour was that we should maybe have been treated a bit more like adults as opposed to naughty kids who couldn't be trusted.

There is a great respect for New Zealand rugby and we didn't want to look like we were shoddy, and I don't think we did. But Scottish players, generally, are always very honest and relatively well behaved, and maybe being treated with a little bit more respect might have allowed everyone to work through the process of turning professional together. It was a little bit them and us.

There was one meeting in Southland which was kind of heated. I think Scott Hastings and David Johnston were just saying, 'Look, there is happy medium here, if the boys want to have a glass of wine with their meal, or want to stay up a little bit later and relax and chat, then it should be allowed.'

DODDIE WEIR

Now that we were in the professional world we had a dietician come of tour with us for the first time and we were told that we weren't allowed to eat this or that or that or this. And we were told that we weren't allowed to drink. Now, telling grown-ups that they're not allowed to drink is not the way to do things. It brings out the rebellious side in you. At the end of the tour we were told that we could eat whatever we wanted because the tour was over and you found that you didn't actually want to eat a load of rubbish; you would never have a massive drinking session the night before a game, because you could never play as well if you had had a skin-full and it might mean that it would be the last time you would play – and also, we were all desperate to beat the All Blacks, so no one was going to do anything outrageous before the Test matches. But that responsibility was taken away from us and it got a lot of players very annoyed. Looking after yourself is just common sense, but the fact that we were told we weren't allowed to do this or that like a bunch of little kids got a lot of backs up. It was the wrong way to do it. As I've said before, drinking sessions can pull you together as a group. In the old days, between 1990 and 1996, we would meet up on a Wednesday before a Five Nations game, train and then go out on the town. It would pull you together as a group. Remember all that fuss about Danny Cipriani being photographed coming out of a club at midnight before a game? Well, you would never catch a Scottish forward doing that. We knew that the papers went out at 3am, so we always made sure we stayed in any nightclubs or pubs until at least 3:30 . . .

PETER WRIGHT

Scotland had always been very relaxed when on tour. We didn't have curfews and things like that – we were just trusted not to get too carried away. Then suddenly we were being told to be in bed by 10pm, we couldn't drink and things like that. So it was a huge culture shock. I remember travelling by bus from Wanganui to Auckland and we watched the movie *Road House* on the video. At the team meeting that night Jim Telfer lost the plot about that, he just couldn't understand why we wouldn't want to watch rugby videos – because that is the way he did things. But we weren't used to living and breathing rugby every woken hour – we needed some release.

One Tuesday night, a few of us – Derek Stark, Gregor Townsend and myself – got speaking to the manager of the hotel in Hamilton we were staying in and ended up asking him to take us into town for a couple of beers. He told us to meet him in the reception at 8pm, but we said we'd meet him at his car in the car park so we could sneak out the back door. We met him and got in the car and as he was reversing back out of his parking space he looked in the mirror and realised he couldn't see any of us because we were all ducked down. He said, 'What's wrong?' – thinking there was a drive-by shooting or something happening. But it was because Jim was at the front of the hotel and we were hiding from him. We went out and had a couple of beers and came home, it was nothing major. Because we were being told what not to do, it made us more determined to do it.

On another occasion, a local farmer we had gotten to know, offered to take us all horse riding, but we weren't allowed to because it was too dangerous. So we phoned the farmer and told him we weren't allowed and he said, 'Fair enough, how about going wild duck shooting instead? We'll get you a quad bike each and a semi-automatic shotgun and you can drive around my land shooting the wild birds.' We thought there was no chance but decided to ask anyway. And Jim said that was okay. So you had all these guys driving around on quad bikes and shooting guns, but we weren't allowed to sit on a horse!

STEWART CAMPBELL

In the week leading up to the first match of the tour we had an afternoon off, and Doddie Weir went to see some friends he had over there who had taken him horse riding, which I don't think he was meant to do. And I had brought my guitar on tour so we could have a bit of a sing-song which is always good for morale. But we lost that first game, so at the post-match meeting Telfer was giving us hell, and he said, 'As for the second row: Doddie, all you do is ride horses; and Campbell, all you do is play that bloody guitar. You're a couple of cowboys, alright – but you're a long way from being rugby players.'

So I was stuck with this great big guitar case which I had to carry around with me wherever we went, and I had to try to keep it hidden from Telfer because I knew it annoyed him every time he saw it.

Except, that is, when we were given a traditional Maori welcome in Rotorua. They were singing three part harmonies and so on, it was stunning. Then I heard a whisper in my ear, it was Telfer saying, 'Right Campbell, play those bastards a tune.' So out came the guitar and a few verses of Flower of Scotland.

Jim is a fantastic forwards coach, one of the best there has ever been. But on the management side . . . it was just too much. The mental wellbeing of the players was neglected.

TONY STANGER

I would never criticise Jim or the other coaches about that tour. It was the first tour of the professional era so how could they possibly know what was required? But it was a pressure-cooker environment so we needed some sort of release and having a few drinks and letting your hair down is a good thing to do. It was a mistake calling it a dry tour because that wasn't what touring was about at that time. Towards the end of the tour we did manage to negotiate a bit of a night out, not getting smashed but a few drinks and a bit of a laugh together – and it made such a difference to the trip. It was all a learning curve.

ROB WAINWRIGHT

It wasn't really an alcohol issue as such, it was a player-management issue. On the 1997 Lions tour the management was just fantastic. For me, Fran Cotton was the most important man on that Lions tour because of the way he ran things. In the week-long camp before we left for South Africa he sat us all down and told us that this was our tour and so we, as players, should be making all the rules. We thrashed out a set of rules that we were all happy with and we abided by them. A classic example of this was when the bus would leave in the morning for a training session. We were told that the bus would leave at 9am – and it always would, with every player on it, but there would be no checking to see that everyone was there; room-mates would always have a quick look to see that each other were there, but that was it. On Scotland tours we all used to get tour numbers and would number off like school children every time we got on the bus to make sure everyone was there – all of us were grown-up men in our twenties and early thirties, calling out numbers. It's little things like that that can get your back up or, as with the Lions, give you the appropriate sense of responsibility that is your due.

Jim's management was very different to Fran's. He told us about the alcohol ban, he didn't ask us about it – if he had asked, most of us would have bought into it. He told the press that the tour was going to be dry and then he told us. If he had come to us first to talk about it I would certainly have argued a case for a slightly more relaxed approach than the one he took, but still have supported the idea.

Jim was an amazing forwards coach, just unbelievably good at making forward units the best they can be – people go on about how good the '97 Lions' backline was, but as much as Fran and Geech, Jim was the most important man on that tour because he guaranteed the provision of the ball to those backs because of the work he did with the forwards and his contribution to the whole thing was amazing. But he fell down as a manager; it just wasn't his thing.

Jim was one of the most incredible speakers I've ever heard when his gander's up, he is incredibly impassioned and moving in what he says. As a manager those speeches would sometimes be slightly farcical but some were amazing. I remember being in Dublin a few hours before playing Ireland at Lansdowne Road and Jim sat us down at about 11am after our morning run-through and gave the most impassioned speech – real Bannockburn stuff – that had the players climbing the walls, it was just brilliant. And as captain, I just remember thinking, *Jim, why have you told us this four hours before kick-off when we're usually trying to keep the guys calm? This should have been saved for just before we go out to play.* But that was just the way things were organised at the time. On the Lions tour he gave some amazing speeches, many of which have been recorded for prosperity on the tour video, but he actually gave his speeches the night before the Test matches and they would have been so good to hear just before we went out of the changing room. Looking back, I wish I had had the courage to go and speak to him about it and asked him to make his speech in the changing room – it would have been even more sensational for us as players.

JIM TELFER

The idea of the tour being alcohol-free was decided by the management as a group – we wanted to do everything we could to give the players a credible chance of beating New Zealand – which was the whole point of touring there in the first place. Before we left we sat down and discussed the idea of trying something different when we went on tour there because all our previous efforts had ended in failure in the Tests. David McLean, our fitness coach, was doing everything he could to educate the players on diet and nutrition, trying to pull them into the professional era, and he had studies that proved how detrimental alcohol was to player performance. They were still allowed to have fun on tour – play golf and do trips and have a drink at the weekend – but the idea was that they would be more physically prepared to take on the All Blacks if they kept their bodies free from alcohol during the week before a match. It was hardly rocket science, but the players really made a fuss about it in the aftermath of that tour. They were clinging on to amateur ideals which didn't belong in the professional era. Professionalism was new to us all and as a management group we thought it was the best way forward. The All Blacks didn't drink in the build up to the Tests, I can tell you that, and time has proved that this is just basic preparation for Test match rugby in the professional era. I got a lot of stick about it at the time, but my methods were proved to be correct in the end – every country in the world has that outlook these days.

GREGOR TOWNSEND

I actually really enjoyed that trip. It was the first time I had been to New Zealand and I was playing really well. It was a dry tour and it was a mistake telling the press that because they jumped on it and from then on they were keeping their eyes peeled for anyone breaking the curfew.

I don't think Jim appreciated at the time what New Zealand players do after games. When we were there four years later in 2000, we went out after the first Test and were playing drinking games with Justin Marshall, Andrew Mehrtens and Taine Randell, so they have kept that tradition of working hard and playing hard. That is the way rugby is; you have to bond as a team and drinking together can really help that.

To his credit, he was assistant coach on the 1997 Lions tour to South Africa, and when the players making the rules said that going out for a few beers was an important part of the team bonding process he was all for it – so he clearly realised he had maybe got that a wee bit wrong in 1996.

We set a proud record on that tour of scoring the most points ever to be scored against the All Blacks up to that point, during the first Test in Dunedin. Unfortunately that coincided with the dubious distinction of having surrendered more points than any other Scotland side had ever conceded. We lost the game 62-31.

ROB WAINWRIGHT

Scoring 31 points away from home against the All Blacks, especially in a stronghold like Carisbrook, but still ending up on the losing side and with a record margin posted against us, was pretty difficult to accept at the time. We had worked hard and pretty effectively for much of the game, especially around the ruck and maul area, but their back three of Christian Cullen, Jonah Lomu and Jeff Wilson were just incredible and they tore us to pieces whenever they got the ball in space.

GREGOR TOWNSEND

In the second Test, in Auckland, we played really well into a horrible gale in the first-half and we came in at half-time trailing only 17-7, and we all thought we were going to beat the All Blacks, but they just screwed us into the ground in the second-half.

ROWAN SHEPHERD

I scored our first try in that Auckland game. Zinzan Brooke sclaffed a clearance kick and it was a dreadful day with a sodden pitch but I ran it back to their 22 anyway, then sent a kick up in the air. Peter Wright has told me that the subs were all on the bench, burying their heads in their hands and muttering about what I was doing. It took one bounce between Craig Dowd and Ian Jones, squirted up into my hands and I scored under the sticks. So it went from 'For f**ks sake, Shep' to 'Ya beauty, Shep' in a matter of nanoseconds. That's the way rugby works out, sometimes.

DODDIE WEIR

The tour was still a great experience. The people in New Zealand were just fantastic and we had some great moments. At the end of the tour we semi-kidnapped a rally driver we had met in Invercargill and took him up to Dunedin with us. We dressed him up in full SRU regalia like the rest of us and started to

Doddie Weir rises to take the ball against Ireland at Murrayfield, 1998. *Getty Images*

hit some student nightspots. In one there was this big racing car arcade machine that would let you race against each another. So we put this lad in one of the arcades and started to get the students to challenge him to a race. The deal was that whoever lost had to buy a jug of beer. So all these students started eyeing this guy up and seeing him in all his Scottish rugby kit they assumed he was one of us, so they started to challenge him. But obviously this guy was a professional racer so he never lost and we ended up getting around 30 jugs of beer bought for us and not having to shell out for a single one.

ROWAN SHEPHERD

The following season was hellish. Our opponents knew what to expect and things didn't quite click, so we struggled a bit from the dreaded second-season-syndrome. The previous season, we were unbeaten in the autumn and then got off to a good start against Ireland away from home so we were on a roll. Whereas in 1997, with more or less the same team, the momentum went the other way – we lost to Australia 29-19 in November and then struggled against Italy just before Christmas before winning 29-22. I don't remember anything specific being wrong with that season as opposed to the year before, except perhaps that the opposition had sussed us out. We had a great game against Ireland which we won 38-10 at Murrayfield, which salvaged that season and probably the next for the players, but we had gone from genuine Grand Slam contenders to find ourselves in a major slump.

And because we had signed contracts there wasn't the same understanding from the public – they felt they were entitled to expect better. A switch had been flicked and all of a sudden we were expected to be professionals. You shouldn't drop the ball and you shouldn't make mistakes because you were a professional, but we weren't very professional in our approach. The Scottish game was doing its best, but compared to the likes of New Zealand, Australia and South Africa, and even England and France to a degree, the set-up was not geared up for the transition. You look at players now and most of them take a long time to establish themselves in the pro game – you are told that guys are on a year-long conditioning programme, they're certainly not expected to be the finished article straight away – yet with one signature we were pros and that was it . . . and a lot of us were amateurs in the truest sense of the word trying to be pros.

DUNCAN HODGE (Edinburgh Gunners)
26 Caps: 1997-2002

People talk about winning their first cap and what a great moment it is, but I have to say that one of my proudest memories was when I was first selected for Scottish Schools. In those days you used to get a letter sent to you at school and

I remember that I was walking across the courtyard when I opened this letter up which said that I'd been picked to play against France and I just went nuts. Looking back, it was as proud a feeling I had then as I had when I won my first cap. We won that game against France 10-6, which was a great, great result; Craig Joiner, Hugh Gilmore and Cammie Murray were in that team and we all went on to play for Scotland.

I played quite a lot for Scotland A before getting capped; the biggest game I played for them was against the Springboks in 1994 down at the Greenyards when I was 19. It was 21-20 and they dropped a goal in the last minute to win it. Tiaan Strauss played, Dalton played; there were about six of them that went on to win the World Cup the following year, so it was a great memory and a super experience to come up against those kind of players when I was only really just out of school. The week after that was Jeremy Richardson's only Test for Scotland and the Boks ran out 43-10 winners, which put into perspective how good the A result had been.

I nearly got capped on tour to Argentina in 1994. I was 20 and we were in Buenos Aires and Graham Shiel went down with a blood injury; I was sitting miles up in this rickety old wooden-stepped stand and suddenly Jim Telfer was screaming at me to get my tracksuit off and get down onto the pitch. So I started making my way down, absolutely shitting myself about getting on and then Shielie just wiped the blood away and carried on, so I had to go all the way back up to my seat again and get my tracksuit back on – which is how I stayed for the rest of the game.

I eventually got capped in 1997 against France in the last match at the old Parc des Princes – which was some place. If you thought Buenos Aires was mad, the old Parc was even madder – brass bands and trumpets and drums and all sorts, and the crowd going wild. Craig Chalmers got laid out cold about 20 minutes in by Christophe Lamaison, so I got called down to replace him. I don't remember an awful lot about the match to be honest; all I really remember was how terrified I was getting ready to go on and then getting onto the pitch and the game was already pretty much gone by that stage. France were immense that season and went on to pick up the Grand Slam and they ran us absolutely ragged – a typical French display in late March in the sunshine – they were just running the ball from everywhere and were unstoppable.

I flew back straight after the game and headed off to the Sevens World Cup in Hong Kong first thing the next morning, so I didn't really get a chance to celebrate winning my first cap. In days gone by, Hong Kong might have been the perfect place to celebrate it, but because it was the World Cup, everything out there was taken really seriously. We ended up getting knocked out by Australia, who had guys like Campese playing for them. I did get one nice memento from Paris though – Ian Smith knicked one of the old brown leather match balls and gave it me, which I still have.

JAMIE MAYER (Edinburgh Reivers)
8 Caps: 1998-2000

There was a Scottish Thistles tour to New Zealand in the summer of 1997 for young players and when I missed out on that, I thought I was going to have to spend a fairly miserable summer training as hard as I could to try and get myself on the selection radar. But I learned a few days later that I had actually been selected for the main Scotland tour to South Africa, which was just the most brilliant news I could have imagined. I was 20 years old and it was my first involvement with the national squad. It was essentially a development tour and there were no Test matches because it took place at the same time as the Lions tour, but wherever we went the whole place was just rugby mad and the atmosphere around the country was incredible. We were training and playing these provincial matches and then would get together to watch the Lions in action. And there was a great moment when Tony Stanger was called up from our squad to join the Lions for the last ten days of their tour and played against the Northern Free State. If ever there was a tour to capture your imagination about the magic of international rugby and inspire you to work as hard as you could to try and reach those same heights, it was that 1997 Lions tour.

I remember sharing a room with Stuart Reid and, having never been on a tour like that before, I wasn't sure what the etiquette was regarding getting undressed in the room – did I get naked and go to the bathroom to do my teeth, or did I get undressed in the bathroom and go back to bed with a towel round me? Anyway, Stuart sensed my dilemma and in true touring tradition decided to wind the naïve new boy up. So when I came out of the bathroom he threw back the covers of his double bed and patted the mattress. 'Come on Jamie,' he purred, 'there's room in here for two.'

DUNCAN HODGE

My first start was against Australia in the autumn of 1997. I had been part of an extended 25-man squad, but I was one of three guys that got cut from that. Then Rowan Shepherd was injured in a club game the week before, so I got called in on the Tuesday and was picked to start at fullback. I had only ever played two minutes at fullback – for the Barbarians against Scotland in the Dunblane international – but the management played down my inexperience by saying I had played at fullback quite a bit. Australia were some team, but luckily they didn't test me out too much. They put one high ball up and I took it cleanly, but they weren't bothered about whether I was playing out of position and fairly inexperienced – they weren't going to alter how they played for that.

They kept the ball in hand most of the time and if they kicked it tended to be short dinks over our defence. It worked like a dream for them and they blew us away. That was Scott Murray's first Test and I think he scored from a driven line-out and we went into the lead at that stage, although it didn't last.

SCOTT MURRAY (Bedford Blues, Saracens, Edinburgh Gunners, US Montauban)
87 Caps: 1997-2007

I started playing rugby for Preston Lodge when I was about 16 and was selected for the Scottish Schools squad to play Ireland, but didn't get on the pitch. I then quit rugby for a while to focus on basketball, which I absolutely loved and which helped hone my handling skills as well as my athleticism – all things that really helped me in the line-out when I returned to rugby.

I was first capped against Australia in 1997 – alongside George Graham, Stuart Grimes, Adam Roxburgh, Grant McKelvey and James Craig. We were thumped pretty convincingly – I remember that monster Willie Ofahengaue running all over the place causing chaos and then George Gregan, Stephen Larkham and Joe Roff all cruising in for tries as well – but it was a pretty special moment for me because I started that match and scored a try.

ROWAN SHEPHERD

Things went from bad to worse when we played South Africa in the following game. You are always going to take a hiding now and again from a southern hemisphere team which is on top form – I just wish it hadn't been by that much. 68-10 it finished. It was so frustrating. I'd liken it to standing in the middle of the racetrack at Silverstone, one moment Percy Montgomery is flying past you, and you have only just recovered your bearings and then James Small flies past your other shoulder. It was pretty hard going.

We got quite a tough reception that night, we stayed in the hotel and a few fans gave us a bit of stick. They had a point – from their point of view we were dire – but you have to appreciate what we were up against as well.

The southern hemisphere big three transformed the game by having pace and power outside. Guys like James Small, Pieter Rossouw, Percy Montgomery from South Africa, as well as Christian Cullen and, of course, Jonah Lomu of New Zealand burst onto the scene. These guys were different animals to anything we had encountered before, and they were getting the sort of good go-forward ball which anyone would do well with the whole time – so they were virtually unstoppable.

GORDON BULLOCH

That was my first Scotland match and obviously it was a baptism of fire. But people forget it was only 14-3 at half-time – then all of a sudden it was 68-10. In your first game in international rugby you are just trying to stay afloat so maybe it wasn't as tough for me to take as it was for some of the more experienced guys, who had a better appreciation of what it was all about.

ROB WAINWRIGHT

Percy Montgomery put in one of the finest display I've ever seen by a full-back in that game. He was just a devastating attacking force. The Springboks were so powerful that autumn; they wanted to put a marker down after losing to the Lions in the summer and those performances really made people sit up and take notice – they scored a record 52 points at the Parc des Princes, a record 29 points at Twickenham, and then 68 against us at Murrayfield. It was some revenge on the northern hemisphere.

STEWART CAMPBELL

I've managed to block most of that game out of my memory, except for one of their tries, when we kicked-off and Andre Venter caught the ball and ran right back through our whole forward pack to score. I had a hugely strong urge just to walk off the pitch, I was so annoyed with myself and with everyone else. It was the only time I ever felt like that on a rugby pitch. It was horrible.

The southern hemisphere sides were always coming off the back of a season, so they were at their best, whereas we were thrown together with a week's training. So it was often the case that you were best not to play in the autumn internationals because the team would get stuffed and guys would be dropped for the Five Nations, leaving spaces in the side for you to come in without the baggage of having being hammered the last time you played an international match. It worked the same way for Nathan Hines and Euan Murray with the 2009 Lions – they were injured throughout most of the Six Nations and so missed the hidings Scotland took, and ended up being the only two Scots selected in the original tour party.

ROB WAINWRIGHT

In 1997 the team was tinkered with again and then after a run of poor results, which culminated in us losing to Italy in January 1998, the coaches were cut and I was dropped as captain. The SRU's dealings with Ritchie and David were not handled well, but I don't suppose there is an easy way to strip out your team management. What made it worse, from a personal point of view, was that I wasn't only stripped of the captaincy, but I was also stripped of my decision-making roles, such as calling the line-out and the back-row moves from scrums. They gave the task of calling the line-out to Simon Holmes, who was a fantastic player, but an open-side – not the most appropriate person to be calling a line-out – and I thought that that was just daft. They were trying to empower other players in the team, and I can appreciate the strategy, but it wasn't an easy time for the team. Morale was low.

In terms of the captaincy moving to Gary Armstrong, I wasn't too disappointed because I thought that Gary was a fantastic leader and he had been a very important player for me during my time as captain. When he was made captain I remember that Gary used to give me a wry old smile in the changing room after matches when he had just had to do the post-match interviews and I remember him once saying, 'There are some jobs that I wish you still did.' It's a difficult job doing those post-match interviews. It's pretty hellish to have to talk about a game that you've just lost, and you want to be respectful to the opposition when you win – I remember getting seriously annoyed reading or watching a post-match interview with the winning captain and our performance has just been dismissed as a side-show to how well his team has done. But I also remember John Beattie giving me a row once because I apologised for our performance after we lost to Italy in 1998. He said that I should never apologise – perhaps he thought it undermined my authority as captain – but it was something I wanted to do; we had just put in the most appalling performance and I wanted to apologise to all the fans. It was just how I felt.

12

FATE'S FAREWELL
TO FIVE

I NGENUITY. CHEMISTRY. DESTINY.

1999 was the last ever Five Nations Championship. And what a way it was to see off the grand old tournament before it became the Six Nations in the spring of the new millennium.

Despite the central roles played by Gregor Townsend, Tom Smith, Doddie Weir, Rob Wainwright and Alan Tait on the historic Lions tour to South Africa in 1997, the following season's campaign was a washout. In the autumn of 1997, Australia and South Africa hammered the Scots at Murrayfield, running in embarrassing scorelines of 37-8 and 68-10 respectively.

1998 started no better, with Scotland falling to a 22-21 defeat in Treviso to Italy in a precursor to the Five Nations Championship. This result cost Richie Dixon and David Johnston their jobs as coaches and Jim Telfer, reinvigorated by his success as part of the Lions brains-trust, returned to the fold in their stead. His impact was far from revolutionary, however, and Scotland's 17-16 victory over Ireland at Lansdowne Road was the last to be posted for a year. The team was humiliated 51-6 by France at Murrayfield, lost 19-13 to Wales at Wembley (the hosts' temporary home while the Millennium Stadium was under construction) and 34-20 in the Calcutta Cup.

Then came another summer from hell. The team travelled to the southern hemisphere to play Fiji in Suva and two Tests against Australia in Sydney and Brisbane. All three were pitifully one-sided, Fiji running out 51-26 winners and Australia hardly breaking sweat as they recorded 45-3 and 33-11 victories. The poor results were, however, somewhat silver-lined as Scotland were able to blood a number of youngsters and implemented a more expansive style of play which, although coming unstuck in the Test matches, started to show promise in the midweek games, particularly against Matt Williams' New South Wales side in Sydney, which Scotland won 34-10.

When the team returned home, their captain Rob Wainwright announced that the time had come to hang up his boots. He was a major personality in the squad and a hugely important player, but the team was fortunate enough to have a number of ready-made leaders in place to alleviate the impact of his loss. Bryan Redpath

---

Opposite: Alan Tait celebrates with Stuart Grimes after the lock forward scores against Ireland in 1999. *Getty Images*

assumed the captaincy in November, for South Africa's return to Edinburgh, but despite improvements in performance, an annus horribilis was sealed as they were steamrollered by the powerful Springboks 35-10.

So where were the team to turn as the last year of the twentieth century hove into sight? And a World Cup year no less. A World Cup hosted by Wales and in which Scotland would play their pool and quarter-final games at Murrayfield (should they qualify for the latter rounds). Performances had to improve beyond recognition in order for Scotland to pose any threat in the Five Nations and build confidence before the World Cup. The media believed Scotland had no chance of being successful in the 1999 Five Nations tournament and the bookmakers had them at 100-1 to lift the trophy. Yet it is often in times of extreme adversity that a team finds its true sense of collective purpose; when your backs are against the wall, when the whole world is against you, you are confronted with a moment of truth: you can either sink or swim. If you can overcome this adversity, be confident in your ability, belligerent in your attitude and be prepared to push yourselves to the very limit of your physical capacities, you can become a different creature altogether.

Ingenuity. Chemistry. Destiny. Three words that seemed, in 1998, to be totally removed from the Scottish rugby team. But they were three words that would define their season in 1999. Three words that went hand-in-hand with three little quirks of fate that changed the fortunes of the men who bore the thistle upon their chests.

First, thanks to the advent of professionalism, the movement of players looking to ply their trade abroad increased significantly. Either through residential qualification or through ancestry, a growing number of players from the southern hemisphere began to seek out new careers abroad with the hope that they might achieve recognition on the international stage.

Representing a country other than the land of one's birth was not a new phenomenon of the professional era. From English-born James Marsh who famously played for Scotland in 1889 while at Edinburgh University before switching his allegiance to play for England against Ireland in 1892, to the prolific Melbourne-born and New Zealand-bred Ian 'the Flying Scotsman' Smith, who scored 24 tries for Scotland from 1924-33, to the Kilted Kiwi Sean Lineen, and with over 130 internationalists being capped out of London Scottish, Scotland have fielded a substantial number of players born beyond its borders. Now a new generation of faces from around the world were lighting up Scottish rugby and adding depth to the club and international squads. Among the sudden influx were South African prop Matthew Proudfoot, Kiwi back-row Gordon Simpson and his compatriot winger Shaun Longstaff, each of whom made significant contributions to the Scottish cause both domestically and internationally.

Arguably, however, the three most influential imports in the new professional age came in the shape of fullback Glenn Metcalfe, who qualified through his Glasgow-born grandmother, and centre and back-row brothers John and Martin Leslie, sons of former All Black captain Andy Leslie, who qualified through their Linlithgow-born grandfather.

Metcalfe joined Glasgow in 1996 and made his Scotland debut against Australia in Sydney on the 1998 summer tour; his intelligent angles of running, his accurate passing and kicking, and his ability to jink and step at speed made him a dangerous attacking weapon from fullback, where his defence was also of the highest standard.

John Leslie captained Otago to the NPC title in October 1998 and he and his brother travelled north to Scotland shortly afterwards. John was selected for Glasgow Caledonians against the touring Springboks and impressed immediately with an outstanding individual performance. He was then selected to play against the same opposition in the Murrayfield Test match on 21 November while his brother took a place on the bench.

Martin Leslie was the perfect replacement for the retired Rob Wainwright – a powerful ball-carrier, a canny operator at the breakdown and player who always led from the front.

INGENUITY

In the build-up to the tournament, Telfer had adopted many of the lessons he had learned with the 1997 Lions and had made a point of empowering his players as much as possible, encouraging them to take leading roles in training, during the match-day preparations and, crucially, on the field of play itself. One of the initiatives that the senior players concocted as the tournament loomed was to mix-up their approach to kick-offs; they wanted to play as unpredictably as they could, to keep the opposition guessing at every turn and to be bold in their attacking play.

As the dying bars of Flower of Scotland faded into the early evening air on 6 February, Duncan Hodge stepped up to the centre sport on Murrayfield's halfway line, his forwards to his right, flicking the ball lightly in his hands as he prepared to launch the ball high into the heart of the Welsh pack that stood in wait before them.

As referee Ed Morrison blew his whistle, Hodge twisted and dabbed the ball high and left. It soared end over end into open space and began to fall towards Welsh fullback Shane Howarth. Murrayfield was still echoing with the din of the crowd as they settled themselves into their seats after the anthems. Now the noise rose again like a torrent as the tall, rangy frame of John Leslie, who had been quietly stationed to Hodge's left, stretched out his long legs, his eyes never leaving the rotating ball as it soared, peaked and began to make its decent. Howarth scuttled to place himself under the ball, but just as he reached to gather it, Leslie extended one long arm and snatched the ball from the former All Black's grasp. After a slight juggle, Leslie adjusted his stride and the final 30 metres to the try-line lay open before him. The thunder of the crowd erupted around the stadium as he glided effortlessly across the final yards to the whitewash and into rugby history with the fastest try ever to be scored in an international match.

Wales were a good side, filled with Lions and all-time greats in Scott Gibbs, Rob

Howley, Neil Jenkins, Alan Bateman, Scott Quinnell and future stars in Martyn Williams, Colin Charvis and Dafydd James, but they were undone by a brilliant side inspired from the off by Scotland's ingenuity and, ultimately, from the second quirk of fate that was to strike Scotland's campaign.

It was a quirk which was tainted by misfortune; 24 year old Hodge was Scotland's fly-half incumbent, having taken possession of the pivotal shirt from Gregor Townsend for the South African Test in November. It is a testament to the cruelty of sport that the broken leg that he sustained during the match against Wales was the key factor that turned around Scotland's ailing fortunes of the previous two years. Despite their wonderful start, the team had gone in at half-time 13-8 down. When Hodge was injured in the 48th minute, Townsend was moved in from outside centre to fly-half and Alan Tait came off the bench to fill the space at outside centre. In the final quarter of the game, Townsend gathered a loose ball just inside the Welsh half to dart under the posts, Tait ran a clever line off his stand-off to score, and the game was sealed by a rumble from a lineout by second-row Scott Murray, securing a 33-20 victory.

CHEMISTRY

A cruel twist of fate had robbed Duncan Hodge of any further involvement in the tournament that year and the introduction of Tait also robbed promising young centre Jamie Mayer, who had emerged during the tour to Australia, of any chance of a starting place. Gregor Townsend at 10. John Leslie at 12. Alan Tait at 13. It was a combination that clicked so seamlessly that it was as if they had been playing together for years. If ever three players were made to play together in the blue of Scotland, it was these three. Townsend was the conjuror, Leslie the steady and intelligent co-conductor, Tait the bustling powerhouse outside them. All three were capable of magic with ball-in-hand and incisive running angles in attack and together they proved to be an obdurate brick-wall in defence.

But while Townsend, Leslie and Tait were the pivots around which the Scottish attack thrived, the ball that was supplied to them was often first-class and the finishing outside them was deadly.

Throughout the tournament, the front-row of Tom Smith, Gordon Bulloch and Paul Burnell were powerful and dynamic. The second row of Scott Murray and Stuart Grimes were maestros on their own lineout ball, rapacious snafflers on the opposition's throw, and athletic around the park. The back-row combinations of Peter Walton, Martin Leslie, Eric Peters, Budge Pountney and Stuart Reid were powerful, cunning and skilful. Gary Armstrong, the bull-necked controller at scrum-half, was the perfect link between his mobile forward pack and his mesmeric backline, and out wide the running skills of Kenny Logan and young Cammie Murray combined wonderfully with the mazy running of Metcalfe.

The following week, Scotland travelled down to Twickenham for the Calcutta

Cup. In the opening quarter of the match, it seemed that Scotland would be blown away by the mighty English team as Nick Beal and Dan Luger ran in two quick tries and the Scottish pack were pounded by their physically superior opposition.

But the self-belief garnered from the win over Wales had penetrated deeply and the will to attack with flair, speed and aggression had been imbedded throughout this Scotland squad. Minutes later, Eric Peters secured a loose ball at a lineout and it was swiftly fed by Armstrong to Townsend who was flat on the gainline. He offloaded out of the tackle to Martin Leslie who in turn slipped the ball out of contact to Scott Murray and the lock was able to deftly move the ball just as Tait was hitting the line outside him to cross for the score. It was full of energy and skill and was thrilling in every way.

The teams retired to the changing rooms at half-time with England ahead 17-7 thanks Jonny Wilkinson's penalty adding to his two conversions of the early tries. Despite the ten-point deficit, Scottish confidence remained high. They were beginning to gain parity in the forward exchanges and their angles of running were causing the English defence all manner of problems.

Shortly after the match was resumed, Townsend ran a wrap-around move with Armstrong and used John Leslie as a decoy runner to release Tait into space. The former rugby league giant hit the gap like a bullet train and then arced away from the covering defence. As he surged to the try line, he was met by Luger and as if in defiance to the winger's earlier try celebrations he stepped towards him, dipped his shoulder and thumped him back as he crossed to score.

England extended their lead through a converted try by Tim Rodber, but Townsend soon ensured that the match would finish with a thrilling dénouement as he intercepted a pass between substitute scrum-half Kyran Bracken and Mike Catt to dart home under the posts.

In the end, England held out to retain the Calcutta Cup and to extend their unbeaten run of victories at Twickenham over Scotland to 16 with the 24-21 scoreline. It could have been different had Logan, who was carrying a leg strain, not missed three eminently kickable penalties, while Wilkinson – as he would do so often during his career – produced an immaculate kicking display.

Scotland had a month's break between the England game and Ireland coming to Edinburgh in March. The SRU arranged a fixture at Murrayfield against Italy on 6 March, which Scotland won 30-12 thanks to tries from Logan, Cammie Murray and, again, Townsend. It was a stuffy game, as Scotland-Italy fixtures tend to be, but it provided a good work-out for the team in preparation for the Ireland match.

Ireland were also a team full of confidence, with a monstrous and talented front-five, and wit and skill out wide. Ulster had won the Heineken Cup in 1998 and their domestic game was in rude health. They were captained by Paddy Johns and boasted several Lions in the talismanic Keith Woods, Paul Wallace, Jeremy Davidson and Eric Millar, and in fly-half David Humphries they had one of the finest controllers of the game in Europe. The game was only minutes old when Humphries scored a try to put the visitors in the lead. In the first three rounds of the competition they had lost to France and England at Lansdowne Road but had beaten Wales at Wembley and were playing some decent rugby. For the crowd, things looked ominous. And then Scotland came alive. Over the next 70 minutes they played with control, ambition and wondrous skill, battering their visitors with relentless waves of cleverly angled runs, superb territorial kicking, quick rucking and offloading, eating up the yards towards the opposition try-line with a seemingly unstoppable rhythm and tempo. The majesty of their play that day was epitomised by a length-of-the-field try which began in the shadow of their own posts and swept irresistibly up field before Stuart Grimes dived over in the corner. Townsend continued his impressive scoring run, dotting down after collecting an offload from John Leslie and stretching through a despairing tackle from Keith Wood. Two tries for Cammie Murray plus two conversions and two penalties from the boot of Logan saw Scotland home 33-13 and into second spot on the table behind England.

And so the final weekend of the tournament approached. Ireland had completed their fixtures at Murrayfield, leaving Scotland to play France in Paris and Wales to host England at Wembley. Scotland's preparations for arguably the toughest venue in the whole competition were marred by Tom Smith's leg break in the Ireland match, followed by the withdrawal of Eric Peters after he shattered his kneecap playing for Bath. David Hilton was brought in for Smith and Budge Pountney and Stuart Reid came in to win their second caps at blind-side flanker and number eight.

Although France were having a disappointing season by their standards, they had won back-to-back Grand Slams in 1997 and 1998 and were always incredibly strong when they played at home.

Parisian mind games were in plain evidence from the start of proceedings as the famously jovial brass band produced a slow funereal dirge for Flower of Scotland before sparking into life for La Marseillaise. The partisan French crowd were in the mood for blood and the game was barely two minutes old when Thomas Castaignede, the elfin genius of the French backline, sniped through the Scottish defensive line and deep into their 22 before setting up a ruck from which a series of delightfully delivered passes released Emile Ntamack to score in the corner.

Scotland had been here before. Away from home they had leaked two soft tries to England and then fought back to the brink of victory. Against Ireland they had opened their arms to allow Humphreys to score early before surging back into the ascendancy. Going down by five points to France was not ideal, especially in somewhere as imposing at the Stade de France, but there were still 78 minutes on the clock. They would strike back, they were sure. No one, however, not even the players, imagined that they would strike back in quite the manner that they did.

In the act of setting up the ruck from which his team scored, Castaignede had twisted his knee and was carried from the field. His departure cast a shadow over the hearts of the French team and supporters while serving as a catalyst to galvanise the Scottish effort. And what followed was perhaps the most extraordinary 17 minutes in Scottish rugby history.

Scotland scored five mesmerising tries and four conversions in that short period. Attacking from deep with the flair and élan normally so associated with their hosts and with an accuracy that had typified so much of Scotland's play during the season, they scored three tries in the space of six minutes from Martin Leslie, Tait and Townsend – who, in doing so, completed a remarkable run of scoring in every Championship match that year, making him only the fifth player ever to achieve the feat, and the first British player since Scotsman AC Wallace in 1925. Martin Leslie's try came only two minutes after Ntamack's opener and Tait's almost immediately after the resultant kick-off thanks to a coruscating break by Metcalfe after he was released by a deft offload from Tait, who returned the ball to the British and Irish Lion seventy metres later to score.

French number eight Christophe Juillet then added to the score-fest off the back of a powerful scrum on the Scottish line, but in the spirit of this truly bizarre match, Tait crossed for his second try only minutes later after another dazzling break from Metcalfe, Tait's expression almost bemused as he stared out into the crowd behind the posts and sunk to his knees to touch the ball down.

Just minutes later Scotland were on the attack again, Townsend scything through the French ranks on a fifty metre run only to be brought down just shy of the tryline. He popped the ball up to the supporting Martin Leslie who slid through to score his second try.

Gavin Hastings, up in the media gallery commentating for the BBC, was rendered virtually speechless by the events unfolding before him.

As the final moments of the first-half drew to a close, Christophe Dominici lanced off his wing and through flailing Scottish tackles to score the eighth try of the half and to raise some hope for the home team. As Clayton Thomas blew for halftime the score stood at 22-33.

If the first-half had been an exhibition of attacking flair and dynamism, the second-half was an outstanding display of attritional and full-blooded defence. 55 points had been scored in the first-half; in the second there were only three – one penalty from the boot of Kenny Logan – and at no point did the Scottish defence look like breaking. They left Paris triumphant, joint top of the table with England and with their highest-ever points win over their Gallic cousins.

DESTINY

On Sunday 11 April, Wales hosted England in the last ever match of the Five Nations, 89 years after the tournament had expanded from the four Home Unions to include France among their number. The following year, Italy's inclusion would see the tournament rebranded as the Six Nations.

As the Scotland players, management and fans awoke bleary-eyed from celebrating their Parisian triumphs, thoughts turned to their place in the Five Nations table. They were currently top after their win over France, ahead of England on points-difference. If Wales were to do the unimaginable and topple the mighty English, Scotland would win the tournament. It was a wild speculation. A dream. But the greatest draw of any sporting occasion is the capacity to hope and to dream; and on that spring Sunday morning, Scots around the world dared to do just that.

England, however, were in no mood for the speculative optimism of those from the north. They were heading into the match full of confidence, looking to seal their twelfth Grand Slam. Despite enduring their own summer of hell in 1998, they had recovered their poise and class to defeat South Africa 13-7 in the autumn, to hold out in their tournament opener against Scotland, and then to overwhelm Ireland 27-15 at Lansdowne Road and France 21-10 at Twickenham.

Wales, after promising so much at the outset of the season, had had something of a mixed tournament. They had lost to Scotland and Ireland, but had then defeated France 34-33 in another Stade de France thriller and backed up that victory by thumping Italy 60-21 in a friendly in Treviso.

England looked formidable, but there was something in the air in the spring of 1999. It was as if Serendipity herself wanted to bid the Five Nations farewell in her own inimitable way. Injury had both colluded against and inspired the Scottish campaign, and twists of fate had wound ethereally to bring together combinations that seemed to the manor born.

England started the match at Wembley as strongly as they had done against Scotland at Twickenham, scoring two scorching early tries through Dan Luger and Steve Hanley. They were all power and speed, dominating proceedings with muscle and intelligent running angles and passing.

But despite their supremacy, they couldn't shake Wales from their coat-tails. The prolific boot of fly-half Neil Jenkins kept the dragon's fire smouldering and his team in the game three-points at a time. As half-time approached, Jenkins had pulled back the deficit to bring the score level at 15-15. A Wilkinson penalty and a converted Richard Hill try looked to re-establish some breathing space for the English going into the break, only for Jenkins to strike again with another penalty to take the teams in at 18-25.

Emerging from the tunnel, Wales burst back into life and after a period of sustained pressure they at last crossed the English line through Shane Howarth. Jenkins' conversion took the score to 25-25. But England were soon back in the ascendancy again with two quick-fire Wilkinson penalties and were beginning to look stronger and stronger as the closing stages drew in.

The clock ticked to 75 minutes. And the final quirk of fate in Scotland's campaign showed itself. England were awarded a penalty halfway between the

Welsh 22 and the ten-metre line. A penalty kick at goal would stretch their lead to 34-25, more than a converted try clear of their opponents. Captain Lawrence Dallaglio glanced up at the posts and tossed the ball to Wilkinson. 'Go for the corner,' he said. 'We'll take the try.'

Ninety seconds later, after a powerful rolling maul, Mike Catt hoisted a Garryowen under the Welsh posts, which was only just gathered by Welsh centre Mark Taylor. Tackled in the process of taking the catch, Wales were awarded a scrum; Rob Howley swept the ball to Jenkins who put in a booming kick, and the Welsh lines were cleared.

Wales had survived. But time was running out. They were six points adrift and needed a converted score to steal the victory. Save for a few rampages from the giant brothers Scott and Craig Quinnell and Howarth's try, the English defensive line had held strong all afternoon. The talismanic figure of Scott Gibbs, a hero of the Lions tour two years previously, had been well-marshalled by the English midfield and back-row and his efforts to scythe through their ranks in the way that Tait had done at Twickenham just a few weeks earlier had been met by staunch English tackles time after time. There seemed no way through.

But then Tim Rodber offered a chink of light with a high tackle on Colin Charvis 40 metres from the Welsh line, which gave Jenkins the opportunity to stab a penalty kick down to the English 22.

Two minutes to go.

Could one of the Quinnell boys or Gibbs or Jenkins conjure something in the dying seconds of the match, something to sneak the win, to break English hearts and deliver ecstasy to their Celtic brothers in Scotland? In the stadium, and all around the world, rugby fans were on the edge of their seats, their eyes fixed on the dramatic closing moments playing out on the Wembley turf before them.

And above the stadium, as twilight set over the Five Nations, Serendipity smiled a fond farewell to the old tournament and made her final play . . .

Chris Wyatt won a shortened line-out, Howley fed Scott Quinnell, Quinnell juggled the ball for control and managed to slip it to Gibbs who hit an identical line to the one Tait had taken off Armstrong at Twickenham. He burst through Rodber, fended off Neil Back, arced his run around Matt Dawson, slid past Wilkinson and skipped past Matthew Perry, raised his arm in triumph and dived into history. 30-31.

Jenkins lined up the ball for the conversion. Stepping back, he picked a bit of mud from his studs, wiped his palms on his shorts and subconsciously waved a guiding hand towards the posts. Three steps. Contact. The ball sailed straight and true.

There was less than a minute left on the clock as England kicked-off. They were lucky. Wales spilled the ball and England were awarded the scrum. There was still time for them to snatch the win. Dallaglio controlled the ball at the base and

Dawson fed to Catt, who struck a drop at goal. It went wide. Howarth gathered, called the mark and then rifled the ball into the sea of red beyond the touchline. The Championship was Scotland's.

DUNCAN HODGE

We went on tour to Australia in the summer of 1998. It was a first tour for guys like Jamie Mayer, Gordon McIlwham, Matt Proudfoot, Glenn Metcalfe and Gordon Simpson. We had a great time out there and although we struggled in the Tests, we did pretty well against the midweek teams. I remember playing against Queensland in Brisbane and Jim Telfer gave us an absolute rollicking before we went out, picking on players and saying how bad they had been playing in previous games and that if they ever wanted to play for Scotland again then they would have to pull their socks up and go out and perform, which luckily we did and I remember Glenn Metcalfe having a fantastic game. Jim's bollockings were pretty scary, I have to say – even though a lot of the older boys said that he was mellowing by that time. It's true that he didn't victimise certain players time after time as he supposedly did in the old days with guys like Kenny Milne and Derek White, but you still didn't want to get on the wrong side of one of his bollockings.

The trip to Fiji was ridiculous. We left the dirt-trackers in Melbourne for three or four days to have a great time while the match squad flew over to Fiji. We arrived at around midnight the night before the game and didn't manage to have a run-through or anything beforehand. It was meant to be one of these SAS in-and-out jobs but it completely backfired. We arrived late, as I say, and then the next day we had this four-hour long trip in a roasting bus, got to this massive bowl of a ground which was as hard as concrete and then took on a Fijian team that were totally in their element. I could see the idea behind the way the trip was organised, but it didn't work and they were all over us for the whole 80 minutes. That was Hugh Gilmore's only cap and Derrick Lee was doing the goal-kicking . . . although he didn't get many opportunities.

ROWEN SHEPHERD

I came on as a sub and it was a classic Scottish disaster. We had all flown to Australia for a week acclimatising on the Gold Coast, which we thought was the dog's bollocks, then 22 of us flew to Fiji to play in that game, and we were caught cold. We'd had to sit in a rickety old bus with no air-conditioning – windows open to try and generate a draft – right across Fiji; turned up at the ground without a clue as to what to expect and discovered a hard, bumpy pitch; the crowd were going bananas as every bounce of the ball went their way; they were throwing it about all over the place and we were chasing shadows. Back then teams didn't run it from their own 22 and off-load the ball like they were doing, and against rugby like that you have to be up to speed from minute one because you can't play catch-up. It finished 51-26.

STEWART CAMPBELL

The ground in Suva was basically a big natural bowl, no seats just huge grassy slopes, with about 20,000 folk there. And if anybody made a mistake, all the crowd did was laugh at the top of their voices. It was the weirdest sensation, because you were expecting the sort of groan we were used to at Murrayfield, but they would just hoot with laughter. It didn't matter if it was us or the Fijians who had messed-up, they just found it hilarious.

They are brought up with rugby so they know the game and they know the skills. They were good supporters – there was no noise when the kickers were lining up their shots at goal – and when they laughed it wasn't malicious, they were just enjoying themselves.

ROWAN SHEPHERD

It was a bit of a wake-up call because we ended up having quite a good tour of Australia. We beat New South Wales in Sydney, a very young midweek team lost to Queensland by a single score, and quite a few guys earned their spurs on that tour – which was valuable for the next season.

JAMIE MAYER

That tour was a fantastic trip and it was probably the first time that I became a serious contender for the Test team. I spent several weeks before the tour working specifically on leg drive and power training which enabled me to literally hit the ground running when we arrived in Australia. I

Rowan Shepherd makes a point to his teammates during the 1998 Test match against Australia at Ballymore. *Getty Images*

spent the first two weeks of the tour training because I wasn't included in the mini tour party to Fiji – which given the feedback from that trip was probably a good thing – and so I was as fit as I'd ever been and raring to go by the time they got back. The result against Fiji meant that the management decided to shake things up a bit in the team and it gave me an excellent opportunity to show what I was able to do. I played well in the midweek games and was disappointed to miss out on a Test place against the Wallabies, but I knew that I was making progress and was becoming increasingly comfortable in the Scotland environment. The tour itself was mainly dry, but we still had one or two great nights out, particularly in Melbourne while the Test squad were in Fiji and again at the end of the tour, and those nights were fantastic for bringing a young squad together and integrating them with the old hands.

GLENN METCALFE (Glasgow Hawks, Glasgow Warriors)
38 Caps: 1998-2003

I came to Scotland to play club rugby with Glasgow Academicals as the coach at the time was the former Waikato rugby coach Kevin Greene. My Gran was from Glasgow which allowed me the work permit to stay and also qualified me to play for Scotland. My initial intention was only to stay for a year or so and travel Europe at the end of the season. I worked at Greaves Sports in Glasgow for a year before gaining a district contract with Glasgow. Then with the formation of the Glasgow Hawks in 1998 and the success that coming season things started to change for me and I got selected for an extended Scotland training squad and then I was selected for the summer tour to Australia – so suddenly I went from bumming around Europe for a year and playing a bit of club rugby to realising that I might actually get a chance to play international rugby. It wasn't something that had even crossed my mind as a possibility six months earlier, so it was a real whirlwind experience.

I remember after not being selected for the Fiji match the remainder of the squad flew to Melbourne while the Test squad flew out to Fiji. We had a great night out in Melbourne and I think it may have ended with some tackling practice in the hotel hallway . . . which resulted in a rather large hole made in the wall. When the Test squad returned from Fiji the hotel management had a word to our management; Jim Telfer wasn't in the best of moods after the Fiji trip and this just made matters even worse. So all the dirt-trackers were summoned for a meeting with Jim. Well, I thought my tour was over before it had started as he completely tore strips off of us. He was furious. I can't remember what he said now – I think I've blocked it from my memory – but I'm sure you couldn't print it anyway. After that I never used the hotel lift at all just in case I got trapped in it with Jim.

I arrived on the tour after a successful year with Glasgow Hawks in Div 2 and had a real spring in my step. I was selected for the Victoria and New South Wales matches and after having won both games well I gained selection for the first Test against Australia. I couldn't believe that in such a short space of time I was about to run out in an international match. What made it even better was that most of my family had flown over from New Zealand and were there to watch. I admit I went from brimming with confidence to being a nervous wreck at kick-off. It wasn't really a memorable result as we were trounced by the Wallabies but I was immensely proud to play in front of my family and playing Test rugby was the most thrilling feeling I had ever experienced.

ROWAN SHEPHERD

The Tests against Australia were fairly credible despite the score-lines and a big learning curve. I remember David Johnston trying to get the backs to play a bit more of an expansive game. It was one of the last old-fashioned type tours – we went to play New South Wales Country away out in the sticks and Victoria down in Melbourne. And I don't think it is any coincidence that we had quite a good season after that trip.

DUNCAN HODGE

We got back and Rob Wainwright decided to retire. There was a bit said in the press about it – such an influential guy deciding to retire when we were only a year out from the World Cup – but in the squad we just got on with it. When a guy decides to retire, it's very much a personal decision. For whatever reason – be it a physical thing that the body just can't take it any more, or a personal reason that the fire for the game has gone, or for family reasons or whatever – once that decision is made you can't feel aggrieved about it. Rob was a great player and a great leader, but there are always guys coming through that will step into any retiring player's shoes. It's the nature of the game. No, we were all sad to see Rob retire, but no one questioned his decision; it was his to make and he was able to retire on his own terms, which is a rare thing in this game.

ROB WAINWRIGHT

If the game had still been amateur I would have announced my retirement after the last Test against the Wallabies. I had been reinstated as captain on that tour because Gary was injured and it had been nice to lead the team again. But as it was, I felt that I needed to speak to Jim Telfer about my decision to see what he thought. He said that I was still an important player and he wanted me to carry on for another season. It was a nice boost to my ego so I decided to stay on, but by the time the autumn came around I knew that my time was up – my body just couldn't take any more punishment – and I realised that it would be better for the team if I dropped out. Martin Leslie obviously then came in in my stead and although I didn't approve of the manner in which he was brought in, he was a fantastic player and great servant to Scottish rugby and his brother helped create the most exciting midfield Scotland have ever had. Seeing the success they had the following season wasn't frustrating as such – I felt no desire to be out there, so I knew my decision to retire had been right, and I was so pleased for them to achieve what they did because I was still very close friends with many of them – but at the same time, when Wales beat England I just thought, *Why couldn't they have done that in 1995 or 1996?*, because a result like that would have allowed me to experience a Championship win with Scotland, which I think those teams in '95 and '96 deserved.

I have to admit that I regret agreeing to play for Dundee High at the tail-end of my career because I never played well for them. I'm not one of those players who could drop down into club rugby easily and perform well – my focus was always on a higher level and I couldn't gear myself into that kind of rugby in the same way. I do remember playing alongside a young Jonny Petrie though and thinking how electric he was – it was a rather poignant moment for me because I could relate to the way he was playing, the energy and the intensity, because I had been just the same at his age and you could see that he would go on to play international rugby; but at the same time it made me realise that my body really had had enough – all the injuries I'd carried for years had slowed me down and I just wasn't that effective any more. I knew then that my decision to retire from professional and international rugby had definitely been the right one to make.

Looking back, the North and Midlands was my favourite team. One of my greatest enjoyments of playing rugby was being part of a team which had great team-spirit and produced more as a group than the constituent parts suggested we would – as we did with Scotland in '96. That North and Midlands team was filled with great characters and players like Danny Herrington, Jonny Mason, Stewart Campbell and Dave McIvor. It was a shame when that North and Midlands team was subsumed into the Glasgow set-up, but if ever I wanted a club name to appear next to mine – and because my job in the army moved me around a lot, I played for a lot of clubs – it would be that one.

JIM TELFER

We are not the only team to scour the earth looking to strengthen our quality and depth by finding players born outside our borders. And it is not a new phenomenon either – it has been going on for years all over the world and the teams like New Zealand and Australia are probably the best at doing it by recruiting all the Pacific Islanders, but they get little or no real flak for it. Guys like Glenn Metcalfe and Shaun Longstaff were playing club rugby in Scotland and you could see that they would make a difference to our team on the international stage. They were qualified, so they were selected. Simple as that. We did look to bring in some other players, though, but I was comfortable with that as long as we didn't go overboard with the concept. We were lacking real depth in some positions and so were recommended players who qualified for us – like tight-head Matt Proudfoot and back-row Gordon Simpson. They all bought into Scottish rugby and were fully committed to the cause. I was as happy to select them as I was to select Damian Cronin or Budge Pountney. They committed themselves to Scotland and were legitimately qualified, so that was all I needed to know. It was the same with guys like Cammie Mather, Andrew Mower and Nathan Hines and I'm sure other coaches have had the same attitude towards guys like Simon Danielli, Simon Webster, Dan Parks, Scott Gray, Jim Hamilton, Alex Grove, Hugo Southwell and Thom and Max Evans.

The next two players to emerge on the radar at that time were Martin and

John Leslie attacks the Springboks' defensive line for Glasgow Caledonians. His form was so impressive in this match that he was picked for Scotland's Test match against the tourists on 21 November. *Getty Images*

John Leslie. They had great pedigree and were keen to come to Scotland and they made an immediate impact. In his first game for Glasgow Caledonians against the touring Springboks, John looked like the only home player who actually wanted to take the game to the South Africans. He was intelligent and forthright and made of exactly the right kind of stuff that I wanted in a centre. I knew that he would help raise the standards of those around him, and the same was true of Martin – he was hard working and abrasive and a very intelligent player.

JAMIE MAYER

I will never forget that game against South Africa in the autumn of 1998. I was 21 years old and was winning my first cap in my home stadium against the world champions. It was the most incredible experience. And the speed of the game was something else. I remember being tackled by Bobby Skinstad early in the first-half and then getting up and sprinting across the field to the next breakdown . . . only to see Bobby running past me and beating me to the breakdown with some ease. I knew then that Test rugby was a completely different ball-game to anything I had been involved in before. That game was a hard lesson in international rugby for the whole team, but it gave me a salutary lesson that I would have to raise my game at least two or three notches just to be competitive.

I had a relatively short international career and I cherish the memory of every minute of it. We had some great players coming together at the end of the nineties and into the next decade. Players like Tom Smith, Scotty Murray, Gregor Townsend, Alan Tait and John Leslie get spoken about all the time, but the whole squad was full of quality. Duncan Hodge had a fabulous service and he could pass the ball off both hands onto a sixpence – his passing allowed me to take gambles on the opposition defence and he was able to put me

Alan Tait in action against South Africa in November 1998.
Getty Images

through holes. I played with Duncan at club and then district level, and I wish we could have played more together at Test level. Martin Leslie and Budge Pountney, although quite different players, both read the game brilliantly and were always close by to get me out of a scrape. Graham Shiel was probably the best centre I played with – we just seemed to understand each other on the pitch. Sometimes that happens, without any work or previous game-time together and I think it was the same with us as it had been for John Leslie and Taity when they played together.

GORDON BULLOCH

For a lot of guys, 1998 had been their first Five Nations, so in 1999 they were a bit more experienced. On top of that the Leslie brothers had arrived from New Zealand, which gave us a lot more nous around the field.

Toony was at his peak, Taity could always sniff a try out, and John Leslie was the missing link we had been crying out for to get that backline really firing. He and Toony were on the same wavelength and I think they saw things – opportunities – that nobody else in the team would see. We scored 16 tries in four matches that year which is an unbelievable statistic when you think about it. We really had a cutting edge – which we've probably not had since.

The forwards were all good, good players and we worked well as a unit. Scott Murray and Stuart Grimes were a tremendous partnership in the second-row, Paul Burnell had been there and done it all before and in Tom Smith we had the best loose-head prop in the world.

TOM SMITH (Dundee HSFP, Watsonians, Glasgow Caledonians, Brive and Northampton Saints)
61 Caps: 1997-2005

When I joined Dundee High after I left school at Rannoch, there was an old prop, a bit of a local legend, called Danny Herrington. Danny took the view that a young prop should have his share of bad experiences before trying to inflict them on other people and he basically shoved my head up my arse in training twice a week every week for what seemed like years. In my position, you need brute strength and a highly-developed survival instinct. That's what Danny taught me. It was a hell of a learning curve and the lessons that he taught me were carried through the rest of my career.

I've suffered from epileptic seizures – Grand Mals, they call them – since I was 18. Until around 2006, the attacks always happened in my sleep, but then I had a waking attack, which meant I had to forfeit my driving licence for 12 months. I had to be careful not to return to rugby too quickly after an attack, because the short-term memory loss can be very acute. I played a Calcutta Cup match after having a seizure on the day of the game, which was not the best idea I've ever had and it definitely affected my performance. But I am incredibly fortunate to have had such a long career in professional sport in spite of my epilepsy. I am involved with a number of charities these days and I think that it's very important to talk of it openly because I want other sufferers to know that epilepsy doesn't have to be a barrier to achievement. You just have to manage your life in a different way, but that is something that all sorts of sportsmen and people in other walks of life have to deal with as well, and it should never inhibit your aspirations to achieve your goals.

GORDON BULLOCH

Momentum is everything, and we got the 1999 Six Nations off to the best start we could possibly hope for against Wales with John Leslie scoring that try within 10 seconds of kick-off. We had decided beforehand that we wanted to use the kick-off as an offensive weapon – whereas now they tend to use the restart to establish field position. We also knew the right winger, Matthew Robinson, was coming in for his first cap, and with a huge atmosphere the last thing he would want was to get stuck under a high ball.

John Leslie stretches his legs as he prepares to make history with the fastest try to be scored in international rugby. *Press Association*

So it was a planned move for Hodgey to kick it that way and fortunately it came off – Shane Howarth came forward to cover for Robinson but it was just too far for him to take it comfortably before John snatched the ball away from him and galloped home unchallenged to break the record for the fastest try in the history of international rugby. It gave us such a huge boost. When something you have worked on earlier in the week comes off it is great for confidence.

SCOTT MURRAY

1999 was my first Five Nations. I had been in and around the squad for a while, but that was my first taste of the Championship – and to experience it for the first time at home against Wales was a great way to start – and then to score just capped it all, it was brilliant. It was my first win for Scotland at Test level; I had also played against Wales eight times at various age-grade levels, but it was the first time I had beaten them, so all-in-all it really was a fantastic day – although really, really tough on Doddie and Hodgey.

DODDIE WEIR

1999 was just one of those things. I broke my ankle in the first 40 minutes of that game against Wales, which wasn't very clever, and Duncan Hodge and I ended up in hospital together. *C'est la vie.* It was the same with the '97 Lions when I had my knee injured – that's life. It was a great achievement by the boys on both occasions and I can at least say that I managed to play some part in the '99 Championship, even if it was only for a half.

DUNCAN HODGE

We got a penalty about ten minutes into the second-half and I kicked to touch . . . and missed. Shane Howarth caught it and, as you do when you make a mistake like I had, I hared after it. He started running towards me and all that I can remember going through my mind was the video analysis we had done on him – that he always stepped off his right foot. So I was chasing up on him thinking, 'He's going to go off his right foot . . . his right foot,' and getting ready to tackle him with my right shoulder. Now, I don't remember very much after that. Gregor is convinced that I was concussed; Scott Gibbs had taken a crash ball into me in the first-half – which I don't remember, which pretty much vindicates Gregor's assessment – and shortly after that Gregor made a call on one of set-pieces. He called 'Wasps' which was just a 10-12 cut, just a basic move, and I was apparently asking him what a 'Wasps' was. Well, I was chasing up on Howarth and he stepped off his right foot; I adjusted my weight to hit him with my right shoulder but I was wearing blade-studs in my boots and they just caught in the ground; all my weight went to the right but my foot stayed where it was and *snap* . . . there went my fibula.

ALAN TAIT (Kelso, Newcastle Falcons)
27 Caps: 1987-1999

I knew that the 1999 Five Nations would be my last Championship, so I wanted to try and go out in a big way and coming off the bench and then scoring against Wales was a great way to start.

It was tough on Hodgey getting injured. John Leslie was a world-class centre and I knew from watching him that we would work well together, so I was pleased to get a chance to have a run alongside him – he always made the right decision, either to give you the ball at the right time or to hit back into the forwards if it was bad ball. And when Gregor moved to ten he proved once again, like he did for the Lions in South Africa, that stand-off is his best position. And all three of us just gelled.

GREGOR TOWNSEND

The way we built-up that season demonstrates what Five and Six Nations rugby is all about. We hadn't performed particularly well during the autumn, losing pretty heavily to South Africa, and our first game of the Championship was Wales at home. They had pushed South Africa all the way in November and had beaten Argentina fairly comfortably, and were one of the favourites to win the Championship that year. But we completely outplayed them.

Duncan Hodge hurt his leg that day, so I was moved inwards to stand-off, with Alan Tait taking over from me at outside centre. Combinations are very important in selection, which doesn't necessarily mean picking your best fifteen players but getting guys who play well off each other, and we were lucky because that injury meant we stumbled upon a formula that worked during the rest of the Championship.

We were actually 13-8 down when that change was made and we went on to win 32-20. Winning that first game gave us so much momentum because the pressure was off and we felt we could try things a bit more.

JIM TELFER

It was a huge relief to beat Wales – that was the overriding feeling. A lot had been said in the press in the build up to that game that Graham Henry had got

Wales back to their best, so it was widely felt that if we beat them it would be a sign that we were starting to turn the corner and that after a few tough years, Scottish rugby would begin to regain some credibility.

GREGOR TOWNSEND

We went down to Twickenham next, and were blown away by England's huge pack in the first quarter; but the self-belief from the Wales game helped us fight back, and although we never led we came really close to stealing our first win down there since 1983. It was really frustrating, but we had done enough to feel that our growing self-belief wasn't misplaced.

ALAN TAIT

Going down to London for the England game was my first and last game at Twickenham and, again, I wanted a big performance. So it was great to score two tries. The first was really just getting on the end of a broken play move, and the second was from a set-piece move that we had improvised on the Friday before the game during our run through, and it worked like a dream.

Dan Luger, Richard Hill, David Rees and Matt Dawson can do nothing to stop Alan Tait from powering over for his second try in the Calcutta Cup clash at Twickenham. *Getty Images*

JIM TELFER

That game at Twickenham was disappointing to lose in so many ways – we had bounced back to get into the game and scored three tremendous tries with Alan Tait going in at each end and Gregor Townsend picking off a lovely intercept and racing in from halfway. We converted all three but unfortunately Kenny Logan missed with a couple of penalty attempts. It was during that game that I first really registered the impact of the Leslie brothers. At half-time I said a few bits and pieces and then John took the backs into one corner and Martin took the forwards into another and they laid out exactly what had gone right and wrong in the first-half and told the rest of the players what they needed to do to beat England. All the other players listened and understood what they were being told and then they went out and did it – and very nearly managed a famous victory. Both John and Martin were very technical and analytical in their approach and they knew exactly how to go out and win games against different opponents. That kind of insight and experience is absolutely invaluable and demonstrated exactly what they could bring to the squad.

GARY ARMSTRONG

Looking back, it was a real missed opportunity at Twickenham. Not many Scottish sides have gone down there and won and when the dust settled after the last game, we realised the implication of not winning that game because it could have been another Grand Slam – we ended up four points away in a game that we should have won.

GLENN METCALFE

I guess in all the highlights of my international career, that 1999 season ranks right at the top. We were actually pretty close to a Grand Slam and looking back on that result at Twickenham is a bit of a sickener as we were only a few points away from toppling England.

The balance that we had throughout the team that year was perfect for our game and playing at fullback I could see the experienced decision making and skill of John Leslie amplify the talents of Gregor and Taity around him – I was in the best position in the world to see the holes the three of them would open up against seriously talented opposition. I was happy for my mate Gregor to have such a great season as a lot of people were critical of his play prior to that year, even though he had guided the Lions to a Test series victory in 1997. People were often on his back about the risks he would take and the mistakes that would sometime come from those risks, but that year he really came into his own and his performances against Ireland, England and France were almost impossible to fault.

IAN McGEECHAN

In a sense, the problems that Gregor experienced as a playmaker were not his problems at all. He has long been branded as being a 'mercurial' player, but the fact of the matter was that his thought processes always tended to be half a yard in front of everyone else's and if the other players were not on their toes, his best ideas could backfire. I wasn't involved with Scotland for that Five Nations, but watching it from the outside I could instantly see the difference that John Leslie had made to Gregor's play – they had an intuitive understanding with one another about how they wanted to play the game and it worked well with Alan Tait outside them, too. They were a super combination and Gregor was really able to show the breadth of his talent.

GREGOR TOWNSEND

We beat Ireland 30-13 at Murrayfield in what was the most accomplished all-round performance by a Scotland team I was ever involved in. John Leslie, Alan Tait and myself in the midfield were getting a lot of praise, but Glenn Metcalfe and Cammie Murray were also excelling in the backline, and we were all benefiting from the quick-ball the forwards were consistently producing. We had great leaders all over the park, which made a huge difference. The Leslie brothers were fantastic to have around and then we had guys like me, Taity, Tom Smith and Gary Armstrong who had all been around and achieved great things with our clubs, with Scotland and with the Lions. That kind of leadership and experience is very hard to come by, but it tends to be one of the key ingredients to any successful side.

The team was full of strong personalities who wanted to play rugby so we were as player-led as we had ever been. Nowadays, teams are even further down the line in terms of the players making decisions, but back then coaches would still have a big say right up to the moment you ran out onto the pitch. However, with the likes of Gary Armstrong, myself, John Leslie and Alan Tait in the side, there was a lot of experience there to say, *we are going to play it this way because we know it is going to work.*

We started taking charge of the Friday run-through, which is called the captain's run but back then was still really taken by the coach. I have really fond memories of those sessions, we would work at a really high pace and there would be no mistakes. We'd be buzzing coming off the park, and the coaches would be buzzing as well even though they weren't involved. They could see how sharp it was.

The try Grimesy scored against the Irish was epic – we started it under our posts and went the length of the field, inter-passing all the way. It was electric stuff.

STUART GRIMES

I got up from the bottom of the ruck that we had turned the ball over in and saw Gregor making a break out of the 22 and I just legged it after him – I was lucky that the ball just came my way in the end and it was nice to get the final touch because Kenny Logan was right beside me and he had never scored in a Five Nations match, so it was good to help keep that record in tact – although I had to put up with all manner of abuse from him later that night.

Glenn Metcalfe slices through the French defence on a glorious day for Scotland in Paris. *Getty Images*

GREGOR TOWNSEND

Our final game was against France and it was Scotland's first appearance at the Stade de France, which is an incredible venue. I wonder if we were slightly over-awed by the whole experience of playing there because we were very loose in the first five minutes, and lost an early try. Then, suddenly, players started reading off-loads and anticipating breaks – the understanding was just there and everything began to click again.

We called the same 'miss-one-blind' move as we had called at the very beginning of the 1996 game against France. This time Alan Tait got smashed just as he passed to Glenn Metcalfe but he got the ball and away and Glenn ran 70 yards up field and we scored off it. Rugby is all about fine margins. If you get caught in your own 22 while trying to execute a move then the next time you are in that position you are less likely to try and move it, but if you go through with it – if your skills are up to the job – then all of a sudden the whole team are looking to have a go. And fortunately, on both those occasions our willingness to have a go paid off.

We scored five tries in twenty minutes. When we came in at half-time the buzz was amazing and the coaches didn't know what to say – they couldn't possibly have planned for that scenario. We wanted to keep playing with the same pace and flair but it was inevitable that France would come back at us. In the end we won the second-half 3-0, which is almost as impressive as what we achieved in the first-half because we defended so well.

Kenny Logan missed a conversion from pretty close in-front of the posts that day. Later that night, Kenny admitted that as he ran up to kick the conversion he looked up at himself on the big screen behind the posts, and he fluffed the ball. He could have kept that to himself, but I suppose he could afford to joke about it because we won.

JIM TELFER

I had never seen anything like it. It was as if every time we had the ball we scored a try. For a time it was like the other team wasn't even on the park. That first 30, 40 minutes was just unbelievable. It was all down to the positivity of the players – the more positive you are in attack, the more chance you will have to get the result.

GARY ARMSTRONG

We wanted to play a wide game, the sort of game that they used to such good effect against us the previous year. It worked, and we cut through them like a knife through butter.

Gregor Townsend celebrates becoming only the fifth player in history to score a try in each match during a single Championship season. *Getty Images*

JIM TELFER

I think we had a vague notion at the back of our minds that we could still win the Championship, but it was no more than that. Everyone expected England to stroll to victory over Wales and although I knew many of the Welsh players very well from the Lions tour and knew how good they were, I also knew many of the English players and couldn't see them fluffing their shot at a Grand Slam.

We travelled back from Paris that morning and each of us managed to get home or to a pub or a clubhouse or wherever to watch that final game of the tournament. I was back at home in time for the kick-off and settled in for what I thought was the inevitable England win.

But even at the hour mark of that game Wales were still very much in it, although I still thought that England would pull away at the end. Neil Jenkins was keeping them in it as only he could and then when Scott Gibbs crashed through to score. I nearly hit the roof.

ALAN TAIT

I looked up at the TV screen in the pub to see Gibbsy flash through the line and I just started jumping all over the place. People started saying that it was too early to celebrate because there was still the conversion to go, but I knew Jenks well from the Lions and I knew there was no way he was going to miss it – he was the best kicker I'd ever seen.

JIM TELFER

It was a tricky conversion to take the lead, but I knew Neil would get it. He slotted it and they held out to deny England at the final whistle. It was quite something to suddenly realise that we were champions, and the phone didn't stop ringing for hours.

The squad gather at Murrayfield to celebrate their Five Nations triumph. *SNS Pix*

13

TELFER'S LAST STAND

SCOTLAND *were Five Nations champions and looked to be in a strong position going into the 1999 Rugby World Cup – they had battled through the adversity of injury and defeat to England to win the Championship and were playing a thrilling brand of rugby.*

Instead of scheduling a run of major Test matches in the build-up to the World Cup, Scotland elected instead to tour the provinces of South Africa with a development squad in an effort to build some strength in depth. Most notable of the young players to gain experience within the squad were future captains Jason White and Chris Paterson. The tour was a mixed success results-wise, with Scotland defeating Border and Northern Free State Griffons but losing to Mpumalanga and the Golden Lions, yet it proved invaluable in introducing these young players into the international set-up.

In the weeks before their first Pool 1 match, Scotland played Argentina at Murrayfield, losing 22-31 before facing Romania at Hampden Park in an encounter which they won 60-19 but at which barely 5000 supporters turned up to watch – an ominous signal of what was to occur during the World Cup itself.

Jim Telfer had indicated the previous year that he was only taking the head coach role until the conclusion of the World Cup, after which he would return to his job as director of rugby for the SRU. After a long and eventful career with Scotland and the Lions, the World Cup was to act as the final chapter in Telfer's esteemed coaching career. Fate and luck had conspired so wonderfully for Scotland in the spring, allowing them to overcome the trials of injury to emerge, ironically, even stronger. But luck is a fickle thing and Fate's wheel was beginning to turn.

The injury that Tom Smith suffered against Ireland and which ruled him out of the sensational victory in Paris also ruled him out of the World Cup and while Doddie Weir had recovered from a broken ankle he had sustained against Wales in the Five Nations opener, he was still some distance away from full fitness. Finally, Scotland were struck down by another serious leg injury that reduced their chances still further. John Leslie, the pivotal rock of the midfield, twisted his ankle against South Africa in the opening pool game and was ruled out of the rest of the tournament. Scotland were leading the world champions 16-13 at half-time but in the second-half the Springboks moved into a different gear and swept the hosts aside, finishing the game with six tries to their name and a 46-29 win over their main rivals for the pool.

Scotland's next two matches were against Uruguay and Spain and they were little

---

Opposite: Jim Telfer bids farewell to his role as Scotland's head coach. *Getty Images*

more than training exercises as the home team ran out 43-12 and 48-0 winners in each game. Finishing second in their group behind South Africa, Scotland played Samoa in a quarter-final play-off at Murrayfield. In the opening ten minutes Scotland won a scrum on the Samoan line. After the scrum was collapsed by the Pacific Islanders, Scotland were awarded a free-kick and elected to re-scrum. Over the next few minutes the scrum either collapsed, awarding the home team another free-kick, or was reset for a technicality. Scotland, trusting their superior fitness and technical ability, elected to scrum and scrum and scrum. It was tactic that was limited as a spectacle but was a tactical master-stroke which resonated through rest of the match, as it not only depowered the fiery Samoan forwards, it also sapped their energy, negating the impact that they had in broken play over the next 65 minutes. Scotland dominated proceedings and went on to win 35-20 to book a quarter-final place with the All Blacks at Murrayfield.

On a wild and windy night in late October, the All Blacks showed their outstanding class and superior skills in dreadful conditions to extinguish the Scottish challenge by half-time, where they retreated to the changing rooms with a 25-3 lead under their belts. Scotland showed enormous courage to rally in the second-half, scoring fifteen points to New Zealand's five, but they had too much ground to make up and the 30-18 defeat was a disappointing way for Telfer to bid farewell to his role as Scotland head coach and for the curtain to fall on the international playing careers of three mighty servants to the Scottish cause. Gary Armstrong, Alan Tait and Paul Burnell all bid an emotional farewell to the Murrayfield crowd as they and Telfer performed a final lap of the pitch and the lights dimmed on their theatre of dreams for the last time.

GORDON BULLOCH

Jim Telfer was a world class coach, one of the very finest that Scotland and the Lions ever had, but he would sometimes try to push things onto us that had worked for him – and he is a very different character to most human beings; not many people can be as single-minded as he is. For example, during one Six Nations he had everyone getting up for a run at 7am every morning – apart from the guys with bad backs, which was Taity and Brush [Bryan Redpath] who were determined not to do it – and he would have us out on the golf course at Dalmahoy, freezing our bollocks off, running round six or seven holes. Nowadays the players would laugh at any coach who suggested that, but because it worked for him he thought it would work for everyone else.

On one occasion during the build-up to the 1999 World Cup, we were staying down in Troon at the Marine Hotel, and he wanted everyone out for an early morning walk round the golf course. So the players got together and organised everyone to turn up in their number ones, we had big duffle-coats and hats on as well, and we ended up walking single file, with one hand on the shoulder of the guy in-front, singing, 'Hi-ho, hi-ho, it's off to work we go.' Then we spread out so we were walking a line abreast, 50 yards behind Jim, down the fairway. In fairness to Jim, he found it amusing and laughed about it as well.

JAMIE MAYER

What was Jim Telfer like as a coach? He was a very good man – although I was probably too young to really understand him and his style at the time. He expected the highest standards of skill, effort and commitment and I believe that any great and well-respected coach gets that delivered consistently from his team. Jim's teams over the years, whether as a player or a coach, have always displayed these qualities and that, above all else, is a testament to the kind of man he is.

GORDON BULLOCH

We spent the Welsh World Cup of 1999 in the Dalmahoy Hotel just outside Edinburgh. I know finance was a factor, but as a player that didn't make sense. We didn't go to the opening ceremony, we didn't do anything, and we played all our games at Murrayfield. The last game against New Zealand was fabulous but in the quarter-final play-off we played Samoa on a Wednesday afternoon in front of 15,000 people – it was a bizarre experience. You couldn't really buy into the excitement of being at a World Cup because Edinburgh, as a city, wasn't really that fussed about having a few World Cup games there. Come game day it was good – for the South Africa and New Zealand games, at least – but apart from that you didn't really feel you were at a World Cup.

GREGOR TOWNSEND

The crowd for three of our games was less than 20,000, which was shocking. We were European champions and playing at our home ground in what was meant to be the biggest event on the rugby calendar, but Edinburgh as a city hadn't really been enthused with the World Cup spirit and a few of the games were on weekday afternoons so people were naturally at work. More people had turned up to see us collect the Five Nations trophy a few months earlier than for two of our World Cup games. In South Africa's pool match against Spain only 6000 turned up at Murrayfield and crowds throughout the tournament in Scotland were hugely disappointing. Things got so desperate that the SRU started to filter recorded crowd noises through the speakers at the stadium. It was embarrassing.

Duncan Hodge lines up a conversion against Spain during the World Cup pool game – with Murrayfield's stands hauntingly empty in the background. *Getty Images*

DUNCAN HODGE

It was a real shame. The ticket pricing and match scheduling were all wrong, so you were playing at Murrayfield in what was supposed to be the premier rugby tournament in the world. It was just a nondescript tournament. It was very disappointing. The World Cup is supposed to be one of the highlights of your career and we were playing in front of crowds of five or six thousand. We didn't even go down to Wales once, all our games were at home and we were staying out at Dalmahoy. It was all just really weird and a huge disappointment.

JAMIE MAYER

The squad's preparation for the World Cup was very good and we worked hard to get ourselves into the best shape we could, even though it was a bit weird being in Edinburgh while the rest of the tournament's focus was in Wales. But we just had to get on with things and focus on our own preparations. We knew that despite winning the Five Nations that the World Cup would be another step-up altogether, particularly as we had to play South Africa in our opening game. I got injured in a training session down in Troon and I genuinely thought my World Cup was over before it began. Fortunately over the next few weeks the physios, particularly Stuart Barton and Stephen Mutch, worked absolute wonders and helped me back to full recovery in time for the tournament's opening.

JIM TELFER

We opened our World Cup campaign against South Africa, which was fairly huge to have first-up – they were the defending champions and had put more than 100 points on us in our previous two encounters. But we were the reigning Five Nations champions and despite losing to Argentina in one of our warm-up matches, we looked in good shape. We played pretty well to begin with and went in at half-time with a 16-13 lead, but we lost John Leslie to an ankle injury and South Africa stepped it up a level after that. The lead exchanged hands a couple of times after tries from Martin Leslie and Deon Kayser and then we were ahead for the final time after Kenny Logan scored with a penalty. They then scored two tries within three minutes which was a fairly killer blow and except for a nicely taken try by Alan Tait after a neat offload from Gregor, they went on to sweep us aside after that. Bobby Skinstad, Joost van der Westhuizen and Brendan Venter were all very influential that day and they looked strong contenders for the World Cup at that stage.

In the aftermath of that game we played Spain and Uruguay and won comfortably in both to set up a play-off game with Samoa.

Battle of the scrum-halves – Joost van der Westhuizen tackles Gary Armstrong during the key Pool 1 match at Murrayfield. *Getty Images*

GLENN METCALFE

Playing in a World Cup is just an awesome experience. In '99 we had a good season and took a lot of confidence into the tournament. First up against the defending champions and we really needed to hit the ground running. We came up short in the end but played some great rugby in that match; a key moment was when John Leslie stretched out to score a try near the posts and in the process severely damaged his ankle that put him out of the tournament. He was a huge loss to the campaign.

DUNCAN HODGE

After one training session we went into this team meeting out at Dalmahoy and everyone sat down. Then Jim grunts at Grimesy and says, 'Come with me.' They went to the room next door, and Jim asks him to roll up his sleeves, then Jim gets out a red marker pen and starts scrawling up and down Grimesy's arm. Then he rolls his sleeves back down and sends him back to the team room.

Then during the meeting Jim says that some people just can't believe they are at a World Cup, they've been pinching themselves so hard they are bleeding. And he makes Grimesy roll up his sleeve to show us this arm with red pen all over it. It was just bizarre. You knew what Jim was trying to say but he wasn't trying to be funny, so you didn't know how to react to it.

Jim had some odd ways about him sometimes. It was quite hard keeping a straight face because he would have a bit of a problem remembering guys names or not pronouncing them properly – he used to talk about Darren Garforth and call him Darren Garfield, or would be telling us about Lawrence Dallaglio and pronounce his name Lawrence Dall-aj-leo.

He had an all-encompassing presence in the squad when he was head coach. Unlike today when training is mainly position-tailored, so the front-row do different training drills to the back-row and the backs mainly run through game situations, it used to be full squad sessions under Jim so that the backs would be hitting as many rucking pads as the forwards – we would do hours of rucking training, while in a game I would be lucky to hit one ruck in 80 minutes.

JAMIE MAYER

Some of my best memories were getting together with the boys during down-time in the hotels and just talking through the opposition and the strengths and weaknesses of the guys we were coming up against. I then loved playing out these pre-game discussions on the pitch, and that was particularly true of the Samoa game – I do not think there is a more satisfying feeling that when a plan you've been working on comes together. We knew that we had to depower them up front and then target guys like Tuigamala, Brian Lima, Stephen Bachop and Pat Lam to make sure they never got into their stride. They were fantastic players, real stars, and although we weren't able to hinder them completely, for the vast proportion of that match they had nowhere to go and we felt comfortable all the way through.

Jamie Mayer powers through the tackle of Terry Fanolua during Scotland's victory over Samoa. *Getty Images*

GREGOR TOWNSEND

We played our best rugby of the tournament against Samoa, but again the crowd numbers were bitterly disappointing – only 15,000 supporters turned up to watch us.

Fortunately they have subsequently done away with the quarter-final play-off game because none of the three teams who won those fixtures progressed beyond the quarter-final stage. I'm not saying that the results in those games would have necessarily been different, but it certainly hampered our chances, as well as England's and Argentina's, as we had to play an extra fixture just four days before the quarter-final while our opposition in those fixtures were able to rest and focus their training without distraction.

JIM TELFER

The atmosphere at Murrayfield for the quarter-final against the All Blacks was incredible. It was one of the best feelings from a crowd there that I had felt in years and the atmosphere in the dressing room was just as powerful. It was my last game in charge and the last game for several of our leading players – and it was some challenge for us to face the favourites for the tournament.

The weather was dreadful and I think our players froze a bit in the first-half, giving them too much respect before trying implement our own game – and New Zealand were away and gone by then. When we turned it on we played some great stuff, but the All Blacks were just flawless and deserved the win. They scored three outstanding tries – one where Christian Cullen flipped the ball out the back of his hand to Tana Umaga which would have been impressive on a bright summer afternoon, let alone a freezing October night in Edinburgh in the lashing rain.

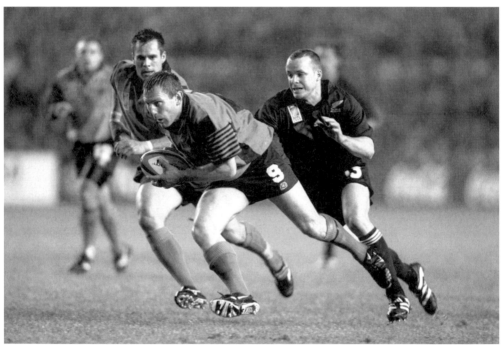

Gary Armstrong snipes past Christian Cullen in the World Cup quarter-final. *Getty Images*

DUNCAN HODGE

That last game has long stuck in my mind. Before we went out Gary Armstrong made this speech about his career coming to an end and what it meant for him to play for Scotland. He was hugely emotional about the whole thing and it really made me realise what it was that I was a part of, playing rugby for Scotland. Right from that letter I got when I was a teenager telling me that I had been selected for Scottish Schools, I was in the system and it just carries you along, you barely have time to really think about it. But that speech that Gary made really made me take stock of what I was doing and where I was and I carried that with me for the rest of my career. When someone like Gary spoke, you listened. In his own way, that quiet way that he has, he remains the most passionate Scotsman I have ever met, the most passionate rugby player I've ever played with. He laid it on the line what it meant to him to play for Scotland and he was in tears talking about it and after that I never took anything for granted. He really put everything he had into the jersey when he played and the emotion on his face when he came back into the changing room after the game . . . it's something that I'll never forget.

GREGOR TOWNSEND

We went in at half-time 25-3 down and I remember saying to Jim Telfer that I didn't think that we could play any better than we were; we were playing right at the top of our game but they were just on a different level and we both knew it. But Jim said that we couldn't let up in the second-half. It was a World Cup quarter-final and you can never just lie down in a fixture like that.

JAMIE MAYER

It was a horrible wet day at Murrayfield but the All Blacks seemed to be able to handle the ball like it was dry summer's day and they constantly played out in the wide channels, while we struggled a bit in the conditions; we were having to use our bodies to receive the ball and because of that we were limited to a tight game. But you have to remember that this was one of the best All Black back divisions of all time. Marshall and Mehrtens had been at their heart all through the late nineties and to see them in action was incredible. They played Ieremia and Cullen in the centre and while many felt that Cullen was wasted there, they ended up having an amazingly quick partnership that worked really well together. Lomu, Umaga and Wilson in the back three . . . need I say more? Those three scored all their tries which, given the weather, was some feat. Jonah scored eight tries in the tournament and really was a superstar, but he was backed up by some fabulously evasive running from the 'lightning bolt' Jeff Wilson and the guile, strength and clever feet of Tana Umaga. They were some team and I still can't believe that they didn't go on to win the tournament.

Once again, Jonah Lomu proves too much for Scotland in a World Cup as New Zealand's superior power overwhelms the home team. *Getty Images*

GLENN METCALFE

I remember lining up against the Haka and feeling a bit odd facing it as an opposition player. That was one game that I would love to play again. My whole family had flown over for the World Cup and to have them there in the stand at Murrayfield dressed in Scotland rugby tops and scarves, cheering us on, was great, but I had a poor performance out there and felt I offered very little to the team that night. As a whole we played fantastically in the second half to outscore the All Blacks, even though we went on to lose – but maybe we took too much out of the ABs as they lost to France in the next match!

GORDON BULLOCH

I was very proud of the way we played in the second-half, we kept them to one try and scored 15 points ourselves. Martin Leslie went over, which was a special thing for him, and it was a great moment when Cammie Murray made that break late in the game and dummied Jonah Lomu to go over. The noise in Murrayfield was like a thunder storm.

It was an emotional moment for the guys who were retiring and it was a super testament to them that despite the weather and the result that so many of the crowd wanted to stay on and cheer them farewell. Gary tried to make a speech to us in the changing room afterwards, but he couldn't manage it. All those years of putting everything into the jersey and he was about to take it off for the last time. Everything that it meant to him was written across his face. Sometimes, you don't need speeches.

14

THE LION MASTER'S SCOTTISH SWANSONG

A S ONE OLD *master retired from the post as Scotland's head coach, so another stepped back into the breach. In the build-up to the World Cup, Ian McGeechan had come aboard the coaching panel with Telfer, John Rutherford and Hugh Campbell and he took over from his old partner-in-crime at the conclusion of the tournament to become commander-in-chief of Scotland's fortunes.*

Scotland's first game of the 2000 Championship was momentous as it welcomed Italy into the tournament for the first time – an event that was celebrated in style in Rome as the home side were kicked to victory by their Argentina-born maestro Diego Dominguez. It was a devastating blow to the defending champions and shook their confidence to the core. Two weeks later they travelled to Ireland and played as poorly as their hosts were mesmeric, the home side inspired by their new wunderkind, Brian O'Driscoll, marched to a 44-22 victory.

Next up was a home encounter with a French side seeking revenge for the humiliation they had endured in Paris the previous year. For all of McGeechan's artistry as a coach and man-manager, he was unable to inspire much of an improvement in his troops' performance and Scotland lost 28-16.

The team hit the road again for the match in Cardiff and although they managed to give a better account of themselves, they failed to turn the corner and were beaten 26-18.

So it was that the media had completely written off Scotland's hopes going into the final game of the 2000 season. England were determined to put right the errors of the previous season when they had lost out on a Grand Slam and the Championship by losing to Wales at Wembley and to atone for their exit from the World Cup when South Africa's Jannie de Beer had spectacularly kicked them out of the competition at the Stade de France with a world-record five drop-goals. England were unbeaten that season as they travelled to Edinburgh and had seared through every previous match in the tournament. In The Sunday Times, *esteemed rugby journalist Stephen Jones wrote: 'Will England be denied as they were in 1990? The odds are against such a notion. No miracle, just a massacre. In the Six Nations showdown at Murrayfield, England to win by 44 points to take the Grand Slam today.'*

Opposite: Jon Petrie thanks the fans for their support following the 2003 World Cup quarter-final. *Getty Images*

But McGeechan and his charges were determined not finish the Championship with a whimper and there was a steely ambition to prove that their previous results had been an aberration rather than a reflection of their actual ability. Save for the thumping that they received at the hands of a rejuvenated Ireland at Lansdowne Road, they had lost the other games narrowly and had actually played some very positive and attractive rugby. It would be incredibly difficult to stifle the English game-plan and impose their own style over the 80 minutes that lay before them, but the squad knew that it was not a deluded flight of fancy to believe that they could. McGeechan met with his players after their loss to Wales and told them simply that the events that had occurred earlier in the tournament were now past; all their focus must now turn to defeating England.

After a relatively mild start to the year, the heavens were open and a chill wind had swept across the east coast of Scotland as the plane carrying the English team touched down at Edinburgh airport. For twenty-four hours the rain fell, covering the city in a thick, swirling miasma. In the hours before kick-off the rain at last relented and watery sunlight filled the cavernous bowl of Murrayfield. But at two o'clock, just as the anthems were drawing to a close, the clouds began to gather once more, pressing in over the Firth of Forth and rolling out over the city, bringing with them a light but persistent drizzle which set in over Murrayfield towards the end of the first-half. By the time the second-half kick-off was hoisted high into the darkening sky that drizzle had developed into a downpour. Very soon it became a deluge. Despite conceding a soft first-half try off the back of a scrum to Lawrence Dallaglio, Scotland were succeeding in their tactics to stifle the English quick-ball and slow their backs' lightening attack at its source. And as if to make up for the tragedy that had struck him the previous season – which had inadvertently acted as the catalyst for Scotland's Championship success – the rugby gods cast their eyes over that Calcutta Cup match and through the mists and swirls of rain, resolved that the day should belong to Duncan Hodge.

In the summer, Scotland travelled to New Zealand for a five match tour which included two Tests against the All Blacks in Dunedin and Auckland. It was a chance to blood new players Ross Beattie, Iain Fullarton, Graeme Beveridge, Steve Scott, Jon Petrie and Nathan Hines and to give some more game time to the recently capped Chris Paterson, Jason White, Richard Metcalfe and James McLaren in the toughest rugby environment on the planet.

At the start of the new season, Scotland defeated the USA and Samoa but were unable to overturn the Wallabies despite virtuoso performances from Scott Murray, Stuart Grimes, Simon Taylor, Jon Petrie and Gregor Townsend.

Results in the 2001 Six Nations improved on the previous year and after losing narrowly 16-6 to France in Paris, the Scots drew 28-28 with a strong Welsh team at Murrayfield thanks to Tom Smith's late equalising score. They were hammered 43-3 by one of the all-time great English performances at Twickenham, but recovered *their composure to defeat Italy at Murrayfield. Because of the outbreak of the Foot and Mouth epidemic in the late spring of 2001, the tournament went into hibernation until September. On the 22nd of that month Ireland at last arrived in Edinburgh, chasing a Grand Slam. In a remarkable performance, Scotland completely outplayed the visitors to win 32-10 and scored four scintillating tries through John Leslie, Budge Pountney, Tom Smith and debutant Andy Henderson.*

That November, Scotland opened their autumn international programme by beating Tonga 43-20 in a game where debutant fly-half Gordon Ross controlled the game expertly and kicked flawlessly at goal. But this opening win would be the only one in the series as the team went on to lose 25-16 to Argentina before being obliterated by the All Blacks 37-6. That latter game was particularly memorable as it saw the introduction of New Zealander Brendan Laney into the Scotland team, just a short time after his arrival from his native shores. McGeechan had originally picked him for the Argentina match but after concern from the senior players that this act would not be received favourably by the wider squad, the media or the fans, McGeechan changed his mind and selected Laney instead for the A team encounter with New Zealand. However, after Scotland fell to the Pumas, the head coach felt that the team needed Laney's Super 12 experience and selected him to play against his countrymen for the second time in a week. The decision was, as predicted by his senior players, widely derided and cast a long shadow over both the remainder of McGeechan's term as coach and, unfortunately (for he was not himself at fault for the decision), over Laney's career in Scotland.

England were the first opponents scheduled to play Scotland in the 2002 Six Nations and they won comfortably 29-3 at Murrayfield, and although Scotland also lost in Dublin and against France in Edinburgh, they defeated Italy and Wales on the road.

In November that year Scotland enjoyed a unique hat-trick of wins against Romania, Fiji and, most notably, South Africa. Lazarus-like, Jim Telfer was back once again in a tracksuit, assisting Hugh Campbell and Pat Lam with the forwards as a specialist contact coach. Gordon Ross started at stand-off for both the Romania and South Africa Tests and played very well. Although there were two dubious tries in the latter match that were awarded to Nikki Walker and Budge Pountney, Scotland had played a very cute tactical game to negate the aggressive Springbok defence, dominating their large forwards with incredible ferocity in the contact areas while the backline put pressure on a number of the Springbok's more inexperienced players by kicking well in the rain.

In the build-up to the 2003 Six Nations, captain Budge Pountney announced his retirement from the Scotland team. It was an acrimonious affair as Pountney renounced the shambolic set-up of the SRU, citing unprofessional conduct that was detrimental to the progress of the team. Among his grievances were simple incompetence such as a lack of water at training and a continued reissue of an invoice from the SRU for a tie that he had given away to a young fan after an international, to more serious ones about player welfare. This concluding point had come to a head when Telfer had flogged the forwards to a standstill in the wake of their victory over the Springboks and had then berated them for a poor performance against Fiji, which Pountney had vocally claimed was down to fatigue brought on by Telfer's brutal training sessions.

Scotland had a fairly inauspicious Six Nations tournament, only registering wins against Wales and Italy at home, but by the end of the Championship they were developing an expansive attacking game which showed some real promise and was a vast tactical improvement to the limited game plan they had been employing earlier in the season.

The squad headed to South Africa in June for a two match series, and once again they displayed their attacking intent and played some wonderful rugby – which included a Chris Paterson score in the first Test which was voted the IRB's try-of-the-year – that deserved so much more than the two narrow losses that were returned. As has so often been the case in Scottish rugby, the team were just inches away from securing a famous first win in the first Test, only for the ball to slip agonisingly out of Nathan Hines' grasp as he reached through a ruck to touch down in extra time. Travelling home with their heads held high, the squad were pleased with their continued progress but knew that they had let two golden opportunities slip in losing just 29-25 and 28-19.

Preparations for the World Cup now stepped up a gear and the squad embarked on a ten-day training expedition to the Olympic institution in Spala, Poland. Intense training was threaded around sub-zero cryotherapy which was designed to speed up the process of muscle recovery and so allow the players to train longer and harder while they were at the institution. On their return to Edinburgh they moved to the other extreme and endured humidity training on running and cycling machines in the hothouses at the Royal Botanic Gardens as they prepared for the conditions in Australia.

In the final weeks of their build-up, they played three World Cup warm-up games against Italy, Wales and Ireland, but worryingly only managed to register a win against the Azzuri.

In what would prove to be England's landmark year, Scotland enjoyed a solid but unspectacular World Cup campaign, once again reaching the quarter-finals after defeating Japan in Townsville and the USA in Brisbane before tumbling to a heavy defeat by France in Sydney. They needed to defeat the flying Fijians in their final pool match to ensure qualification to the last eight. An injury-time try from Tom Smith, which was converted by Chris Paterson, saved the day and they were through to play the hosts who, after a mighty battle, defeated them 33-16 in Brisbane. This game was to be Ian McGeechan's last in charge before he became director of rugby at the SRU. His final stint at the helm of the national team had come nowhere near scaling the *heights that his previous tenures had enjoyed, yet nevertheless, Scotland had played some fantastic attacking rugby at times and had posted some gritty, hard-fought victories, none more so than in the wins over England in 2000 and South Africa in 2002, as well as in their credible performances in the summer of 2003.*

TOM SMITH

There were factors we couldn't control in 2000. We had a few injuries. John Leslie was out after only playing a few minutes of the opening Six Nations game; Gary Armstrong, Alan Tait and Paul Burnell had retired; and there was a change of coaches as well. Our environment changed and unfortunately our performances did too. Ideally you want to have a legacy where you have enough people knocking at the door that success becomes continuous and you can survive the loss of star players, and maybe we were a little bit fragile on that front – perhaps we still are.

Maybe we spent too long patting ourselves on the back after we won the Championship the previous year instead of saying that this time we want the Grand Slam. It took us a while to build confidence in the 1999 season and I think maybe we forgot how tough it was grinding out those performances before it clicked.

2000 had been a pretty dismal season for Scotland. Having won the last Championship expectations were quite high, but we went down to Italy for game one of the new Six Nations and got brought back down to earth with an almighty bump – and things deteriorated from there. The whole 'Grannygate' thing was blowing up at the time – Shane Howarth and Brett Sinkinson, the Welsh players, had no link to Wales through their grandparents' as they had claimed, and the IRB's rigorous checks that followed revealed that David Hilton's grandfather's birth was registered in Bristol, rather than Glasgow, which was where all his family had believed him to have been born. David was forced to withdraw from the Scotland squad, but he took the decision with incredible bravery and fought for his place by qualifying through residency a couple of years later. It was tough on David and tough on the squad, but it wasn't a mitigating factor in our performances. We just weren't performing anywhere on the pitch.

JIM TELFER

The situation with David Hilton was incredibly unfortunate and devastating for him because he and his family were convinced of his qualifications. David still maintains that his grandfather was born in Scotland several weeks before his birth was registered in Bristol.

DUNCAN HODGE

That first game was obviously huge for Italy and they played very well to win, but we really didn't help ourselves. There was the saga of John Leslie playing when he had hardly trained after coming back from injury and was named as captain, and then after only a short time he broke down injured and had to go off. It was a shambles, the whole thing, and none of us were at the races.

JAMIE MAYER

What happened against Italy in 2000? Poor preparation and too much confidence following a successful previous year. I still remember posing for a photo eating pasta a couple of days before the game. I looked like such a chopper, especially in light of the result. I remember a fan approaching me after the match and announcing that I had ruined his expensive weekend. Funny how everyone celebrates when we win but we stand alone in defeat. It was a valuable lesson for the whole team.

TOM SMITH

After falling to Italy in Rome, we went to Ireland and started well, with Kenny Logan scoring a cracking try – his first ever Championship try, would you believe – but then it all fell to pieces. Brian O'Driscoll started to show what a special player he was going to be over the next decade and they just ran wild.

GREGOR TOWNSEND

Those first games were tough, really tough. After the high of the previous year we really sank to the depths – like many of the Scottish teams of the past, the season following a Grand Slam or Championship win has tended to be something of a disaster. We seemed to forget that all the glamour play of the year before had been built on hard work and graft. It didn't help that Kenny missed a lot of kicks in Rome or that John Leslie wasn't fit when he took the field as captain – he had only had one week's worth of training in him before we travelled to Rome because he was still coming back from the ankle injury he picked up at the World Cup. He didn't last the first quarter of the game before he went off. But the blame didn't rest at their doors – the whole team's performance was dreadful and we were all accountable for the result.

Against Ireland we tried to pick ourselves up and had a good start, but we were completely outplayed after that. Nothing we tried worked and confidence dropped through the floor.

France came to Murrayfield and we improved on our performance in Dublin – although that wouldn't have been hard – but they ended up winning 28-16.

DODDIE WEIR

As it transpired, those games against Italy, Ireland and France turned out to be my last games for Scotland. It was maybe not the ideal way to bow out of international rugby and it would have been nice to finish the tournament, especially with the England game. I played them eight times and never beat them.

I still keep in touch with a lot of the boys I played with. Rugby is like that – it's a membership. You can not see a boy for ten or fifteen years and then when you do, it's like no time has passed. When you've slogged your heart out with these guys on the training pitch and in matches, when you've had these great experiences with them away from the game and on nights out together, it bonds you. No matter what the level, it's the same – be it at school, or at Melrose, with Newcastle, the Borders, Scotland or the Lions – the bond is just as strong and the friendships just the same.

I have been very fortunate in my career. I've experienced some great, great moments and met some super people who have become lifelong friends. But, unlike many former players, I wouldn't want to go back and start again from scratch. I never did like training, so the idea of going back and doing fifteen or more years of training . . . no thanks. I'll take the memories instead.

GREGOR TOWNSEND

We went to Wales hoping to take advantage of the furore surrounding Sinkinson and Howarth, but it seemed to galvanise them; we were starting to play much better but we still ended up losing 26-18. We couldn't buy a win.

DUNCAN HODGE

I got into the team for the Wales game and we actually played some really good stuff and I remember Glenn Metcalfe just carving them up from all over the field. I hit the posts a couple of times and we ended up losing by eight points, so it was a tough one to take. We were obviously staring down the barrel of the gun at the wooden spoon then and were completely written off by the time England came to town.

TOM SMITH

By the time we met England, they were chasing the Grand Slam and we were facing a white-wash. They were extremely confident and let the whole world know how confident they were – despite having had a bit of a shake-up the year before when they lost to Wales at Wembley to gift us the Championship.

We all went to the cinema the night before the match to see the Al Pacino film *Any Given Sunday*, which is all fire and brimstone about inspirational sport. I don't know what effect that had on us. I know that when we woke up on the morning of the match and looked outside to see it bucketing down that gave us all a huge boost.

In fairness to England, they still wanted to play rugby. Clive Woodward had had a few moans about our pre-match entertainment and things like that. He'd had done quite a good job of irritating everybody as only he knew how.

Everyone was pretty low and it took a little while for the belief to start to develop. England kept trying to run it out of positions where they probably should have just hoofed it up the park, and we kept pinning them back, and slowly everyone stated to think maybe . . . just maybe.

DUNCAN HODGE

It was the end of a nightmare season, and that was the first time ever we were given a day off during the week leading up to the game. I think it was because it was a Sunday game. We went clay pigeon shooting.

We'd actually played fairly well the week before down in Wales. We had a bit of a go and hadn't been beaten by a lot. In the lead up to the game I can remember certain bits of analysis. Dawson was massive on his quick taps, so McGeechan said that whoever was back ten – which was more likely to be a winger or the full-back – was to come in and smash Dawson. And that was pretty important – Glenn Metcalfe took it upon himself to cover Dawson during these top-penalties and he completely neutralised that threat.

There weren't that many spectators at the game as far as I can recall. I think it was one of the first games to be held on a Sunday, so it wasn't the usual Calcutta Cup sell-out – probably not helped by the way both teams were playing – the usual home fans stayed away to avoid seeing the inevitable drubbing. England were averaging the high 30s in every game while we had lost every game and no one gave us a shot.

During the game, it was all England. The thing for them at the time was that Dawson was captain of Northampton, Dallaglio was captain of Wasps, Johnson was captain of Leicester – with England they were used to winning, with their clubs they were used to winning – and they used to rule the refs. So the first half went almost all their way, then just before half-time we got a penalty five yards from our own line, we ran it then kicked it to around about halfway and we got another penalty which we kicked for three points. So it could have been 17-6 but we went in at 10-9. Then in the second half we started well, and the silence amongst the English boys was deafening. Whereas in the first half they had all been chirping away, and swaggering around – then there was no chat whatsoever, there was just nothing. Everything so far that season had been on Easy Street and all of a sudden, for the first time – partly because of the weather, partly because of us, partly because they weren't playing the conditions as well as they could have – they were in a situation that they hadn't been in before, and for all the experience that they had throughout the team, they didn't know how to change track to Plan B. Plan A had worked every time and they kept thinking that eventually it would click and come right and they would start running in half a dozen tries or more. Their tactical play was as poor as ours was good in the conditions. For the first time they were thinking to themselves: *Hang on a minute, we're in a serious game here.*

TOM SMITH

On a day like that, it is all about blood and guts and territory. Skill doesn't really come into it. And I think England misread it by trying to play great rugby inside their own half. Scotty Murray and Richard Metcalfe were doing a tremendous job on their lineout which meant that they were struggling to secure any set-piece authority, which they had been enjoying all season – and it rattled them. We kept up in their faces the whole time, keeping possession for long spells and when we kicked we kept it low and awkward. Andy Nicol did one great little grubber through which had their defence at sixes and sevens.

DUNCAN HODGE

The rain really set in and it started to hinder their attack – they had been throwing the ball around at will in the previous games, but our defence and the rain were slowing them down. As the game wore on and the weather got worse, they struggled to impose themselves and their lineout really started to struggle.

TOM SMITH

All through the second-half the rain was just bucketing down – it was like standing in an ice-cold shower – and we just kept on pressing them. Duncan Hodge kicked brilliantly and kept us in it. Then towards the end we really started to camp out in their half. We pushed hard to their line with some bursts through the forwards; the ball squirted out just as we were inches away, but Gordon McIlwham reacted the quickest and secured the ball back. Hodgey had come forward to gather the same ball and he grabbed it from Gordon and dived over. And the rest, as they say, is history.

DUNCAN HODGE

It was just luck that I was there – I was following the play in as we approached the line hoping to help, but suddenly the ball was there, I grabbed it and I dived over. The ground was so wet that the ball slid out of my hands as I touched it down and for a moment I wasn't sure if the ref was going to give it. I have a picture at home of me looking up at the ref to see what his decision was going to be and it was a great moment when he signalled the try. It was something really special.

Duncan Hodge looks up to see whether referee Clem Thomas has awarded his clinching score against England. *FotoSport*

GREGOR TOWNSEND

It was great to beat England in 2000 because it was the only time I managed that in ten years in the international game – but, speaking personally, it doesn't really stand out in the same way as some of the other notable successes of that era. That season we only won that single game out of five – so you have to remember to keep it in that context

Having said that, it was a fantastic performance, with Duncan Hodge immense at stand-off – he controlled the game really well. They were Grand Slam favourites, but we matched them physically during the first-half when it was still relatively dry, then in the second-half when the weather deteriorated we managed the conditions really well.

It was the coldest I have ever been on a rugby pitch. I was at outside centre and the ball just didn't come out that far. Afterwards, I was one of three or four outside backs who just ran straight into the changing rooms and jumped into the showers with all their kit on. So we weren't there to witness Andy Nicol being presented with the Calcutta Cup outside.

After ten long years of trying, Scotland, at last, regain the Calcutta Cup. *Getty Images*

DUNCAN HODGE

It was a Sunday and there was just a buffet after the game, so everyone just had a quick bite to eat and then went off to do their own thing. All my family had been at the game so we went to Montpelliers in Bruntsfield. I was sitting at this table with my family and three or four different strangers came up during the time we were there and put a bottle of champagne down at the table. I was saying, 'What are you doing?' And their answers were all pretty much the same: 'You don't need to ask that. You and the team have made our day. Just drink it and enjoy it.' Then they'd just turn around and walk away.

That was a big moment of realisation for me. Because you are so immersed in international rugby, you don't realise, or you forget, what it means to other people.

Later that night we met up with all the Scottish guys at the Sports Bar in the Grassmarket, which was owned by Gregor Townsend, Derek Stark and Rowan Shepherd at the time. Then we went to Espionage and met up with all the England guys, so there was all this stuff about them refusing to shake our hands and so on, but that was nonsense.

JON PETRIE (Glasgow Caledonians)
45 Caps: 2000-2006

Despite a fairly dismal Six Nations, Scottish rugby was nevertheless on a bit of a high after reclaiming the Calcutta Cup for the first time in ten years. My first cap came at a time when I wasn't really expecting anything at all. It was only my second year as a pro and I somehow squeezed onto the New Zealand tour during the summer of 2000. I was 22 years old and there were a lot of older guys who had been there for a pretty long time, so I suppose a few people would have viewed me as being there to make up the numbers. But once I got out there, it was like nothing I had ever experienced before. Other than going out for the Hong Kong Sevens I had never been on a senior tour, so it was kind of hard not to get overawed by the whole experience.

It was one of the last tours to have games outside the Test matches and it gave us a chance to establish some patterns of play and get used to playing with each other – either as new players or as players coming together for the first time since the Six Nations. We travelled all over New Zealand, playing matches against East Coast/Poverty Bay, the Maoris, the New Zealand Barbarians and then Tests against the All Blacks in Dunedin and Auckland. All of those games were incredibly tough and we only managed to post one win all tour, against East Coast/Poverty Bay.

DUNCAN HODGE

It was the last long tour that Scotland have done. There were mid-week games in North America and in Australia in 2004 but since then it has just been Test matches. We were away for six weeks in New Zealand and travelled all over the place playing games. It was a great experience, but very, very hard to do after a long season. Your body is just in pieces and your knackered all the time – and there are simply no easy games in New Zealand, every team was very, very strong.

Scotland line up to face the Haka at the House of Pain in Dunedin. Carisbrook's nick-name once again rang true for the tourists. *Getty Images*

JON PETRIE

In the Tests, the All Blacks were just unstoppable – I remember sitting in the stands during the first Test and watching Anton Oliver, the hooker, rampaging in like a train from the halfway line, just swatting our defenders aside.

I started off in the midweek team and had a couple of really good games, so made it onto the bench for the Saturday side, and I ended up being a bit hacked off that I didn't make it into the squad for the first Test. We were absolutely hammered in that match at Carisbrook but even despite that I didn't really think that I would be involved in the second Test.

Usually they'll give you a hint that you might be coming into the team or being dropped out of the team before the final selection meeting, but nobody had spoken to me at all. Geech read out the team for the second Test, and when they read these things out you are listening intently for your own name, and I was picked at number eight which tends to be the last name read out, so I didn't have any knowledge for about a day and a half afterwards of who else was in the team. It was a fairly long meeting, with a discussion about tactics and the mindset we needed to adopt, but I had to go to Geech afterwards and ask him to give me a summary because I hadn't heard anything. It does get a whole lot of emotions going. Obviously you are really excited and you know your family are going to be really excited as well. I phoned my Dad at 4am GMT, and I think he thought someone had died.

That second Test was played during a horrible night up in Auckland with gale force winds and the rain just lashing down. It was one of the proudest moments of my life. I had read French at university in St Andrews but cut short my studies after my third year when I was offered a contract with the Caledonia Reds. It had been a hard decision to make as I was only a year away from graduating with an honours degree, but I realised that the opportunity might not arise again and my burning ambition was to play for Scotland. You can never tell if you're going to be good enough to make it, if you'll get the luck of the bounce in front of the selectors and all the rest of it. So to finally pull on the jersey was a magnificent feeling and one that I knew I would cherish forever.

I remember the first kick-off and Andy Nicol was at scrum-half so we were standing close to each other. Andrew Mehrtens launched the ball way up into the floodlights, it seemed to hang there for an age, and as it started to come down I remember Andy shouting, 'Your ball Jonny.' So that was my introduction to international rugby, collecting this slippery ball which was plummeting to earth like a meteor, with the entire All Black pack charging towards me. I suppose it is good to get into these things straight away.

To be capped against the All Blacks at Eden Park, in a starting jersey, is about as good as it gets. We were playing at night in this iconic stadium, facing a Haka from the likes of Christian Cullen, Tana Umaga, Andrew Mehrtens, Justin Marshall, Jonah Lomu, Anton Oliver, Todd Blackadder, Norm Maxwell, Reuben Thorne and Josh Kronfeld – all of them absolute legends of the game, many of them the best-ever to have played in their positions.

They completely outmuscled and outran us, of course, but we did well to score a couple of tries through Cammie Murray and Chris Paterson.

DUNCAN HODGE

We were destroyed in both the Test matches, but I look back now at that team that we played against and it was just phenomenal. In the backs alone you had Justin Marshall and Andrew Mehrtens at half-back, you had Pita Alatini and Alama Ieremia in the centre who were perhaps not legendary names but were still super players, and then you had a back-three of Jonah Lomu, Tana Umaga and Christian Cullen, which would be a lot of people's all-time dream team back-three. We weren't close in any of those games at all. It was tough because we had had a long season and although they perennially come over to play us in November at the end of their season and whip everyone they come up against, they play less matches than we do in the northern hemisphere and they have a much bigger playing pool so they can rotate players. They have 30 or 40 guys capable of playing top-class Test rugby, but we don't have those kind of resources. We have to keep Test teams and squads together as much as we can and rotation isn't an option in the same way as it is for them. I remember after we got hammered in the first Test Jim Telfer flew into New Zealand on the Monday. We had a training session on the Sunday morning and then got flogged by Jim as soon as he arrived. The dirt-trackers played on the Tuesday, but Cammie Murray got injured, so I had to go on and play about an hour of that game; then on the Wednesday Jim got the Test team together and he flogged us again and we didn't have any days off so we were training on the Thursday and Friday too. There was no categorisation of training at that point – so we all did big sessions together no matter what and they were killers. And for three or four of us who had to back up games with the midweek team because of injuries, it was even harder. So I remember running out onto Eden Park on the Saturday night for the second Test and just thinking how completely shattered I was and wondering how on earth I was going to make it through an entire match against the best team in the world. I have never played as tired as I was in that match.

JON PETRIE

After the game I asked to swap jerseys with my opposite man, Ron Cribb. Cribb said that because the All Blacks only ever play in white when they play Scotland or France, he might not get another, so he wouldn't swap. I went back to the changing room a bit disappointed. Swapping jerseys was an act that I had long watched and admired as a fan and one that I had hoped to emulate – I thought that it was a kind of standard etiquette. I was sitting in my space in the changing room, starting to take my boots off when there was a knock at the door. In walked Josh Kronfeld, who had just won his 50th cap for the All Blacks, which, considering the depth of competition in New Zealand, particularly in the open-side position, was a testament to what a magnificent player he was. He walked over and congratulated me on a great game and on winning my first cap . . . and handed me his jersey. 'You hold on to yours,' he said. 'I'm sure it'll be the first of many, but the first one is always special.'

It was some gesture and I will never forget it. We went out in Auckland that night with all their players and had a superb time. It was something of an eye-opener that they were boozing away and playing drinking games; there was a culture developing in Scottish rugby at the time that drinking of any sort was a real no-no, but the All Blacks appreciated that if you played hard you should be allowed to party hard, too. The life of a professional player can be fairly robotic, and in many ways it needs to be because to achieve anything in the game you have to be very disciplined in your approach to training, diet, lifestyle and playing. But at the same time, it is a game played by young men and if you restrict yourself too much you miss out on a lot of the things that you need to properly enjoy in your teens, twenties and your early-thirties like anyone else.

Without those experiences, your life becomes a void that is only filled with rugby and that's no good for anybody. You are only young once and can only play the game to the highest level for a finite number of years, but at the same time, all your friends in other walks of life are gaining other experiences that shape and round the rest of their lives, and you cannot retire from the game and then try to catch up on what you missed out on. The world moves on, so it's important to strike the right balance or else you can lose out forever.

DUNCAN HODGE

The 2001 Six Nations was a really mixed affair. Gregor got injured after about five minutes against France and there then followed a whole goal-kicking debacle that lasted for a few matches. In that France game I came on for Gregor and Kenny Logan was doing the kicking and took a couple while I was on and then a message came on that I was to kick the goals. Then in the next game Kenny was kicking the goals against Wales and he kicked something like three from eight and I remember at around 75 minutes when Tom Smith scored, Andy Nicol turned to me and said, 'You take the next kick,' and I looked at the scoreboard and realised that it was 28-26 to them and I had to kick the goal to draw level. So it was the only kick I had taken all day and there was obviously huge pressure on it, but I managed to get it, which was a huge relief – although in the very last act of the game I had a drop-goal to win it, which was charged down. It wasn't to be, but the organisation of it all from the sidelines wasn't good. They should have either asked me to start kicking earlier – or I should have just carried on the goal-kicking duties from the France game – or just left it with Kenny. Neither of us were very happy about the sudden change-over. I'm just glad that my one effort went over because it could have made it a whole lot worse if I'd missed.

Tom Smith really showed his full range of skills in that game. He was bossing the Welsh scrum and the lineout was functioning really well – and he was charging all over the place in the loose. At one stage he got the ball down the blindside wing and he and Mossy [Chris Paterson] were on their own and outnumbered by about four or five Welsh defenders . . . and Tom put in this beautiful grubber kick behind them that Mossy latched onto over the line to score. And then, right at the death he took a ball out in the centre again and broke away from their defence on the 22 and rounded Neil Jenkins to score. It was some performance.

JON PETRIE

My first Six Nations game at Murrayfield was against Wales when we drew 28-28. We were 18-6 down at half-time and we just sat in the changing room and I don't remember anything anyone in particular said, but I remember the

After a virtuoso performance, Tom Smith slides in for the score to draw the match with Wales at Murrayfield. *Press Association*

feeling that it was going to have to be all or nothing. We knew we had to put everything out there. There was just this collective sense that we didn't want to lie down. That's the thing about international rugby, you get so drained physically and mentally out there that sometimes you are left thinking that you don't know how you are going to manage to get back to your feet. It's not that you don't want to, it's just that you don't know where the energy is going to come from – but there is something that makes you do it.

I had come straight from the summer tour into the autumn Test, and I remember being struck at that point by how good the atmosphere was at Murrayfield – but I was soon to learn that that was nothing compared to the buzz of a Six Nations match. You come in to stay in a hotel in the middle of town the night before the match and suddenly you realise just how many people have paid a hell of a lot of money to travel and watch you play. It is kind of difficult to deal with mentally – but I found it really enjoyable. And the atmosphere around the stadium when you arrive is just a whole different level.

DUNCAN HODGE

We went down to Twickenham for the next game and were absolutely stuffed. They well and truly got their revenge on us for the previous season and the way they played was one of the best performances I've ever seen. I remember that we were about 30 points down and they had been running us ragged and they brought on Jason Robinson for his first cap with about 15 minutes to go, which was the last thing we needed to see. He came on and within about 30 seconds had made a 60-yard break out his 22 and had set up a try. And then he did it again virtually from the kick-off. There can't be many first cap impacts like that one.

I remember on the morning of that game waking up in my hotel room and opening *The Times* to see an article by Will Greenwood, who I had gone to Durham Uni with along with Tim Stimpson, and he was comparing me and Jonny Wilkinson and our approaches and attitudes to the game – although he was comparing the Jonny Wilkinson of then, who was a fitness fanatic and perfectionist, with the 18 or 19 year old me who he knew at Durham – and his whole profile of me was basically harking back to the days of uni rugby when we were going out on the town after every game. At the time I was one of the younger boys in the uni squad so every Wednesday they said it was my birthday and I always had to chin a massive amount of this and that in every pub we went to. So he was comparing my student days at Durham with Jonny's professional approach, which was pretty funny on the morning of an international when we were going to be facing each other on the field. Will and I had a good chuckle about it at the after-match dinner.

We played Italy next and it wasn't a great game, but we did what we had to do and won – I kicked six kicks from seven and Tom Smith picked up another try and we managed to put them away – although it was far from a classic.

And then the Ireland game was called off because of Foot and Mouth. When we played them it didn't really feel like a Six Nations game, more of a one-off Test, but it was a great performance – albeit I had been dropped to the bench! I obviously hadn't had a good preseason or something because there had been hardly any other games in the interim.

IAN McGEECHAN

Our victory over a strong Ireland was no fluke – it was good rugby, played well. We put in another strong performance against Tonga and then fell away against Argentina and the All Blacks, but it should be remembered that we lost our middle five to injury around that time. If you can't put your best back-row and half-back combinations on the field, you will invariably struggle, especially against teams like Argentina and New Zealand, who excel in that area. We were entering something of a transitional phase at the time, with new players coming into the set-up and a change of focus developing on the way we wanted to play the game. The results were mixed at the time, but we came third in the 2001

Six Nations, which was probably higher than most people expected us to, and it remains one of the highest finishes we've had since the tournament expanded in 2000.

JON PETRIE

That was a year and a half since we had been Five Nations champions, we had beaten England in April of the previous year, so at that stage there was still a fairly high level of expectation. And despite suffering a massive loss to England, who were just on a different level that day, we recovered to beat Italy at home and then, once the authorities were satisfied that the Foot and Mouth epidemic was under control, we played Ireland at Murrayfield and absolutely stuffed them. It was tremendous performance and one that I still remember very fondly, even though I didn't start the match.

Things were looking up for the squad, but then things turned a bit sour in the autumn with the whole Brendan Laney affair.

GREGOR TOWNSEND

Several of us let Geech know about our concerns surrounding Brendan Laney's selection, but he seemed absolutely determined to play him. I think he looked at the almost instant success that John and Martin Leslie had been and thought that Brendan would do the same. And unfortunately there had been a precedent set there – John and Martin had only played one game for the Caley Reds before they were picked to play for Scotland against South Africa – and we all thought that it was a dangerous road to take. What good does it do any up-and-coming youngster to see their dreams of playing for their country dashed by some guys flying in from across the other side of the world and straight into the team? And not just for the youngsters; it wasn't good for the team as a whole. Geech placated us for a week by putting Brendan in the A team, but it was pretty obvious what his thinking was when Brendan was subbed halfway through the game – he was clearly being rested for the Test team. So no matter how Derrick Lee played against Argentina, it seemed a foregone conclusion that Brendan would take his place the following week.

DUNCAN HODGE

I was kind of caught up in the middle of the whole thing because I was captaining the A team at the time and Graham Hogg was basically told that he had to play Brendan against New Zealand as soon as he arrived.

It was tough on Dez [Derrick Lee] because he got awarded man of the match against Argentina and was then dropped for Brendan – and it had nothing to do with Brendan either because he wasn't the one picking the team. It was just so short-sighted. There was no way that one guy was going to make the difference between us beating the All Blacks or not. Even if he had been a new Christian Cullen, it still wouldn't have been enough – no one player can make that kind of difference on his own. It was totally pointless throwing him in like that and it had a huge impact on how he was regarded in Scotland – when he could easily have missed that game and had three months earning his stripes at Edinburgh before the Six Nations and been integrated into the Scotland squad then.

It was a tough time for everyone involved. I like Brendan a lot and always enjoyed playing with him, he was a good player and he was a great talker and communicator and was great at taking the ball up hard and flat – a typical New Zealand-reared rugby player – but he was put in a nightmare situation as soon as he got off the plane – as were the other players involved. He was a great player for Edinburgh but never quite did it for Scotland – but whether that's because of the atmosphere he experienced when he played Test rugby, which was down to the way it all started, I don't know.

GREGOR TOWNSEND

It wasn't Brendan's fault. There aren't many people who would turn down a chance to play international rugby and he wouldn't have wanted to anger the coaches by refusing to play – he might never have been selected again. It was tough on everyone – Derrick and Stuart Moffat were shoved down the pecking order and there were strong feelings of animosity from the crowd and the media directed at Brendan that lasted for the rest of his time in Scotland; it was felt that he hadn't earned the right to wear the jersey and he became a caricature of the rugby mercenary.

BRENDAN LANEY (Edinburgh Gunners)
20 Caps: 2001-2004

To be honest, I should maybe have been firmer and refused to play – and I really did think long and hard about that – but I had just arrived in the country, wanted to make a good impression and push for international honours as soon as I could. Hindsight is a wonderful thing. I know that I should have played a few games for Edinburgh and for Scotland A before even being thought about for Scotland, but if you're handed the opportunity to play against the All Blacks, how do you turn that down?

It was really tough for Derrick Lee and young Stu Moffat. Derrick was the Scotland fullback for the game against Argentina, which was the same weekend that I played for Scotland A against New Zealand. Despite the fact that Scotland lost, I thought that Derrick had played outstandingly well. But I think my game for the As was just a token gesture by the coaches – for whatever reason they were determined that I was going to get capped and like some great white hope, be the missing link to glory. The whole thing was handled very badly and I don't think the Scottish coaches would make that mistake again. I felt very bad about the whole thing and it really affected how the crowd took to me as well. It wasn't good.

GLENN METCALFE

I thought it was odd to rush Brendan into the Scotland set-up so quickly. He was undoubtedly a very good player and we all knew he could bring something positive to Scottish rugby, but the manner in which he was introduced wasn't ideal. I'd like to think the management would handle that type of situation differently now. Brendan was handed an incredible opportunity to play against the best rugby team in the world and it would have been extremely hard for him to turn that down. I think it put him in a really hard position. But from someone who has trodden that path before him, I think that it would have been a lot better for him to have served out an apprenticeship of some sort in the Scottish club game. Without doing that I don't think there is any way that you can go into Test rugby with any affinity to the jersey you're wearing or to the players you're playing with – especially when wearing that jersey means so much to them. There should be no easy routes to Test match rugby. And also the game is very different in Scotland to the rugby played in New Zealand. Every country has a different culture and approach to the game and you need time to settle into that environment and attune yourself with the type of rugby that your teammates and coaches are playing.

In New Zealand, rugby is the national obsession as well as the national sport. From the age of five, for most kids, it's just what you do – after school kick-arounds, Saturday games, Sunday tournaments, watching club, provincial and international rugby whenever you can and just dreaming about being an All Black. The focus in Scotland is very different because it's not the national sport. When I started playing in Scotland I felt the game was not as physical and the players were not as big as they were back home – although that is no doubt partly to do with the heavy Polynesian influence we have in New Zealand rugby. One thing I did notice was at one training session we pulled out a football to have a kick-around and I couldn't believe how good all the boys were – I was totally out of my depth; but you could see a fundamental difference there which has a knock on affect to senior rugby – as kids in Scotland all the boys spent much of their spare time kicking a football around. Football teaches you great spatial awareness and hones your peripheral vision, but as a Kiwi I spent my life passing and kicking a rugby ball around so I was always innately comfortable with it – as all boys in New Zealand are – and I think that's why New Zealand rugby is so strong across the board.

IAN McGEECHAN

New Zealand still pose the ultimate threat to any team on the planet's psychological and physical well-being: they can destroy you, at any time, in a dozen different ways. Every team in the world has experienced it when playing them. Over the years, Scotland have played some of their best rugby against the All Blacks – basically because the players know that if they don't raise every aspect of their game, they know that they'll be blown away. More often than not, the game can be fairly even for much of the 80 minutes, but the All Blacks excel at sucker-punching teams out of the game with relentless efficiency near the try-line. So often they score two or three tries in the space of just a few minutes, which wipes out the hopes of the opposition, even if the rest of the game is fairly evenly matched. It is a clinical efficiency that every All Blacks team seems capable of. That is the challenge that you have to meet, prevent, and then implement yourself if you are to stand a chance of victory. It is that innate self-belief that the All Blacks have – they will weather any storm because they know that they will get chances to score, and they will invariably deliver on those chances when they materialise. When the All Blacks are in full-flow they make it look so easy. Passes are timed to perfection, running lines carve open space and it all looks so simple. When they are in full-flow they play rugby the way it is supposed to be played.

GREGOR TOWNSEND

Argentina won that first autumn match 25-16 and afterwards we had a great dinner – they were a good bunch of guys. Right at the end Omar Hasan, their 19 stone prop, sang a song and everyone loved it. The Samoans and Fijians used to do that quite a lot as a team, but he did it on his own and he had this fantastic operatic baritone voice.

Scott Murray must have said to Tom Smith, our captain, that he'd give him £100 if he got up and sang at the dinner the following week when we played New Zealand – not ever thinking that Tom would have the guts to do it.

Now, the All Blacks are always very serious and professional in the way they conduct themselves after games – they are always very respectful to their hosts – and that was especially the case this time. Their captain, Anton Oliver, spoke about the game and congratulated us on our performance. It wasn't mere lip service. We'd actually played quite well, even though we lost 37-6 in the end. We stopped them from scoring any tries until the 71st minute before they got three quick tries to give the final score quite a misleading slant. So he was very complimentary about us – and it was genuine, which is a huge compliment from an All Black captain.

Then he talked about being in France on Remembrance Day a few days earlier and visiting the battlefields of the Somme and the graves of the many New Zealanders who had fallen in the First World War. He spoke really well and it was obviously very emotional for all of them. At the end he sat down to a solemn ripple of applause.

Then Tom got up, and the All Blacks were all very quiet and respectful. He walked straight to the front, and without a word of introduction he began to sing, 'Start spreading the news . . .'

He got through about half the verse, then said, 'That's £100 you owe me, Scott. Thanks.'

The All Blacks didn't know how to react. They couldn't believe what was happening. We were all going wild.

Tom may not speak that much in public but he certainly used to come out his shell in the squad environment. Every Friday, after the captain's run, you had to get up and sing on the bus back to the hotel if it was a significant occasion for you, like your first cap or your birthday. Tom always used to sing Kylie Minogue songs, and he was terrible – but he used to like getting up there and deliberately being terrible.

JON PETRIE

Jim Telfer was back coaching for those November games. When I first came in he had moved upstairs to be director of rugby, and you could see him up in his office with a pair of binoculars looking out, then after a few week he started coming out and standing in his suit at the side of the pitch, then it got to the stage he was standing at the side of the pitch with his boots on, and eventually he was back doing what he did best.

On the morning of a Test match the forwards used to go out and do some line-outs on the hotel grounds, then Jim used to take us into the team room to give us his big motivational speech. I remember before the All Blacks game in 2001, we were staying at the Roxburgh and he decided to sit all the forwards in a circle facing out the way, and he was marauding around the middle of the circle going through his speech and he kept on slapping boys on the back of the head. It scared the daylights out of you. He went through every player, telling them how tough they were and what he expected them to do to the opposition. Then he got to Badger – Gordon Simpson – who had been brought in when

Simon Taylor was injured, and he'd run out of things to say, so he ended up slapping him on the head saying, 'Badger, we didnae want you in the team, but you're the best we've got.'

Some of the drills he did were just plain stupid, but he loved boys getting worked up and almost injuring each other – and he seemed more delighted when boys did actually get injured.

He had this drill called the 'four corners of the earth', which was just basically a standard grid with a guy in each corner with a ball. Jim would shout go, and everyone at the same time had to run as fast as they could towards the middle in an effort to get through – you weren't allowed to side step, you were supposed to collide with the other guys. It was a completely pointless drill – other than Jim getting the satisfaction of seeing boys hurting each other.

He did mellow in later years, though, which was just as well because that intensity he had couldn't have been good for his health.

BRENDAN LANEY

I really enjoyed my first Six Nations, which was in 2002. I felt more comfortable to be in the team having got some game-time for Edinburgh under my belt. I got my first Scotland man of the match award when we beat Italy in Rome and managed to score 24 points, which was a record haul at the time for

a Scottish player. I then played pretty well when we beat Wales in Cardiff, which was a great experience – silencing a crowd as rowdy as the Millennium Stadium's is pretty special. We really took the game to the Welsh and snuffed out their hopes through our forwards – Gordie Bulloch got two tries from driving mauls – it may not have been pretty, but that's what you've got to do when you go on the road.

Brendan Laney kicks for goal at the Millennium Stadium. *Getty Images*

JON PETRIE

Greco [Graham Hogg] was always a bit of a legend for Scotland A, and one of his specialities was a firebrand speech in the changing room before a match. On this one occasion he went round the room saying to Duncan Hodge, 'Who is the best stand-off in Scotland?'

'I am, Greco.'

To me, 'Who is the best number eight?'

'I am, Greco.'

And it got to Derrick Lee, and he said, 'Who is the best fullback in Scotland?'

'Well, actually, I think Glenn Metcalfe is playing pretty well at the moment,' – which obviously went down like a sack of shit with Greco.

DONNIE MACFADYEN

My Scotland career started with Scottish Schools, who I played for on and off for a couple of years. I didn't get selected for the under-19s but came back into things for the under-21s. I played against France, Italy and Ireland but missed the Wales and England games because of injury and then went out for the under-21 World Cup in New Zealand in 2000 – which took place at the same time as the Scotland tour there, so we got to go to both Test matches to watch them. We had a great team that year and several of us went on to play for Scotland – in the forwards alone there were Bruce Douglas, Dougie Hall, Andy Hall, Simon Taylor and myself and we also had Tom Palmer who played for us at under-21 level before moving to Wasps and eventually getting picked for England. But at the same time Australia had guys like Phil Waugh and George Smith playing for them, South Africa had guys like Butch James, Marius Joubert, Adi Jacobs, Jo van Niekerk, Wikus van Heerden and CJ van der Linde, and New Zealand had Ben Blair, Riki Flutey, Seilala Mapasua, Aaron Mauger, Mils Muliaina, Jerry Collins, Carl Hayman, Richie McCaw, Kevin Mealamu, Rodney So'oialo and Tony Woodcock, as well as about four or five other guys who went on to become All Blacks. That New Zealand side absolutely thrashed the South Africans in the final, 71-5, which was played as a curtain-raiser before the second All Black-Scotland Test at Eden Park when Jon Petrie got capped, but looking back at the quality of that New Zealand under-21 team now you realise why.

As a team the Scotland under-21 side I was in had a lot of potential that we didn't really follow through on. I think the main problem any Scotland under-21 side, or under-20s as it now is, will have is that the big southern hemisphere teams have their players playing professional rugby by that stage, while in Scotland you have one or two academy players, maybe one or two guys on the books at a pro club and the rest come from amateur clubs. They get blown away in these competitions because they're not ready for the speed and intensity that the southern hemisphere guys play at. But it's not because they're bad players – within a year or two those same guys in the Scotland under-20 team will progress through to Test rugby and perform well there, so you realise that in many cases it's just a case of the Scottish guys getting used to playing at that faster, more intense level. After all, only a year after that under-21 tournament, Simon Taylor was a Lion in Australia. Looking at the results in these under-20 World Cups people often panic about the state of Scottish rugby, but the southern hemisphere guys are just exposed to professional rugby at an earlier stage, so really we just need to find a way for these guys to play more intense rugby and live a more professional life in terms of their fitness and conditioning, and they could easily compete – because they can do it in full blooded Test rugby just a year or so later.

I was first involved with the senior Scotland side when we toured North America in 2002. It was a good young squad that went out there and we had a great time as well as getting our first experience of the Test match environment. It was particularly special for me because I'd spent a year out after school in Canada working and playing on Vancouver Island and there were a few guys who we came up against who had been former teammates of mine. That season I spent there was also the first time that anyone had turned to me and said that they thought I would go on to play for Scotland – so to be able to go back there to actually win that first cap was fantastic and to see those guys again felt like a nice completion to a cycle in my life.

The coaches on that tour were Pat Lam and Ian McGeechan and I thought they were brilliant – although at the same time I had grown up watching Ian McGeechan in charge of Scotland and the Lions, so to begin with I was a bit awe-struck by the whole experience.

MIKE BLAIR (Edinburgh Gunners)
64 Caps (to date): 2002-still playing

My first involvement with Scotland at any level was the under-15 trial. I didn't get selected. Rory Lawson didn't go to the trial but he ended up as captain, which was pretty good going. I was behind Calum Cusiter for the under-16s and then Rory and I shared the scrum-half role for Scottish Schools. I played for Scotland under-18s a year young and wasn't involved for the first game, but I started the last game against Ireland at Thomond Park. Paul O'Connell was playing for Ireland that day and it was the most horrible, horrible weather . . . and we lost 51-0. But that was the first really big game that I was involved with for Scotland and it was played out in front of an 8,000-strong crowd. I was one the very few, if not the only guy, to go on and play professional rugby from that team – which was in total contrast to the England team we played that year, who had fourteen of the starting fifteen who went professional and eleven of them got full England caps and some also went on to play for the Lions. They had guys like Andrew Sheridan, Andy Goode, Hall Charlton, Joe Shaw, David Flatman, Alex Sanderson, Adam Balding and Steve Borthwick. That game was the first time I saw the difference in how Scottish players were being developed in comparison to other countries. The England players were all getting fast-tracked into Premiership clubs straight out of school and were being looked after in academies and so on – while only a handful of Scottish players, and I was lucky enough to eventually be one of them, were linked to the Scottish Institute of Sport. It comes down to funding in the end, but at that stage of your development, it's night and day been the haves and the have-nots – and our guys' main focus was on where they were going to go to university, as opposed to which club they'd play professionally for.

The following year we had several guys in the team who went on to play for Scotland. Rory and I were in the squad and we were playing with guys like Phil Godman and Al Kellock. We did much better that year, but still continued to struggle against most of the other bigger countries.

The year after that I was involved with the under-19s at the Junior World Cup in France, and Frank Hadden was coach. I was the only guy out the 32 in the squad not to start a game; I was reserve stand-off. I was originally picked as a fullback because Frank said we didn't have any fullbacks and he wanted to play me and Rory in the same team and I said, 'What about Neil Stenhouse?' Neil played for Hawick at the time and had been in their team since he was about 16 and he was a huge goal-kicker. And Frank just said, 'Oh, we want more than just a goal-kicker, we want your running and your game management.' But then when the games came around they obviously wanted a goal-kicker and because I hadn't been playing at nine to challenge Rory, Rory played at scrum-half and Stennie played at full-back and I covered stand-off. So that was quite a frustrating time.

But at the end of the tournament things started to get better because I was chosen to play in the sevens team and that was really the big springboard for my career. I was working with Rob Moffat and Roy Laidlaw and we had a reasonable seven playing, so it was all a good, positive set-up. We went to Amsterdam, played in the Henley sevens, played in Cardiff and at Twickenham, so I got a lot of game-time and it made a big difference to my fitness, speed, handling and defence. As a 20 year old playing in the Twickenham tournament I was up against guys like Lomu and other high-quality opposition, so it really allowed me to get some experience against good players, play with some freedom and in lots of space and basically just show what I could do – which hadn't been happening when I was coming off the bench in the age-grade stuff.

The sevens was also tremendously good fun. All the teams stayed in the same hotel and I remember walking through the lobby the day before the Twickenham tournament and seeing Joeli Vidiri, who has literally one of the biggest heads I've ever seen, and Jonah Lomu just chatting away, while I looked like some kind of lost child who had borrowed someone's kit and was just wandering vaguely around the place. The tournaments themselves were great fun, the rugby was exhilarating and the crowd were always in great spirits – and then afterwards all the players went out and mixed together; it really was a super experience.

After the sevens I played two games for the under-21s and was then fast-tracked into the Scotland A side – and although now it wouldn't be such a big deal being involved with the A team that young, at the time it was kind of unusual. We lost to Wales A in Wrexham, but starting that match was brilliant for my confidence and I played pretty well.

My first game for Scotland was against the Barbarians at Murrayfield in the summer of 2002 and although we lost, I started and scored a long-range try which was another boost for my confidence – especially as it was my first involvement with the senior side. But all these things are about luck and right-time-right-place opportunities because Bryan Redpath had decided not to tour North America that summer and Graeme Beveridge was injured, so I got selected for that tour and was suddenly number one scrum-half for the Test matches – while in other circumstances I might easily have not made the squad at all.

TOM PHILIP (Edinburgh Gunners)
5 Caps: 2004

I signed for Edinburgh in 2002 and in the summer of that year I was selected to tour North America with the senior Scotland squad. Hoggy [Allister Hogg] was selected as well and it was an incredible experience for us both because we were only 18 at the time. It was sort of a development squad and it was brilliant. I was chuffed to bits to be there. I didn't know if I was going to get capped or not, but Hoggy and I were really just called up to get some experience and it was great for us both.

I don't sleep well because I have constant pain in my back – it's a problem that I've had since my early teens – and it was a really long flight to Canada; on those kind of journeys, where you have to sit or lie still for long periods, the pain can get excruciating, so I spent most of the flight awake. But I just remember looking around at all these guys who I had seen playing on the TV or from the stand at Murrayfield ever since I had been a young kid and it was a special moment to realise where I was.

It was great being on tour with so many young guys and especially good that Hoggy was there because we had been through age group stuff together, and of course Mike Blair was there too, which helped because we had known each other all the way through school.

I played against Canada East, Canada West and USA A. Playing against Canada West I put Nikki Walker in for a try with a nice little pass; it was just the two of us and one of their defenders and everyone spent the next few days telling Nikki how well he'd done. Then, against USA A, I put Nikki through another gap, three-on-two, and then followed up my pass; it was then two-on-one with us and the fullback and all I was thinking was, *I'm going to score for Scotland, this is just awesome!* And then Nikki sold a dummy and got absolutely melted by their fullback. *Cheers, Nikki . . .*

MIKE BLAIR

I remember before my first cap against Canada saying to my mum and dad that if I scored, I would wipe my nose to let them know that I was thinking about them. I had all these visions of scoring a similar try to the one I'd scored against the Barbarians. We had a driving maul from about five metres out and were just about to plop over the line when I joined the maul, knicked the ball and fell over – so it was great to score on my debut, but it was not in quite the manner I had envisioned.

When you dream about what your first cap might be like, I definitely didn't imagine it to be the experience that I ended up having. We played in a field which was in the middle of nowhere in Canada with about 2000 people watching. It was baking hot and we lost. It wasn't the most auspicious of starts.

BRENDAN LANEY

The summer tour to the USA and Canada was great fun. It was good to get away with the boys and we had a great time – it was as much about building team spirit out there as it was blooding young players and trying new combinations.

MIKE BLAIR

The following week we played against America, went 7-0 down after five minutes and then Wagga [Nathan Hines] got sent off for punching. All the new guys were just thinking, 'Cheers, Wagga!' But we were able to pull it back and ended up thumping them, so it was a good way to haul the trip back on the tracks after the Canada game.

DUNCAN HODGE

It was a good fun tour out in North America. It was fairly short, with a couple of midweek games and two Tests – which will always be remembered in trivia questions because of Wagga getting sent off. It was a good tour to blood some new players and a lot of the older guys didn't tour – guys like Gregor didn't go and Tom Smith didn't go, and a few others.

I didn't have any idea at the time, but that game against the USA turned out to be my last cap. From winning 64-23 against the USA on the summer tour and scoring two tries, to the first squad session the following season – which was about two weeks of holiday and four weeks of pre-season training later – I somehow went from first choice stand-off to fourth choice. I remember being down in Connacht in the first or second game of the season with Edinburgh and overhearing a couple of the boys talking about a squad session, and I didn't think too much about it at first, but then I realised that they were talking about a Scotland session. So I went to speak to Frank Hadden about it, who was the Edinburgh coach at the time, and he told me that he had just heard as well but hadn't wanted to tell me about it until after the game. We had a bit of talk about it and I had a bit of a rant, but I figured I would just work my way back into the squad. Unfortunately that never happened – Matt Williams selected me for his first squad but I broke my foot before I even took part in a training session, then by the time I came back I was 30 and I was too old, in Matt's book, to be playing Test rugby. Which is a little frustrating when you look at how long someone like Mike Catt played, or even that Simon Shaw is *still* playing and he's older than I am.

No, it was a disappointing way to end things with Scotland. I was 27 at the time that Geech cut me from the squad and many people would think that that's a pretty good age to be playing international rugby. But so be it. I just figured at the time that I would get a call to explain why I was dropped and what he wanted from me to get back into the team – but to this day I'm still to hear from him.

BRENDAN LANEY

Coming back from the summer tour and preparing for the autumn internationals I really started to feel that I was beginning to change people's perceptions about me. The autumn series was just fantastic that year, something really special to be a part of. I equalled Gavin Hastings' record of reaching 100 Test points in nine matches, which was a proud moment for me – it really showed that I was contributing to the Scotland effort and hadn't come to just pick up a few caps and a pay cheque. And then to go unbeaten through all three games of the series was a real achievement and to beat a side like South Africa was epic. It was a really gutsy team effort and we deserved to win on the back of the courage that the guys showed out there.

MIKE BLAIR

When we came back from North America I thought I had done OK – not brilliantly, but OK – and I thought that I might have a shot at playing in the autumn Tests. But Brush and Graeme were back, so I dropped out of the squad

The squad celebrate their victory over the Springboks at Murrayfield in November 2002.
Getty Images

and I suppose it was fair enough – if they had been fit for the tour I wouldn't have been capped at all. I ended up playing for the A team throughout the autumn and played pretty well and it was probably better to have done that than just sit on the bench for three games and maybe only get one or two minutes at the end of each match.

One of my favourite ever memories, however, was a phone call I got from Dougie Morgan a few weeks before the 2003 Six Nations to say that I was going to be involved in the squad for the Ireland game, because it wasn't something I had expected at all. I didn't get on in that match, but being involved full stop was just amazing.

We had France away in the next game and Brush got stitches in his eye after about 20 minutes and I came on – and I was absolutely shitting myself. The noise in the Stade de France is one of the most unbelievable things I've ever heard, it's like the Millennium Stadium when the roof is closed – thunderous, thunderous noise and this incredible energy. The atmosphere at Murrayfield is a different kind of environment; in France and Wales there's a real carnival mood during the build-up to the game, but at places like Murrayfield and Twickenham there's a much more eerie, almost pre-battle kind of atmosphere.

So I came on, shaking to pieces and almost immediately a gap opened up at the side of a ruck and I sneaked through it and hared off up field on this forty metre run before eventually getting hunted down by these monstrous Frenchmen. There's a point on the video that you see me running and the only other people you can see around me are these ten French guys that are about to pound me into the ground. I remember speaking to Simon Taylor after the game and he said that he had had the weirdest thought when I made my break because he hadn't really been aware that I had come on; he had got up from the ruck and looked around and the first thought that he had was: 'Why is the ball boy running away with the ball?' I can understand his thinking – I was barely pushing 11 stone, had a ridiculous haircut with a Tintin quiff and looked about 12 years old. I probably haven't changed all that much physically over the years, but at least the quiff has gone.

BRENDAN LANEY

We thought we would do better in the 2003 Six Nations than we did, but we picked up good wins at home against Italy and Wales and controlled things well. We lost to Ireland in the opening match at Murrayfield and to France and England away, but all three of those teams were hitting a purple patch, especially England and France – and looking at their impact later in the year, you could see how well they were building towards the World Cup at that stage.

IAN McGEECHAN

In the two or three years building up to their World Cup triumph, England were playing the best rugby in the world. They evolved their game brilliantly to suit the qualities that they possessed – an incredible back-row, a shuddering and dynamic front-five, and intelligent backs. They dismantled us at Twickenham in 2001, thumped us clinically at Murrayfield in 2002 and snuffed out our challenged with ease again in 2003. They were so consistent in their performances and every player knew that he had to be at the top of his game to keep his place in the team. The only way to challenge them was to get hands on the ball and not give possession away, because they could keep it forever if you did. And during those two or three years, not many teams managed to get the better of them. It was the pinnacle of English rugby and they pushed the game on into whole new levels of excellence.

GREGOR TOWNSEND

We toured South Africa in the summer and although we lost both Tests we played some of the best rugby that I had experienced with Scotland – it was right up there with the '99 season. Our forwards picked up where they had left off when they last played the Springboks and really took the game to them physically. The back-row of Jason White, Simon Taylor and Andrew Mower were just brilliant – they were smashing these huge South African forwards all over the place. And our back-play was pretty electric too. In the first Test we outscored them three tries to two, with Andy Craig, Chris Paterson and Jason all scoring. We were leading 25-12 at one stage, but Louis Koen was keeping them in the game with his kicking – and a freak moment from one of his kicks got them right back in it. He took a penalty from around 30 or 40 yards out and hit the post – Trevor Halstead had been following up the kick and he reacted quicker than we did and got to the ball to score. They then pushed on and got into the lead after Stefan Terblanche scored another try. Going into injury time we were just four points down and were pressing on their line for several minutes. They kept giving away penalties that we decided to run and although I think we should have been awarded a penalty try for the number of times they infringed to stop us scoring, we eventually got another ruck right on their line and Nathan Hines picked up the ball and reached out through the ruck to score . . . but he just dropped it before grounding it. It went to the video ref and they were awarded a knock-on, which finished the match. It was a real gut-wrencher that we were that close and we definitely deserved more from our performance than that.

We headed to Ellis Park in Johannesburg the next week and the Springboks played much better than in the first Test, although we matched them in most areas again. I think the biggest difference came down to our fitness levels. They were ahead of us at that stage and they were able to close out the game in the final quarter. Terblanche and Koen did all the damage – Terblanche with a try and Koen with his boot – but Andy Craig scored again and Mossy's kicking was superb as ever. He was really starting to come into his own as a goal-kicker at that stage.

MIKE BLAIR

We had a couple of weeks at home after we got back from South Africa and then we began our pre-tournament training for the World Cup – which was all pretty novel. We flew out to the Olympic training camp in Spala in Poland for ten days of cryotherapy-based training – which basically involved heavy training sessions followed by three-and-a-half minutes in a cryogenic freezer, with temperatures at around -140 degrees centigrade while we just wore shorts, earmuffs and facemasks and a pair of clogs. The idea is that such extreme temperatures allowed for better muscle recovery after an intense work-out, allowing you to fit more training into a day. Those three-and-a-half minute bouts are the longest minutes and seconds of your life when you're in there. I found the whole Spala thing a bit weird, to be honest. You go out there for ten days and because of the whole cryotherapy thing they tell you that instead of doing five sessions in a week, you can do ten sessions. But they fail to tell you at that point that you then need a week to recover. So I always thought that we should just have stayed at home and done ten sessions over two weeks as normal.

But I have to say it was fascinating being in Spala and seeing all the other athletes who were there – there were a lot of Olympic pole-vaulters, hurdlers and sprinters, and seeing how they went about their training and preparation was very interesting.

Once we were back in Edinburgh and began training again we started doing a load of cardio work on bikes and rowing machines in the Botanic Gardens so that we got used to the heat and humidity levels that we would be facing out in Australia – it was obviously the complete reverse of what we had been doing in Poland, but it was just as hellishly difficult. We played one game in Townsville where the humidity was meant to be at its worst – but it wasn't humid at all. We then played the rest of our games in Brisbane and Sydney and again there was no humidity, so all those sessions in the Botanics had been a bit pointless.

Looking back, the South Africa tour earlier in the year had kind of felt like our break-out tour. We weren't miles away from the Springboks and Mossy scored that try of the year; then we did all the training in Poland and the warm-up games in Edinburgh and things just felt like they were building and building . . . and then it never really happened in Australia. I'm not sure if it was a case of pressure, or what, but we never got into our stride and only showed in very occasional glimpses what we were capable of – which was so, so much more than what we showed in that tournament.

GREGOR TOWNSEND

We had a warm-up game against Italy at Murrayfield, which we won 33-25, but then played Wales and Ireland, also as warm-ups, and lost them both, which wasn't exactly an ideal preparation for the World Cup. But we still felt in pretty good shape after all the training we'd been doing and our trips to South Africa, Poland and then being based back in Edinburgh had focussed everyone's minds on the challenges of the World Cup that lay ahead and had also been brilliant as a bonding exercise for the whole squad. I think many of us had been guilty of worrying about injuring ourselves in the warm-up games and so didn't play as well as we might have. It may have been the wrong attitude to have, but you can appreciate our concern – especially when the reality of what might happen hit us when we played Ireland.

MIKE BLAIR

I still feel bad about it, although it wasn't remotely intentional, and looking at the replay it wasn't even a bad tackle – but Geordan Murphy took a high ball against us and then went on a counter-attack and I just hit him with a good, solid low tackle. It was how he landed that was the problem – his leg got caught as he fell and his leg snapped. He was one of the most exciting fullbacks in European rugby at the time, so it was a huge blow to him and his team, but it also cost the tournament one of its potential stars. You don't get a chance to play in many World Cups and he had been coming into some serious form that year, so I felt awful about it. It's not something you would wish on any player.

STUART GRIMES (Watsonians, Glasgow Caledonians and Newcastle Falcons)
71 Caps: 1997-2005

We played the USA in the group section of the 2003 World Cup. The game had stopped while one of the players got some treatment and we were all in a huddle listening to Gordon Bulloch, the captain, speak. Ross Beattie arrived a bit late and was going on about needing water. He grabbed what appeared to be a bottle of mineral water out of our physio Stuart Barton's bag and gave it a good powerful squirt into his mouth. Little did he know that the bottle was filled with massage oil for player rubs. Within seconds Beattie was coughing and spluttering all over the place.

Bryan Redpath and Andy Craig celebrate with Gregor Townsend after he scores a try against the USA. *Getty Images*

It was one of those moments when everyone was trying to be serious and avoid cracking up with laughter . . . but it was hard! I remember looking at Nathan Hines and us having a little wry grin at each other.

MIKE BLAIR

The World Cup in Australia was one of the best experiences I have ever had with Scotland. It was my first World Cup and the whole atmosphere of the tournament was incredible – the number of fans who had made the journey from all over the world, particularly from the UK and France, was amazing and I thought that some of the initiatives that the organisers had for drumming up support for the lesser teams like Namibia, Georgia and Uruguay were superb. Namibia and Romania played each other in Tasmania and Uruguay and Georgia played at Stadium Australia in Sydney; ticket prices were lowered for the matches and they would be advertised over the radio, on TV and in the newspapers, encouraging the locals to adopt one or other of the teams – and the fans turned out in their thousands all wearing the colours of their adopted team for the day, so there was all this amazing vocal local support for these more minor matches, which was such an improvement on the previous World Cup.

It was hard work and a very intense environment at times in the Scotland squad, but it was also incredibly good fun. We trained hard in baking hot conditions and we didn't really do ourselves justice in any of the games, but the whole experience of being out there was brilliant and we also had some great nights out as a squad. These nights out are sometimes frowned upon from the outside, but it makes a real difference to team-bonding as well as giving players some time-out from the game. In Test match rugby, and particularly during a tournament like the World Cup that goes on for several weeks, you can get consumed by the game, it's all you think about and that's not healthy or productive for anyone. You need to be able to blow off some steam at times and think about other things. We got a bit of flak about our drinking from the press back home, but none of our behaviour was unprofessional. The dirt-trackers would only go out if they knew they weren't going to be playing, or if we went out as a squad it was after a match when we would have a week or ten days before the next game. And the drinking never affected our training or our games – the boys who had been out would always be at training and backing the starting squad up, and obviously if you were involved in a game you didn't go boozing. But the media played on it a bit, which was a shame. I can tell you, we weren't the only team who had dirt-trackers going out on the piss, every team had it.

We ended up staying near the Welsh and English guys and all the dirt-trackers in each team would get together and have a great time – it was like being in Faliraki!

GREGOR TOWNSEND

I really enjoyed the 2003 Rugby World Cup. The way the Australians organised it was brilliant. The USA game was a highlight, which you would never have expected, with 50,000 people in Suncorp Stadium on a Monday night.

But it hadn't been a great couple of seasons for Scotland, Ian McGeechan was under a lot of pressure and we got some stick in the press over a few things.

We started off staying in these apartments in Coloundra near Brisbane. The food wasn't great but you could cater for yourself if you wanted, and the idea was to give the players space and freedom to do what they wanted to do when not training. However, three days before we were meant to move on anyway, this biker gang called the Bandidos turned up to stay in the complex. There were over 150 of them, and they had apparently all paid $1000 each in advance for damage they might cause. So we moved into the city centre, and then after the USA game we moved down to Sydney and stayed in a place called Cronulla to the south of Sydney. This time the hotel couldn't really cope with the demands of a rugby team and it was just a bit too far out of the way to be convenient, so we moved again into Darling Harbour, close to the city centre. The fact that the management had responded to the situation was a real positive for the squad and raised spirits after our heavy 51-9 defeat to France – but it was written up in a very negative way by the press as an organisational disaster.

Somebody wrote an article about some of our wives coming out and how this mucked up the tour, but from our point of view it was great, my family and Basil's family stayed at a hotel down the road and it was a lovely boost to have them around. The England squad had their families staying with them – and they won the tournament. Seeing players enjoying themselves in those days tended to be portrayed as a sign of weaknesses.

There was also a bit of sniping about players going dirt-tracking – but that is just what happens on tours and it didn't get out of hand. I remember we turned up for our captain's run at Suncorp Stadium and the dirt-trackers were going for a fitness run and you could smell the rum coming off them, but as I say, that's what happens and they were all there ready to sweat it out. Unfortunately, with any tour there are always going to be guys who aren't involved in the big games, so they should be allowed to enjoy themselves, and the stories coming back from what the dirt-trackers got up to helped boost team morale.

MIKE BLAIR

In terms of playing, the World Cup was a bit disappointing for me as I didn't get an awful lot of game time. I started the game against the USA, but had a bit of a shocker. Bryan Redpath was the regular captain so I knew that I had to play out of my skin to get in front of him. It wasn't to be, but the experience of being at the tournament was fantastic and it was great for my development to be training so closely alongside Bryan during those weeks. I'd played against Italy and Ireland in the warm-up games and thought I'd played well but, as I say, the USA game wasn't great. I'd hoped to get on against France, especially when we were 30 points down with 20 minutes to go and it became clear that the Fiji game was going to be the crucial match, but it didn't happen. It was much the same with the Australia game – it would have been nice to get on and show what I could do when the game was gone, but it was Brush's last game, so I suppose they wanted to let him have the full 80, which is fair enough.

The whole tournament was still a lot of fun and socially we had a great time. Gordon Ross invented a drinking game that has been doing the rounds ever since. He bought a plastic toy shark that had this big gaping mouth full of teeth which became known as the 'Shark o' Skite'. To play, you opened the shark's mouth and one of the teeth in its lower jaw would be spring-loaded at random. The shark would then be passed around each player in turn and they would each have to press down on a tooth of their choice; if the tooth went down and nothing happened then you got to pass the shark on to the next man, but if you hit the one that had the spring in it, the shark would bite down on your hand and you would have to see away your drink. As you can imagine, that shark took down a lot of good men over the course of a night out and it was directly responsible for some of the more outrageous moments of the tour.

GORDON BULLOCH

While we had a great time at the tournament, one of the harder things to take was when Martin Leslie was suspended for twelve weeks after the USA game because he'd banged his knee into an opposition player's head as he cleared out a ruck. We all felt it was a pretty harsh punishment because there hadn't been any intent and the guy he hit wasn't injured, so for some reason we decided to pay tribute to him by mimicking his facial twitch as the camera came down the line past us

Gordon Bulloch vents his frustration during a World Cup campaign where Scotland stuttered rather than sparkled. *Getty Images*

during the national anthems for the France game. And we were absolutely slated for doing that by the press.

I suppose, if we had won the game it would have been forgotten about – but we got 50 points put on us and suddenly you were left thinking, *Jeez, that wasn't too good an idea.*

GREGOR TOWNSEND

It's a tough one because I know certain players back home thought it was a bit disrespectful. But if you want to judge how Scotland performed after doing that then look at the score after 30 minutes, we were only 6-3 down – it was only in the second-half that game really got away from us.

It really bonded us as a team. We wanted to make a statement that we were a strong group and we thought the punishment was harsh.

The master and the apprentice. Gregor Townsend lines up with Chris Paterson against France. *FotoSport*

All the press in Australia said it was a really good gesture, that it was a great thing to do for a guy who had had a hard time. I know the coverage back home was negative, but outside of Scotland it was seen as a dignified, silent gesture.

JON PETRIE

We'd had quite a long build-up out there but it just didn't click in the first game against Japan in Townsville. We came round to it a bit more in Brisbane against America, and then there was the France match. We didn't cover ourselves in glory at that World Cup, we made it to the quarter-finals but only by the skin of our teeth after we had been hammered by France at Stadium Australia. We just didn't play very well, which was particularly disappointing because we'd had such a good build up.

MIKE BLAIR

In the wake of the France game it was decided that Mossy [Chris Paterson] would get a run at stand-off for our last pool game against Fiji. Geech said in a press conference that it had always been our intention to play him at ten at

Gregor Townsend in action against Fiji. *Press Association*

some point during the tournament, but it seemed to come a bit of the blue for all of us, including Mossy, because he hadn't trained in that position even once during the any of team training runs. It was pretty tough on Gregor to be moved out to outside centre for our most crucial game, pretty tough on Mossy because he was being brought into a hugely pressured environment with hardly any time to adjust to it, and pretty devastating for Gordon Ross who had been leapfrogged altogether after playing well in the first game against Japan. They said it was pre-planned, but it seemed like it was more of a knee-jerk reaction to the criticism that the press were dishing out after the France game and an effort to assuage them by picking Mossy, which certain quarters of the press had been calling for for ages. But fair play to Mossy, he took it all totally in his stride and really showed his class as he looked completely comfortable and confident out there controlling things.

CHRIS PATERSON (Edinburgh Gunners, Gloucester, Edinburgh)
100 Caps (to date): 1999-still playing

I loved my time out in Australia – it was the best six weeks of my international career up to that point and we all had a great time. The French game was obviously a huge disappointment and on the back of that there emerged all these reports that there were problems in the camp. But the truth of it was that France were outstanding and deserved to win that well. After that game I genuinely thought that they would go on to win the tournament.

JON PETRIE

A lot of people made a lot out of the atmosphere in the camp and claimed that we were not very professional while we were out there, but I would completely disagree with that. We were out there for seven weeks so there were a few occasions when a few guys went out for a few beers, but these would be the guys that weren't playing that week. Everyone knew they were at a World Cup and understood what an honour that was.

GORDON BULLOCH

Our final pool game was against Fiji, which was a must-win match after the France debacle. They were a strong side and the conditions in Australia were suiting them perfectly – they were throwing the ball around and having a go from everywhere. Their forwards were massive but could sprint as fast as most international backs and their skills were unbelievable. And in Rupeni Caucaunibuca they had one of the stars of the tournament. He was short and barrel-like, almost chubby, but he could shift, really shift. He had scored the most unbelievable try against France when he just blistered around their cover defence from around 70 yards out. So we were well aware of what he could do and were determined not to give him any space . . . so of course he went on to score two tries against us. For the first one he took the ball down the touchline and managed to make it past Simon Danielli, Glenn Metcalfe and Kenny Logan despite having about three inches of space the whole way. And if that was good, the second try he scored was even better. They flung the ball wide to his wing on their 22 and he broke outside Tom Smith and then stepped inside Jim McLaren, leaving him flat on his face, and then cut back towards the posts, passing Glenn Metcalfe, who is no slouch, and he made it look like Glenn was jogging as he was coming across – he just burned him.

Chris Paterson looks to unleash his backline against Fiji. *FotoSport*

STUART GRIMES

We were staring down the barrel of a gun then. We were creating spaces to attack them with Mossy playing at stand-off for the first time in the tournament and he was doing well, but Fiji were all over us. They were running it from everywhere and Caucau was just on fire. Going into the final five minutes we were 20-15 down and looked like we might be exiting before the quarter-finals for the first time in our history. Basil [Bryan Redpath] took us aside and said that we had to keep it tight and look to score through the forwards, which was where Fiji were at their weakest. It wasn't a pretty way to win the game but it was immensely satisfying. We worked incredibly hard to get ourselves into position and then kept our heads to force Tom Smith over – what a way it was for him to celebrate his 50th cap. Mossy had to kick the conversion to win and he kept his cool – and we were through.

JON PETRIE

We were under a hell of a lot of pressure by the time we played Fiji and thankfully Tom came up with the goods.

The winger, Caucau, was at his peak and could have scored a barrel-load of tries, but Glenn Metcalfe tackled like a demon that day. He absolutely wrecked his body, throwing himself at guys who were about to score in the corner. We were actually quite lucky to sneak through, with Tom Smith going over from a line-out drive in the 79th minute. There was a huge sense of relief at that stage that we had made it through the group stage.

MIKE BLAIR

It was a tough game to watch from the sidelines. Caucau was a sensation – he made it look so easy when he got the ball but he was also incredibly aggressive in defence – there was one sickening moment when he smashed into the line and shattered Simon Danielli's nose with a forearm. It was brutal.

And that final quarter was utterly nerve-wracking. It was a great bit of disciplined play from the forwards to control the ball through so many phases before Tom Smith powered over. He had to stand up on the bus and sing a song the day before because it was his birthday – he absolutely murdered Kylie's I Should Be So Lucky, and that song turned out to be a bit of an omen for the Fiji game. We were through to the quarter-final to play Australia, but we had ridden our luck to get there.

One of my favourite memories came out in the aftermath of that game. Alan Tait showed us a video of the Fiji game as we got ready for the quarter-final. He put a couple of clips together of Glenn Metcalfe making two try-saving tackles.

We watched them a few times and then Taity stood up and said, 'Fookin' Snowy Metcalfe! Two tackles: still in the comp!' Session over. It was brilliant.

STUART GRIMES

So we had the hosts, who were also the defending champions, in the quarter-final. It was about 40 minutes before the match and the kickers were already out on the field getting a bit of practice in. Then the rest of us started heading out of the changing room for the warm-up and as we walked up the tunnel we saw Chris Paterson getting carried past us in the opposite direction. He was one of our main men, playing stand-off that day and our main goal-kicker, so we were wondering what the hell was going on.

It turned out Mossy had been practicing his kicking, with Ben Hinshelwood returning the ball to him. And Ben had launched this huge torpedo kick which had struck Mossy right on the side of the head just as he was lining up another kick. He collapsed on the spot – out cold.

These were in the days when you only took the 22 men in the squad with you on match day, so, while we had a lot of people in the stand, none of them were prepared to play.

They got Mossy into the changing room and were splashing his face with cold water, saying, 'Oh my god, what are we going to do?'

Andy Craig was called down from the stand: he was in his number ones and was struggling a bit after being out on the tiles the night before. His boots were back at the hotel, which was half a mile away, so someone was sent to get them.

But in the meantime Mossy began to recover his senses, and with only five minutes to go before kick-off they decided to go with him. He played a blinder and struck one of the finest drop-goals ever by a Scottish player, but we ended up losing 33-16.

A few years later, when I was playing at Newcastle with Matt Burke, we spoke about that day. He said he had been out there at the other end of the pitch with his Australian teammates doing his own kicking drills and he couldn't believe what had happened. There had been three or four of them who all saw the ball hit Mossy on the side of the head, and they all instantly started to fall about the place laughing. Apparently they were talking about it in the changing room just before they ran out.

From then on, two travelling reserves have always been included in the Scottish squad for Test matches, ready to go if some freak accident like that happens again.

GREGOR TOWNSEND

It was 9-9 at half-time, but we were lucky to be level. We were playing our hearts out, but Australia were a much better team and we were still in the game largely by dint of their mistakes. Our forwards were superb though and there was an awe-inspiring moment when Stirling Mortlock, their talismanic centre, crashed into the line only to be met by Jason White, who halted him dead in his tracks, picked him up like a doll and smashed him backwards.

We were unlucky in a couple of facets of the game – Kenny Logan had broken free to score but Steve Walsh, the referee, brought us back for a penalty which he awarded to us because he hadn't see that Kenny had made the break. Australia scored a fairly dubious try that then lifted their confidence and they then ran amok for fifteen minutes. We fought back and scored a try through Robbie Russell, but it was too little too late – much like the last World Cup quarter-final against the All Blacks.

JON PETRIE

We didn't do too badly against Australia. They were obviously favourites, they were at home, and the Suncorp Stadium is just a fantastic place to play rugby.

Clash of the Titans. Jason White thunders into Stirling Mortlock. *Getty Images*

It was a tough time because we were getting pelters from the press. But it was a great tour, and a great time to be out there – even if the rugby was tough. You keep yourself pretty insular from what's going on outside, but you were aware of some of the negativity in the press which was disappointing because you do want people to be on your side going into something like that, and it didn't feel like that. Having said that, we have to be aware of how we are perceived and recognise that we play a roll in that.

GLENN METCALFE

The World Cup in Australia was a disappointment for me; as a squad we were fitter and stronger and better prepared than ever due to the fitness camp in Spala and the tour to South Africa where we played well in both Tests, but we seemed to misfire through the pool games against Japan and the USA and got crushed by France. All the hard work and prep wasn't paying off. I couldn't believe we weren't able keep pace with France and for much of that match it seemed like we were just spectators out there. Then we played Fiji, which to this day was one of the toughest matches, physically, I've played in. We held on to win . . . just . . . and went on to face Australia in the quarter-final. Again we suffered a defeat that I felt shouldn't have happened. I don't mean that we should have won, but we should have made a much closer contest out of it considering all the hard work we put in prior to the tournament and the quality of the squad that we had.

I went off with an injured shoulder and now looking back and knowing that it was my last game for Scotland, it was a disappointing way to end my international career.

GREGOR TOWNSEND

It was an emotional end to the game. We did a lap of honour to thank the fans, and Bryan Redpath and Kenny said their goodbyes as the tournament was their swansong before hanging up their boots. It was also the end of the coaching road for Geech and Telfer; Telfer was finally standing down from the SRU and Geech was moving up to become the director of rugby. Matt Williams had already been named as his replacement and we had been implementing some of his structural play and tactics during the World Cup. Many of his instructions had been confusing and somewhat over-elaborate, often over-complicating areas of the game unnecessarily, which was a terrible decision to try and introduce mid-tournament. We weren't particularly impressed by very much it, but had little choice but to get on with things. In retrospect, it should have served as a warning of what was to come.

CHAPTER FIFTEEN

THE AUSTRALIAN REVOLUTION

A S HE MOVED *up to take the helm as director of rugby from Jim Telfer, who was, definitively this time, retiring from active involvement in Scottish rugby,* Ian McGeechan's final act as head coach was to appoint the Australian Matt Williams as his successor. McGeechan would not last long in his role behind a desk at Murrayfield – the siren call of the tracksuit and the training paddock would prove too strong and he was soon heading south to take up a new position with English and European champions, London Wasps, an appointment which, in turn, would eventually lead to his return to the Lions den, first as midweek coach on the 2005 tour to New Zealand under Clive Woodward and then as head coach for the 2009 tour to South Africa.

As part of a continued shake-up at the SRU, chief executive Bill Watson was sacked and team manager Dougie Morgan stepped aside. Matt Williams had been brought in as a technical advisor during the 2003 World Cup so that some of his systems and initiatives could begin to filter into the team. He appointed former All Blacks skipper, and the incumbent Edinburgh captain-coach, Todd Blackadder, as his assistant. Alan Tait had been working with the squad as defence coach, but Williams wanted to take on that role himself, and so the Kelso man was soon on his way out of Murrayfield as well.

The Australian had a mixed track-record as he came into the post as Scotland's head man. He had been head coach of New South Wales from 1997 to 1999 and in his first season in charge he took the Waratahs to their worst-ever Super 12 position of ninth. In his final season the team finished their campaign with a dismal six losses in their last seven matches, extinguishing any hopes that they had held earlier in the season of a semi-final place, and he left the post with a year still to run on his contract.

From Sydney he moved to Dublin to become assistant coach to Mike Ruddock at Leinster and succeeded the Welshman at the helm the following year. After an inauspicious first season in charge, when his team finished third out of four in their Heineken Cup pool, he led the Irishmen to the inaugural Celtic League title as well as the Irish Inter-Provincial championship, and followed this up by guiding them into quarter and semi-final appearances in the next two Heineken Cup campaigns. On the

---

Opposite: A disconsolate look from the Scottish team – one that was all too familiar to them during Matt Williams' time in charge. *Getty Images*

back of these performances he was approached by McGeechan to ascertain his interest in moving into international rugby and was finally named as his successor on the eve of the World Cup.

Williams was initially affable and charismatic in his dealings with the media and could certainly talk a good game; his eloquent southern hemisphere cadences added weight to his statements about how he thought Scottish teams should play the game, and helped expound his vision for Fortress Scotland – an initiative to strengthen the domestic teams by only selecting players for the national team who plied their trade within Scotland – as well as his targets for 'up-skilling' the players who were now under his charge. No one could hide from the raw truth of many of his statements – Scotland had been underperforming for a number of years, and save for an upsurge in the 1999 Five Nations, had been on a downward spiral since the mid-nineties. However, there were some doubts cast about his approach when he claimed that the Scottish rugby public should not expect to see any notable improvement in the team for some 18 months as the players adapted to the new systems and worked on improving their skills; he predicted that throughout this transitional period that there would be very few, if any, positive results registered. The revolution would be painful, he said, but in the end the team would emerge into a bright new dawn to bathe in success for years to come.

His approach was indeed revolutionary and with every revolution there are casualties. Dougie Morgan and Alan Tait had already been cleared from the management and coaching side. Now Williams turned his attention to the playing staff.

Following his announcement that huge improvements would have to be made in every position in order for the team to stand a chance of success in the future, Williams phoned Glenn Metcalfe, James McLaren and Gregor Townsend, three of the most experienced players in his squad, and recommended that they should each take the opportunity to announce their retirements from international rugby on their own terms – as he had no intention of picking them for any of his future squads. With little option before them, all three players duly announced their retirements, immediately removing 144 caps worth of experience from the squad.

For all that the coach may have been misguided in jettisoning many of the more experienced campaigners that were still willingly at his disposal, he certainly didn't hold back in his promise to give youth its head by selecting a team brimming with young talent for the 2004 Six Nations opener against Wales at the Millennium Stadium.

In the months preceding the World Cup, and during the tournament itself, Mike Blair was seen as the heir apparent to succeed the retiring captain, Bryan Redpath. Williams wasn't so convinced and as he studied the players in the Scotland squad and compared them with their rivals in the opposition ranks, he came to the conclusion that the Scottish pack was going to struggle to impose themselves in any of the forthcoming Tests. Williams believed that Blair was getting something of an armchair ride at Edinburgh; Chris Cusiter at the Borders, however, was getting anything but that. In selecting Cusiter ahead of Blair for the opening match of the 2004 Six Nations, Williams said that he needed a scrum-half who was used to playing under the pressure of a retreating scrum. There was no doubt that Cusiter deserved his shot at glory and since his debut he has gone on to prove his class for both Scotland and the Lions, but it was a mixed message that Williams was sending out – it boosted Cusiter's confidence certainly, but it also revealed that he did not rate his forwards as an international unit.

Other youngsters brought into the team included centre Tom Philip and back-rower Ally Hogg, and in a bold move he selected Chris Paterson as his stand-off and captain. As well as the added responsibility that the role of captain brought, there was a lot of pressure on the Gala man to repeat the form that he had shown at fly-half during the World Cup while simultaneously leading a team shorn of much of its experience. To compound matters, Williams had devised what he believed to be an ingenious defensive system whereby Paterson would retreat to fullback in defensive situations, centre Andy Henderson, who was playing out of position on the wing, would shuffle into the number 12 channel while Philip moved to stand-off, and fullback Ben Hinshelwood would come into the vacated wing birth. In reality the system was disjointed, confusing and added doubt in the minds of the players as they lined up to stifle the Welsh attack. In the end, the hosts were able to unpick the system with relative ease. This type of over-complication became emblematic of Williams' tenure in charge of the national side. Despite positive showings from Cusiter, Philip, Hogg and a late introduction by the Australian-born stand-off, Dan Parks, Wales strolled to a 23-10 victory.

It was a story that would become a trend throughout the remainder of the tournament as Scotland finished the Championship without registering a single win.

During the summer, the team recorded their first victory under Williams against Samoa in, uniquely, Wellington, but then crashed to two defeats to the Wallabies, going down 35-15 and 34-13 in Melbourne and Sydney.

Chris Paterson was injured during the Samoan match and was replaced as captain by Scott Murray for the remaining two Tests. When Paterson retuned to the team later that year he regained neither the fly-half shirt nor the captaincy; he was selected on the wing and on-field leadership responsibilities were passed to hooker Gordon Bulloch.

In November, Scotland faced the Wallabies for the third successive time and although Williams attempted some trickery to contain the expansive Australian game plan by reducing the width of the Murrayfield pitch to its legal minimum, his countrymen ran out 31-14 winners. The Scotland team then had something of a morale boost by beating Japan 100-8 in Perth. But normal service was soon resumed with the team losing yet again to Australia, 31-17, before facing South Africa in the fourth and final Test of that autumn series. The visitors atoned for their 2002 defeat in Edinburgh by scoring five tries in a 45-10 victory to conclude a wretched year for the Scots.

The 2005 season opened with a moment of promise as Scotland ran France close in Paris and had Ally Hogg not been called back for a much debated foot-in-touch, the Scots might have recorded a famous victory.

Any hint of progress was dismissed the following week, however, when Ireland came to town and hammered their hosts 40-13. Two weeks later, Williams finally broke his Six Nations duck by defeating Italy 18-10; for all that it was positive for Scotland to claim the win in what had already been dubbed the wooden spoon play-off, it had once again been an uninspiring performance from the home side who had clawed their way to victory thanks to the steady boot of Chris Paterson. The lack of any real progress was once again highlighted the following week when Wales came to Edinburgh and, as Ireland had done, inflicted a humiliating defeat over the hosts, running out 46-22 winners as they marched towards the Grand Slam.

Williams was holding true to many of the promises that he had made when he was appointed coach. He was encouraging players back to Scotland, preferring to pick home-based players over those who played from clubs abroad; he was implementing his own style of play and tactics and was sticking firmly to his guns that his was the right way for Scotland to play; and his team had managed to achieve just two wins, against fairly limited opposition, during the entire course of his tenure. Now, in the wake of the Welsh defeat, Williams claimed that it might well be another year before the team would make its breakthrough.

A final daunting Six Nations trip to Twickenham loomed for the dispirited and battered Scots. England were on the wane after their triumphs in Sydney two years previously, but they were still a mighty and intimidating prospect for a Scotland team at such a low-ebb.

26-10 down at half-time, a decision was made after the coaching team had left the changing room to discard the over-regimented game-plan; the Scots were going to attack and counter-attack for all they were worth, seek to throw the offload whenever they could and not be afraid to have a go. The result was probably already beyond them; they had nothing to lose. They had come to Twickenham to play rugby and before Alain Rolland blew his final whistle, that was exactly what they were going to do.

And so it was that the man who tried to revolutionise the Scottish game was, finally, revolted against by his own players. As Woodrow Wilson famously said, 'the seed of revolution is repression' – and it was against the repressive structures and game plans imposed by the Australian that the players finally turned. They hit back and ran free and in that second-half they played some of the finest rugby that the Scottish fans had seen from their team for years. It may not have resulted in victory at Twickenham, but it freed their power of expression and allowed them to turn the *corner as Williams was dethroned and a new coaching structure came into play. The idea that they did not possess the necessary skills for international rugby was wrong; they simply lacked the courage of their convictions to go out and play as they could. And it was with that simple truth that the new regime would seek to reignite the floundering fortunes of the thistle.*

GREGOR TOWNSEND

Coming back from the World Cup, I was excited and invigorated about the season ahead. I was very pleased with the way that Mossy had finished the tournament at stand-off and although I still wanted to contest for the jersey with him, I could also envisage us building a new partnership with him at fly-half and me outside him at inside centre – in a kind of mentoring position that England employed with Jonny Wilkinson and Mike Catt and Australia used with Matt Giteau and Elton Flatley.

On the back of the World Cup I had turned down a chance to play in the Super 12 with the Natal Sharks, choosing instead to stay on at the Borders and continue to push for a place with Scotland.

I was aware that there had been a few Scotland sessions at the start of the new season, but I had been recovering from the thigh injury and so didn't read too much into my exclusion from these. And then I received a call from Matt Williams. When we had last met, out in Australia just after our quarter-final exit, he had talked positively about his plans for the Six Nations and was looking forward to throwing some ideas around with me in due course for the upcoming Championship. Well, his call put a slightly different complexion on things. He told me that we had a dearth of international experience in midfield and that he wanted to blood new players in that position so that they could start building that experience. He was about to announce his Six Nations training squad of 44 players . . . and I wasn't in it.

I told him that I wanted to fight for my place but he was worried about the PR side of things – that the press would focus in on my exclusion rather than his positive selections. He said that because of my reluctance to just disappear into the background, he would publicly pick me for the squad but that, in reality, I was banned from attending any training sessions and that I would not be considered for any match-day squads.

So, where was I to go from there? I was being retired from international rugby and there was nothing I could do about it. For all that I was prepared to fight it out for my place, it was clear that no matter how well I played over the next few weeks and months, I wasn't going to be picked.

I went to Murrayfield for a meeting with Williams and told him that I had decided to retire. What else was I to do? It was hardly retiring on my own terms, but it was less ignominious – and less damaging to the progress of the rest of the squad – to publicly deride Williams for his decision.

MIKE BLAIR

It was a tough pill for Gregor to swallow. He was being put out to pasture and yet he was only 30. He was also, at the time, the most capped player Scotland had ever had. All that experience and class just went out the window. It also didn't help that guys his same age were still getting picked in the squad – guys like Brendan Laney and Derrick Lee – and yet he had been told that he was now too old for the international game. It was crazy. You look at someone like Mike Catt who was still getting capped by England at 36, or even guys like Yannick Jauzion playing for France – they are the steady generals in the team who help the young guys through their first years of international rugby; and they're not in the team just to mentor either, they're still class players in their own right, just like Gregor was.

Gordon D'Arcy once said that while Matt Williams was at Leinster, he could talk to you for half-an-hour and you would walk away thinking: 'What was he trying to tell me?' It was a fairly accurate summation of many conversations I had with him. He could talk a great game full of nice little sound-bites and buzz-words, but the actual content of what he was trying to put across could get lost quite easily – if it was even there to begin with.

Ian McGeechan at a press conference with Matt Williams and Todd Blackadder. *SNS Pix*

It's hugely important for rugby players to enjoy the game they play, to enjoy training. If you don't, the monotony of training can really begin to get to you; if there is no break from the hard physical exertions, if there is nothing to relieve the intensity of endless video analysis, then there's none of the freedom that's required to draw the best out of you. Rugby is first and foremost a game; if there is no enjoyment, it is impossible to play it to the best of your ability. Of course, the perspective on all-out enjoyment changes somewhat now that we live in an age of professional rugby, but nevertheless, there must remain some semblance of enjoyment – without it, players become automatons and there is no creative spark, no freedom to express yourself.

ANDY HENDERSON (Glasgow Warriors)
53 Caps: 2001-2008

When Matt Williams took over, as a changing room, we were keen to be positive about it. We were excited about the prospect of a new challenge.

But things didn't really work out. One of the big things for me was that training was simplified an awful lot, and broken down to basic skills. When you come together before an international match you really need to be working on what you are going to do as a team and not spending your whole time practising your spin passing, which really should be the sort of day-to-day stuff you do at your club. I always thought that was a bit bizarre.

As things went along a growing issue was the drop-off in confidence within the squad – which in international sport is probably the most important factor in teams realising their potential. It is a vicious cycle because unless you win a few matches it is really hard to instil confidence, but without belief you are going to struggle to win.

TOM PHILIP

After I came back from the 2002 North America tour I dropped out of the senior Scotland squad and played for the under-21s for a season. We had a great team that year with guys like Graeme Morrison, Phil Godman, Chris Cusiter, Hoggy, Kelly Brown, Nikki Walker, Gareth Morton, Dicko [Alasdair Dickinson], and Ali Strokosch and we beat England, which was a huge result – I'd been dropped for the previous game against Ireland but came back for that England game and played really well. I then played some good games for Edinburgh and Matt Williams came to see the Edinburgh-Glasgow game when I made a few breaks, put in some good tackles and scored a try, and from there I got selected back into the senior squad again for the Six Nations. I held my own during the training sessions and I think I impressed with my defence because there were a couple of rugby league guys from Australia who had been brought in to advise on that area of the game and they liked my approach to tackling and making big hits. I thought I might be in with a chance for making the extended squad for the Six Nations, and I couldn't believe it when I was selected to start against Wales.

CHRIS CUSITER (Border Reivers, Perpignan, Glasgow Warriors)
52 Caps (to date): 2004-still playing

It was a surprise to get the elevation into the Scotland squad so soon after signing for the Borders and I definitely didn't expect to be the first choice for the opening game of the Six Nations. Standing there in the Millennium Stadium gave me a feeling that I had never felt before and I had a tear in my eye during the anthems. After you taste international rugby all you want to do is experience it again and again. After I picked up my first couple of caps I reassessed my goals and it became incredibly important to me that I held onto the shirt from all-comers. I wanted that number nine shirt and I would work as hard as I possibly could to keep it.

MIKE BLAIR

I was obviously massively disappointed not to be starting under the new regime, but Cus [Chris Cusiter] definitely deserved his chance – he was playing very well for the Borders at the time and although I didn't agree with the coach's reasons for picking him ahead of me, on playing merit he certainly deserved his shot. But the thing that really annoyed me about it all was that Matt Williams told me about six weeks before the Wales game that Cus was going to be starting. There wasn't much I could say to change his mind. He'd said that line about Cus getting the nod because he was playing behind a weak pack, which I found pretty baffling, because while Edinburgh were having a good season that year, our forwards were by no means dominant up-front. Even when we won against Toulouse we were virtually running backwards in the set-piece and it was really the excellence of our back-row that meant that we held in there because they were able to tidy things up so well. So it was frustrating to be given that as an explanation. If he had just said that Cus was playing better than I was, then I would have accepted it – if that was his opinion, then so be it. But if you're given a reason based on external factors that don't really add-up, it makes it more difficult to accept.

Every generation seems to have had its major battle for the Scottish scrum-half berth, and ours is no different. There's me, Cus and Rory Lawson all fighting it out and there will be other guys who will emerge in time too. It's a challenge, but it's a great feeling when you're picked to start – you know you've definitely earned it to get ahead of those other guys.

I hadn't played well during the World Cup and there was a bit of a hangover from that. Once Cus was selected I knew that I had to just get my head down and work hard and look to play as well as I could when I came off the bench.

But while I was disappointed not to start that opening match against Wales, I was so pleased to see Tom Philip get capped. We had played together at school – he was only 14 when he first turned out for our 1st XV and I was captain, and he was probably the biggest guy in our team; his one thigh was like both of mine put together – and it was great when he got his contract with Edinburgh. He's an absolute beast physically, with great skills and pace and a huge heart. He looked really comfortable out there right from the start and he made a big impact, carrying strongly and absolutely murdering some of the Welsh boys in the tackle.

ALLISTER HOGG (Edinburgh Gunners)
48 Caps (to date): 2004-still playing

Tom and I made our Scotland debuts together in that Wales match. We'd been playing for Edinburgh together for a wee bit by then and so having him making his debut too was very reassuring – because we knew each other well but also because of what he could bring to the game in terms of physicality. He'd walk out on the pitch and even though he was only 20, he would dwarf just about any other player out there. You knew just by looking at him that he would make an impact.

Because we were both new to the whole scene I think we helped keep each other calm through the whole experience, which was a pretty massive thing for us both because playing in somewhere like the Millennium Stadium was a hell of an atmosphere to earn your first cap in.

TOM PHILIP

I don't sleep well anyway because I'm always in such a lot of pain with my back, but it was even worse before a big game. Matt Williams was really understanding about it and they roomed me with Mike Blair because they knew that by having such a familiar face around it would help settle my nerves.

On the day of the game I just remember being really nervous and not speaking much while the rest of the boys were having banter in the meeting room. The most infuriating thing was that while I was sitting there shitting myself, Hoggy was the coolest man in the world, it was like he was about to go for a game of golf with his mates – he was just fooling around and making

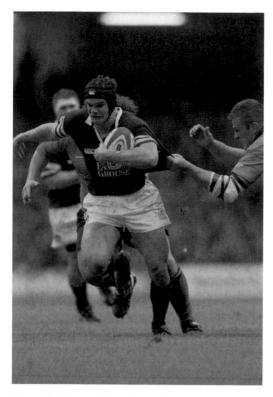

Tom Philip uses his size and pace to power through a gap in the Welsh defence. *Getty Images*

jokes, just the most confident guy, totally nerveless.

I could never really relax before games because I was always carrying injuries. I never had that usual period that other players have to relax and get themselves ready mentally because I had so much to do to get my body in the right sort of shape for the game. As soon as I got in the changing room I just dumped my kit down and then started to warm up, getting all my strapping done, getting my back cracked by the physio, warming up all my muscles properly, that was always my focus, and it was quite a lonely experience having to go through all that. I got all that out the way and then we went out and you just can't imagine the noise that hits you in Cardiff, with those steep, steep stands that just tower up all around you, it's unbelievable. In modern sport, and especially in rugby, much of the game is based on communication, but in a place like the Millennium Stadium, you can't hear anything that anyone else is saying to you – it was one of those games where guys would be running the length of pitch long after the whistle had been blown because they couldn't hear anything. It was an amazing feeling to be right at the centre of it all.

I remember that after ten minutes I was absolutely knackered. I'm not sure if it was because if the pace of the game – it was probably more to do with the nerves and the atmosphere, the whole build up, the fact it was on TV and everyone's watching you – but I remember looking up at the stadium clock and seeing that only ten minutes had gone by and I honestly thought that I couldn't go on and that I would have to be replaced before half-time. Fortunately about five minutes later I got my second-wind and I was able to settle into the game – and after that, that was exactly what it felt like – just another game of rugby. You do your job and you do what you've been practicing and you settle into it. In terms of pace and physicality I didn't notice all that much of a step-up from playing in the Heineken Cup or in some of the domestic games, but the main difference was that when you play for your club you will target one or two guys in the opposition as their danger men – say, the fullback or the big centre, and you make sure you watch everything they do – but in international rugby everyone is a danger man, so you just have to take every phase of the game one step at a time. The key is to remember to fulfil your personal goals as opposed to trying desperately to shine. If you do that well then you're onto a winner and if you happen to make a break or score a try or whatever, then great, but you can't try to force these things because that's when you'll make mistakes.

I was moved to the stand-off channel defensively because I always liked making big hits and I was looking forward to them sending guys down my channel, but it never happened – they moved the ball wider and exploited us out there, which was frustrating because I wanted to make my contribution defensively. It didn't work out the way we thought it would – which was pretty much the story of that whole Championship. It was a hard, hard season.

I remember Will Greenwood was playing at inside centre against me in the Calcutta Cup and he looked over at me from the half-way line just before the kick-off and gave me a wee smile to say *have a good game* – it was a nice thing to do, but at the time I think I just scowled at him . . . I wish I had been more comfortable in the whole environment to smile back, but I was still pretty new to it all.

There was a lot of anger going around the camp towards the end of the Championship because we were playing some quite good rugby at times but just weren't getting the results, and the coaches and the players were getting the blame to varying degrees from the press and the public – and we were all just annoyed that it wasn't happening for us.

I remember going out for that final game against Ireland in Dublin and I was just really, really angry, desperate to win, and I hit Brian O'Driscoll with a pretty dodgy tackle early on . . . I was lucky not to get carded for it. We should have won that game and again there was this incredible sense of frustration that things just weren't happening. By this time I was really hurt – I didn't warm up properly and my back and groin were just in pieces – and it all added to the anger. O'Driscoll gave me some good write-ups afterwards saying that hopefully I'd be the future in the centre for Scotland and whatnot, which was nice of him – especially after I'd bumped him one early in the game.

DONNIE MACFADYEN

Partly due to injury, partly due to form, I had dropped out of international reckoning after the 2002 summer tour to North America. But Matt Williams brought me back into the fold when he took over and he selected me for the 2004 summer tour to Australia.

I was picked to play Samoa for the opening Test in Wellington – it was played there because it has the highest Samoan population outside Samoa and it wasn't too far for us to travel from our main base in Australia, so by hosting it in Wellington it guaranteed a good home crowd. The atmosphere throughout that whole match was brilliant – right from the start when we lined up to face their Manu Siva Tau, the Samoan version of the Haka, all the way through the game. We played some really good running rugby that night and scored some great tries. I had been injured the previous season and had missed out on the World Cup, so it was a very special moment to come back into the team. I had actually been pretty close to going to the World Cup. I missed out on the initial squad but Andrew Mower got injured in the first game so the coaches phoned home to speak to the medics in Scotland to decide whether to pick me or Cammy Mather to fly out as his replacement. I had played for Glasgow the day before and had a slight shoulder knock when the call came through; the knock wasn't too serious, but Gerry Haggerty our team doctor, was asked, 'Would he be fit to play against the USA in four days time?' Gerry said that he couldn't 100 per cent say that I could, so they went with Cammy instead. That was obviously a pretty heart-breaking moment, especially as I then played for Glasgow the following Friday night, so to get back into the Scotland shirt a year later was immensely satisfying.

Todd Blackadder was the forwards coach on that tour and he was, without doubt, one of the finest coaches I ever dealt with. I've mentioned before the aura that Ian McGeechan had when I came into the team, and it was just the same with Todd – he was an absolute giant of the game; he had not long been All Blacks captain and he was one of the all-time great provincial captains for Canterbury; his knowledge and insight were staggering and having him sit down for one-on-one sessions helped my career and understanding of the game so much.

TOM PHILIP

I was picked to play against Samoa and a couple of days before the game we had a full-contact session on the beach. It wasn't a clever session – two guys were concussed and then I wrecked my knee. But because of all the pain that I was in with my back and my groin, when my knee went it was incredibly painful, but it wasn't as bad as my back and groin, so I just kind of thought that I would get on with things. Matt Williams came over to me and said, 'Come on, get up, Tom, you're tougher than that.' So I got up and tried to walk it off – I was out in the sea trying to get it moving – which is not the best idea when you've just ruptured your cruciate ligament. We had the afternoon off and it was only hours later that I went back to the physios to see about my knee and that was when they realised how badly I'd damaged it. I flew home and it was all a bit disappointing because no one had arranged for me to be looked after medically when I got back and I had to sort out the operation and everything myself. I then remember watching the first Test against Australia just after I'd had my operation . . . and I was just in floods of tears.

ALLISTER HOGG

Tom's injuries have been devastating, but ever since we first started playing together you could see that he was always in pain. The fact that he was able to carry on training and playing through that pain is incredible. With all that he's been through, with all the operations, having to stand down from Edinburgh, all his efforts to come back . . . I think about him a lot and I still hope that we'll see him out there playing again. He's a real talent, a game-breaker and there aren't many players in the world, let alone in Scotland, who have the attributes that he can bring to the game.

TOM PHILIP

I played for years in all sorts of pain with my back and my groin, my hamstrings and my knee and it was only when I went to see a specialist off my own bat that they diagnosed all the problems I had. I had these scans done on my back and they found all these fractures and burst discs, a couple vertebrae were described as having the same consistency as chalk, and my whole back was a mess – and when your core stability is affected like that, it has a huge knock-on effect on the rest of your body, which was the reason behind all my other problems. I don't think that playing rugby or doing weights when I was young was the cause – although it may not have helped – it was more the fact that it went undiagnosed for so long so that I continued to do the kind of things that were making it worse. That was the most disappointing thing for me. The surgeon told me that I could have been paralysed, and thankfully nothing like that happened, but I still don't sleep well and am in chronic pain all the time – and it's not going to get any easier as I get older. I've had titanium screws inserted into my spine to stabilise it and then had to have another operation to replace them when those first screws bent. I now can't sit in a car for more than 20 minutes without it getting fairly excruciating – and that's something I'm going to have for the rest of my life.

I came back from the surgery on my back and I still didn't really get the treatment that I needed. I was kind of made to feel like I was complaining and wasn't looking after myself properly, which was ridiculous. I had six months left on my Edinburgh contract by that stage and the physio told them that I needed about an hour of treatment a day to get myself right. I got that, but by the time the six months were up I still wasn't quite ready to play again . . . and that was it.

I've kept going, trying to get myself right. I've had silicone injections in my spine to try and relieve some of the pressure on various nerves and I played a few games for Edinburgh Accies while coaching there before having a season in rugby league as a semi-pro down at Whitehaven. I've loved playing rugby league, it feels like a more honest game – there's no sly play around the tackle area or any confusion with what's going on with rucks and mauls; a penalty is a penalty and what you see is what you get. You need to be fitter to play league than union and it's really tough; I was playing semi-pro but the physical intensity was right up there with Test match rugby union. But again I found my season was limited by injuries – the back affects so many other areas that I still have problems with my hamstrings and my groin. I suppose that as time goes on I'm going to have to make a decision about whether to pursue a career away from rugby, or to keep giving it a go. Some people will think that it's a crazy idea to keep going, but the thing about playing sport at the very highest level, when you dedicate your whole life to it, it's hard to let go and I don't ever want to look back and think that I didn't do everything I could to try and reach that level again. People say that they would give their right arm to play for their country; I think I've given enough . . . but the aspiration to get back there has never diminished.

DONNIE MACFADYEN

In the Test matches against Australia I was up against my old under-21 rivals in Phil Waugh and George Smith, who both established themselves as two of the greatest open-sides the game has ever seen. We lost quite heavily in both the matches but again we were playing pretty well and were throwing the ball around effectively, but they just ran away with it in the end in both games. They were a great side and had real strength in depth on the bench. In both Tests I remember battling away against George Smith for around an hour and then just as we were both beginning to tire, they would bring on Phil Waugh; I remember standing there on both occasions and just thinking, *Oh come on, give me a break!*

Those games also showed me just what a canny operator George Gregan was. He always seemed to pick the right option and was in total control of every facet of the game that he was involved in. But he was also a master of gamesmanship. I was running around for the whole game trying to win as much ball on the deck as I could and I remember in one ruck, going in on a fairly isolated Aussie player and was just about to turn the ball over when all I heard was, 'Hands off blue seven!' Obviously not wanting to get pinged by the ref I let go and backed off and when I looked up I saw that the ref was about 20 yards away and Gregan was just grinning to himself as he box-kicked the ball clear.

He was at it again in the second Test as well. Andy Henderson scored a totally legitimate try but the referee didn't see it because as Andy broke through the line, Gregan, very subtly, tackled the ref. The ref didn't see Andy go over and then Gregan started chirping away saying that the ref had obstructed his efforts to tackle Andy; and in the end the try wasn't awarded. I suppose you learn these tricks on your way to winning 139 caps for your country . . .

Chris Cusiter in action in 2005. *Press Association*

CHRIS CUSITER

I played four of my first eleven matches for Scotland against Australia, so it was a great to be playing up against someone like Gregan on such a regular basis – you learn so much from watching him. Because of the experience that he has, you can see the authority that he carries on the pitch and it's similar to playing against guys like Martin Johnson and Lawrence Dallaglio because you can see how they are constantly managing the referee. It is something that all international teams work on, but those three were pretty much the masters at it.

JOHN BARCLAY (Glasgow Warriors)
20 Caps (to date): 2007-still playing

I was first selected for a Scotland training squad when I was 18. I was fresh out of school and had yet to play a single minute of professional rugby, but Matt Williams selected me for the extended squad for the 2004 autumn internationals. I knew that I wasn't really there on merit and if I had played I probably wouldn't have done myself justice. To be honest, it wasn't the best thing for me at the time and it took another three years before I was capped, which was probably a good thing in the end. You can't just get thrown in there. I know that Richie McCaw played for the All Blacks before he had played for the Crusaders in the Super 12, but he had at least played a fair number of games for Canterbury in the NPC – and to be fair, I think he is probably fairly unique, not many players would deal with it as well as he did.

I was thrown in at the deep end at Glasgow as well, but it worked out much better to have it that way at club level rather than in Test rugby. I was still pretty young and still learning and I hadn't played much for the first team. Donnie Macfadyen and Andrew Wilson got injured and Jon Petrie dislocated his shoulder so all the experienced guys were out. Myself and John Beattie were thrown in to play, that was my break into the team and I was given a good chance.

A lot of success is put down to skill and talent but a lot of it is also drive and determination. When I was at school I was going out and doing fitness and weights and running every second day by myself. If you can't drive yourself by yourself then the chances are you're not going to get very far.

DONNIE MACFADYEN

I remember when John Barclay and Johnnie Beattie came into the Glasgow squad in 2004, you could instantly recognise that these guys were talented players but were still a little raw – but they got some games under their belt and very quickly got up to speed with what professional rugby was all about in terms of the speed and physicality of the games and you just saw them flourish – which was in turn helped by the fact that they were doing properly managed and monitored strength and conditioning work behind the scenes. But you could tell as soon as you trained and played with them that they would both go all the way.

ALASTAIR KELLOCK (Edinburgh Gunners and Glasgow Warriors)
27 Caps (to date): 2004-still playing

My first cap was against Australia in the autumn 2004. We were staying in the Sheraton Hotel and I went to bed at seven o'clock on the night before the match because I was so nervous. When I got to my room I found Gordie Bulloch, the team captain, had put a letter under my door. He was basically wishing me luck and saying that I should do what I had been doing at club level because that's why I had been picked. But he also highlighted that I had a role to play in the team, that it wasn't just my first cap but a big international match for all the other members of the squad as well – and he wrote that if we all did our jobs to the best of our ability we would win the game.

I don't know if that happens for every player on their first cap, but I thought it was a really nice touch. It helped settle my nerves.

DONNIE MACFADYEN

One of the few victories we had under Matt Williams came against Japan at McDiarmid Park. It was a great game to play in and I always enjoyed playing at McDiarmid Park – we played there quite a bit as the Glasgow Caledonians when I first went pro and it's a great pitch, a pretty hard surface so you get quick games, which always suited me. We showed in that game – as we had done against Samoa – that we could play when the shackles were off and there was no pressure, and we racked up what remains the highest Scotland score in Test rugby. I think there was always a feeling in the camp that we were always going to struggle to overturn the big teams, and in retrospect that was probably partly to do with the fact that the management were continually telling the press that we weren't ready yet as a team to beat those kind of sides.

I do remember one very clear feeling after scoring my try in that game – complete fear. Because when you first get capped and when you first score a Test try you have to stand up on the bus and sing a song. And I remember panicking as soon as I had scored, knowing that I had to do it again. I'd sung Fly Me to the Moon by Frank Sinatra when I first got capped, which was pretty much the sum total of my repertoire. I'm nothing like Euan Murray, who is a human jukebox and can remember the lyrics to hundreds and hundreds of songs – I can hardly remember anything. So in an act of desperation, I sung R Kelly's remix to Ignition, which was a fairly awful choice and I was *slated* for it by the boys.

Donnie Macfadyen makes a break against Japan at McDiarmid Park. *Getty Images*

ANDY HENDERSON

We played Australia four times in 2004 – twice on tour in the summer and twice in the autumn. I remember coming out for the team run the day before the fourth match of the year, and the old touchlines at Murrayfield had been painted over and new ones had been put in, meaning the pitch was a good few metres narrower than it normally was. It was pretty obvious for everyone to see because the lines which had been painted over were a completely different colour to the rest of the pitch – I'm sure they could have been a bit more subtle about it with a bit of forethought. But it was a pretty negative thing to do – Matt Williams and the rest of the coaches obviously wanted to stop Australia going wide, which was where their real strength was – and although I didn't think about it too much at the time, it sent out another dispiriting message to us all. Apparently we weren't good enough to defend against them on a full-width pitch so the management had decided to bring them in to the minimum width allowed. It was humiliating that they felt they had to go to such extremes to cover our deficiencies.

Chris Cusiter whips the ball away from the back of the scrum during the first Test against the Wallabies in November 2004 as Allister Hogg breaks off in support. *Getty Images*

DONNIE MACFADYEN

It was a really cringe-worthy moment when we realised that that was the plan – and it made no difference in the end because they still trounced us. It was so embarrassing, the whole thing, and it did really make you question how much faith the coaches had in the team – that they were prepared to go to those kind of measures to try and give you an edge, any edge, over the opposition – it smacked of desperation and it still makes me cringe to think about it.

MIKE BLAIR

Matt loved to try and think outside the box and I actually really enjoyed a lot of the stuff he did, but some of it was just ridiculous. We all had the number 27 embroidered on our training kit – which represented the fact that we were Scotland players 24 hours a day, 7 days a week, 365 days a year. You add them all up: 2+4+7+3+6+5, and you get 27. But you'd look at that number on everyone's kit and it just didn't strike a cord psychologically, it was just a meaningless number.

TOM SMITH

I got injured during the November 2004 internationals so I missed them all, and I came back in at around about Christmas before the 2005 Six Nations. We went to Stobo Castle in the Borders for a team get-together and that's when I really noticed that something had changed. They did a review of the South Africa game and it was a really unhappy atmosphere. They had lost the game, Matt was picking the team to bits on the video, but there was a variety of contradictions in what he was saying.

You can go to a player and say, 'That was the wrong decision, you got away with it that time but nine times out of ten you wouldn't have.' Similarly, you can say, 'That was the right decision, nine time out of ten it would have worked, but on this occasion it didn't. You were unlucky.' But Matt would judge an action by its consequences and not by whether it was the right decision. He would fire into a player for doing the wrong thing because it didn't work and then five minutes later another player would do exactly the same thing and if it worked he would say nothing to them. A bit of an argument sparked up with a few players pointing out the inconsistency of this, and it actually got quite unfriendly.

It was all part of this need to have too much control. The coaching team wanted to say, 'In this situation this is what you do and in that situation that is what you do – if you don't deviate from this plan you will be fine.' But rugby doesn't work like that and rugby players don't work like that.

CHRIS CUSITER

My first couple of years of Test rugby were pretty disappointing in terms of results. Going into the 2005 Six Nations I had picked up 13 caps but had only won against Samoa and Japan. It was a frustrating time, there were games when we didn't perform as well as we could have, but there were others, like the France game in 2005, when we played well but still ended up losing. We defended very well and they got a lucky try late on when Hugo Southwell's clearance kick was charged down and Damien Traille flopped over to score – while at the other end, Ally Hogg had been called back earlier in the game for a foot in touch, which was a pretty dubious call – on the replay it definitely looks like he kept himself in play. You compare that to the try that Jonny Wilkinson was awarded in 2007 against us at Twickenham when his foot was clearly out of play well before he grounded it and yet he was awarded the try. It felt like everything was conspiring against us. It was a tough time.

JON PETRIE

It might have been a relatively poor France side, but we had played really well and Hoggy had scored that try which was disallowed. If the touch judge hadn't thought he had spotted that foot in touch, we would have won – I'm certain of that.

Then, towards the end, we were defending our line pretty hard but definitely staying on side. The referee gave a penalty, which I didn't question although I hadn't seen who had been off-side. Then he looked around a bit, then pointed at me and got this yellow card out. I couldn't believe it. It was such an important point in the game. I was pleading like a little schoolboy, trying to change his mind. So off I went to the bin, with 80,000 Frenchmen booing me. They kicked the penalty and we lost the match. It was bitterly disappointing – particularly because I knew I hadn't done anything wrong. Grimesy came straight in afterwards and said, 'I think that might have been me, by the way.' I thought, 'You could have said that out on the pitch, you bugger.'

It was good of Matt to come straight out afterwards and say that it wasn't me. But, strangely, I still felt bad. I went to the length of getting that yellow-card cleared off my record, but it doesn't offer much comfort. I'll never get those last ten minutes of that international match back.

GORDON BULLOCH

It was a difficult time. As captain I felt caught between a rock and a hard place. You are trying to support the coach and support the players at the same time but at one stage they were pulling in completely opposite directions. My problem, I felt, was that I wasn't being told everything by both sides. The senior players would be chatting amongst themselves and I'd be hearing about the unhappiness second or third hand. Matt is actually a terribly nice guy, it just didn't work out in terms of the methods he employed. He had ideas he had picked up in Australia and Ireland and he tried to force that into a Scottish system, and we weren't ready for that.

JON PETRIE

The first-half against Wales was just embarrassing. Matt Williams had come in and read the riot act, telling us we needed to do this, that and the other, but sometimes it is more about the players, and perhaps the more important things were said after Matt had gone. I remember Tom Smith being a part of that, he was one of the senior guys in the squad and, because he isn't that talkative a character in general, when he does decide to say something people listen. He is very good at speaking his mind and he tends to have something worthwhile to say. He's an intimidating character before you get to know him. He is a big sleep walker so they used to put the new boys in the squad with him, and nobody would tell them about his nocturnal activities, so they'd wake up in the middle of the night and discover him practicing his line-out lifts.

Matt had a lot of faults. He was very process-driven. I remember having a team meeting once because Hugo Southwell had thrown a miss-pass which hadn't worked out. So we all sat through this video analysis and an hour long meeting about why Hugo had thrown the miss-pass when it hadn't been agreed that that was a move we were allowed to do. He was taking responsibility away from the players to express themselves on the pitch. He wanted us to agree beforehand to do this, this and this in certain areas of the field, but you can't do that – which is the wrong way to go about it because you have to let the players play their game.

Having said that, I always felt he was a good guy, and you could see he was trying to bring a Clive Woodward type business approach to it – but it didn't work. And in that particular game against Wales, everyone had got so hacked off with it, that the attitude was: *let's just go out there and play.*

What I liked about Matt was he was very good at stating this is what I want from you and this is what you are doing wrong, and that is why I am not picking you. I appreciated that, but I know that it rubbed some people up the wrong way. Another positive thing was how many young guys he brought into the squad. The jettisoning of older, more experienced players who still had a few years left in them was the wrong thing to do though. The young guys should certainly have been brought in, but any successful side brings in young guys by integrating them into the team slowly with guys who have been there and done it many times before. Getting rid of the experience and then asking the young guys to perform in that furious Test match environment without older players to help guide them is a recipe for disaster. Which is exactly what we got.

MIKE BLAIR

It was the half-time talk against Wales that started to get the ball rolling a bit with regards to forgetting the structures that the coaches had put in place and just playing what was in front of us. We had been hammered in the first-half and Wales were leading 38-3. It was humiliating. So we decided to just go out and have a go. We scored three tries in that second-half and the fact that we had done so was definitely in the back of our minds as we went into half-time at Twickenham. The tactics just weren't working – they were wrong for us, so we decided to change our style, just as we had done against Wales. Again, it worked and it showed us even more clearly that the style, the structure, the whole system that the coaches were trying to enforce on us wasn't right.

JON PETRIE

After we played down at Twickenham and lost quite heavily, there were a few issues in the changing room, particularly with Willie Anderson and Robbie Russell. Willie had gone round shaking all the forwards' hands and thanking them for their efforts because it was the last international that season. But because Willie hadn't previously engaged with Robbie at all – had never discussed his non-selection and had refused to put him on the pitch in some games – Robbie saw no reason why he should shake hands. That was kind of a big moment, a fairly stark example of how the coaching staff had lost the changing room. After that, it was really hard to pull it back. It was a really difficult time because everyone was desperate to do well, but it just didn't work out – there wasn't any understanding between the coaching staff and the rest of the squad.

International rugby is all about getting together, running through the plays and making sure that everything is slick, but we were still doing technical stuff on Test week. They were trying to coach us how to pass, when we needed to be focussing on what we needed to do tactically.

Matt got a reputation within the squad that when things went well it was because of him, whereas when things went wrong it was our fault – and that doesn't sit well with players.

I'm sure Todd must have found it difficult. It is a shame he went home because he was a great guy and had a lot to offer.

Chris Paterson leaves Lewis Moody in his wake as Scotland throw Matt Williams' tactics out the window in the second-half of the Calcutta Cup match at Twickenham. *Press Association*

TOM SMITH

I think, essentially, Matt didn't have enough faith in the players around him. He didn't trust them to do the right thing. He had a response for every scenario on the field, and it became stifling.

There was a lack of trust between players and management. From our point of view, it didn't feel like we could say what we thought, we felt that if we wanted to keep our position we had to shut up and tow the line. Ultimately, it was inevitable that the wheels would fall off after the relationship between the players and the management broke down.

He had a small group of staff around him that he kept very tight and I don't think they questioned each other enough, and I don't think they realised that they were steadily losing the faith of all the players. It became very much a *them and us* environment.

Matt's very articulate and his presentation skills are excellent, but if players don't have faith and they've heard the same speech again and again and again, then it is only going to end one way.

IAN McGEECHAN

I have to hold my hand up and admit that I made a mistake in taking on Matt Williams as my successor as head coach. He talked a good game and I was impressed by that, but when he took over he never respected Scotland or the players and spent most of his time telling them what they couldn't do. But that's the wrong approach to take to coaching and it totally misses one of the keys to unlocking Scottish sporting potential – we'll always be the underdog, but we relish that and we'll always put up the biggest fight. It was something that Matt totally missed and the team suffered badly as a result – and it was something that has taken many of them an awfully long time to get over.

MIKE BLAIR

Looking back I can see what Matt was trying to do in terms of changing the way we played and I liked a lot of his training and some of his ideas, but to totally try and reinvent the way we played rugby was the wrong approach. He didn't understand the Scottish psyche at all. It's all very well telling someone they're crap to try and get a reaction, but you have to then tell them they've played well if they have, not just continue to tell them they're crap. Jim Telfer apparently used to shout people down a lot, but the difference was that he then focussed on building them back up again – which is something that Matt just expected us to do on our own . . . and it didn't happen.

    Matt over-thought a lot of aspects about the game as well, particularly the media side of things. He always used to talk through various agendas that we would have – for example, Agenda A was what we would tell the press, while we really thought Agenda B and would put Agenda C into practice in the next game. It was all smoke and mirrors and many of us felt uncomfortable with it all. And there were other things that he would do that weren't great. After the Wales match in 2004 he came into the changing room and told us that he was about to go out and face the press and that he would shoulder all the blame for our performance and the defeat. Then he went out there and said that as players and as a squad that we were very inexperienced, that we weren't ready for this type of rugby yet and that it would take a year or so before we would be capable of winning. That whole situation raised a lot of eyebrows in the squad. It wasn't the way to instil our trust in him and it felt like his support of us was just another artificial agenda of his.

ANDY HENDERSON

In fairness to Matt Williams, he brought in guys like Chris Cusiter, Allister Hogg and Ross Ford, who have gone on to have pretty big careers for Scotland, but his first year was a transition period.

If you are told enough times that you are not very good at something then eventually you start to believe it. So that was a big change when Frank came in, he talked the team up and that had a huge effect as we saw in his first season.

Chapter Sixteen

OLD SCHOOL VALUES

B ACK TO *basics. That was the mantra of the former master of Merchiston Castle School who was appointed interim head coach alongside Hugh Campbell, forwards coach George Graham, backs coaches Steve Bates and Sean Lineen and defence coach Alan Tait. Frank Hadden's remit was to rebuild the battered confidences of the Scotland team. From his seat as head coach of Edinburgh, he had watched the disintegration of his players' performances as they moved from club to international colours. They were all good players, he knew that first hand. Yet when they took to the field for Scotland something was missing – their spark had been dampened, their nerves were looking frayed. They had the skills – he knew it as their coach and he also knew it as a Scotland fan for he had seen the demonstration of their skills as clearly as anyone else when they played on their wits in the second-halves of the Wales and England games. Having spoken to his senior players and conferred with his new assistant coaches, there was a realisation that the Matt Williams and Willie Anderson regime had stifled the players' creativity and had shot their confidences to pieces. They had witnessed what the team could achieve with just a modicum of belief that they could play. So Hadden reverted to his schoolmaster's pastoral past and began the rebuilding of the Scottish team's battered psyche.*

In a radio interview with Ireland's Keith Wood, Hadden stated simply that there was little point complaining about the lack of resources at the disposal of the Scottish coach or that player depth was relatively shallow when compared to other nations; it was how things were and it was important just to get on with the tools and facilities at his disposal. It was an admirable statement and one that he built upon when he said that the Scottish players were certainly not short of talent, as his predecessor had continually alluded, but instead needed to have a structure put in place that would support their creativity and allow it to shine.

That summer, Hadden and his coaching staff led Scotland to their first-ever victory over the Barbarians on a beautiful afternoon in Aberdeen. The players looked invigorated under the new coaching system and ran in five tries for an emphatic 38-7 win. Two weeks later they flew to Bucharest for a one-off Test match against Romania. It saw first caps for Kelly Brown, Scott Lawson, Phil Godman, Euan Murray and Andy Wilson, and a first captaincy stint for the experienced war horse Jon Petrie. The squad's preparations were hardly affected by the Lions tour to New Zealand as only Chris Cusiter, Simon Taylor and Gordon Bulloch had been selected

---

Opposite: Mike Blair snipes down the side of a ruck against South Africa in November 2008. *Press Association*

in the original tour squad of 44 players, while Jason White would fly out as a late replacement in the last week of the trip. The only particularly significant change was at scrum-half where Mike Blair took advantage of Cusiter's absence to regain his place in the team after Cusiter had held the number nine shirt for 16 uninterrupted starts under Matt Williams. It was something that Blair maintained, more or less, for the next four years, until, ironically, he himself was selected for the Lions in 2009 and Cusiter took advantage of his absence to usurp him for the shirt. In a commanding performance over the Romanians, Scotland emerged 39-19 victors.

In the autumn, Argentina, Samoa and New Zealand came to Edinburgh, and although only the Pacific Islanders were beaten, 18-11, the team at least looked competitive and confidence continued to grow in the squad.

As the 2006 Six Nations loomed, the pack was reshuffled and Jon Petrie dropped to the bench, with the captaincy handed to the towering figure of Jason White. It would prove to be an inspired appointment.

Scotland's first fixture was against France at Murrayfield. It has been a long established rule of thumb that France started slowly in the tournament before getting on a roll: if ever there is a good time to play Les Bleus, it is first up and at home.

In a pulsating encounter, Scotland stood up to their celebrated visitors to score two superb tries in either half through Sean Lamont. The first of these followed a break by Jason White who was tackled short of the line; the ball was recycled quickly and Lamont stepped between centre Florian Fritz and prop Pieter de Villiers to score under the posts. The second try was even more impressive. With Mike Blair strutting and marshalling his troops with aplomb, the Scottish pack drove a lineout from outside the French 22 all the way to the try line where, at the last moment, Lamont joined the shunt, collected the ball and dived over to score.

Scotland's defence was aggressive and held firm but for two lapses that saw number eight Julien Bonnaire and replacement hooker Sébastien Bruno score for France, and the back-row of White, Ally Hogg and Simon Taylor were immense, while out wide Mike Blair and Chris Paterson combined magnificently on more than one occasion to scythe through the French ranks and the wide passing of centre Marcus di Rollo had their defence stretched. Having led 13-3 at half-time the home team held onto the lead to secure a famous 20-16 win.

A week later the team were in Cardiff and were looking good until Scott Murray was knocked to the ground without the ball by Ian Gough. Murray flashed a leg out in frustration and connected with Gough's head; he pleaded that it was accidental, but he was shown a red-card and left the field with more than an hour left to play. Scotland's fourteen men were eventually over-powered by the fifteen of Wales, despite a late rally which brought tries for Hugo Southwell and Chris Paterson.

Unperturbed, the team readied themselves for the Calcutta Cup clash at Murrayfield two weeks later. In one of the all-time great defensive displays, Scotland battered their visitors into submission while Paterson once again displayed his pre-eminence with the boot, kicking the home team to glory, 18-12.

Following the joy of this victory, the team travelled to Ireland but were beaten narrowly 15-9 thanks to five penalties from Ronan O'Gara to Paterson's three.

In the final round of the tournament, they faced off with Italy in Rome. As has so often the case with this fixture, the encounter was something of a slugfest and very low on entertainment value, but the visitors crawled their way to a 13-10 victory with a try, a penalty and a conversion from fullback Paterson and a drop-goal from Gordon Ross, which took Scotland to third-place in the Championship table and, in terms of points, their best-ever finish in the Six Nations.

In May, Scotland scored nine tries at Murrayfield in a record 66-19 win over the Barbarians which set them up for their summer tour to South Africa. While both Tests were lost, 36-16 in Durban and 29-15 in Port Elizabeth, Scotland once again demonstrated their attacking capabilities and ran the home team much closer in the second Test than the score-line suggested.

That autumn Scotland faced Romania, the Pacific Islands and Australia. They won the first two games comfortably, 48-6 and 34-22, and although they then lost heavily to the Wallabies, 44-15, the coaches had used the series to hand a number of new players their first caps, including Johnnie Beattie, Rob Dewey, Dave Callam, Jim Hamilton, Rory Lawson and Alasdair Strokosch, all of whom would become important players in the squad over the following years.

In 2007 the team endured a poor Six Nations, only managing to secure a victory at home to Wales. They began the Championship with a 42-20 drubbing in the Calcutta Cup at Twickenham before making something of a recovery to defeat the Welsh 21-9 at Murrayfield.

On 24 February the Italians arrived in Edinburgh and took part in one of the most memorable opening quarters ever witnessed at Murrayfield. For the home team, it was for all the wrong reasons. In seven extraordinary minutes Italy were gifted three tries – one from a charge down of a Phil Godman chip which was snaffled by Mauro Bergamasco, and two interception passes thrown by Chris Cusiter, who had reclaimed the scrum-half jersey from the injured Mike Blair. Although Scotland fought their way back into the match with tries from Rob Dewey and Chris Paterson, the visitors sealed a 37-17 win – their first on the road since joining the Championship – with a late try from scrum-half Alessandro Troncon.

The very foundations of Hadden's new feel-good administration were beginning to tremble. And the situation did not improve in the final rounds of the tournament as Ireland squeaked a 19-18 win at Murrayfield and France overpowered Scotland 46-19 in Paris.

The downturn in results opened up the pressure valves in the coaching set-up – and as the 2007 World Cup loomed, Hadden began to compromise.

A relentless training camp made sure that the squad would come second to no one in terms of strength; but at what cost? The emphasis on player freedom had *disappeared and the limited style of play Hadden was looking to enforce was reflected in his comments before the team's last game of the 2007 Six Nations when he spoke gleefully about the three-quarter line being the biggest ever assembled by a Scotland team. Few would ever question the strength and courage of Sean Lamont, Rob Dewey, Andy Henderson and Nikki Walker but as an attacking unit there was precious little guile there. Scotland could now physically compete with any side in the world, but the confidence in their strength and power meant that they focussed on bludgeoning sides rather than combining their new attributes with the running game they had employed so successfully in previous seasons. It wasn't pretty rugby, but it was effective. Scotland swept past Portugal and Romania and then fielded a weakened team against the All Blacks. This caused outrage in both Scotland and New Zealand as well as other corners of the rugby world, many feeling that the decision to rest players against the All Blacks to keep them fresh for the crunch game against Italy was demeaning to the Scottish shirt, negligent to the paying fan and undermining to the spirit of the World Cup. But Hadden simply stated that he was ultimately judged by how the team finished in the tournament. It was doubtful that even his first team would be able to run the All Blacks close and to risk them to injury before the Italian game would serve no one. A brave fight against the Kiwis and a loss to Italy might placate the ire of the purists, but it would cause even greater anger to the majority of Scottish supporters than that incited by the fielding of a weakened team against New Zealand. The All Blacks duly ran amok in Edinburgh against what many termed a Scottish second fifteen. Despite the accolade, the team still contained vast experience in Chris Paterson, Chris Cusiter and Scott Murray, but they fell to one of the favourites for the tournament 40-0.*

And so the focus turned to Saint-Etienne. On a cold wet night Scotland fell behind to a controversial Alessandro Troncon try as Andrea Masi took out Rory Lamont in the air as he went to gather a high ball, allowing Italy to establish a platform on Scotland's line from which their talismanic captain slithered over.

Thanks to the steady boot of Chris Paterson, however, who impressively finished the tournament with 100 per cent kicking accuracy, Scotland pushed on to secure a narrow 18-16 win. It wasn't beautiful, by any means, but it was effective, and Hadden had secured Scotland another quarter-final place that just two years earlier had looked a distant dream.

In the quarter-final at the Stade de France, Scotland faced the might of Argentina. The Pumas had been the surprise package of the tournament and had become a fan favourite across the world thanks to their passion, verve and power. Their pack were monstrously effective and in the backs they fizzled with glamour, skill and pace with the luminous Juan Martin Hernandez, Felipe Contepomi, Ignacio Corleto, Lucas Borges and Agustin Pichot dazzling on the fields of France. They had already shocked the tournament hosts by beating them 17-12 in Paris and had turned over Ireland 30-15 on their way to the top of Pool D.

Again, Scotland looked to outmuscle their opponents but they were soon trailing the South Americans 13-6 thanks to a charge-down try from number eight Gonzalo Longo and the boot of Contepomi. In the final quarter of the match Scotland finally seemed to realise that the most effective way to play the game was to imitate the style of their opponents – to combine their new-found physicality with a wider running game. As the ball began to fly across the width of the pitch, the Pumas soon began to look stretched and Chris Cusiter, on as a late replacement for Mike Blair, fastened onto a ball from Kelly Brown after a wonderful break from prop Craig Smith to slide in at the corner. Paterson's boot was clawing Scotland back into the game and as the final seconds ticked in Dan Parks delivered a cross-kick into the Argentinean dead-ball area for a match-clinching try . . . only for Sean Lamont to fail to gather the punt before it went out of play. 30 seconds later, Pichot kicked the ball high into the Paris stands and the Latin locomotive steamed into the semi-final. In that last twenty minutes, Scotland played with a style and panache that might have seen them into only their second World Cup semi-final; their approach had been reminiscent of the way they had played when Hadden had first come on the scene in 2005 and many felt that if they had just held onto that style while combining it with their new power, things might have been turned out quite differently. There was a lingering sense of frustration that the team's tactics against Argentina in the quarter-final was geared around avoiding defeat rather than securing victory – at least until it was too late.

2008 saw a continued slide in Scottish fortunes as France won at Murrayfield 27-6, Wales beat them in Cardiff 30-15 on their way to a second Grand Slam in four seasons, and Ireland ran away with the game at Croke Park after an adventurous start by Scotland, with Paterson making a rare start at stand-off, going on to secure the game 34-13.

In a game with remarkable similarities to the clash of 2006, the Calcutta Cup was re-secured with a 15-9 triumph at Murrayfield. Any progress that might have been made on the back of that victory, however, was thrown away in Rome as Sergio Parisse intercepted a telegraphed Dan Parks pass to send Gonzalo Canale home, before Andrea Marcato stole the match with a last-minute drop-goal for a 23-20 victory. Scotland avoided the wooden spoon on points difference.

In what would prove to be a sign of the changing of the guard, there was something of a shake up in the coaching panel that summer. Andy Robinson came on board from Edinburgh to assist with Glasgow's Sean Lineen as the team travelled to Argentina for a two Test series. They lost the first match 21-15, but roared back in Buenos Aires to win 26-14 with outstanding performances from centres Graeme Morrison and Ben Cairns, the front-row of Allan Jacobsen, Ross Ford and Euan Murray, the back-row of John Barclay, Ally Hogg and Alasdair Strokosch, and half-back pairing Mike Blair and Phil Godman.

In November, New Zealand, South Africa and Canada came to Scotland and although the only victory that was posted was against Canada at Pittodrie in

Aberdeen, the team had only just fallen short of South Africa and the front-row had announced their credentials to the world with magnificent performances against the All Blacks and the Springboks. On the back of these showings, much of the Scottish pack and a number of the backs were heralded as certainties for the Lions tour to South Africa in the summer of 2009, and Mike Blair became the first Scottish player to be shortlisted for the prestigious IRB Player of the Year award, alongside 2005 IRB Player of the Year Dan Carter, Italy captain Sergio Parisse and Wales pair Shane Williams and Ryan Jones.

Going into the 2009 Six Nations, hopes were once again flying that Scotland could make a push for the title. They had a mighty pack, arguably the best kicker in the world, and a number of exciting and powerful strike-runners. The signs all looked positive.

But it was not to be.

Two of the monoliths in the pack, Nathan Hines and Euan Murray, were injured and missed much of the tournament. The team lost to Wales at Murrayfield 26-13, the visitors playing what BBC pundit Jeremy Guscott called 'the perfect half of rugby' by outmuscling, outrunning and outthinking the hosts before a late surge in the second-half saw a superb individual try awarded to Max Evans shortly after he came off the bench.

On St Valentine's Day in Paris, winger Thom Evans latched onto a lovely inside ball from Phil Godman to score his first international try, but with an omen that Hadden's luck was terminally on the wane, the home team powered through to win 22-13, with the clinching score from Fulgence Ouedraogo awarded despite a clear forward-pass from Maxime Medard which was inexplicably missed by both referee George Clancy and touch-judge Wayne Barnes.

Two weeks later, the side picked up their sole win of the campaign with a solid if unspectacular 26-6 victory over the Azzurri at Murrayfield, with Simon Danielli and Scott Gray running in scores to compliment Paterson's kicking.

On 14 March, the Irish hit town on the hunt for their first Grand Slam in 61 years. They duly picked up the Scottish scalp on a drizzly evening with Jamie Heaslip crossing to add to the 17 points scored from the boot Ronan O'Gara, securing a 22-15 victory for the men from the Emerald Isle.

The final round was played out at Twickenham and after some sledging in the press from English captain Steve Borthwick, who derided Scotland for the manner of their celebrations following the previous year's Calcutta Cup success, the home team powered home for a 26-12 win. The opening exchanges of the match were keenly contested, until giant winger Ugo Monye turned the fortunes of the game on its head in the space of five minutes. The Harlequin scored a sizzling first-half try down the left flank and then minutes later scorched across the pitch to tackle Thom Evans into touch just shy of the line when the Scottish winger looked a certainty to score.

The result at Twickenham, although spirited, was the final nail in Hadden's *coffin. Now roundly criticised in the media, it was felt that the head coach had brought the team as far as he was able. He had resurrected their fortunes in 2006, saving them from ruin and guiding them to some memorable victories; although hounded at the time for his decisions during the World Cup, he had nevertheless taken the team to the quarter-final and had Sean Lamont collected Dan Parks' cross-field kick, Scotland might well have snuck through to the semi-final. The last two seasons of his reign had been less successful, but he had secured Scotland's second-ever win in the southern hemisphere by guiding his charges to victory over the Pumas in Buenos Aires and had come incredibly close to toppling the world champions in 2008. But it was felt that the time had come for a change and although the SRU touted the names of Australian Eddie Jones and South African Jake White around as they conducted their interviews for Hadden's replacement, there was already a man waiting in the Murrayfield wings ready to step back into the limelight of international rugby.*

JON PETRIE

When Frank came in it really was like a breath of fresh air. We went on tour to Romania that summer and he made me captain for that and for the Barbarians game. His whole attitude and approach made my job really easy because it was such a refreshing change. If you tell people they are crap enough times they are going to start believing it and they don't play well, and that is what happened with Matt.

All Frank did was come in and say, *Actually, you know what guys, I am going to put faith in you to play the game as you see fit. I'll give you the shape but you express yourselves. Go out there and play rugby, you are good players.* And that was all it took to turn things around at that stage. It made my job a hell of a lot easier because we had guys playing rugby with a smile on their face for a first time in a long time.

MIKE BLAIR

The best thing that Frank did was to come in and say that we were actually good players. He simplified everything and just told us to go out and play and enjoy ourselves, to give the ball some air and look to attack whenever we could. It was such a release.

With Matt Williams it was all about structures and angles and detail, with loads of meetings all the time. Frank came with a very simple game plan – *let's just enjoy ourselves and throw the ball around.* I think the massive contrast between them was that around Frank everyone was just able to relax and play their own game. As opposed to being told how crap we were all the time and focussing or what we couldn't do, Frank came in and told us how good we were and he developed a game plan around what we could do instead of trying to foist a completely alien style of play on us.

I remember before we played New Zealand in 2005 we didn't do any video analysis on them. Frank sat us down and said that he could show us reams of film showing how good they were or he could show us film of them dropping passes and missing kicks etcetera, but in the end neither really mattered – what was important was how we played and the type of game plan we wanted to implement.

You can over-analyse things. Often when you analyse a team you don't watch the bad stuff that they do. You can over-do the analysis to a point where you begin to wonder how you could ever possibly beat the team you're watching – because all the flaws in their game are removed. You forget that they're fallible, so Frank was trying to dispel that whole aura around the All Blacks and it was very refreshing. In the end we lost the match, but New Zealand were a great, great side that year. They destroyed the Lions in the summer and that autumn they completed their first Grand Slam tour since 1978. But Frank's approach really liberated us and we felt invigorated going into that match – and that attitude definitely helped set things up for the success we enjoyed the following season.

Frank Hadden. *Getty Images*

ANDY HENDERSON

France at Murrayfield was the first game of the 2006 Six Nations and expectations weren't too high because we hadn't done particularly well under the previous regime. Frank had been in charge during the summer in Romania and during the Autumn Tests, but the Six Nations is a very different proposition.

There was a feeling of confidence in the squad at the way we were being asked to play and the clarity and freedom of the game-plan – so it was a very different mood, but we still realised that we were huge underdogs.

MIKE BLAIR

That France game was just brilliant. We played some really great rugby and our

Mike Blair clears the ball from a ruck against France at Murrayfield. *Getty Images*

expansive style took them totally by surprise. I think the French expected to just turn up and thump us, and they just weren't prepared for that open style we played. There were a lot of gaps around the rucks and mauls and I remember making several breaks down the fringes which got us in behind their defence. They really started to look shaky in defence and there were times that we were just lacerating them all over the park.

The biggest moment was the driving maul that Sean Lamont scored his second try from. We drove the ball from about 25 yards out against one of the most respected forward units in the world – and by the end we had them running backwards. I was desperately trying to get my hands on the ball so that, like any good scrum-half, I could capitalise from all the forward's hard work and claim the glory moment, but Sean had the same idea and he flew in at the last moment and pinched the ball and then flopped over.

ALASTAIR KELLOCK

Frank Hadden's first Six Nations in charge was mine as well and we beat France in the first game. The forwards drove a line-out for 25 metres and just when we got close to the line Sean Lamont came in at the back and touched the ball down. We were delighted that we had scored, but not overly happy that Sean had come off his wing to steal our forwards' try.

MIKE BLAIR

Mossy was running great lines from fullback and kicking like a dream and our ball-carriers were all over the place giving us options off nine, ten and twelve, and in the wide channels as well. It was just brilliant rugby and the crowd noise was incredible. Then Sean went over for his second try and you could see the French were gone in that moment – they just wanted off the pitch and a chance

Sean Lamont goes in under the posts for his first try. *Getty Images*

to regroup back at home. When you break a team like that, when every part of the game is going your way, it's a great, great feeling. And to do it against the third or fourth best team in the world made it all the sweeter.

ALASTAIR KELLOCK

We then went down to Wales and competed pretty well considering Scotty Murray kicked Ian Gough in the head and got sent off. Scotty still claims he didn't, but the video evidence is there. We don't give him stick about it because getting sent off in an international is no laughing matter – and the thought of Scotty doing something as rash as that is completely out of his character. We gave a good account of ourselves as we played with 14 men for most of the game and we began to think that we might even sneak it at the end, but it wasn't to be and they managed to close the game out 28-18. But we were playing some really positive stuff and I have no doubts that we would have won if we had had our full complement of players on the field for the full 80 minutes.

SCOTT MURRAY

It was a stupid thing to do, but it was reactionary. I didn't mean to kick him in the head. I got a three week suspension because the disciplinary committee didn't think that it was accidental which was a pity because it was. Ian was very decent about it and he and several of the Welsh players came out in support to say that they didn't think that I meant to do it, but it didn't cut any ice with the disciplinary committee.

ALASTAIR KELLOCK

Then came the Calcutta Cup match, which was . . . just . . . unbelievable. Scott MacLeod and I started in the second-row, I think it was the first time we had played together. We were both pretty young and skinny playing against a typically massive English pack – so we were under the cosh all afternoon. But we stuck in and all I really remember is the massive feeling of elation afterwards.

ANDY HENDERSON

I remember pitching up for training before the England game and seeing big queues outside the ticket-office at Murrayfield – which was a bit different. It was nice to see public interest growing after what we had achieved in the France game and the manner of our defeat in Wales – so it was particularly good to follow that up with another win. It was a tough old game, but we deserved to come through it with the victory. England are famed for their forward power and their backline at the time was also pretty huge, so to neutralise their physical threat was a great thing.

MIKE BLAIR

You could argue – as many in the press did afterwards – that England played into our hands in that Calcutta Cup match. They said that they should have kept the game simple and pinned us back with a solid kicking game. Maybe they should have; but I have often wondered if it would have made any difference – sometimes you just know a game is going to go your way and as we jogged down the tunnel, I just had this confidence, which you could sense through the whole team, that we were going to win.

The defence in that game was one of the most outstanding I've ever been involved in with any team, and the back-row were on a different level. The impact that Simon Taylor, Ally Hogg and Jason White had on the game cannot be overstated – they were just unbelievable. Ally stole and slowed down so much ball, all three carried really well and some of the hits that Jason and Simon put

Jason White and Simon Taylor flatten Ben Cohen during the 2006 Calcutta Cup triumph. *Getty Images*

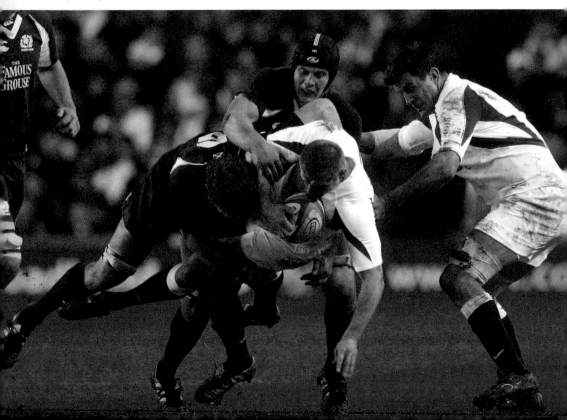

in were just incredible – it was like watching the England boys running into a swinging sack of bricks; they were just pounded back every time they tried to break through. And the most impressive thing is that it didn't let up for a moment – even right at the end, Joe Worsley ran into Jason who lifted him up and hammered him backwards. When the guys on your team are making hits like that, and especially when it's your captain doing it, you gain such a level of confidence and it spurs you on through the next passage of play – and with it the crowd noise rises and that lifts your spirits even more. The noise that day from the stands was amazing and it really felt like we had a sixteenth, seventeenth, even an eighteenth man on the pitch with us.

I think the tackle stats were something like 112 tackles completed by us to their 36, which is astonishing. And Mossy's kicking was flawless – he kicked five penalties out of five attempts and Dan Parks scored a drop-goal. It was a game of attrition, but the satisfaction that comes from grinding out a win like that is huge. It was a real case of punch, punch, and counter-punch from both teams. It was savage. But the key was that we never backed down and against teams like England, that is exactly how you have to take them on. The atmosphere was incredible – it was suffocating for them and completely energising for us.

ALASTAIR KELLOCK

We went out in Edinburgh afterwards and I remember walking home and people were shouting out the window to us, calling us legends and that sort of thing. We were getting clapped into pubs, which, looking back, was a bit cringe-worthy, but it was great at the time. Normally when you go out in Edinburgh or Glasgow no one recognises you, but that night . . . we were the toast of the town.

JON PETRIE

That match against England is actually one of my worst rugby memories. I had missed the autumn internationals with a dislocated shoulder and I hadn't played very much since coming back but made it onto the bench right through the Six Nations, behind Ally Hogg, Jason White and Simon Taylor, who were all playing really well.

I got on in every match except the England one – I was the only substitute not to get on. With about thirty seconds to go I was told to get stripped and I pretty much opted against it. I didn't feel part of it at all. It was a huge disappointment.

Afterwards everyone was celebrating with the Calcutta Cup and while you don't want to bring the other boys down, it is hard to share their excitement when you don't feel you have done your bit. I took myself off for a shower, and I must have stood in there for about an hour and a half, while the rest of the guys were chucking the Calcutta Cup around the changing room and getting their photos taken with it. I just didn't feel a part of that at all but I didn't want to impose that on the rest of the boys. I went out and showed face that night, but didn't really feel that celebratory.

ALASTAIR KELLOCK

Scott Murray was back from suspension and Nathan Hines had come out of retirement by the time we played Ireland, so I got dropped to the bench and Scotty MacLeod was dropped out of the squad altogether. I remember getting the phone-call from Frank on the Monday morning telling me to come and see him, and it was devastating.

The Monday morning call is the worst. They don't phone you to say, 'Congratulations, you're playing really well and you're in the team.' It is just torture. Other players claim it doesn't bother them, but I wake up and I just can't help but stare at the phone, waiting for it to ring.

There was also a time when Frank used to stand at the bottom of the lift in the hotel and wait for you coming down to breakfast. You'd come out the lift and try not to look at him, it's almost as if you are thinking, *If I don't make eye contact he can't see me and he can't drop me.*

MIKE BLAIR

The Italy game was another one of those fairly drab matches between Scotland and Italy but it was great to get the win over there to finish the tournament. We ended up in third place in the Championship, which was the best we had ever done because that third place the team got in 2001 was shared. It gave us a huge boost going into the tour to South Africa that summer. As often happens on these tours to the southern hemisphere, we were brought back to earth with a bump in those two Tests against the Springboks, but we were still playing with adventure and were causing them real problems when we threw the ball wide from side to side and stretched them.

We carried that style of play into the Romania and Pacific Islands games in the autumn of 2006, but we found that, as a style, it was beginning to creek when we lost heavily to Australia. They played a wide game as well but they were also very physical and their backs outmuscled ours at the gain-line contacts.

The success that we had with that wide style of play had been brilliant and we all enjoyed playing that way, but continuing to play that way definitely affected us the following year because other teams had cottoned onto how we played and analysed our wide game, so they would work on pressurising us around the breakdowns to prevent us getting quick ball and many teams adopted a press defence coming from out to in so that the wide channels were cut off unless we threw a long looping ball to the outside centre or the wings, or kicked it in behind the defence for those wide players to run onto it – both of which are unpredictable tactics and can cost you possession or put you under a lot of pressure.

It was when that started to happen that the coaching staff started to look at a more physical and confrontational style of play. That was aided by some injuries and we had guys like Jim Hamilton coming into the team, we had Rob Dewey at inside centre, the Lamont brothers out wide, it was a huge team. You can only play with the squad you have, so the bigger our team got the more we focussed on keeping things tight and dominating through our size and the less we began to throw the ball around as we had been doing. Some people felt that it was wrong to change our tactics, but we had been worked out so we had to mix it up. What we needed to do, looking at the whole situation retrospectively, was to work on a balance between physicality and the wide game – which is what teams like the All Blacks have always done so brilliantly.

RORY LAWSON (Edinburgh Gunners, Gloucester)
20 Caps (to date): 2006-still playing

I was first capped off the bench against Australia in November 2006 and I then made my Six Nations debut against England at Twickenham in 2007, but I didn't get a chance to make a start in the number nine jersey until we played France in the final game.

Some people might have the perception that it has been hard for me to try and carve out a career in the shadow of both my father and my grandfather, but really it has been an inspiration rather than any kind of albatross around my neck. Dad's been great to have around throughout my career – as a former scrum-half, he has always known exactly what I need to do and his reading of scrum-half play is second to none. We have a photo in the house of him diving over for one of his Calcutta Cup tries and it's a great incentive to want to follow suit. And having Bill McLaren as your grandfather is something I am very, very proud of and I am so pleased that he got a chance to see me play for Scotland.

ANDY HENDERSON

The Calcutta Cup match at Twickenham was our first game of the 2007 Six Nations and Jonny Wilkinson's first game back since he had kicked the drop-goal to win England the World Cup – it had been something like 39 months that he had spent out of the England starting line-up. It was something of a fairytale comeback for him and a complete nightmare for us. They absolutely destroyed us. It was disappointing to lose so heavily after our efforts to wrestle the Calcutta Cup from them 12 months earlier – especially as the try that Jonny scored should never have been given. In the replay and in a whole ream of photographs that came out after the match, you could clearly see that his foot was well in touch before he placed the ball over the line. But these things happen and you have to look back on them after a while and be philosophical about it. Jonny had been through a torrid, torrid time with injury and if anybody deserved a bit of luck to swing back his way, it was him. But as far as Scotland-England encounters are concerned, I hope that that's his dues paid.

Jonny Wilkinson's controversial try. The score was given and England went on the rampage at Twickenham. *Press Association*

PHIL GODMAN (Edinburgh Rugby)
23 Caps (to date): 2005-still playing

During the week leading up to the Italy game at Murrayfield, we had spoken a lot about what our game-plan was. I'd played the week before against Wales – that had been my first Six Nations start – and we'd had a really good solid win against them and I'd done reasonably well getting the backline moving. We didn't score any tries but we had forced a lot of penalties and Mossy had kicked the points, so the Italy game was one we had pinpointed as an opportunity to take our attack onto the next level, and really put some points on them.

We worked at training all week on this game-plan of going wide quickly to lap their rush defence, and to kick over them as well, and it had gone like a dream. Then I got the ball in the first minute and I remember thinking at the time that I might be a bit deep – I was right on our own line – but at the same time a well executed chip kick would have really caused Italy problems because there was absolutely nobody there, and we could have been scoring at the other end. It was a risky option, but it was only a matter of inches away from being the right one.

I had played against Mauro Bergamasco before – for Newcastle against Treviso – and all he did was hit me all afternoon, whether I had the ball or not. He's an animal. So I knew he was going to come at me and as soon as I hit the chip I knew I hadn't put enough on it. And even when he got the charge-down I was thinking, *most of the time charge-downs don't result in tries.* But it bounced perfectly – and all you could hear was this big groan reverberating round the ground.

But I wasn't panicking at that stage.

CHRIS CUSITER

Then I threw two interception passes – and they scored off both. The first one wasn't a planned move. I was at first receiver and I just tried to draw the man and pass, but Andrea Scanavacca read it and was left with a clear run to the line. The other one was off a move from a line-out. One of the options we had discussed was throwing a pass over the top, and I chucked it because there was nothing else on. I don't know if somebody had run the wrong line or not, but it didn't come off. In retrospect it was the wrong decision.

PHIL GODMAN

Suddenly we were 21-0 down and you're standing there wondering how this could have happened. The chat under the posts was not to panic, but in that situation it is hard not to. Anyone who played in that game will agree that it was the strangest rugby experience of their lives. We had the ball but were gifting them the scores. We got back into it – but there was an element of shell-shock there, which was hard to cope with at the time.

CHRIS CUSITER

It was horrible, but at the same time you are conscious that there is another 75 minutes to play so you have plenty of time to make up for your mistakes if you keep your focus. You know that the only good thing that can come out of the game is coming back and winning it, so you have no choice but to knuckle down and get on with that. There is no place to hide out there in front of 50,000 people. All I could do was try to block what had happened out of my mind and concentrate on helping Scotland get back into it. You don't have time to think about the implications of what is happening when you are out there. It is only afterwards that everything catches up with you.

At one point we got back to within one score of them, but they upped their game and we had worked so hard to get close that there was nothing left in the tank. It was really tough.

KELLY BROWN (Glasgow Warriors)
37 Caps (to date): 2005–still playing

It was the most surreal experience. I remember jogging up to the halfway line after the third try, looking up at the scoreboard and thinking to myself, *What the hell is going on here?* It was like an out-of-body experience. You were genuinely wondering if it was all a dream . . . or should I say nightmare. We had only made three mistakes but they had all led to tries. It took quite a while to get past that.

PHIL GODMAN

That game still haunts me. I didn't play for Scotland again for another sixteen months, and during that period every time my name was mentioned that one incident was always spoken about. I suppose it was the way that game went afterwards which made it such a hot topic. At the end of the day, I got a kick charged down – that's all. I'll get kicks charged down again, I can guarantee that – but hopefully I won't be on the wrong side of a game like that ever again.

I was walking along the street not long ago and walked past a group of boys who clearly recognised me. I could hear them nudging each other and pointing – so I was feeling quite chuffed because us rugby guys don't have the same sort of profile as the football boys. Then one of them shouted, 'Hey, Phil, well played against Italy!' And they all laughed. I just know they weren't talking about the 2009 match!

CHRIS CUSITER

As we got closer to the 2007 World Cup we changed our approach and I never really understood why because I thought the way we were playing worked pretty well. It stretched teams. But we went back to a more physical, confrontational style of game and really focussed on bulking up.

ALASTAIR KELLOCK

It was a combination of what had happened against Italy in the 2007 Six Nations and the fact that we drew them in the World Cup. As the World Cup got closer and closer you could sense that everything was focussing on that game.

MIKE BLAIR

Mark Bitcon was our conditioning coach and it was quite amazing the difference that he made with everyone's physiques. Well, everyone except me. I had injured my shoulder the year before playing against the Scarlets and I have never recovered the same kind of strength in my arm as I had before. Certain weight-lifting movements are fine, but others are just impossible. Mark would keep a big wall chart up in the gym recording every players' weight-lifting stats and as we got closer and closer to the tournament some of the boys were lifting the most ridiculous weights – and then right down at the bottom of the chart, miles away from everyone else, was my name.

It was amusing in many ways and I got a lot of abuse from the boys about it, but at the same time I quite liked being there at the bottom. I was performing well when I played despite my lack of size – and it showed me that I didn't have to be the biggest guy in the world to compete on the international stage. I had gone on a weight-gain programme a season or two before and the more weights I did the more sluggish I felt around the pitch. My passing wasn't as good and I didn't feel as sharp. After my shoulder injury prevented me from lifting all those weights I felt faster in everything I did. I still pride myself on my defence and it's a wonderful feeling putting guys that are much bigger than you on the ground and I like the fact that it is down to technique and bravery rather than just brawn. And it's reassuring to know that in the modern game, there is a still a place for the little guys. Guys like Chris Custer and Mike Phillips are superb to have in your team; in Mike's case, he's big and powerful and attracts a lot of attention whenever he gets the ball, which releases space out wide; Cus is smaller but he's nuggety and tough, much like Rory Lawson, and in many ways he and Rory are like another back-row forward when they play because they can take the ball into contact and actually make a dent. I suppose it all depends on the style of play that you want to go with. I like to bring players into the game as often as I can and only take the contact when I need to – it switches the defensive focus and when that happens space opens up elsewhere – you snipe in a different way. Chris, Rory and I all like to run and look for a break, but we do it differently, and we defend slightly differently as well – they're better at taking on defensive duties around the fringes, while I like to organise things a bit more and look to do a bit more cover defence should the opposition break through. It means that we all bring something slightly different to the table and although it's tough when you're not the one selected to start, if you get a chance to come off the bench, you know you're bringing something different that might change the course of the game. And having the three of us all vying for the one shirt certainly lifts your game and stops you from ever resting on your laurels.

JASON WHITE (Glasgow Caledonians, Sale Sharks, Clermont Auvergne)
77 Caps (to date): 2000-still playing

Mark Bitcon used to call himself the Guru and he put together an absolutely tremendous programme for us in the build up to the competition. He was well supported by guys from the Scottish Institute of Sport and the whole thing was just superbly structured and managed. It allowed us to compete physically with any team in the world whereas before we maybe suffered in one or two games because we were outmuscled. That base he gave us allowed us to go and develop other areas of the game and you don't hear talk of people saying that we can't compete physically with any team any more, which is fantastic and a real tribute to the work that Mark and his team did for us.

CHRIS PATERSON

That game against Ireland before the World Cup was brilliant in many ways, because size and being dominant physically was something we had lacked before and we really showed what a difference it could make in that game because Ireland were completely blown off the park. That lack of physicality had cost us games in the past. But because it worked so well that day against Ireland, I wonder if it maybe held us back over the next couple of years. It took away other parts of the game that had been really quite effective for us.

MIKE BLAIR

Dan Parks was fantastic for us during the World Cup. Phil Godman and I go back a long way and I love playing alongside him, but he runs a very different kind of game to Dan. As stand-offs, both are great weapons to have within your squad – Dan plays a largely kicking-orientated game, while Phil likes to run and pass to break down defences. The way the rules were working at the time of the 2007 World Cup, particularly surrounding the tackle laws, teams that were kicking well were tending to be the ones that were winning games. Teams like Argentina, France, England and South Africa progressed through the tournament because they kicked superbly and then used a fast, aggressive defence to push up and force turnovers or penalties. The game has changed since then, but in 2007 kicking was king and Dan is one of the best in the world when it comes to putting boot to ball. He can do the most unbelievable things when he kicks – the kind of things he does in training, little tricks and so on, are incredible, and he can literally put the ball on a sixpence. In the aftermath of the tournament we all voted for our Scottish player of the World Cup and it deservedly went to Dan. He has had a tumultuous time in a Scotland shirt, he has been to darker places than any of us can imagine and some sections of the public and the media have been appalling to him, really poisonous, but his positivity despite all of that has been inspiring. No player goes out to play badly, but we all have bad days and when you play at stand-off you are more open to criticism than anyone else in the team. In international rugby you can go from hero to zero in no time; as Alan Jones, who coached of the Grand Slam winning Wallabies of 1984, used to say, 'today a rooster, tomorrow a feather-duster'. I'm just so pleased for Dan, on both a personal and professional level, that his star in the ascendency again.

And it's good for Phil too – just as Cus, Rory and I push each other on, so do they. It's what every team needs to be successful – players pushing each other to new heights just to hold onto the jersey.

Ally Hogg, Simon Taylor and Scott Lawson look to exploit the frail Portugal defence. *FotoSport*

KELLY BROWN

We improved throughout the World Cup, certainly. We came into it having recorded a good win against Ireland and come pretty close to South Africa. We weren't particularly great against Portugal or Romania, but each game showed positive signs of improvement. For all the fuss that was made about our team selection for the All Blacks game, I still thought that we might have a chance to do something special against them because we had been written-off. In the end they took us apart, but they had a nearly full-strength team and we had a few injuries – like Mossy having to go off early with a head bang. It's pretty special playing against a side like the All Blacks – they make rugby seem so easy and that's a sign of their class – but I'm confident that with the group of players that we have coming together that we will have as good a chance as any Scottish team in the past to get a win over them in the near future. It's all about cutting out your mistakes – which All Blacks teams always punish you for – and making sure we keep them contained. That's how teams like South Africa, Australia, England and France have beaten them in the last few years. When you put the pressure on them they're as fallible as any other team.

That loss to New Zealand was disappointing, but it wasn't a disaster. We blooded some new players and guys on the fringes got to have a run-out. The big game was always going to be against Italy and that's exactly how it worked it.

JASON WHITE

We had two solid wins against Portugal and Romania to start the group stages and they were good games for settling people into the tournament and starting to get our patterns of play going. We had played South Africa and Ireland and had done well in both games, particularly beating Ireland which is something we hadn't done for four years. The decision had to be made for the third game against New Zealand as to whether we would field a full-strength team or not, or to rest the majority of our front-line players as we had a short turnaround between that game and the final game against Italy. In the end we decided to rest a number of our first-choice team to allow them plenty of time to recover from the first two games and prepare properly for the Italy game.

It was a pretty tough environment for John Barclay and Alastair Dickinson to win their first caps, against New Zealand. But they both really stood up for themselves and looked comfortable out there among some of the very best players in the world. There was a bit of talk about us throwing lambs to the slaughter out there, but that wasn't the case. Some people felt that it was a negative attitude not to field our best team; yes, we might have beaten them and proceeded to the quarter-finals with a great win; or we might have given a good account of ourselves and lost and also lost a few of our key players to injury, which would have hampered us massively going into the Italy game, which would then still be a must-win. I can understand people's arguments, but I think it was the correct tactical call; and after all, it paid off in the end.

MIKE BLAIR

The Italy match was a huge game for many reasons – we had to win to go through to the quarter-final, we had backed our whole pool strategy around this one fixture after deciding to rest most of the front-line players against the All Blacks, we were the only Celtic nation still in with a chance of making it out of the pools, and Italy have something of a voodoo sign over us – especially after the debacle we had against them earlier in the year during the Six Nations. It was do or die for both teams. I remember the Italian centre, Gonazalo Canale, referring to it as 'the match of death' during the build up.

Both sides were understandably nervous going into the game and fortunately for us the Italian nerves were the more frayed and they gave away an early penalty that allowed Mossy to get us on the scoreboard, and then we got another one shortly afterwards so that we were 6-0 up after only four minutes or so. We might have scored a try shortly afterwards after Troncon had a poor clearance kick but Mauro Bergamasco put an end to things with a professional foul and was yellow-carded. Not that that did us much good – a few minutes later Ramiro Pez fired up a high Garryowen and as Rory Lamont went to take it in the air he was smashed by Andrea Masi; Italy won the ball and it was chaos for a few seconds around the ball before Troncon forced his way over. They converted and then added a penalty and out of nowhere, it seemed, they were 10-6 ahead.

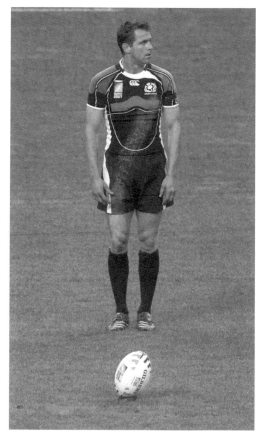

Dead-eye Chris Paterson achieved the remarkable feat of finishing the World Cup with 100 per cent accuracy in front of goal. *Getty Images*

Mossy pulled us back in it before half-time with a couple of long-range penalties and we went in 12-10 ahead, but it was a nervous old time.

JASON WHITE

The game ended up being dominated by kicking and trying to dominate territory, which was the absolutely correct thing to do in the conditions. You have to play what's in front of you, no matter what the game or the opposition.

They got a try to go into the lead but we all felt that we could and would beat them, so nobody panicked, which was a very pleasing thing to see as captain. We all kept our composure and worked ourselves into the right areas of the pitch. Mossy kicked brilliantly and we kept in it.

MIKE BLAIR

Mossy and David Bortolussi exchanged penalties in the second-half, but lucky Bortolussi also missed a few and going into the final few minutes we were 18-15 ahead. Then, with only a couple of minutes left, Italy were awarded another penalty.

It was real stomach in boots time. I wondered whether Scotland would be making history with Italy again – we welcomed them to the Six Nations by losing in Rome, were we about to be the team that would see them into their first ever World Cup quarter-final? It was a tricky kick – out to the right of the posts near the ten-yard line and it was cold and wet, which would make the flight of the ball through the air heavier and there was a bit of a breeze, but you could never tell. They're agonizing, those moments, because there is nothing you can do to influence the kicker – you just have to stand there, impotent, and hope and hope and hope.

JASON WHITE

It was a bit nerve-wracking at the end, but Bortolussi put his final kick wide and we came through and that was the important bit. Our target was the quarter-finals and we made it – which is something that neither Ireland or Wales managed, so it shouldn't be underestimated as an achievement.

It was tight – tighter than we would have liked and it was disappointing to lose a try while failing to score one ourselves – but the win was the thing that mattered. We knew that we would have to improve against Argentina the following week to have a chance of progressing to the semi-finals, but at that stage we were more than happy to accept substance over style.

Jason White, Simon Webster and Kelly Brown celebrate Scotland's victory over Italy. *Getty Images*

ALLISTER HOGG

In the build-up to the quarter-final we really felt that we had the beating of Argentina. We had some real chances in that match to seal the result but we let them slide and didn't play as we might have, so it was hugely disappointing not to go any further in the tournament. They were a good side, well drilled and knew each other very well – as a team they had been together for a number of years. We tried to play a bit of a territorial game, but it didn't come off. We should maybe have tried to throw the ball around a bit more earlier on.

DAN PARKS (Glasgow Warriors)
53 Caps (to date): 2004-still playing

We probably started to play too late in the game – and we had a chance at the end but didn't take it. It was a heart-breaking way to go out, but they took their chances and we didn't. At the end of the day that's what rugby so often comes down to. They lit up that tournament and deserved to go through, but we'll have a chance to level things in the pool stages of the next World Cup and that's something focus on.

MIKE BLAIR

Unfortunately we looked to counter the way Argentina played rather than looking to impose our own game on them. We knew that they kicked a lot and pressed in defence but didn't create an awful lot. Our game plan was to kick into their half and once we had any set-pieces in their half we would attack, all out, go wide and get a decent balance in our play of ball carriers and wide runners. The only problem with the plan was that we didn't get a set-piece in their half for virtually the entire first 60 minutes; all we did was gain possession in our half and kick it away. As predicted they didn't create very much – they got a few penalties and a try from a charge-down clearance. But we were as guilty of a lack of creativity. You look back now and consider the styles of play that we had in 2006 and 2007 – the wide game and the physical game, with almost exactly the same personnel, give or take a few players. If we had married up those two styles we could have been in the semi-final of the World Cup and would have been a dangerous proposition for any team. In terms of a path to a World Cup semi-final, you couldn't have asked for much of a better one than the one we had that year. So yes, it's pretty hard to look back on now and know what we missed out on.

Kelly Brown and Simon Taylor try to stifle the Argentinean attack. *Press Association*

JASON WHITE

The players enjoyed the World Cup and the guys who were experiencing the competition for the first time thought it was immense. It was obviously disappointing to lose to Argentina because we didn't play to our potential in that game. In many ways it came down to experience on the big stage and Argentina had more players who were used to performing at the highest level, particularly for their clubs – but also in that competition because they had faced the hosts in the opening game, a huge, huge occasion, and had won and then they had beaten Ireland as well, who many people had as dark horses for the competition. And they backed up how good they were by giving South Africa a bit of a scare and then beating France again to finish third.

It's a matter of developing a cool head in these big occasions, but it was a fantastic experience for a very young squad, and all going well the majority of the squad will still be together for the 2011 World Cup and can use these experiences positively there. We have to learn to develop beyond relying on Mossy and Dan to kick all our points, but at the same time it was an unbelievable statistic that Mossy went through the tournament with 100% record at goal. His overall stats just defy belief and although we want to develop our try-scoring ability, having him in your team is incredibly reassuring.

CHRIS PATERSON

I don't like to talk too much about my kicking – it's just something that I see as part of my job on the field, not the main thing I do at all. And I never over-think it either, I just go through my routine and focus on keeping my rhythm the same. Mick Byrne, who is now with the All Blacks, was the one that made the big difference with my kicking while he was Scotland's kicking coach. He was very philosophical when it came to kicking practice – just do small amounts, 20 minutes a

Agustin Pichot and Nathan Hines acknowledge a hard-fought battle as Scotland's World Cup campaign comes to an end. *Press Association*

day or so, and if you're having a bad day just leave and start again the next day. He used to say that if things aren't working for you on a certain day, don't try to force it because that's when you'll change your timing and your technique and just pick up bad habits. So I'm not obsessional about it in any way, it's just something that I've become very comfortable with doing.

ANDY HENDERSON

We lost our opening game of the 2008 Six Nations to France at Murrayfield and didn't play at all well. We then went down to Cardiff and lost again and then had to travel over to Ireland to play at Croke Park on the back of Ireland's massive – and historic – win over England the week before.

Frank picked Mossy at ten for that game and we had a brilliant opening ten minutes when we were all over them and Mossy was looking really good. But then, as that Ireland team always seemed to do at the time, they rode the storm and managed to stop some of our more promising attacks by giving away penalties, and then they broke against the run of play and scored up at the other end. I think that both of Tommy Bowe's tries and Rob Kearney's try were all scored after we had been on the attack and they turned the ball over. It's always a fairly shattering moment when you get yourself into a good position and you think that you're going to score, only for someone to drop a ball or get turned over at a ruck or for a kick not to go to touch and the other team are suddenly 60 yards up the other end of the pitch scoring.

It felt that that happened to us a lot in 2008.

MIKE BLAIR

The Ireland game was as disappointing to lose as the previous games, but at the same time it was one of the proudest moments in my life because I took over the captaincy after Jason White was injured playing in our loss to Wales in Cardiff. I'm the 108th captain of Scotland and it was such an honour to be given the role – although following in Jason's footsteps was quite a daunting prospect – the team had to go from looking to this great big beast who could knock the stuffing out of any player in the world to scrawny wee me.

To lead the team out was just amazing and Croke Park was some place to do it. But it was even better the following week against England at Murrayfield. It was lashing it down and I remember standing in the tunnel waiting to go out and the lights were mostly off in the stadium and this lone piper was playing up on the top of the East Stand and all I could see was the rain pouring down almost horizontally.

That was another sensational defensive performance. It was a kind of re-run of the 2000 game in terms of us having gone through the Championship without picking up a win and then playing to the conditions. It was funny, just like the 2000 and 2006 victories, I was astonished by the fact that England didn't change their tactics to suit the weather or to counter the way we were playing. They had these hardened campaigners in Jonny Wilkinson, Iain Balshaw, Andrew Sheridan, Phil Vickery, Simon Shaw and Steve Borthwick, who had all been there and done it before at the highest level – and who had also lost to us in the same manner in 2006, and some of them again in 2000 – and yet they didn't say, 'Look, this isn't working, what we have to do is change this and do this . . .' They just carried on playing in the same way and that suited us perfectly.

DONNIE MACFADYEN

I eventually decided to hang up my boots at the end of the 2007-08 season. 2004 was really the only year that I played without suffering a major injury and getting

Mike Blair hoists the Calcutta Cup aloft after another mighty defensive performance from the home team seals the bragging rights over England for the second time in three years. *Press Association*

a good run of games I started to feel like I was beginning to show some of my potential. But then my knee got wrecked in training and I was out for 15 months. I took the ball into contact and tried to spin out of the tackle and just tore it to pieces. When that happened the initial diagnosis was that it wasn't very serious. I went in for keyhole surgery and was told that I would be walking out later that day and would be fine for the first Six Nations game that year, which was about six weeks away. I woke up after the operation and one of the first things I remember was seeing a pair of crutches and just thinking, *uh-oh.* Gordon Mackay, the surgeon, told me that he was staggered by the damage he found when he opened the knee up and I had to have a total reconstruction, which required three more operations and over 15 months of rehab before I was back playing.

It was a long old road back from that first injury and then in a pre-season game against Wasps, Graeme Morrison made a break and I was trailing behind him and one of the Wasps guys dived in to tackle him. They both hit the deck right in front of me and I jumped over them both – and when I landed my knee just buckled and bent backwards. The first knee injury I had was sore but not terrible. The second one, well . . . it really wasn't good.

Surprisingly it didn't take as long to come back from that injury as it did from the first one and I was fit by the end of the 2007-08 season, but I knew by then that I didn't really have any other choice than to call it a day, which was a tremendously sad and disappointing way to have to finish your career. It had been four years of pretty much constant injury and there's only so much you can put your body and your mind through. It got to the stage when I just couldn't trust my body any more and in a contact sport that's no use at all. I found that I was always worrying about getting injured, it would be in the back of my mind every time I went into a contact situation, and that was no good for anyone playing rugby, but especially so if they play at open-side flanker where you have to throw your body recklessly into anything. So I don't think I was ever as effective again – and also my speed, which had been one of my most defining aspects as a player, was definitely affected by having two knee reconstructions. Neil Back was always a hero of mine growing up because we played in the same position and were of a similar stature. He was always the fittest man in the England and Leicester squads he was involved in – he knew that because of his size he had to bring something else to the table to compete and get ahead of his rivals. I adopted that same philosophy and became incredibly focussed on my strength and speed. After I had been out of the Scotland squad for a few years I was invited to a training session by Matt Williams as a kind of 37th man. But in the fitness tests we did I was running times with the wingers and my fitness was in the top two or three, so it made Matt sit up and take notice and I was back in the team shortly afterwards. But once that speed began to be diminished I didn't feel that I could offer the same qualities that I could before.

My knees still aren't right, to be honest – they hurt to walk downstairs and my wife Rosie, who's a doctor, is constantly worrying about me developing arthritis in them, which would be incredibly debilitating in later life.

The sad thing is that suffering major injuries season after season is quite a common occurrence in professional rugby – and the repercussions that it has on the rest of your life cannot be underestimated.

I still wonder now and again about taking up some kind of social rugby because I do really miss the game, but I know that my knees are too vulnerable and if I want to have any quality of life in later years then I have to take a step back from it all. I still watch rugby, mainly with my mum because she loves it, but it's difficult to see your friends out there still playing at the highest level when you want to be out there with them. I think it will get easier when the next generation of player comes in that I don't know, but at the moment I think Alex Grove, who was capped in the autumn Tests in 2010, is the only current Scotland player who would walk past me in the street because he doesn't know who I am.

It's a hard thing to adapt back into the real world and I think it is something that a lot of ex-players struggle to deal with. In terms of global sport, struggling with retirement from a professional career is nothing new; but professional rugby is still pretty young in this country and I'm part of the first generation to go straight from school or university into a professional team, and now come out the other side. Pete Sampras famously said that there's no playbook for retirement and he's absolutely right – everything you do as a professional rugby player is planned meticulously, from what you wear, to what time you're supposed to be places, to what you eat and how you train. You drop out of that system and suddenly you're alone. When I started, the older guys around me all had careers – they were lawyers or teachers or whatever – but I went straight from school into ten years of rugby, and then out again, and it was a huge culture shock. No backroom staff, no manager to phone, no crowds knowing who you are . . . It's not a prima donna complex, it's just the way it is. Everything and then suddenly nothing. And no matter who you are, it's hard to deal with.

I never played abroad during my career, so it wasn't until I retired that I really got a chance to consider the professional game in Scotland, how it's run and so on; and it's an incredible fish-bowl. There are two teams, everyone knows everyone, there's no threat of relegation in the Magners League, you always get into the Heineken Cup, and I think there is a real comfort zone there that not only stops people pushing themselves as they might, but also just allows them to settle into routines – so when your career is over, unless you have something that helps ease the transition, it's an incredible culture-shock. There is a lot of focus on helping players with career advice now, but there also needs to be mental and medical support. Myself and a few other ex-pros, and some guys still in the game, are speaking to the SRU about the need for a support structure for players when they retire and they are being very receptive. It's important to help other guys out who might be going through the same thing, or to help prepare the guys for when they have to go through it themselves. There is shadowing in businesses, courses, and guys are encouraged to do part-time degrees, but there needs to be more focus on the mental aspect to make sure guys understand how dramatically their lives are going to change; but we're working towards that as well, so the future is looking brighter for the current and future generation, which is great.

ALASTAIR KELLOCK

In the summer of 2008 we went on tour to Argentina and they mixed things up by bringing in some new coaches to assist on the tour. It was refreshing to work with Andy Robinson as well as my club coach, Sean Lineen, out on that tour with the rest of the Scotland coaching staff. They brought in new ideas and focus, and Andy's attention to detail – especially for the forwards – was just incredible. Little things like adjustments in technique and little tricks can make such a difference at Test level and Andy's insights really did help to improve our technique and efficiency in the set-piece and around the contact area both collectively and individually.

I came off the bench in both those summer Tests and to win the second match was a brilliant, brilliant feeling. It was also one of the toughest, most physical games I've ever played and the crowd were just mental. There's real passion in Argentinean rugby, right from the clubs and the crowd through to the players. They all stick together like brothers in the trenches and that sense of a team ethic is very inspiring. The challenge when you play them is to match that passion and the ferocity that they bring to a game. Their sense of loyalty to each other keeps them fighting for the full 80 minutes and they never give up thinking that they will win. That is why they did so well in the 2007 World

Mike Blair secures a high ball in the first Test in Argentina. *FotoSport*

Cup, why they continue to do so well on the international stage even though they, as yet, do not take part in a regular annual tournament, and why they will be such a dangerous opponent to our hopes in the World Cup in 2011.

MIKE BLAIR

The second Test out in Argentina was particularly special for me. It was my 50th cap and the performance we put in was superb – it is always so satisfying to see the hard work done during an intervening week between matches come out and we were more intense and more precise and we played a quicker ball in the dangerous areas. In many ways, the landmark of the 50th Test wouldn't have meant anything if we hadn't won that game. The fact that we did, playing good rugby, to achieve only the second-ever Test victory Scotland has had in the southern hemisphere, was just brilliant.

GRAEME MORRISON (Glasgow Warriors)
25 Caps (to date): 2004-still playing

To come across to somewhere like Argentina where rugby's a very passionate game, the crowd were pretty hostile; both arenas we played in in each Test were pretty intimidating. So to bounce back from the defeat in the first Test to win

Graeme Morrison carves through the last few metres to the Argentinean try line in the second Test for the clinching score after Dan Parks intercepted the ball in his own half. *FotoSport*

in the second was a very memorable occasion and to score made it all even better. Dan Parks had just come off the bench and he intercepted a pass inside our own half and ran about 40 yards into their territory, then just as he was about to get tackled he looped a lovely ball inside to me and I had a clear run to the line. It was a tremendous moment and a nice little Glasgow one-two.

JOHN BARCLAY

Everything just went right for us in that second Test and it was one of the most enjoyable games that I've played for Scotland. We played some great rugby and I never felt at any time that we looked like losing, which is a fantastic feeling to have in somewhere like Argentina with the crowd going crazy all around you and their players throwing everything at you.

MIKE BLAIR

At the start of the following international season we had a good run-out against Canada up in Pittodrie. It's great being able to take games to other venues around Scotland and we have always had excellent vocal support from the crowds up in Aberdeen – although sometimes the weather can make it a fairly arduous experience. In the days leading up to the match there had been blizzards sweeping across the country and when we arrived to play the game they were shoveling snow drifts off the pitch – so it was bitterly cold and really soft under foot. To make matters worse, the ground staff at Pittodrie had decided to paint the pitch-markings red to help distinguish them from the snow – but the only problem was that I'm colour-blind so I couldn't see any of the markings at all. I had to go through the whole game trying to guess where the lines were from the flags, and I wasn't all that successful, to be honest.

We recorded a good win against a physical Canadian side and it was great to see Max Evans getting his first cap and right from the off he showed what a dangerous runner he could be.

EUAN MURRAY (Glasgow Warriors, Northampton Saints)
32 Caps (to date): 2005-still playing

The autumn of 2008 was fantastic, although it was bitterly disappointing not to beat either the All Blacks or the Springboks considering the dominance we had over them in the set-piece. Those games were the biggest challenge I had faced in my career at that point and as a team it was the biggest challenge of most of our careers. I wish we'd had New Zealand last in the three-Test series though, because I really feel that we could have beaten them if we had had a few run-outs before facing them.

Mike Blair prepares to feed the ball to the scrum while his front-row turn the screw against the All Blacks. *FotoSport*

Ross Ford rampages into the All Blacks' defence. *FotoSport*

MIKE BLAIR

We started that game very strongly and took the game to the All Blacks right from the off, which is something that I don't think they expected. I took a quick tap in the first minute or two and put Mossy through after he took a great angle off my shoulder and he was dragged down just short of their line. A wee while later we had a good strong scrum right on their line and Ally Hogg picked up, drew their back-row and passed to me – I was on the move, ready to accelerate to the line with Thom Evans outside me and I think we would have almost definitely scored . . . except I knocked the ball on. It was a killer moment in the game. It was just before halftime and would have taken us in at 13-18 and with our tails up, but as it was we went in 6-18 and all our possession and dominance had barely registered on the scoreboard. The All Blacks scored some clever opportunist tries, as they always do, and the game got away from us in the end. But the forwards had stood up and sent a message to the world about the kind of power we possessed and in the backs we made some nice breaks and got into good field position. It was all part of a learning curve – learning to turn that dominance into scores and reacting when the ball goes loose, just as the All Blacks do. It is a painful curve to be on, but every team has to go through that at some stage.

It was agonisingly close against South Africa the following week. We had played superbly during the first-half and were winning 10-0 at half-time. Phil Godman had made a fantastic break deep into the Springbok's 22 and was hauled down just short of the line. We recycled the ball quickly and Nathan Hines was bundled over by the posts.

Mossy was injured early on in the game and Phil took over the kicking duties. He had to go off for some treatment and was replaced by Dan Parks. It was pretty shocking how the crowd reacted to Dan coming on – booing and shouting abuse – it was appalling. I was ashamed by it all, to be honest. He missed two kicks at goal while he was on – and you can understand why. Goal-kicking is the loneliest duty on a rugby field. You have to shut out all distractions and go through your rhythms while 70,000 people are staring at you from every angle and millions more watch you on TV. It's all very well to say that you need to shut out the world, but if you have 70,000 people – *your own supporters* – baying for your blood, booing you and then letting out a collective groan when you miss, you would have to be a machine not to let it affect you. The crowd is a fickle thing. They booed Dan off the pitch again when Phil came out of the blood bin, but Phil had a kick late on to nick the lead which he also missed, and there was nothing like the same reaction from the crowd.

It's tough on them both playing at stand-off. Phil was the golden boy then and Dan was totally reviled. Now, in 2010, it's a complete reversal. It happens in most countries – look at the reaction that people have to Jonny Wilkinson or Danny

Cipriani in England. The apple of the fans' eye one day, a waste of space the next. I understand the passion that people invest in us as players, the money they spend to watch us, and I understand that we are representing them on the international stage – it is all part of the magic of sport – but I wish there was more of a sense of perspective about their reactions to us. It kills us to lose, to make mistakes, but things can and do go wrong. We spend our lives trying to be the best we can be in every moment that we play, but we're all fallible and we all make mistakes. If we were all perfect there would be no chance of an upset, the game would just be a series of phases between scores. I don't expect the crowd to cheerfully applaud us no matter what – the passion that they bring to the arena is what international sport is all about – but to boo a player, to insinuate that he's worthless . . . that, I find, is unacceptable and goes against any grain of sportsmanship and good conduct that has been such a fundamental part of the history of our game.

I thought a lot about the crowd's reaction to Dan after that game and why public opinion has been so split on him over the years. I think in many ways it boils down to the fact that he was born and raised in Australia and when he was first capped in 2004 he got hit by the backlash of the Brendan Laney thing. Later, when Matt Williams finished with Scotland, Dan was tarnished by his brush too because of their shared nationality and partly because he had been brought in by Matt in preference to Gregor. Because of that, I think people picked more holes in his game than they might have if he had been born and raised here. With people like Andy Irvine and Gregor, the fans remember more of the good than the bad – and there certainly were bad elements in their play that cost Scotland tries, or even games. With Dan, for many years, fans only saw or remembered the bad and would forget the good. I'm glad that there is more of a sense of perspective about it all these days – and that is due largely to Dan. He plays to his strengths, he doesn't try to be the ultimate all-rounder, and in doing so he has proved how good he is at what he does well – and Scotland have benefited hugely from it.

PHIL GODMAN

The key moment in the first-half of that Springbok game for us came when Mike made a break off the back of a ruck and he sliced right through their defence. He fed the ball to me and I managed to step through the cover defence; I thought I might just make it to score, but then Pierre Spies came out of nowhere and absolutely hammered me. He's a monster; he's 6′3″ and around 18 stone and can do the 100m in just over 10 seconds. He smashed me. Luckily I was able to place the ball back and our support runners were there to clear out the ruck. We kept the ball tight and Wagga went over. I picked myself up and knocked over the conversion and we were 10-0 up.

MIKE BLAIR

It had been quite a loose game with both sides making handling errors and it was only thanks to some good scramble defence that we managed to prevent them scoring an early try.

Our pack was playing superbly though, absolutely beasting them in the scrum and were doing well at the ruck, which is normally a real area of strength for Springbok sides. It was hard work for the forwards, but I felt confident that if we could continue to match them in those areas we could push on with our lead.

Afterwards the press claimed that we had frozen because we hadn't expected to be ten points ahead, but I think that it was more of a case of the Springboks showing their class as world champions to grind out the win. They got a couple of pretty quick penalties that Ruan Pienaar slotted to bring them within reach and then Jaque Fourie, who had just come off the bench, scored in the corner. It was a similar move to the one that Fourie scored from against the Lions in the second Test in 2009, and it was heartbreaking on both occasions.

Pienaar missed the kick, so we were a point behind but still very much in the thick of it.

We regained some control in the final quarter and Phil started an attack from behind our posts which ended up with Ally Hogg going on a run into their 22. Five minutes later we won a scrum on their line and were shunting them backwards. We should maybe have tried to keep the ball in the scrum and gone for the pushover, or even a penalty try, but it looked like the ball had come out the back of the scrum so I had to play it. We ended up getting turned over and our last chance was gone. It was one of those things – you have to react instinctively and I thought the ball was out, but on reflection – which is always the easiest standpoint to judge these things – the ball was probably still in and we should have kept it in the forwards.

EUAN MURRAY

Looking at the final section of the game we made some errors of judgment. The pushover was the plan, but we didn't stick with it and the ball was spun wide. From the forwards point of view it felt like we were going well and we were confident; our aim was to push them backwards and they were going backwards, so it was disappointing we didn't score from there. But I think the more we are in these positions the more experience we will have, and the more we will make the correct decision under pressure.

Scotland's scrum showed the world how powerful and effective a unit they were in the 2008 autumn series, particularly against the Springboks. *Press Association*

PHIL GODMAN

We then won another penalty a minute or so later and I had a kick to take the lead, but it was quite a tricky angle and I missed. Pienaar then scored with a penalty and shortly after that I had a chance to close the gap back to a point with a kick from about 30 yards out, slightly to the right of the upright. It was a fairly straightforward kick, but I didn't catch it cleanly and at the last moment in bent away from the posts and slid wide. I watched it all the way, knowing it would be tight, and it was gut-wrenching to see it just miss. If it had gone over we would have received the ball back at the kick-off and might well have got ourselves into a position to score again through another penalty or a drop-goal, maybe even a try. But it wasn't to be and it was devastating to be that close to toppling the world champions.

MIKE BLAIR

It was a tough result to accept, but having been fairly comprehensively beaten by the All Blacks the previous week, it was a great turnaround by the boys. We had all stood up to the physical confrontation that the Boks pride themselves on and had played some really positive rugby – and the pack had been fantastic. They were rightly receiving plaudits from all around the world for their performances that autumn.

PHIL GODMAN

We went into the 2009 Six Nations pretty confident. We had shown in the autumn that we had a pack to compete with anyone in the world and we were starting to get a fluid running game coming together with some really dangerous strike players out wide. We had a huge choice of players in the back three, all who were proven match-winners and who all brought different qualities to their position – Thom and Max Evans, Sean and Rory Lamont, Simon Danielli and Simon Webster, Nikki Walker, Hugo Southwell, Chris Paterson. So the way we played against Wales at Murrayfield was a bit of a shock and it brought us back down to earth.

MIKE BLAIR

The Wales game was a bit of a confidence-killer. It was the first game of the Championship and after the autumn series and the way that both Edinburgh and Glasgow were playing in the Magners League and the Heineken Cup, we genuinely thought that we were dark horses for the Championship. We were missing Euan Murray and Nathan Hines, but we still had a strong squad and Geoff Cross, who came in on the tight-head for his first cap, had been playing really well for Edinburgh. It was a fairly demoralising debut for him in the end. About twenty minutes in, he chased an up-and-under clearance kick and knocked himself out on Lee Byrne's knee as Byrne leapt to take the ball. We all watched the replay as a team afterwards and you can see that Geoff was just charging up field, thinking that the ball was probably going to land about 30 metres further away than it did. It was a fairly sickening impact to have to watch in slow-motion. He was stretchered off and given a yellow card at the same time for dangerous play.

GEOFF CROSS (Edinburgh)
2 Caps: 2009-still playing

Starting that game for Scotland was one of the proudest moments of my career and I remember everything about that game – for the first twenty minutes, anyway. I remember the huge emotions I felt during the anthems and the tears rolling down my face; I remember preparing for the kick-off and focusing all my thoughts on doing well in the scrums and at the lineouts, winning the contacts and collisions and sticking with our planned shapes of play. I remember everything until I ran into Lee Byrne's knee. It was hugely disappointing that I made a poor decision but I haven't got too worked up about it since then; there's no point. It's a game and these things happen. You make mistakes and you just have to move on from them. It was my first cap so I was very pumped up and it affected my decision-making. What you need to take from that experience is that you use that same energy and passion and temper it with improved decision-making so that you do the right things at the right time.

MIKE BLAIR

Shortly after Geoff had gone off Lee scored after some neat inter-passing between Tom Shanklin and Shane Williams. They scored again a few minutes later – our scrum was struggling because we were still a man down and Wales won a strike against the head; Martyn Williams picked up the ball and fed Stephen Jones who almost made it to the line. Ally Hogg put in a smashing cover tackle, but the ball came back quickly on the Welsh side and Alun-Wyn Jones powered over.

We went in at half-time 3-16 down and with Simon Webster also off after clashing heads with Martyn Williams.

The second-half was no better than the first. Jamie Roberts was huge all day for them, cutting great lines and busting through tackles. Leigh Halfpenny went in at the corner after Jamie smashed the ball up and Shane Williams released Leigh into space with a wee backhand flip. It was a neat try, but one that we should never have allowed to happen. They were winning 3-21 and ten minutes later Shane Williams was scoring for them again. It was a shocker.

We did manage to salvage some pride when Max Evans came on for Ben Cairns and scored a superb individual try, stepping through Shane Williams' tackle and shimmying inside Lee Byrne to score. It was a cracker. We almost scored another try when Mossy dived on a kick through, but the ball bounced away from him. It wouldn't have made any difference though, the game was already long gone and our pre-match aspirations were in pieces.

ALASDAIR STROKOSH (Edinburgh Gunners, Gloucester)
17 Caps (to date): 2006-still playing

We made a big improvement in our attitude from the Wales game when we went to Paris. We upped our intensity and did much, much better in the collision area and dominated much of the physicality of the game. In the end we lost again, but we had definitely improved. We had two tries disallowed, which would have changed the whole face of the game. But at the same time we gave away a lot of penalties and made a lot of errors which cost us the result.

PHIL GODMAN

We played with a lot more adventure and composure in the second match that season against France in Paris. Right from the start we looked to stretch them

and attack as much as we could. We almost got off to a dream start when Max
Evans, who had come into the starting line-up after his impact off the bench in
the Wales game, did a super chip and chase and forced a five-metre scrum.
France cleared their lines, but there's no doubt that the way we came out of the
traps had them rattled. It was nip and tuck throughout that entire first half, but
we felt that we were in the ascendency as we went back into the changing rooms
– so it was incredibly frustrating to see France score a try at the start of the
second half that should never have been given. The whole thing was a bit of a
mess – the ball was pin-balling around on the ground and it bounced up into
Lionel Nallet's hands and he fed it to Maxime Medard who cut a lovely angle to
our line – but the space for his run was created because their flanker, Fulgence
Ouedraogo, was running a block on our defence and then as Medard was
tackled he gave a blatantly forward-pass to Ouedraogo to score. These things
happen in rugby – they happen in most sports – but it doesn't make it any
easier when you're on the wrong end of the decision. And that try really fired
up the crowd and gave the French a lift. They had been on the ropes up until
that point but it gave them a footing at 13-3.

But we continued to play and were making good ground around the ruck and
were using the maul to good effect. Mike Blair and John Barclay were playing
really well and made one great break between them right up to the French posts
– but the rest of us were too slow to get to them and John was turned over.
But we were playing ourselves back into the game and Stroker [Alasdair
Strokosch] made another break soon afterwards and I was able to follow that up
with another good run into their territory. From there we recycled the ball a few
times and then the ball came out to me and I popped it inside to Thom Evans
to score. Mossy converted it and we were right back in it at 13-10. Or so we
thought. France stopped throwing the ball around after that and really tightened
up their game – and ground us out of it. They really began to batter us and our
injuries began to tell then. Jim Hamilton had gone off injured early in the game
and because Jason White was playing in the second-row with him, we lost our
only genuine lock in squad. Kelly Brown came in at number eight and Simon
Taylor moved into the second-row, so our pack was suddenly pretty light-weight
in comparison to the French and they started to really dominate the scrum and
lineout as the game wore on. They won penalty after penalty in the last quarter
and Lionel Beauxis just stroked them over whenever he came into range of the
posts and they ended up winning 22-13. It was disappointing for so many
reasons – their try, simple errors we made, and the fact that, on balance, we
played much better rugby than they did. But for all that we had lost two from
two, we were at least playing better and had continued the attacking intent that
had emerged at the end of the Wales game.

MIKE BLAIR

In both 2008 and 2009 we had very disappointing starts to the Championship, and when that happens it's hard to generate momentum in your campaign. Typically of Scotland, we showed excellent signs here and there, but excellent signs aren't enough. For all the frustration – and believe me, we all shared in it – I wasn't too unhappy with my own form. Certainly, I didn't feel it was as bad as some people made out. The problem is the sense of negativity that filters in from outside when results don't come right. There is often a lot of it about and it's not easy to be unaffected.

ROSS FORD (The Borders, Edinburgh Gunners)
41 Caps (to date): 2004-still playing

Against Wales we were bitterly disappointed by our performance and knew we had to make amends against France. The level of effort and the way we approached the France game was more of where we wanted to be, although we still ended up on the losing side. We knew that we would have to up it again for the Italy match. Fortunately we did and we ended up winning 26-6; we were making progress in the competition but it was nowhere near the levels that we had produced in the autumn and that was troubling.

MIKE BLAIR

We had Ireland up next at Murrayfield and they were two games away from sealing only their second-ever Grand Slam. That tells you how the game went. It was a pretty tight match and it was effectively decided when Jamie Heaslip went over to score the game's only try. It was off the back of a great little bit of opportunist-play by Peter Stringer. In the build up to the game there was a bit of controversy about the fact that he had been picked because he had fallen down the pecking order somewhat in Ireland. But he is a player of huge, huge experience and he wouldn't have appreciated the way the press were talking about him – being a link man only, only brought in because of his passing game and that he was incapable of causing any kind of threat around the fringes. Well, I think they probably said much the same about him before Munster played Biarritz in the 2006 Heineken Cup final – and he scored the decisive try when he picked and went from the back of a scrum to score. He took a ball off the back of a lineout against us and John Barclay moved out to attack O'Gara, opening up a gap between him and Stroker . . . Stringer saw it and he slipped through. I ran back to cover him but he stepped and I twisted my back badly trying to tackle him as he released Jamie to score. I had to go off after than and although Mossy had kept us in the game with his kicking, Ronan O'Gara settled the result with his own kicking.

We had played pretty well in that game – especially in the first half and had created quite a few chances – Simon Danielli was dragged down just short of the line after a chip through and Thom Evans and Phil were close to scoring too. There was one moment when Mossy went for a bouncing ball that would have given him a free run to the line but Tommy Bowe just managed to claim it before him. It was tight but it was another loss. We had to go to Twickenham for the final game and although things hadn't been going well for us that season, we still felt that we might be able to cause an upset down there. We have performed well against England on a number of occasions over the last ten years and we really thought we could win. A lot was made about my form and that Ross Ford's form was not particularly good, but I didn't really feel as if I was playing that badly and I'm sure Ross didn't either.

We started brightly and Thom Evans almost got in to score – it was a cracking tackle by Ugo Monye and great work to come over from his wing to haul Thom down. I think the try Ugo scored and then that tackle, all within the space of around five minutes, sealed his place on the Lions tour that summer and in fairness to him it was a super bit of attacking and defensive skill that he had demonstrated. They then scored another try through Riki Flutey which was well-worked, but we were still very much in the game and it was only a late, late try for Matthew Tait that sealed it for them and put a bit of gloss on the result that made it look like we were well beaten, which didn't tell the whole story. Jason White had one barnstorming run that took him right up to their line but his scoring pass didn't go to hand and we were turned over. Later on I fielded a high ball on their ten metre line and broke away from the defence to get into their 22, but again I couldn't get the final pass away and the chance went begging. It was a case of fine margins, but those margins went against us during that Six Nations.

JON PETRIE

I suppose the honeymoon period can only last for so long, because eventually things start going against you and at that stage you have to have a plan B, and that's when things started to fall down a bit under Frank Hadden.

MIKE BLAIR

I felt very bad for a lot of the flak that Frank copped towards the end of his time as head coach. He had really turned things around after Matt Williams had been in charge and had helped us enjoy our rugby with Scotland again – which resulted in some famous victories and our best-ever finish in the Six Nations table. He got us through to the quarter-finals of the World Cup and within touching distance of a semi-final spot. And then luck turned against him. We had a lot of injuries in the squad in 2009 – and losing Nathan Hines and Euan Murray for much of the Six Nations was a real blow – and some of us weren't playing as well as we might, myself included. I stressed it at the time – and it wasn't just a case of the captain supporting his coach – I said that it wasn't Frank or any of the other coaches out on the pitch making the simple errors that cost us games; it wasn't any of them dropping passes or missing kicks to touch or falling off tackles. It was us. People have said that the time had come for a new man to come in with a change of attitude and ideas – Andy Robinson's impact has spoken for itself, so maybe there was some truth in that statement. But the level of abuse that went Frank's way was totally unmerited. He did all he could to help us win, but it wasn't him out there making the mistakes that meant that we ended up losing in those final games of his tenure. He saved Scottish rugby when it was at one of its lowest ebbs and he did great, great things to bring our game back out from that depression. Some of my fondest memories as a rugby player happened because of Frank and the fans who watched those games will never forget the results we had while he was in charge, particularly our win against France and our two Calcutta Cup triumphs.

But it's always the man at the top that gets the chop and every coach and manager in any sport goes into the role in the knowledge that his head is first on the line when things go wrong. Andy Robinson is a very different character to Frank and brings different credentials with him. Andy's general knowledge of rugby is unsurpassed, and his knowledge of Scottish rugby specifically is also very good too. As a player and then as a coach of a number of teams who have come up against Scottish sides, he has done plenty of analysis about how Scottish teams play and the merits and deficiencies of our players – and I can tell you, the depth of his analyses is just incredible – and then his experience as Edinburgh and Scotland A coach has given him an insight from the other side of the fence. Once it was decided that Frank's time was up, there was only ever going to be one man for the job and since Andy has taken over there has been a really positive feeling growing in the squad.

CHAPTER SEVENTEEN

POACHER TURNED GAME-KEEPER

T HE ROAD *to redemption is a rocky one.*

In the autumn of 2006, England coach Andy Robinson sat stony-faced in the Twickenham stand as flanker Pat Sanderson crashed the ball into contact. His team were trailing 10-12 to the visiting Argentineans and were looking to build a platform from which to strike a killer-blow to their visitors' hopes and get the game back on track. It had been a tough two years since Robinson had assisted Clive Woodward in leading England to World Cup glory in Sydney on 22 November 2003. In October of 2004, Woodward had stepped down from his position after a fall-out with Francis Baron, Chief Executive of the RFU, over player access and greater support for his plans from the RFU establishment; wishing to leave the team in as healthy a state as possible, however, Woodward recommended that Robinson should succeed him as head coach. It was the job of Robinson's dreams and he clutched it with both hands. But England's star was in decline. The core experience that had led the team to triumph in Australia had either retired or were on their last legs and bad luck had bedevilled Robinson's tenure. He had named the iconic Jonny Wilkinson as his captain, but the star fly-half had been beset by injury and failed to take to the field even once under the new regime. The English clubs were also making life hellishly difficult; they felt that they had bent over backwards to help England etch their name on the William Webb Ellis Trophy and now they wanted recompense – they wanted their stars back playing for them more, not less. Robinson's player access was slashed, yet the expectations to continue the wonderful ride that English rugby had long enjoyed continued unabated despite clear warnings from the head coach that the team was entering a transition period as they sought to replace the experienced campaigners shuffling into retirement. But understanding and patient support in sport are fickle friends, and once triumph has been tasted, defeat and mediocrity are too bitter for many to endure. While Robinson was in charge, England lost thirteen matches and won just nine. Although this was a better ratio than that to be recorded by Martin Johnson a few years later, it was not enough to slake the demanding thirst of England's supporters now used to seeing their team as the world's best. After six consecutive Test defeats, Robinson was on his last legs and he needed his team to show that they were turning a comer.

Opposite: Scotland's front-row prepare to take on the Wallabies. *Press Association*

So there he sat as his charges moved in to kill the Pumas' challenge. As Pat Sanderson was tackled by Juan Manuel Leguizamón, England's forwards set up a quick ruck ball for their backs. Scrum-half Peter Richards moved the ball to replacement fly-half Toby Flood who in turn looked to the open spaces outside him. A step, a shuffle and the ball was fired out to release the flying Anthony Allen as he raced into space.

Up in the stand, Robinson could see it a mile off. The step and the shuffle had wasted precious milliseconds and Federico Todeschini had read Flood's intentions like an open book. Todeschini pushed up, reached out a grateful hand and gathered the ball as it arced towards Allen. An echoing cry of horror rolled around Twickenham as the home crowd watched the Argentinean sprint away into the night to drive over the English line.

Shortly afterwards Ian Balshaw struck back for the hosts, but Todeschini kicked his fourth and fifth penalty goals of the game to move his side into an 25-18 lead. A few minutes after his final strike, the game was over. And so was Robinson's reign.

In October of 2007, after a long year in the rugby wilderness where he took some time out from the game to lick his wounds and ponder the agonies of the final months of his England tenure, Andy Robinson finally put pen to paper on a new deal that would bring him back to the game he loved, joining Edinburgh as their new head coach on a three-year deal. The move was not one without its own pains as Robinson decided that it was too much to ask his family to uproot themselves from their home in Bath, where his children were still being schooled, so he made the move to Edinburgh independently and lived a commuter's life.

After just 18 months at Edinburgh, where he led them to their highest-ever Magners League finishes of fourth and second, he was appointed as head coach of Scotland in June of 2009.

His mantra for Scotland was simple – it echoed the qualities that he and Woodward had successfully instilled in the England camp in the build-up to their World Cup triumph: international rugby is all about winning, no matter how well or badly the team plays; substance would come first, style later.

While Robinson was at pains to stress that his tenure would be a case of evolution rather than revolution from the Frank Hadden era, one thing that would definitely change was that Matt Williams' Fortress Scotland policy would be entirely dispelled. While the policy had been watered down somewhat by Hadden, there continued to be a preference to select home-based players over those playing elsewhere if all other factors were equal; under Robinson, players would be picked entirely on merit, no matter where they were based.

With a coaching style that is epitomised by a furious intensity and attention to detail, Robinson declared that his primary remit was to empower his players, driving them to take full responsibly for their actions on the field while seeking to inspire the nation through their performances.

Robinson's tenure got off to a very promising start. In the autumn of 2009

Scotland defeated a Fijian team ranked above them on the IRB table, and then beat Australia for the first time since 1982 thanks to an incredible defensive display, before falling just short against Argentina.

In the 2010 Six Nations Scotland finished a disappointing fifth in the table, but the devil was in the detail. They came as close as any other team to beating eventual Grand Slam champions France at Murrayfield and but for two defensive lapses might well have caused an upset. In Wales, they suffered a severe injury to Chris Paterson, who sustained deep bruising and two tears and lacerations to his kidney only fifteen minutes into his 100th cap, an ankle injury to Rory Lamont that ended his season, and a near-fatal spinal injury to wing Thom Evans which forced him to announce his retirement from the game a few months later. It was horrific. In what will be remembered as one of the most extraordinary conclusions to a game, Wales recovered from 9-21 down to sneak the win 31-24 in the last seconds of injury time against a 13-man Scotland.

Unsurprisingly shell-shocked by their Cardiff encounter, Scotland tumbled to a limited Italian side in Rome before picking up the pieces to draw 15-15 with England at Murrayfield. In the final round of the competition they travelled to Dublin for Ireland's farewell match at Croke Park. Irish hopes for a second successive Grand Slam had been shattered in the second round by France in Paris, but they were looking to sign off in style with the Triple Crown before their return to the redeveloped Lansdowne Road. They still had hopes of winning the Championship, requiring England to win heavily in Paris and for them to hammer the Scots by an equally hefty margin. In pursuit of this golden points margin the hosts threw the ball around with abandon in the opening half, only for their adventure to be clinically punished by the visitors, who regained the lead after Brian O'Driscoll's try with one of their own as Johnny Beattie thundered down the touchline and over Geordan Murphy and Paul O'Connell to score in the corner. The metronymic boot of Dan Parks, the comeback kid of the Championship, kept Scotland in the hunt and then stole the show with a last minute penalty, sending the Scots into raptures as they claimed a famous 23-20 win, their first in Ireland since 1998. It was a campaign that could have been so different. But for injury and misfortune, Scotland might well have finished second in the table – they did not lose a game by more than nine points – and had the catastrophic injuries suffered in Cardiff not knocked them off their stride, who knows what they might have achieved.

In the summer, the team journeyed to South America for a two Test series against Argentina. The country had been a happy hunting ground for Robinson on his previous trip there as assistant coach with Scotland in 2008, but that second Test win, although very welcome, had been achieved against a home lacking many of its best players who were still playing club rugby in France. For the 2010 series, the Pumas would be at virtually full-strength. On a balmy afternoon in the rugby hotbed of Tucumán, where Argentina had never lost a Test match, Dan Parks kicked

Scotland to a magnificent 24-16 victory and, in doing so, also picked up his fourth man of the match award in five consecutive Test matches – a remarkable feat considering he had only been on the winning side twice in that time.

The tour was completed with the second Test in Mar del Plata, and a win that gave Scotland their first run of three consecutive wins on the road since 1982, as well as their first-ever series triumph in the southern hemisphere. In a match that was played out for much of the eighty minutes in driving rain, Dan Parks' kicking game came to the fore once again while the visiting pack dominated a wily and experienced Argentinean unit. An early Jim Hamilton try and eight points from Parks' boot gave the Scots a 13-9 victory. It was a display of calm control, flourishing adventure on occasion, and steely defence throughout, and was no less than the team deserved after a season where their character and courage had been tested to the limit.

Robinson's men had orchestrated a stunning recovery both in Dublin and in Tucumán and had backed up those performances with a pragmatic and controlled victory in Mar del Plata to add weight to the belief that the beetle-browed former flanker was forging a team in his own image – bristling with industry and commitment and an overriding will to weather any storm, to overcome any obstacle and conquer any adversity in the pursuit of glory. His first season in charge had seen him chart a perilous passage between Scylla and Charybdis, and while the Scottish ship had listed perilously towards disaster – most notably in Cardiff – he had steered the team to victory in three consecutive Tests away from home, matching his extraordinary achievements from the autumn.

And so to the future. In the autumn of 2010 the All Blacks, the Springboks and Samoa come calling to Murrayfield. In the spring of 2011, Scotland face Wales, Italy and Ireland at home and England and France on the road. The World Cup in New Zealand follows and Scotland face an intriguing pool containing England and Argentina as their main rivals for a quarter-final berth. Scotland look as well placed as they have ever been to continue their proud record in the competition; but time, as ever, will tell.

For Andy Robinson and his Scottish charges, the road to redemption has proved – and will no doubt continue to prove – rocky indeed, but like any destination worth reaching, it is the wonder of the journey that really matters.

ALASTAIR KELLOCK

One of Andy Robinson's first acts in charge was to lead a Scotland A party to Romania for the Nations Cup. There was no main Scotland tour that year because of the Lions tour to South Africa, so we took a pretty strong team to the Nations Cup. He asked me to be vice-captain and it was a great trip, really enjoyable – helped no doubt by the fact that we won the tournament and played some decent rugby. It was good to get a chance to work with Andy again as well because since the 2008 tour to Argentina, I had only really known him as the opposing Edinburgh coach. He is very easy to work with because he knows exactly what he wants from you as a player and lays it on the line. He's been there and done it as a player and as a coach and so there are no doubts in your mind that what he is telling you is spot on. He is incredibly passionate as a coach and has a desperate desire to win, which we can all relate to.

CHRIS CUSITER

It was great working with Andy out at the Nations Cup. I was captain and we did well out there, playing some good rugby to win the competition and I think that stood me in good stead while Mike was away with the Lions.

You have to take your opportunities when you get them, so it was important to play well when I was selected to start against Fiji in the autumn. Mike has had opportunities before me and he's taken them and held onto that number nine jersey for a long time. It's the same for Rory Lawson. After the 2010 Argentina tour he has become the incumbent and the one that Mike and I have to play better than to get the jersey back. Ultimately it comes down to our own performances in the build-up to games and on the day itself if we're chosen to play – but above all we all want Scotland to win and we all support each other

Rory Lamont bursts through the Fijian defence. *Getty Images*

through everything we do. We've all known each other a long time and get on very well; yes, there's an element of rivalry, which you would expect, but it's a friendly, healthy rivalry which has been good for us all.

Going into a new season, we knew that we needed to put a marker down. There was a new coaching regime in place and a new focus. It was an exciting challenge to play three teams who were all ranked above us on the IRB table. We played Fiji first up and they are always tricky to play against – all their players are big and fast and athletic, with great ball-handling skills. The early try that Johnnie Beattie scored was well worked and set the tone. Graeme Morrison's try in the second-half was perhaps a little fortuitous to be awarded, but there have been plenty of tries scored against us over the years which should never have been allowed, so maybe that one went someway towards redressing the balance. It was a good win against a good side, although we knew that Fiji hadn't been at full strength and so we were all aware that it was crucial that we upped our game for the following week.

We had great pace and tempo in the first-half against Fiji which opened up a lot of gaps, we scored a good try and Rory Lamont came very close to scoring off a set-piece, so that was all very pleasing. What was frustrating was that in the second-half we turned over a lot of ball; we wanted to come out in the second-half and impose ourselves, but we never really got back into our rhythm. But we held out to get the win and at the start of any series of games that is crucial.

The plan going into the Australia match was to spread the ball wide a little bit more, to be ambitious, and to speed things up with quick taps. We knew that we needed to be ambitious to beat a side of that quality.

ALASTAIR KELLOCK

We spoke about passion, about the need to lift the crowd by giving absolutely everything. Andy had made a big thing about inspiring the nation in the build-up to the game and we all know what a difference it can make to your performance if you can get the crowd lifted and cheering you on. We were very aware of that about 20 minutes from the end when we were defending on our line and the noise from the crowd was just fantastic. Then Nick de Luca broke out and sent a kick down into their corner and the noise was incredible, it gave me an extra yard. When they scored in injury-time, I thought it was all over, but when you defend like that you deserve to win games.

PHIL GODMAN

We showed ambition in attack but it was the way we stuck in in defence that really won it – it was comfortably the best defensive performance I've ever been involved in. International rugby is all about winning, and the courage the whole team showed in pursuit of that was fantastic. By the end, when they went over after two or three minutes of defence, the whole experience was a bit surreal. We were all so shattered after working so hard that we just stood there as Matt Giteau lined up the conversion. I was in a bit of a daze, and was shocked to see it not go over, but the feeling of realising that we had won the game was just incredible.

Andy Robinson relishes his return to Test match rugby before Scotland face Australia at Murrayfield in November 2009. *Getty Images*

CHRIS CUSITER

I took a knock tackling Stephen Moore, their hooker, and had to go off, and it was pretty horrific having to watch the rest of the game from the touchline, but the boys played brilliantly and their defence was something else. The effort, the urgency and the passion were unbelievable and I just wished that I had been out there at the end.

Everyone worked tirelessly throughout the game to get up on their feet as quickly as possible after they took contact to make sure that we were constantly putting pressure on their attacks. Yes, they missed a couple of kicks and the last one was to win it, but we had been up in their faces for 80 minutes, knocking them off their stride, making sure that they were never comfortable and that there was no rhythm to their game – and that will have affected their kicking game.

They scored a try right at the death but it hadn't come easily for them. They had two tries held up over the line and one called back for a forward-pass and that was all down to the pressure of our defence and the never-say-die attitude. It wasn't perfect rugby by any stretch of the imagination, but we did what we had to do and to win a game like that was just the most fantastic feeling.

RORY LAWSON

I only found out that I would be on the bench the day before when Mike failed a fitness test on his ankle, which was a great shame for him but a great opportunity for me. And again,

Phil Godman and Nick de Luca look to unpick the Wallaby defence. *Press Association*

it was terrible for Chris that he had to go off with a head-bang, but it gave me a chance to show what I could do and to be involved with a game like that is just unbelievable. There was this amazing feeling all across the team when I came on – you sensed the belief that we could win the game, right across the board, everyone knew that they were going to be working as hard as they could and that there wasn't a man out there who was going to drop off anything. It was the most incredible defensive display that I've ever been involved in.

It was a strange feeling after the game. It was a real high, but we also knew how close we were to recording another valiant defeat – which would have taken away from the defensive effort, from the guts and the passion, and everyone would be continuing to talk of the decline of Scottish rugby. I am tremendously proud to have played a part in the first Scotland team to beat Australia since 1982. I came off the bench quite early on in the game because of Chris's injury. It can be frustrating having to bide your time for opportunities, but that's what happens when you have guys like Chris and Mike in front of you – they are both world class players – and so it's important to take your opportunities when they come. It was unfortunate that Chris took a bang on the head but it was good to feel I had time to make an impact. To a man, everyone gutsed it out in that game; that's what that performance was entirely based on – hard work and guts.

Chris Cusiter makes a break down the side of a ruck as Will Genia comes across to cover.
FotoSport

CHRIS PATERSON

You have to take that win with a pinch of salt – we won because of a mistake at the end. Yes, we played our hearts out for 80 minutes and defended tenaciously, but we had very few opportunities to score tries and it very nearly went the other way. You have to keep your feet on the ground about these things. It was a great win, there's no doubt about that, but we still have a lot to work on and we're a long way yet from going into games against the likes of Australia and expecting to win.

We said under the posts that we would rush out and try to charge down the conversion, but I still expected Giteau to kick it. I turned at the last second and saw it go wide, but I didn't jump for joy – it wouldn't have been courteous to do so, especially to a player of his standing and class. People have talked about Giteau missing a couple of kicks which kept us in the game, but it was very windy out there and I think the praise should be with the kicks that went over from both sides rather than focussing on the ones that missed. Phil Godman kicked outstandingly and although he had a miss, the ones he hit were great strikes and not easy.

Alex Grove and Nick de Luca celebrate as
Matt Giteau realises the consequences of his
last-minute missed kick. *Getty Images*

Great defence and great tenacity, that's what I remember most about that game. As I say, the fact that it ultimately came down to them missing a final kick to win the game slightly took the gloss off things a little bit, but nevertheless it was a great result. I spoke with Jason White after the match and we realised now that the only top-ranked team that the Scotland team of the 2000s hasn't beaten is the All Blacks – so for all the doom and gloom that has gone around Scottish rugby over the years, that is something pretty significant to bear in mind.

ALASTAIR KELLOCK

The third game that autumn wasn't much of a spectacle, but credit to Argentina, they did exactly what they needed to do to win. They disrupted our ball at every turn in the rucks and mauls and they played to the referee's interpretation, which shut us out the game and broke down any momentum we tried to generate. Their defence was outstanding as well, but it was frustrating not to complete the hat-trick of wins that autumn as it would have been a great – and well deserved – achievement, and it was all the more frustrating because we knew exactly what to expect from Argentina and still didn't manage to combat it.

CHRIS CUSITER

We produced some great build-up work against Argentina, but we just didn't finish things off and that is what cost us. I don't doubt that we have the skills to finish things off, but we just weren't able to execute under pressure in that match. We created and played some good rugby, but we just weren't able to turn that into tries – they stifled us at key moments or turned us over as we were getting into dangerous areas of the field; that was streetwise from them and naive of us, but it was a good lesson and one that we would remember in future games with them, particularly on the summer tour.

The team gather to celebrate Scotland's first victory over the Wallabies since 1982. *Getty Images*

ROSS FORD

We played well in the first half but didn't kill them off. We were throwing the ball around well and our off-load game was working well, but then they started to stifle our offloads and that interrupted our continuity and our rhythm. They then started to get the upper hand in the scrum and the lineout in the second-half and we let them back into it. They started to get the go-forward at the breakdown and that gave them the initiative to go on for the win. We had chances to score in the second-half but didn't deliver on them. That's the difference between good teams and average ones and we knew that we would have to improve before the Six Nations or it would be much the same story again.

CHRIS CUSITER

After the autumn, we had built ourselves up for a big opening game in the Six Nations against France, but it didn't come to anything. We dominated a lot of the play in the first-half but still went in 6-15 at half-time. We lost a try to Mathieu Bastareaud but came back into it and Johnnie Beattie made a tremendous break but he couldn't quite get the offload to me cleanly and I knocked it on with the line begging. Phil put in a grubber kick a little bit later for Sean Lamont but it didn't come off and we ended up back in our half – it was two inches difference from us scoring to suddenly being on the defensive.

Our scrum was struggling a wee bit and France kicked a few penalties, and then Bastareaud went over for his second. But we still felt that we were well in the game. But instead of upping our intensity in the second-half, we fell away. It was touch and go for much the match and we really felt that we had the beating of them, but two errors in defence really cost us and Bastareaud went in for two pretty soft scores that we could easily have stopped. People made a big deal out of the fact that Euan Murray had elected not to play on Sundays because of his religious beliefs, but I thought Moray Low did very well against a crack French outfit who proved throughout the Championship that they were the best pack in the competition.

The Basque warrior Imanol Harinordoquy crashes into Max Evans. *FotoSport*

MIKE BLAIR

Euan Murray's decision not to play on Sundays was well accepted by the players and the coaching staff. A lot of guys know Euan very well and when he originally made the decision there was no talk behind his back of, 'What's he playing at?' Everyone knows how serious he is about his religion and certainly we back him up with that.

I know how hard a decision it would have been for him, because he loves playing international rugby. And I guess he does put a bit of pressure on himself because it means Moray Low and Geoff Cross will get opportunities to play ahead of him. But that's something that shows the strength of reasoning behind Euan's decision.

EUAN MURRAY

I took a nasty head knock playing for Glasgow against Munster in 2005 and had convulsions on the pitch. I don't remember anything about it, but I've seen the video. In the aftermath of it all I was just thankful to be still alive. It was pretty scary – the other guys on the pitch told me afterwards that they thought I was going to die. In the months it took to recover from that my religious beliefs were strengthened. The seizure made me realise that life is short, so I started to question things like, *What are we here for?* and *Where am I going when I die?* And then I started reading the Bible and my life was transformed.

I just wasn't happy with myself. I felt like I was living an immoral lifestyle. When I became a Christian my life away from rugby changed hugely. I went to church; I looked after myself more; I used my time better; I prayed.

On the day of the France match I had a good Sunday; I went to church, I cooked, and I didn't watch the game until the next day. I hope things will change in future because I don't see why there have to be games on Sundays. I don't know how many of my team-mates agree with my approach, but I'm happy with my decision and they seem to have accepted it by taking me as I come. They've been with me through good times and bad and seen both sides of my life, before and after I became a Christian. They know how important it is to me.

CHRIS PATERSON

That game against Wales was my 100th capped appearance. It's a strange thing winning so many caps for Scotland. In many ways it doesn't feel like I have as many as I do. I just want another one, and another one, to keep going. Of course, there'll come a point when I finish and I'll look back then on what I've done in my career. Every time there's a new Six Nations, I feel as if I'm starting from square one. I am getting older and everyone is expecting me to drop off a bit, but that drives me on. I want to be the fittest in training. That sounds like a physical thing, but mentally it is probably more important.

Bill McLaren's funeral really brought it all into focus for me. A lot was said about how much he would have loved to have played for Scotland, even just once, and I know that I am hugely fortunate to have done that so many times. In many ways I'm almost embarrassed that I've been lucky to amass that amount when someone like Bill did not get the opportunity to win even one. He was a great, great man, a man who loved Scottish rugby very deeply. It would have been marvellous for him and his family if he had managed to play for the team he loved so much. With all the great memories that he has given people around the world, I think they would all have liked him to have fulfilled that ambition, but it's nice to know he did at least get to see his son-in-law and his grandson play for Scotland and for them to know how proud he was of both of them for achieving that.

You stand on that pitch in Cardiff with 70,000 Welshmen singing and shouting and making this great din . . . and there are only 15 of you staring up at them all . . . but that's what it's all about, that's why you play the game – you want to take them on and if you can silence that crowd, you know you're doing well. To win my 100th cap there really was special. It's a shame that the game itself didn't exactly go according to plan – although it will be remembered around the world for a very, very long time.

MIKE BLAIR

The Millennium Stadium is an astonishing place. The stands tower up around you and you can virtually feel the crowds' breath on your face, they're so close to the pitch. It is an incredible, often claustrophobic atmosphere and the noise is deafening from the moment you step out there to the moment you head back

John Barclay splits the Welsh defence to score in Cardiff. *FotoSport*

down the tunnel. But it's inspiring too – with Land of my Fathers or Bread of Heaven resonating around the ground, the noise sends shivers searing through you – and if you have the right attitude to it all, it can be as inspiring to you as it is to the Welsh players.

It was an incredible game, right from the start. It was Mossy's 100th cap and we all felt that we had a good chance of going down there and getting a win.

We started really well and John Barclay had a storming run that took him right through the tackles of James Hook and Gareth Cooper to score. The way that Dan Parks controlled things at ten was also incredibly impressive – an absolute masterclass in tactical play.

DAN PARKS

It's been a rough ride, my international career, there are no doubts about that. There have been some incredible highs but there have also been moments that I would rather forget. 2008 and 2009 had some big lows, but I am very proud that I have fought back; 2010 has been a great year and immensely satisfying. My teammates and my coaches have always stuck by me and that is what has seen me through the darker times. I've had some tough times out there at Murrayfield, but I've really enjoyed 2010 and the crowd's attitude towards me is now completely different to how it once was. And it's the same with the media – I was totally written-off by some pundits who have then awarded me man of the match plaudits this year. It's a special time, but I'm taking it all with a pinch of salt – these things can't last forever; I'll make mistakes, as anyone playing ten will do, but the secret is not to let it get to me – there are things that I can do and things that I can't. I'm more aware of that than anyone else, so I just need to make sure I keep practicing and doing the things that I excel at and not try to please everyone by trying things that don't suit my style of game. By keeping it simple and sticking to what I'm good at, I've played well this year. It's as straightforward as that.

MIKE BLAIR

Having been criticised for our style of play in previous matches that season, we scored two tries, two drop-goals, two penalties and a conversion in that first-half. It was fantastic. But it all came at a cost. The injuries were just horrifying. Mossy took a knock that looked at the time like he may have cracked a rib or something – when he had actually lacerated his kidney. You could see he was really struggling out there but that he was trying to play on because of the occasion, and he tried to shake off the knock, but now knowing the trauma that was going on inside him, it's amazing that he was able to continue on at all. But you could see the trouble he was in when he went to convert Max Evans' try; he's the best goal-kicker in the world, but he missed it because he was in such a lot of pain. It was the first time he had missed a kick at goal during the Six Nations in three years. It's a testament to his character that he even had a go at the kick – we had real momentum building and Dan was playing exceptionally well – it had been his grubber through the Welsh line that had given Max the score – and it was clear that Mossy didn't want to put any extra pressure on Dan by handing over the kicking duties.

Things were still looking pretty bright for us despite Mossy going off. But then Thom Evans got injured.

Thom Evans lies stricken on the Millennium Stadium pitch. This shocking injury ended his career, but it could have been much worse had it not been for the immediate attention he received from the medical staff. *Getty Images*

THOM EVANS (Glasgow Warriors)
10 Caps: 2008-2010

I've watched the incident a few times and it didn't look too bad from the TV angle. I kicked the ball ahead and chased and as I got to it again Lee Byrne came up to cover and we collided. My head hit his torso and I went down. It looked fairly innocuous on TV but the pain was terrible. I hit the ground hard and I just couldn't move; it was the most awful feeling I've ever experienced. I tried to get to my knees but nothing would move, not even my arms. Then after a few seconds I began to get some movement back but at the same time there was this searing pain between my shoulder blades. It felt like I'd been shot. The next thing I remember is James Robson, the Scotland doctor, at my side talking to me. I could respond to him, but my breathing was so fast that it felt like my insides were being crushed. James told me not to move and he stayed with me, trying to keep me calm. In the end he saved my life. If the injury had occurred even a millimetre further away I would have been paralysed and I'm extraordinarily lucky that I'm able to walk.

I was taken to Cardiff's University Hospital and had an operation on my neck just a few hours later. A few days later they gave me the option of a second operation to help stabilise the injury, so I went for that and they inserted a steel rod into my back – which pretty much sealed the end of my rugby career. It is disappointing but it pales in significance compared to what might have happened. I can jog around now and things are improving all the time. I'll be able to play golf again soon, which is fantastic, and I can't stress enough how grateful I am to James Robson and all the medical staff at the ground and the hospital. Without them things might have turned out much worse.

MAX EVANS (Glasgow Warriors)
13 Caps (to date): 2008-still playing

At half-time I knew that Thommy had been concussed and there might be something to do with his neck, but it was very vague.

I didn't think too much more about it at the time and was just really focused on the game. There was nothing at the time to suggest that it was anything more serious than a knock. I only found out after the game the severity of it.

I got my stuff together as quickly as possible and went straight to the hospital. Obviously you don't know anything until you see it first-hand. I saw him as he went into the operating theatre. He was very frightened. As I got there they were reading out the clearance form, the waiver, whatever, so I knew it was pretty serious then.

James Robson told me that if Thommy had been moved by even a millimetre it could have been fatal or he could have been paralysed. That's why they go through these precautions whenever there is a head collision or an impact to the neck that leaves a player stunned on the ground. More often than not they get up again and everything's fine, sometimes they have a concussion. But sometimes, like with Thom, it's one in a thousand, and something far more serious has happened.

James told me it is the worst injury he has ever been involved in, and that from a man who has been involved in several Lions tours and Scotland tours. To say that shows that Thom was very unlucky.

In the weeks that followed I felt totally helpless, but I knew that the team he had in the Cardiff hospital were exceptional. They started off standing him up. He was obviously very dizzy having been lying down for almost a week. One day he was just standing up for just a matter of minutes. The next day he started doing some paces. He is improving all the time, but it's not something that anyone can put a time-frame on, he just has to take it easy and let it progress naturally.

I've watched the moment it happened back a few times. I expected it to be something that I might not be able to watch. It wasn't. It did not look that bad. It's just the speed he runs into contact and with Lee Byrne running in hard as well. I think it was just one of those things. There was certainly no malice in there.

MIKE BLAIR

Max Evans was our main utility back and he was already on for Mossy. There was just me and Phil Godman left on the bench, so I was put on as a winger.

We held the line pretty well for the remainder of the half considering that there had been such major reworking of the backline and although Stephen Jones got a penalty just on the stroke of half-time, we went in 18-9 up and then got a penalty in the first minute of the second-half to move 21-9 ahead. We were getting back into the swing of things and would have been out of sight after Sean Lamont made a break up the left-hand touchline, but his pass to Kelly Brown was called forward after Kelly had gone over to score so we were pulled back for a scrum. That was a real get-out-jail-free moment for the Welsh and they knew it – they began to up the pressure after that and a few minutes later Shane Williams arced his way across the field to put Lee Byrne in at the corner.

In a bit of a déjà vu moment to the Argentina game in the World Cup, Dan sent over a lovely cross-field kick to the right-hand touchline – it was Shane Williams, the smallest guy on the park, against Kelly and Rory Lamont, two big tall guys. But Shane's leg power is incredible and he sprung up between them and gathered the ball and called the mark. It was a brilliant piece of play and I think that moment was the real turning point in the game. You can rarely put your finger on why the momentum or psychology of a game swings in favour of one team over another, but you could sense it beginning to swing their way after that – although, to be fair, I thought we had managed to stifle their comeback a few minutes later when Dan sent over a monster drop-goal and put us 10 points clear again. It turned out to be a false hope. Scott Lawson was sin-binned and about three minutes later Leigh Halfpenny, who is a very good friend of mine from the Lions tour, shot down the touchline to score.

It was real madness after that. Stephen Jones converted and then we kicked off again. Dan had to go off because he had cramp, so Phil was on at stand-off. Wales went on the attack from deep and Lee Byrne kicked ahead – Phil jumped up to try and charge the kick and just caught Lee with his foot. I was covering the kick from the wing and gathered the ball and when I looked up all I saw was Lee on his face on the ground about ten metres away from Phil and the referee was signalling a penalty – and then he yellow-carded Phil.

PHIL GODMAN

It was never a trip. I'll swear that to my dying day. I jumped up for the ball and my toe had the slightest of contacts with his leg – and five or six metres later he was sprawled on the ground behind me. I won't say he dived; it was a mild contact and at full speed your balance is always fairly precarious, but it definitely wasn't a trip and so didn't merit a penalty, let alone a sin-binning. You are allowed to jump up to try and charge down a kick and as long as you don't change your line to obstruct the kicker as he chases, there is no foul play. That is exactly what happened and I got binned. And the contact that I did have was absolutely miniscule. That one decision really put the nail in our coffin.

Phil Godman leaps to charge down Lee Byrne's chip ahead – the contact that Godman's left foot had with Byrne's leg sent the Welsh fullback sprawling. *FotoSport*

MIKE BLAIR

Stephen Jones kicked the penalty and we were all square at 24-all. But we were in serious trouble now. Dan had been subbed and Rory Lamont was off injured. We were down to twelve men, so Alan MacDonald, our substitute flanker, came on in the centre – although I have to admit that I hardly noticed the change-over because it was such chaos.

CHRIS CUSITER

We wanted to win a penalty and get ourselves back in front. It's easy to say it wasn't the right decision now but we had worked so hard and played so well to get in front that we felt that we deserved to go on and win. We didn't want to accept the draw. In retrospect it was the wrong decision, but if we had got the penalty and won it everyone would have applauded our courage and conviction to back our skills to get the penalty and the win. We had to kick-off. If the ball had gone out, it would have been game over. I decided that we should go for it, so I told Mike to kick it in-field.

PHIL GODMAN

There were a few mixed messages flying about in the heat of the battle and, with hindsight, we would probably have taken the draw. But, at the time, we wanted to win.

MIKE BLAIR

They gathered the ball from the kick-off and set up a ruck. Stephen Jones fired the ball down into our 22 and Leigh Halfpenny absolutely burned his way down the touchline to chase it and got there at the same time as Graeme Morrison just as the ball bounced up. Both of them skidded onto their backs and Lee Byrne collected the ball and passed it to Halfpenny who had got back to his feet the quickest. It looked as if Leigh was going to score in the corner but I just managed to get in his way – I fell over trying to change direction as he stepped and we both sprawled to the deck around five metres from our line. Their players exploded into the ruck and James Hook fed the ball to Alun Wyn Jones who straightened the line and was brought down a metre or two short, but his run had sucked in our outside defenders leaving a huge number advantage to the Welsh out wide. They almost butchered the overlap when Bradley Davies took the ball flat back into the contact when even one more pass would have given them a stroll in, but we were still short of numbers and as the

Andy Robinson looks on in horror as his team's lead unravels in spectacular fashion during the final few minutes in Cardiff. *Press Association*

ball came back again, Richie Rees fed Shane Williams and he danced in under the posts. They say it is one of the most dramatic and exciting games of rugby ever to have been played in either the Five or Six Nations. Maybe so. But it would have been nice to appreciate that judgement having emerged on the winning side. To lose in that manner after having dominated for so much of the match was just devastating.

DAN PARKS

It's pretty rare to get voted as man of the match when you're on the losing side. It was important to me that I played well, but in the end Test match rugby is all about winning. That is the thing that really matters, that is the thing that gets chalked in the history books. From a personal point of view, I was pleased with the way things went after being away so long and it was nice to be able to focus on playing my type of game and just enjoy the day. I thought it was going to be a really special day, and it certainly looked that way for much of the match, but in the end things didn't go our way. There was a bit of a feeling of injustice because we all believed that on the day we were the better team and played the better rugby, but it was Wales that got the result. The most heart-breaking thing was that they managed to score 17 points in six minutes. It was an incredible way to finish a game, but pretty painful for us to take.

MIKE BLAIR

There's not a lot to say about the Italy game that followed. We were all so deflated after Cardiff and were a bit shell-shocked with all the injuries. We still thought we would win and although the game was a typically turgid Scotland-Italy encounter, I thought we deserved to edge it. Josh Sole gave away a cynical penalty to stop us from scoring after a great break by Johnny Beattie, which should have been a penalty try and a yellow-card, but which was just a penalty, and Chunk [Alan Jacobsen] still swears blind that he scored from a maul, even though the video ref didn't give it. It was another disappointing night in Rome – a feeling that I've experienced far more often than I'd like.

CHRIS CUSITER

When we took the lead at 12-9 with around 20 minutes to go I felt that we were moving ourselves into a position to start to kill the game off. But the Italians got themselves back into it with a try – it was one defensive lapse on our part when Jim Hamilton got stranded too far away from other defenders out in midfield and they carved through to score. That's all it was – a minor lapse when we gave them a yard or two too much space and they capitalised on it. That's the unforgiving nature of the Six Nations.

MAX EVANS

I drove back through to Glasgow the night before the Calcutta Cup match to pick up Thom. He couldn't sit still for very long because he was still in quite a bit of pain, but the journey to Edinburgh was just about OK for him to do. We met the rest of the team and Thom said a few words before presenting Dan Parks with his 50th Test jersey and James Robson with his own match jersey from the Wales game, as a thank you for everything he did for him in Cardiff.

Thom did really well to get through all he wanted to say because it was very emotional and all the boys appreciated it – it gave us all a massive lift. And it was great reminding each other of what he said when we were in the changing room before we went out the next day.

DAN PARKS

It was a touching moment when Thom came up meet the guys on Friday night. He is a great guy and I miss playing with him. It was a great occasion, very emotional. I don't think there was a dry eye in the house, but it was great to see him up and walking about. Personally, I felt very privileged. Thom spoke highly of me and of the friendship we have and it gave me a huge boost.

ALASTAIR KELLOCK

The crowd was just awesome for the Calcutta Cup game. Their singing of Flower of Scotland was the best I've ever heard it and the guys were just ready to go after that.

CHRIS CUSITER

Playing against England at home is as big as it gets for a Scotland player and I think the crowd feels that way too. That was maybe the best I've ever heard Murrayfield. It was absolutely fantastic when Dan ran out, they gave him a huge and thoroughly deserved ovation and they were immense again during the anthems.

We were in control for large parts of the game; in the first-half we had a lot of possession and we were attacking really, really well and causing them a lot of problems. We went into half-time with a 9-6 lead and felt that we were in a good position to push on from there.

The set-piece functioned really well and was a great source of possession for us and we made a number of line breaks and came close to scoring on several occasions, but England's defence was immense. It was a draw and strange sort of result to digest – on the one hand we were desperately disappointed not to have gone on and won it which we felt we could have, but at the same time they missed a late penalty and had a drop-goal charged down for them to win it, so we were glad to hold on at that stage.

JOHNNIE BEATTIE (Glasgow Warriors)
14 Caps: 2006-still playing

Everyone was pretty disappointed and it was an odd feeling afterwards. It's not something that occurs very much, a draw in international rugby and especially in a Scotland-England match. It was good to get some points on the table but disappointing not to push on and get the win which we all felt we deserved.

MAX EVANS

I felt very frustrated after the game. In many ways it was great that we at least got a draw and not a loss – a much better feeling than after the Wales game. But like that game I felt that we deserved to win it and had lots of chances to do so, but credit must go to England because they defended very well. There was a good feeling in the changing room afterwards, even if it was a slightly weird one. We had talked all week of how physical we were going to be and how hard we had to run onto the ball – and we certainly looked very dangerous at times, but just couldn't get over the white-wash. Graeme Morrison really stepped up his game, which was great to see. He had been under a lot of pressure before that game, I think he was maybe trying too much. That's a problem that Dan has experienced too in the past – trying to be something to everybody instead of just playing to his strengths. Graeme went back to his strengths and had a fantastic game. He was unbelievable to watch, the kind of speed he was running into people – and it's stuff like that that gives you a big lift on the pitch as well as being something that we can build on in future games.

GRAEME MORRISON

I was playing okay at the start of the Six Nations but not particularly well, and then I had a conversation with Andy Robinson before the England game and he made it very clear to me that I was going to have to make a much bigger impact if I wanted to stay involved in the squad. He told me I had to focus on the things I'm good at – running hard and bringing other players into the game that way – rather than slowing down in front of contact and trying to be a playmaker. It wasn't a case of complacency. I think I just lost sight of what I did to get in the Scotland team in the first place. I knew that I was on my last chance, so there was a lot of pressure – but at the same time I knew what I had to do, and Andy had given me the confidence that I could be an important player for the team so long as I concentrated on the job I was there to do. As Andy says, rugby is a simple game as long as you concentrate on what you are good at.

MIKE BLAIR

Our back-row were sensational all through the season and against England they were brilliant again. They turned-over their ball on at least five occasions at the ruck and we didn't get turned-over there all game, which shows how much we dominated that area.

Graeme Morrison charges the ball up against England. *Getty Images*

Dan Parks had two kicks rebound off the uprights and Toby Flood missed a couple of kicks as well and we basically battered ourselves to a draw, so it was probably a fair result. In the last ten years it seems the way of these Calcutta Cup games. After losing the first three games that year in the manner in which we did, seeing Rory Lawson charging down Toby Flood's drop-goal as he went for the winner was a great moment. A draw allowed us to stabilise and look to build towards Dublin.

Rory Lawson charges down Toby Flood's drop-goal attempt to save the draw for Scotland in the Calcutta Cup. *Press Association*

ALASTAIR KELLOCK

Going into the Ireland game we had good form in the set-piece, which we knew would be essential to claiming a scalp over in Dublin. The lineout was functioning particularly well, which was a very pleasing thing personally and for the forwards as a unit. I think we had managed to win 46 of the 48 lineouts that we threw in up to that point and had managed to steal 11 of the oppositions throws, which is a great platform for the rest of the team. But we knew that going to Dublin we were going to be up against one of the best lineout units in the world. It is a testament to the work that we put in that we managed to steal eight of their throws in that one match. That went a long way in disrupting their rhythm and giving us a chance in the game.

RORY LAWSON

In international rugby, it's no good being a good loser. It may be good sportsmanship, but it is not how you want to be remembered. Being a good sport only goes so far. You want to win. That is how you will be remembered. I'm not advocating foul play or cheating or anything like that, but rather having a ruthlessness in your approach. We lost to Wales and Italy in 2010 because we weren't ruthless enough at the right times – a malady that has affected many Scottish teams over the years – and we could have beaten England if we had been more ruthless at putting away the chances that came our way. So going into the Ireland game, we all felt that we had something to prove. We focused on developing that edge and taking games away from our opponents. I wasn't involved in the match-day squad for that last Six Nations game, but there was a real sense that developed in the build-up to the match that we could go over to Dublin and get the win that we deserved. We had a shaky start and Brian O'Driscoll scored a try after a forward pass from Jonny Sexton, but then we started playing with some composure and Johnny Beattie's try was brilliant – just like something his old man might have done in his prime – and Dan Parks' kicking and all-round control was superb.

It may have come down to that final kick of the game, but we thoroughly deserved the win – it reignited our confidence and showed that the Australia and Fiji wins hadn't just been flashes in the pan. It was nothing more than we deserved after the Championship we had had and it gave us a great boost as we started to prepare for our tour to Argentina in the summer.

DAN PARKS

When we first got to the ground I walked around the stadium before the game and the breeze was going across the pitch – but at each end it was going different ways.

I'd had a penalty early in the second-half just short of 50 metres and it moved to the right when I thought it would have drifted left.

When I lined up the final kick I thought I'd aim it to the left to account for the breeze and it went through. It was a great moment.

I get a lot of abuse from the boys for the way I look after my boots – I take them into the shower after every training session and match and always keep them clean and polished. They say it's excessive, but I look after them and they look after me – well, they did in Dublin anyway.

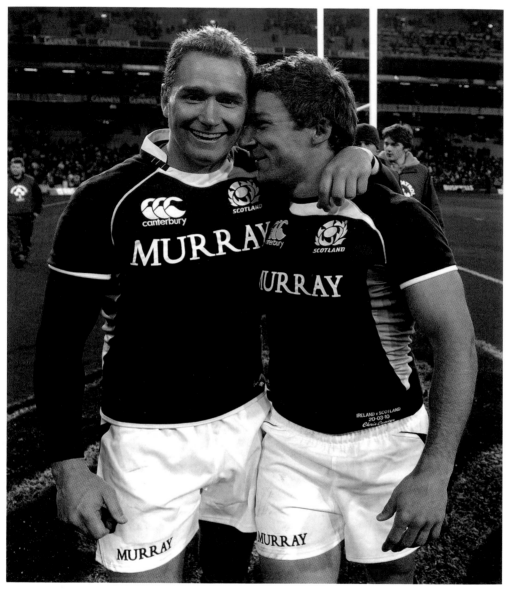

Dan Parks and Chris Cusiter celebrate Scotland's victory over Ireland at Croke Park. *Getty Images*

Jonny Sexton was very gracious after the game. I went over to swap shirts with him; he doesn't have a Scotland jersey but he wanted me to take his shirt and wouldn't swap. He said, 'It's your day'. That was pretty special of him.

ROSS FORD

Going away to Argentina in the summer, we knew that our set-piece had to be absolutely top-notch if we were going to have a chance against the Pumas. The scrum performed well in both Test matches. We didn't exactly take them apart, but we gained parity against them and had some decent shunts that had them going backwards, so it was very pleasing. Certainly an improvement on previous encounters we've had against them and it is very positive psychologically for us as a unit going forward into next season – especially as we'll be playing them in the group stages of the World Cup in 2011.

ALASTAIR KELLOCK

It was a great moment being named as captain for the Argentina Tests. It is a huge honour to captain your country and I was smiling all week after Andy asked if I would do it. There have been a few ups and downs in my career – I didn't make the World Cup squad in 2007 which was a big low, but I just knuckled down and got on with it, worked hard. It's a tough thing to go through but to come out the other side you really appreciate what you've achieved, the reward for all that disappointment and then hard work is so great, it outweighs any bad times that you've been through.

DAN PARKS

The noise of the crowd in both Tests in Argentina was crazy. Some people say that it can be intimidating, but I don't try to shut it out, even when I'm kicking for goal. I actually enjoy it. It's the same feeling that I had in Cardiff and Dublin this year as well – it's what Test match rugby is all about – the ferocity of the noise and the way that the crowd really takes part in the game. And then once you kick the points it suddenly goes silent and I love that most of all.

I've been on five tours with Scotland, including the World Cup in 2007, and Argentina in 2010 was definitely the best, both personally and as a team – I was happy with my performances and winning both Tests was fantastic, but the main thing was the confidence that was in the squad. Comparing it to previous tours, we beat Samoa in Wellington on my first trip with Scotland, but lost both Tests to Australia; we played well when we were out in South Africa in 2006, but the Springboks were always in control of those games. When we went out to Argentina in 2008 we should have won the first Test and although it was great to win the second Test, there was a different feeling to the one we had in 2010. We navigated our way through both matches, knowing exactly what we needed to do to win and implemented our game plan. We knew we could win and we went out and did it. It's a small shift psychologically, but the confidence was there after the win in Dublin and that result has made a huge difference to the mindset of the squad. We should have won other games in the Six Nations, but didn't. That win against Ireland let us turn the corner and it gave us the

Dan Parks maintained his form from the Six Nations throughout the two Test tour to Argentina to guide Scotland to their first series victory in the southern hemisphere. *Getty Images*

confidence to continue playing the way we had because we knew it would work. The biggest difference was in the first Test in Tucumán – we went behind but knew what we had to do to get back in front and we knew that we could do it and in the end it felt pretty comfortable, even if the scoreboard was pretty close. The second Test was a step on again in establishing a consistent winning mentality, especially in the conditions, we showed our character, and the confidence in the squad now is the best I've ever known it. They were two very different games. The first match was played in dry conditions so both sides were able to throw the ball around a lot more while the second was played in heavy rain and was a real dog-fight, so it's good to know that we can win well in both sorts of conditions. It was a great way to finish the season and gives us good momentum going into the autumn.

RORY LAWSON

We jumped two places up the IRB rankings after that series win, which was also a great bonus. It's hugely positive and it proves that we're moving in the direction we want to be going. The key thing is now to keep building on that and setting our targets higher than where we are.

JOHN BARCLAY

We beat Australia in the autumn, we beat Ireland away from home and won our first Test series in the southern hemisphere. We should have won a few more games than we did in the Six Nations and should have completed the hat-trick in November, but with the way we're playing and the atmosphere in the camp, we know this turn-up in results will continue. It's definitely been the most enjoyable season I've had with Scotland and it's great to be a part of it all.

The team celebrate their victory in the second Test against the Pumas in Mar del Plata.
Getty Images

MIKE BLAIR

The justification that a team is making progress despite a continued run of bad results is often wheeled out, in all sports, when players or coaches are trying to defend their approach or their methods. Often it is little more than a smokescreen, a shield that is put up in the face of media scrutiny, but there are times when the claim that a team is making progress towards turning close-run defeats into victories is genuinely made. I think that it is clear for any observer that both as individuals and collectively as a squad, this current Scotland team is making progress. Even looking beyond the victories against Australia, Fiji, Ireland and Argentina, I'll give you an example. In the 2009 Six Nations we went through much of the Championship without Euan Murray and Nathan Hines. The media weren't slow in suggesting that we were underpowered without these two players; the reality of what happened in the games that spring shows that we probably were. They are two international class players, British and Irish Lions, and two guys that would walk into just about any team on the planet. Fast forward fourteen or fifteen months and we went to Argentina with them missing from the squad again. There were noises in the press that we were, once again, going to be underpowered without them. In reality we gained parity and times completely dominated one of the best forward packs in the world, a forward pack of vast experience and technical excellence. That is tangible proof of progress and the developing maturity and skill of the squad. Add to that the quality of the Argentinean team, the intimidating nature of the venues we played in and the fact that that same Argentinean side blew away France by 40 points a week later, and you see a squad that is turning the corner, edging out victories that I am sure we would not have edged out in the past. The depth of our squad is vastly improved, virtually every player now has good Test match experience and has been part of some historic wins in recent years. That experience has been hard-earned at times and we've all suffered disappointment and frustration which is as good a motivator to drive you to succeed as anything – and the experience of winning, of grinding out wins against quality, world-class opposition, gives a confidence that is absolutely invaluable – you can go to the ropes and know that you are good enough to fight back, to punch your way out of the corner and go the distance and deliver the knock-out blow that will secure victory. That is true development – and it has been several years in the making. At the 2007 World Cup we were the youngest team there and it was the same in the 2008 and 2009 Six Nations. We said during the build up to the 2007 World Cup that it may take some time for the results to start rolling in regularly because you need to learn how to cope with and then master international rugby, and if you are a team that is largely made up of young players, you have to learn those things together, you can't rely on old, grizzled players to drag you through the worst of it. But I think that we're starting to see the true potential of the squad coming to fruition. The responsibility we now have is to keep that momentum going and have the confidence to push on to the next level. Only then will we really be able to prove how good we really are . . . and might yet be.

It's an exciting time as we build ourselves up for a new international season: we have the autumn internationals and then, next year, we have Wales, Ireland and Italy at home in the Six Nations, followed by the World Cup in New Zealand.

After being away for the summer, it will be great to get back to Murrayfield; it's always a reassuring feeling to be back on our home ground and in our own changing room. There's a plaque in each players' cubicle which bears the name of greats from the past who have previously worn the shirt – an inspirational reminder of the legacy that we're following. Seeing those great names, I'm always reminded of something that Jim Telfer once said: that the jersey is never really yours; it belongs to the nation and to the history of the team and you are only borrowing it for a time.

To walk down the tunnel and out onto the Murrayfield pitch when it is shrouded in darkness is as special as it gets – the flames of the pyrotechnics billow up on either side of you, the scatter of camera flashes glitter like stars, and the heart-rending melodies of Highland Cathedral echo through your soul while the weight of expectation and the fervour of the crowd beats down from all around you. Can there be anything more thrilling, haunting or inspiring?

To run out onto that hallowed turf is the stuff of dreams of any Scots boy who has ever picked up a rugby ball. I used to practice David Sole's slow march of 1990 in my garden, used to stand ready to sing the national anthem, used to hear Bill McLaren's voice commentating on my every move as I spun passes, sidestepped and kicked the ball around imaginary defenders, scoring points at will as the Murrayfield roar filled my ears.

I will never take for granted the privilege that I have been able to realise my childhood dream. Every moment is exhilarating and in every step you take, every pass you give and receive, every time your foot strikes the ball, and in every contact you make, you feel the nation with you, in the badge on your chest, in the beat of your heart, driving your legs, powering your muscles, electrifying your senses.

When we wear the Scotland jersey, we wear it for the thousands of fans that support us around the world; we wear it for the great players that have worn it before us; we wear it for our friends and our families, for our school teachers and our coaches; but we also wear it for that boy inside of us who has played these games a thousand times in his head, and for those who even now march around their gardens with a cherished dream that they might one day follow us into battle with the thistle on their chest. For me, that is what playing for Scotland is all about.

When you're out on that pitch, you just hope that you can make your own piece of history to add to that legacy . . . and when you get out there, where so many legends of the game have trod before you, and the noise of the crowd is literally trembling through your bones, you know that every one of those faces and voices that are supporting you would do anything to be out there with you. That noise combines with the inspiration that we carry with us and drives all that we do when we play – it is the inspiration of our teammates, our friends and our families, our dreams and our ambitions and the history of those who have gone before us; these are all the things that make us who we are as players and as a team, as a rugby nation . . . it is everything that is behind the thistle.